Bureaucratizing the Good Samaritan

Bureaucratizing the Good Samaritan

The Limitations to Humanitarian Relief Operation

Tony Waters

CALIFORNIA STATE UNIVERSITY, CHICO

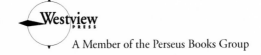

Westview
PRESS

A Member of the Perseus Books Group

Copyright © 2001 by Westview Press, A Member of the Perseus Books Group

Published in 2001 in the United States of America by Westview Press, 5500 Central Avenue, Boulder, Colorado 80301-2877, and in the United Kingdom by Westview Press, 12 Hid's Copse Road, Cumnor Hill, Oxford OX2 9JJ

Find us on the World Wide Web at www.westviewpress.com

Library of Congress Cataloging-in-Publication Data
Waters, Tony.
  Bureaucratizing the good samaritan : the limitations to humanitarian relief operation / Tony Waters.
    p. cm.
  Includes bibliographical references and index.
  ISBN 0-8133-6790-5 (pbk. : alk. paper)
  1. Refugees—International cooperation. 2. Humanitarian assistance.   3. Bureaucracy.
4. Refugees—Rwanda.   5. Refugees—Tanzania.   I. Title.

HV640 .W335 2000
362.87'526—dc21

00-043988

The paper used in this publication meets the requirements of the American National Standard for Permanence of Paper for Printed Library Materials Z39.48-1984.

10   9   8   7   6   5   4

To Dagmar, Christopher and Kirsten Waters

Contents

Tables and Figures

Acronyms and Abbreviations

AAR	Austrian nongovernmental organization
AEF	Africa Education Foundation
AICF	Agence Internationale Contre la Faim (French NGO)
CARE	CARE International (international NGO)
CDR	Coalition pour la Défense de la République (radical Rwandan Hutu party)
COGEFAR	(name of Italian construction company)
CRS	Catholic Relief Services (American NGO)
DRA	Disaster Relief Agency (Dutch NGO)
ECHO	European Community Humanitarian Organization
ELCT	Evangelical Lutheran Church in Tanzania
Frodebu	Front des Démocrates du Burundi (Burundian political party)
GOAL	(Irish NGO)
ICRC	International Committee for the Red Cross (Swiss agency)
IFRC	International Federation of Red Cross and Red Crescent Societies
IRC	International Rescue Committee (American NGO)
IRIN	International Relief Information Network
IDP	Internally displaced person
JRS	Jesuit Refugee Service
JVA	Joint Voluntary Agency (American NGO in Thailand)
LWF	Lutheran World Federation
MRND	Mouvement Révolutionnaire National pour le Développement (ruling party of Rwanda before 1994)
MSF	Médecins sans Frontières (Doctors Without Borders, international NGO)
NPA	Norwegian People's Aid
NGO	Nongovernmental Organization
OAU	Organization of African Unity
ODA	Overseas Development Assistance (U.K. government agency)
RPF	Rwanda Patriotic Front (ruling party of Rwanda after 1994)

TCRS   Tanganyika Christian Refugee Service
TRC   Tanzanian Red Cross
UNAMIR   United Nations Assistance Mission to Rwanda (UN
                  military contingent in Rwanda, 1993–96)
UNBRO   United Nations Border Relief Operation (Cambodia-
                  Thailand)
UNDP   United Nations Development Programme
UNICEF   United Nations International Children's Emergency Fund
UNHCR   United Nations High Commissioner for Refugees
Uprona   Parti de l'Union et du Progrès National (governing party
                  in Burundi until mid-1993 and after coup in 1998)
USAID   United States Agency for International Development
USCR   United States Committee for Refugees
WFP   World Food Programme (UN)
WHO   World Health Organization (UN)

Acknowledgments

This book is the result of my involvement in the refugee business since 1982. Many people have contributed to my thoughts since then. I would like to take this chance to reach back into my memories to acknowledge a few (though by no means all) of them, though of course they may not agree with my conclusions. Nevertheless, in all, I know, there was a heartfelt interest in finding the best way to serve the dispossessed of the world.

In Nan, Thailand (1982): Peter Rees, Steve Haman, Naowarat, Ian Timm, Kouei Cho Saeteurn, Nai Jantnoi, Seng Lor.

In Phanat Nikhom and Bangkok, Thailand (1983): Manit Chiachuabsilp, Father Sanit, Father Boonlert, Jenny Kang, Vongduen Kerdchana, Tony Nolan, Philip Bennoun, Tassanee L., "Uncle" Manu, Meng Chiew Sae Teurn, Manh Cho Saeteurn, Thavinh Phonyapanh.

In Kigoma region, Tanzania (1984–87): Wilfrid and Karin Mahn, Jan and Antje Siemerink, Carolus and Wilma Poldervaart, Willem and Rieke Van Gogh, Heidi Kaletsch, Kalima Mamboshella, Mzee Abdallah, Tobias Siweya, N. P. Mchonchele, Mrs. C. Basongo MB, Cosmas Malugu, Mathayo Balikutsa, Egil Nilssen, Mzee Chamwino, Ramadhani Asedi, Ibrahimu Luziga, Father H. Van der Paverd, Father Tryers, Father Bourdieu, Magdalena Lanz, Ilse Pomranz, Elfriede Mueller, Jan and Catherine Rotte. A special note of thanks to Benedicto for protecting the refugees in Heru Ushingo. He did it without reward or expectations of compensation or acknowledgment, only because it was the right thing to do.

In Ngara and Karagwe, Tanzania (1994–96): Leo Norholt, Philip Wijmans, Lazarus Mezza, John and Suzanne Cosgrave, Adamasu Simeso, Johan Balslev, Mark Ajobe, Bernhard Staub, Gary Sibson, David and Tehira Porter, Everready Nkya, Peter Sweetnam, Ted Berth-Jones, Dietrich and Ulrike Schneiss, Karl Steinacker, Maureen Connelly, Andreas Koessler, Judy Benjamin, Marc Sommers, Steve Njobe, Trish and Rob Wilson, Sister Agnes, Sam and Miranda Gibbs, Antony and Christian Latham, Jaap Antjes, Denise Barrett, Eugene Samuel, Paul Sijssens, Chantal Garand, Colin Pryce, Peter Buchanan, Richard Luff, Mzee Atanase, Mzee Evariste, Mzee Leonidas, Bodil Torp, Edwin and Dorothy Ramathal, Stephan and Gertraud Schaeffer, Sosthenes Bernhard, Brigadier General Sylvester Hamedi, Philip Mangula MB, Bishop and Mrs. Edwin Nyamubi, Matias, Jean-Paul, and Jean-Pierre.

I also want to acknowledge the courage of Eveready Nkyr, Mzee Alfred John, and nine Tanzanian drivers for TRCs who remained in Southwest Rwanda in August 1994 when the French army pulled out. Their courage was to lightly acknowledged.

Ingeborg Tremmel (my mother-in-law) provided a comfortable and peaceful place to work in Leverkusen, Germany, in the summer of 1999. This is where much of the manuscript was written.

Academic debts are more difficult and complex to acknowledge. But a number of people have had influence on this book. At the University of California, Davis, John R. Hall has been the most persistent in seeing that I followed up the subject of the "bureaucratized Good Samaritan" since I first discussed it with him after a graduate seminar in 1990 or so. Jack Goldstone has also contributed ideas, particularly in terms of methodology. I have discussed this work at various times with Catherine Newbury, Goran Hyden, Scott McNall, Craig Jenkins, Tom Johnson, Laurie Wermuth, Clark Davis, Kathy Kaiser, Frank Hirtz, Jim Haehn, Eric Jones, Nelson Kasfir, and others who were interested and encouraged me to continue.

Bernhard Staub, Bent Simonsen, Heidi Kaletsch, and Beth Whitaker all deserve credit as people interested in bridging the gap between academe and field practice. Michael Hyden also assisted with data collection in Chabalisa 2, and Fridtjov Ruden patiently taught me something about hydrogeology. I hope Chapter 10 does what he taught justice; the mistakes are of course mine.

Anne Abramson read and critiqued the entire manuscript. Some important adjustments were made at her suggestion. Bill Travers assisted with Chapter 11. Candy Priano provided the graphics. George Thompson at the interlibrary loan desk at Merriam Library at California State University, Chico, helped chase elusive references quickly and efficiently. Jeff Teeter assisted with conversion of the photographs into black-and-white Photo-Shop files. Billie Kanter, Jolee Liptrap, and Cheryl Vermillion patiently arranged for the bureaucratic threads to be tied together when it came to charges, budgets, and payments. Billie and Jolee also kindly looked the other way when I exceeded my share of the Department of Sociology's photocopy resources.

The interest from Andy Day and Dave McBride at Westview Press provided encouragement and support. I hope that the book does their confidence in it justice. The copyediting of Katherine Scott was sharp and insightful.

The other source of support I have received was the Department of Sociology and Social Work, California State University, Chico—from the staff, faculty, and students. I have never had a more comfortable and collegial place to work.

Tony Waters

PART ONE

THE INTERNATIONAL
REFUGEE RELIEF REGIME

Jesus said, "A man was going down from Jerusalem to Jericho, when he fell into the hands of robbers. They stripped him of his clothes, beat him and went away, leaving him half dead. A priest happened to be going down the same road, and when he saw the man, he passed by on the other side. So too a Levite, when he came to the place and saw him, passed by on the other side. But a Samaritan, as he traveled, came where the man was; and when he saw him, he took pity on him. He went to him and bandaged his wounds, pouring on oil and wine. Then he put the man on his own donkey, took him to an inn, and took care of him. The next day, he took out two silver coins and gave them to the innkeeper. 'Look after him.' He said 'and when I return, I will reimburse you for any extra expense you may have.'

"Which of these three do you think was a neighbor to the man who fell into the hands of robbers?"

The expert in the law replied, "The one who had mercy on him."

*Jesus told him, "Go and do likewise."**

As the Biblical parable of the Good Samaritan implies, the impulse to help a stranger in need is not new; it is a trait long admired. In telling this parable, Jesus tells his listeners that the Samaritan was a better neighbor than the holy men who neglected to assist the stranger. He says it is good and proper to show mercy, and to ignore suffering you encounter is wrong. The lesson is that the morally superior decision was taken by the Samaritan, and not the holy men. This is of course a sentiment shared by many of the world's religions. The requirement to assist is also accepted as moral and right in the modern secular world.

---

*Luke 10:30–37, New International Version.

1

Though the impulse to help the more unfortunate among us is old, our capacity to do so has expanded exponentially with the Industrial Revolution, the modern state, instant communications, and modernity in general. In the modern world, charity is organized far beyond the level of a moral choice made by an individual who by chance passes a robbery victim along the road. In fact, in the situation where charity is most broad, and assists the greatest number of victims, it is organized into a "complex task"—meaning that specialized organizations are established that undertake the relief and rehabilitation of the millions of anonymous victims lying along the world's highways. The ability of the modern world to organize these tasks has resulted in the rescue of millions of victimized strangers in the years roughly since World War I.

To do this, a complex of organizations and agencies such as the UNICEF (United Nations International Children's Emergency Fund), the Red Cross, CARE International, UNHCR (United Nations High Commissioner for Refugees), Oxfam, Médecins sans Frontières (MSF), and other names familiar to modern Western society have emerged, often achieving for themselves a high profile on nightly newscasts throughout the world. More lives than ever are saved because such agencies specialize in treating the victimized quickly and effectively. And because of the wonder of modern transport and communications, trained people specializing in these tasks are sent, often quickly, and far fewer victims are left unsuccored by the side of the road than would otherwise be the case. In response to this perceived need, budgets for relief work have also ballooned: in 1995 about $8 billion was spent on relief. Less predictable is the fact that these spending increases have not been accompanied by a concentration on one or two major centralized agencies; instead there has been a proliferation of groups. In 1980 there were about 1,600 nongovernmental agencies operating out of the 24 economically developed OECD states. By the mid-1990s there were about 4,600 (Walkup 1997:136).[1]

Also more efficient, though, is the other side of a mercy equation, meaning that credit for being a Good Samaritan justifiably is shared by schoolchildren who respond to Red Cross appeals; Western governments that fly in shipments of relief goods to Bosnia, Rwanda, and Albania; and individual Tanzanians, East Timorese, Colombians, or Albanians who quietly protect refugees before the international relief agencies arrive. Each agency connecting "victims" and donors justifies its involvement in the terms of humanitarianism or religion. And in order that it be known to donor constituencies, the popular press broadcasts and disseminates word of the good deed done. Such publicizing of "righteousness" may not be what Jesus had in mind in the parable of the Good Samaritan, but nevertheless it is a prominent feature of how relief efforts are conducted today and cannot be ignored.

The reason that succoring the needy and delivering credit is more efficient for both the victim and the donor, is that, as with other complex tasks, the task of providing relief has become bureaucratized. To do this, the "mercy" function has been broken down into tasks done by specialists hired and trained to do each action efficiently and effectively. In this respect, the work of today's Good Samaritan agencies is not that different from the larger bureaucracies of modern business and government within which the principles of bureaucratization were established. These organizations define a goal to achieve, identify the means to do it, and establish programs to achieve the specified goals.

The nature of these relief agencies—which I call the international refugee relief regime—is discussed in the following chapters. The first chapter is about how and why I've become interested in this subject. The description starts with Chapter 2, which is a brief historical overview of how the bureaucracies of the international relief regime evolved. Chapter 3 is about their strengths and weaknesses, given the inherently bureaucratic nature of the international refugee relief regime. Chapter 4 is about the moral underpinnings assumed by the bureaucracies as they seek to justify their programs. Chapter 5 discusses the methodological difficulties inherent to discussing refugee relief agencies. Chapters 6–8 focus on describing how the international refugee relief regime operated in the Rwandan refugee crisis in Tanzania.

Notes

1. Natsios (1996:68) notes that the United States in particular has seen a growth in the amount of emergency aid given. He uses as an example the observation that between 1989 and 1993 budgets for two U.S. agencies, the Office for Foreign Disaster Assistance and the Food for Peace program, rose from $297 million to $1.2 billion. Natsios's article also describes the specifics of how such money is channeled to a variety of NGOs (nongovernmental organizations) in the United States and Europe.

1

Introduction: The Rwanda Refugee Relief Operation and the Bureaucratized Good Samaritan— A Personal Context

Between October and December 1996, troops across central Africa forced 1.4 million refugees back to their home country of Rwanda. This forcible refugee repatriation was undertaken by Zaire and Tanzania with the acquiescence of the international community. This occurred despite the fact for two and a half years Tanzania, Zaire, and the international community protected the same refugees from such an event.

The forcible repatriation in late 1996 was probably the largest in modern times. Certainly it was the largest since the Allies forced refugees back to Soviet-dominated countries in the period 1945–47.[1] Seemingly forgotten in the intervening 50 years was the fact that some of the forcibly returned European refugees were executed within earshot of the Allies at the time they were repatriated. Indeed, it was out of this experience that the principle of refugee protection emerged: that persons having a legitimate fear of persecution have a right to protection in the country of first asylum from forced repatriation. Why, then, for the first time since World War II, did the international refugee relief community acquiesce to a major forcible refugee repatriation?[2] Why were Rwandans forced back, and not the Cambodian, Afghan, Bosnian, or others who, since World War II, have fled their countries and been protected to some degree from such action?

As a student of refugee history, I find the conventional reasons given for the forcible repatriation (reviewed hereafter) of Rwandans too easy, and therefore dissatisfying. In particular, they were made without reference to a broader understanding of how refugee crises have been created and resolved during the last 50 years. Instead, the explanations address

6

FIGURE 1.1   Map of Rwanda, Burundi, and western Tanzania showing the location of refugee camps, and other places relevant to the Great Lakes refugee crises, 1994–96. (Map by Candy Priano.)

only issues and explanations raised by that one crisis, often offering explanations rooted in the interests of the protagonists, be they the new government in Rwanda, Tanzania, the refugees themselves, the United Nations, or refugee assistance agencies. Some of the common explanations given about what happened to the Rwandans included the following:

- The Rwandan refugees were common people who had nothing to fear in their home country. (The same was said about the eastern Europeans forced back to their countries at the end of World War II and shot by the Soviets. The same was also said of Cambodians fleeing after the Vietnamese invasion in the late 1970s.)
- The Rwandan refugees were manipulated by unscrupulous leaders using them for political ends. (The same was said of Cambodians fleeing with Pol Pot.)
- The home country (Rwanda's) new government established amicable relations with its neighbors; those neighbors were in a better position to judge the new government's intentions than those who had fled. (This was the excuse used by the Allies after World War II to forcibly return refugees to territories controlled by the Soviets.)
- It was noted that the refugees themselves had worn out their welcome in poor host countries that were ill prepared to provide asylum. (But a devastated Central Europe hosted millions of refugees through the 1950s, India hosted 10 million refugees from Bangladesh in 1972, Iran and Pakistan have hosted millions from Afghanistan since 1979, China has hosted hundreds of thousands of Vietnamese, and Central American refugees were widespread throughout that isthmus between 1979 and 1993. All were poor countries.)
- It was claimed that Rwanda had legitimate interests in invading Zaire in order to close the refugee camps because otherwise perpetrators of crimes against humanity would remain free to threaten Rwanda's territory. (Cambodia and Bosnia could have both justified invasions of neighbors with similar claims.)
- It was claimed that host countries can best judge refugee status and home conditions. (The humanitarian community objected to this position in the case of Vietnamese in Hong Kong, Malaysia, etc.; Bosnians in Germany; Guatemalans in Mexico; Haitians in the United States; and so forth.)
- At the end, it was pointed out that Rwanda had a right to shut down refugee camps that doubled as military bases. (Afghanistan, Laos, Cambodia, El Salvador, and Nicaragua could all have

asserted a similar right at various times. The apartheid-era South African regime actually used this excuse for attacks on African National Congress exile camps throughout southern Africa in the 1980s.)

In short, the justifications appear sensible, but are not completely satisfying. There is a sense that something more happened in the Rwanda crisis; that although such commonsense justifications perhaps offer short-term explanations to policy makers, there must be a broader story. The broader story I think is that the Rwanda refugee situation became "bureaucratized" too fast, with the result that the administrative and political compromises erected to deal with the short-term emergency were incapable of generating longer-term visions. Admittedly, this is a dry explanation for a juicy and dramatic subject like the Rwanda genocide and refugee crisis. Certainly it is more dry than recounting the conditions during the genocide, narrating the drama of the military successes of the RPF (Rwanda Patriotic Front, the ruling party of Rwanda after 1994), cheering the downfall of Mobutu, or describing bodies in the river. But I think it is one that explains a great deal more than the off-the-cuff explanations listed above. This book is about how I reached that conclusion.

Excitement, Emotion, and the Rwandan Refugee Crisis

Superlatives dominated discussion of the Rwanda refugee crisis from the start. For the world, the Rwandan refugee crisis started on April 28–29, 1994, with "the largest and fastest refugee exodus in a single day." The camp established in Ngara, Tanzania, was "the largest in the world." The American columnist Roger Rosenblatt (1994:40, 42), writing about Ngara in May 1994, was sensitive to the drama: "Bodies appear in an explosion of spray at the top of a steep falls, and then spin and tumble down like logs on their way to a mill." He continued with the enthusiastic use of superlatives: Benaco refugee camp, he wrote "is a marketplace, perhaps the largest in the world." The *Time* magazine cover was for me particularly memorable. In bold type over the picture of a mother and her child was the dramatic headline: " 'There are no devils left in Hell,' the missionary said. 'They are all in Rwanda.' "

More drama came only a few weeks later when the Ngara records were eclipsed after 2 million Rwandans fled westward to Zaire, and a fast-killing cholera epidemic emerged. The Zairean camps were described in cover stories as "Land of the Dead and Dying" (*The Economist*), "This Is the Apocalypse" (*Time*), and "Hell on Earth" (*Newsweek*). New records for size of refugee camps, speed of cholera epidemics, and size and speed of international relief programs toppled after Ngara had been at the top of the publicity heap for a short two months.

Thus, from the beginning, the international humanitarian response was dominated by emotional superlatives. There was a massive outpouring of relief supplies. Heroic efforts to control cholera were made in Tanzania and Zaire. The unusual coordination between aid agencies and well-organized refugees in distributing relief goods in Tanzania was praised. For the first time Russians participated in an international relief operation in Africa as part of the international team coordinated by the UN. Finally, a report about the Rwanda relief operation, valued at $1.4 billion between May and December 1994, received an evaluation study costing $1.5 million, an evaluation, I was assured, that was the most expensive and complete undertaken of a humanitarian operation.[3]

Capping the drama and requiring more superlatives was the killing preceding and during the refugee exodus, which underlay all analyses. The genocide was "the largest since the Holocaust," and killing in Rwanda proceeded at a pace faster than even Auschwitz was able to achieve. The masterminds of the genocide were also judged in terms of superlatives: their evil, along with that of Bosnia, are the only two war crimes since World War II for which the UN has had the wherewithal to press prosecution. Thus, in the case of the Rwanda relief operation, two emotional subjects became intertwined: pity for refugees and revenge against the perpetrators of the genocide, known commonly by a sinister sounding French word, *génocidaires*.

Pity and revenge are of course two very different emotions. The question for the international refugee relief community became, in effect, how to express the world's emotions effectively for such massive suffering. Can both exist side-by-side? Is a relief operation the most appropriate response? Or are justice tribunals? Whichever was the case, one thing was clear, the only type of human organization capable of dealing with the large task was a bureaucracy, that cumbersome and all-pervasive form of social organization which, as Max Weber points out, we all revile, yet are so dependent upon for modern life to be possible. Thus, ironically, despite the fact that bureaucracies are inherently sterile, conscienceless, and inhuman, they are nevertheless the only tool useful for expressing both mercy and revenge, the emotions the world demands be expressed.

This book is an exercise in assessing policy by looking both at what actually happened and also at what might have happened. Was the forced repatriation inevitable? Would different policy decisions have resulted in different consequences?

In terms of methodology, this book uses traditional historical narrative with a comparative sociological analysis. The book is divided into two sections. Part 1 focuses on the historical underpinnings of the "international refugee relief regime." Chapter 2 describes the institutional limitations within which the regime must operate. Chapters 3 and 4 are both about the nature of bureaucracy in the context of international relief operations. Chapter 3 is about why bureaucracies are effective, even in emotional situations like refugee relief. Chapter 4 is the "yes but" chapter with respect to bureaucracy, and explores why it is difficult for bureaucracies to define the moral differences between right and wrong in emotionally charged situations. The difficulties inherent in studying the regime are the subject of Chapter 5. Chapters 6 to 8 conclude the first section of the book with a description of the Rwanda crisis and how it developed. The focus in this part is a study of how the work in Ngara unfolded, how policies developed, and the criteria on which decisions were made.

The second section of the book shows how the concept of the "bureaucratized Good Samaritan" is an effective one for understanding the limitations of the international refugee relief regime. There are three case studies of how donor emotions and the needs of the bureaucracies interacted in Ngara, Tanzania (Chapters 9 to 11). The subjects covered are purposely disparate, and include one centering on the role of planners (contingency planning and preparedness for an influx from Burundi); one focusing on the role of engineers and public health experts (water provision and well-drilling); and one of general interest to the lawyers (violent death). The point of choosing such broad subjects is to demonstrate how similar bureaucratic and emotional concerns underlay decision-making, irrespective of the technical field involved.

From this analysis, the "bureaucratized Good Samaritan" concept is used to assess what the limitations of the international refugee relief regime are and how these limitations will continue to limit reform. This leads up to a discussion, in Chapter 12, of the question asked at the beginning of this chapter: Why were only the Rwandans forcibly repatriated? The discussion in Chapter 12 leads to a conclusion that refugee crises are inherently political. Nevertheless, the need for an apolitical humanitarian veneer is maintained not only in connection with the Rwandans but in other crises as well. This is the subject of Chapter 13, where it is pointed out that the weaknesses found in the Rwandan case are in fact built into the contradictions of how refugee relief is handled, and that each of the other crises discussed implicitly had a unrealized potential for a forcible repatriation. Thus, as the emergency response system is currently constituted there are certain "decision points" where opportunities are taken advantage of or lost. These points reflect the dynamics of how political and financial support for humanitarian crises is generated, and not the objective needs of the refugees themselves. How these points are dealt with typically has much to do with the effects that the international popular press has on policy and decision makers.

The final chapter asks how the limits of the "bureaucratized Good Samaritan" will shape current efforts at reform. The key point is that until decision-making is rooted more firmly in rationalized bureaucratic norms rather than the dictates of the emotionalized (and necessarily sensational) roving eye of the press, reform efforts are likely to continue to be stymied. In essence, "press management" is the problem, not the solution. The solution is to strengthen bureaucratic rationality, and not delegate authority to the necessarily emotionalized popular press, which is pursuing other ends than the delivery of rationalized services to the refugees.

At the end of the book is a collection of eight essays I wrote about refugees while in Tanzania. Six of them were written on behalf of my employer, the Lutheran World Federation (LWF). The original purpose of these six essays was very consistent with the "bureaucratized Good Samaritan": they were tools to describe our work to donors within the church. As with all such reports, there needed to be a strong human element, which conveyed to lay readers the type of work we were doing, how their money had been used in the past, and how it would be used in the future. In this function, my job was not that different from that of a print reporter.

The seventh essay is about the demographics of the refugee camp with which I was most familiar. Such data, though widely disseminated, were not understood and were ignored by planners who could have used them to make operations more efficient. Nevertheless, I think of this essay as being of general methodological and analytical interest. Likewise, I have hopes that some refugee camp administrator somewhere will see the point in developing such data.

The final essay is adapted from a 1989 issue of *Disasters*, in which I wrote about the difficulty in counting refugees in a remote Tanzanian village. Since much of the usefulness of the "bureaucratized Good Samaritan" concept rests on the accuracy of good counts, I include the essay here as a warning. Things in Africa are not always as straightforward as outsiders assume.

Personal Background

My own interest in the international refugee relief regime goes back to 1982 when, after a stint in the Peace Corps at a Malaria Zone office in Thailand, I was employed by the International Rescue Committee (IRC) as a sanitarian and project manager in Thai refugee camps for Indochinese. A source of continual frustration for me was the inefficiencies and wastefulness in the relief effort. Water systems stood unused while expensive water trucks roared by; poorly designed camps led to fires and floods; refugee families who were going to be resettled abroad endured years of despondency while on the international dole. Like many young people working for nongovernmental organizations in such situations, I began to blame this situation on the two large international organizations most responsible for setting policies for those camps. In the case of Thailand, these agencies were the United Nations High Commissioner for Refugees (UNHCR), who ran the camps, and the U.S. Department of State, which had the largest resettlement program and also funded UNHCR. From this experience, I came away with a belief that the ideals for refugee relief could be realized if it were made more cost-effective and efficient (see Waters 1984).

From 1984 to 1987 I worked on another UNHCR-funded refugee project, one in Tanzania for the Lutheran World Federation (LWF), this time as a special project officer responsible for installing road culverts, managing building supplies, general rural development programs, and supervising agricultural extension agents. Many of these projects were to be undertaken by employing villagers using World Food Programme (WFP) "Food for Work" commodities—which, when they arrived at all, were a year or more late. The point of this project was to settle "spontaneously settled" refugees in Tanzanian villages and regularize their refugee status. Here, too, UNHCR policy did not meet its own ideals. Particularly disruptive was the failure to arrive of promised funding. Neither the promised money from UNHCR nor food from WFP materialized on time, and both were later cut, in the middle of the project. This resulted in a great deal of back-pedaling by those of us in the field.

A final assault on my bureaucratically rational sensibilities occurred when the Tanzanian government in 1987 expelled the refugees for whom we had been building infrastructure (Waters 1988 and 1989; Malkki 1994), and the UNHCR failed to even register a public protest in response to the expulsion. In this context, the LWF project coordinator insisted that a refugee project without refugees should be discontinued, since the refugees had been sent back to Burundi. The Kigoma regional commissioner insisted that the construction projects be continued, even though the refugees were no longer welcome, a position with which the not-so-courageous UNHCR concurred (see Waters 1988). Again, I looked critically at UNHCR's role in this affair. How was it possible for the High Commissioner for *Refugees* to continue a *refugee* project when all *refugees* had been expelled?

My next stop was graduate school, eventually at the University of California, Davis. In a social theory course at Davis, I read Max Weber's (1948, 1958) descriptions of organizational rationality and, elsewhere, Arlie Russell Hochschild's (1983) descriptions of the "emotional labor" of airline stewardesses. Suddenly, my view of what I had seen in the

UNHCR and the nongovernmental organizations I worked for made more sense, and my own youthful passion for insisting on efficiency and predictability a little less.

The connection between the two very different approaches to social theory is this. On the one hand the UNHCR and the agencies around it acted very much like the rational profit-seeking organizations Weber described as existing in both the private and public sectors. In particular, they were organized on the same principles; and as a result there were the demands for accountability, bureaucratic efficiency, reliance on hierarchy, search for precedent and consistency, persistence, expansion, and the need to quantify.

But there was a difference between refugee relief bureaucracies and the more common private- and public-sector bureaucracies. The "profit" (financial or political) was not generated by the sale of what they manufactured or the services delivered, but depended on the size of the donations they received and spent. Hence, the element of the "emotional management" Hochschild described. The amount of money received (and therefore spent) was generated not through the impersonal production and sale of a product or service, or even by the generation of a service for a political constituency, but by "appeals" to "donors" who themselves neither consumed the product produced nor sought conventional profits. In other words, the "rational profit" was instead achieved by soliciting funds from "donors," who typically were the governments and citizens of Western democracies and Japan. These countries had mixed motives: they do value humanitarian values for their own sake, but they also had domestic and international interests. The point is that the "bottom line" for the humanitarian agencies was not financial profits in a price-setting market, but the ability to attract more dollars through appeals to sympathy, friendship, empathy, and the emotional criteria implied by "deservedness." The engine through which this emotion is generated is the international press, which focuses sympathy through its selection of crises to respond to. My expelled Burundians never made it to the *New York Times,* and thus, regardless of the bureaucratic rationality I expected of the UNHCR, were unlikely to command humanitarian interest. Furthermore, this necessity to generate such emotion on a large "bureaucratized" scale was very similar to the way Hochschild's flight attendants needed to use smiles and other emotional cues to sell seats on an airplane. In both cases the results are similar. Just as Hochschild's stewardesses became cynical about the smile they sold, refugee workers become cynical about the refugee projects they implement.

In other words, my Weberian love for making dollars work as efficiently as possible was irrelevant in a refugee context, since organizational inefficiency could be papered over as long as the emotions of the donors were tended to. Perceived deservedness determined the number of dollars available for the bureaucracy, not efficiency. In other words, "emotion" was the implicit product of the UNHCR, whether measured in terms of lives saved, good feelings, press clippings, videos produced, social justice generated, or some other measure. And uniquely for the refugee relief business, the good feelings that were relevant were not those of the recipients (as is the case to a degree in government social welfare programs) but of the distant donors viewing the results of their largesse on television.

A practical chance to test and refine these ideas came to me in 1994 when I was hired by the Lutheran World Federation to help establish their programs to receive Rwandan refugees. I was assigned to Ngara, Tanzania, effective May 2, 1994, and participated in the relief operation for the next two years. Much of this book is the result of what I saw, heard, and thought during that time and is recounted in the ethnographic first person. I also present reports about broader documentation from the operation. The ethnographic portions include discussions of Tanzania, and also a bit about Thailand. Descriptions of what happened in Rwanda and Zaire draw on written sources and some personal communications.

This approach is I think distinct from that of others who have written about the Rwanda refugee relief operation, and as a result I view this book as complementary to two other types of writing about the Rwanda refugee crisis. First are some outstanding, recently published scholarly historical assessments, including Gérard Prunier's *The Rwanda Crisis: History of a Genocide*, Alison des Forges's *Leave None to Tell the Story*, and Peter Uvin's *Aiding Violence*. The first two books use the methods of the historian to describe what happened in Rwanda. Uvin's book implies a comparative approach, but never moves very far beyond the situation in Rwanda. All three books, because of their emphasis on Rwanda, imply that what happened in Rwanda was unique and needs to be understood in its own right, as indeed it can be. This is the nature of "historical particularity," a subject which will be returned to in the discussion about methods in Chapter 5.

The second genre relative to which I position this book is the reporting of the relief community itself. This reporting undertakes to evaluate itself and its operation for its own bureaucratic needs. Some of this reporting is of high quality. The *Joint Evaluation of Emergency Assistance to Rwanda (JEEAR)* is the best known of this type of work, although Oxfam, Médecins sans Frontières, the United States Committee for Refugees, and others also make notable contributions. The strength of this genre is that it was accessible to policy-makers interested in decisions about the Great Lakes region of Africa at the time decisions needed to be made. Such analysis, though, often ends up describing the proverbial trees rather than the forest. These reports tend to describe the administrative and political difficulties in particular circumstances and times, rather than the assumptions and weaknesses inherent to the broader operation. Thus, much has been written about the breakup of the Rwandan camps in Zaire, but little as to what the breakup tells us about the organizational capacity of the UN and the NGO agencies who supervised the camps.

My aim with this book is to draw on the strengths of both genres, to combine a historical perspective with a general sociological understanding of the bureaucracies.

Notes

1. There has been some controversy about how the Rwandan repatriation was conducted. At the time, interested parties (including the United States and Rwanda) insisted that the repatriation was by and large successful and was accomplished without significant loss of life. More recent estimates indicate that between 200,000 and 300,000 of the refugees are unaccounted for. Estimates by UNHCR (the United Nations High Commissioner for Refugees) and MSF (Médecins sans Frontières, or Doctors Without Borders) indicate that as many as 200,000 Hutu refugees may have been killed by soldiers from Rwanda and/or by Zairean rebels (Lemarchand 1999:196).

2. Louise Holborn (1975) has written the most comprehensive history of refugee program administration in the period following World War II. John G. Stoessinger (1956) has written about the evolution of the international refugee regime in the period starting after World War I and extending to the early 1950s.

3. See Special issue of *Disasters*, 20(4) 1996, for a discussion of the study, especially the Introduction by Macrae. Fifty-two consultants were hired to produce the study, which took a little over one year to be published. John Borton alerted me to the magnitude of the expense in a conversation in Ngara in July 1995.

2

Refugees, International Politics, and the Good Samaritan

The Origin of the Good Samaritan's Bureaucracies

Programs of refugee relief and resettlement are not new. One can imagine Moses in the Sinai fussing with Israelite recipients over the quality and quantity of food rations, in the same way refugee administrators do today. Records about the American Tories who fled to Nova Scotia at the end of the American Revolution are clearer. Soon after their arrival in Nova Scotia, their British benefactors began to moan about the danger of the refugees' developing an unhealthy dependence on the relief distributed by the military (MacKinnon 1986). But, these efforts, while commendable, were not like those today; they were not carried out by permanent organizations like the Red Cross or UN agencies whose only job is to seek catastrophe and provide succor on behalf of "donors." This chapter is about how relief bureaucracies emerged in order to mediate relations between donors and beneficiaries.

A few of the modern relief agencies have their primary origin in wars that took place in the nineteenth century (Shawcross 1984:100–101), but the really large and efficient process of mass famine relief began in earnest during and after World War I (Kaplan 1988:29–30; Smith 1984:80–97). A complex of agencies developed together, often in fits and starts, as the international refugee relief regime moved from crisis to crisis, coping with changing definitions of "refugee." As we seek explanations for how it developed, the period since World War I is perhaps best divided into four eras.

First was the period between 1914 and 1939, when famine relief was first undertaken by the American businessman Herbert Hoover, first in Belgium during World War I, and later in Russia after the war (see Smith 1984). He went beyond the efforts of the Red Cross, which had ministered to combatants, and organized food deliveries to civilians trapped by military blockades. Following this effort the Arctic explorer Fridtjov Nansen became the League of Nations' first "High Commissioner for Refugees," and issued 1.5 million "refugee passports" to stateless White Russians, Armenians, and Greeks in the 1920s (Shawcross 1984:80). The limitations of this system, which was dependent on the goodwill of "host" nations, faltered when Nansen's successor as High Commissioner could not duplicate this achievement in the 1930s after Jews were expelled by Nazi Germany.

In the period immediately after World War II the focus shifted to resettling European refugees. Twelve million refugees were resettled and repatriated by the Allies following World War II. Also at this time, the United Nations Relief and Works Agency was established to help Palestinian refugees (Harrell-Bond 1986:xii; Holborn 1975). This was followed in 1951 by the Office of the United Nations High Commissioner for Refugees (UNHCR), which was charged with providing legal protection against forcible repatriation and the coordination of relief activities, and was provided with a $300,000 budget (Cunliffe 1995). At the time, UNHCR activity was limited to providing assistance only to those who were refugees as a result of World War II, a million of whom remained in Europe at that time.

A third period, which began in the 1960s, marked a move into refugee relief in the Third World. This was first done by the International Committee for the Red Cross (ICRC), which became deeply involved in the provision of relief to both sides in the Nigerian Civil War (Shawcross 1984:102–103). The ICRC, a Swiss organization, is unique among the Red Cross societies because international treaties give it responsibility for visiting prisoners of war. In part because of this duty, ICRC has principles of "confidentiality" and "neutrality" in its relations with the combatants, the UN, NGOs, and the press. Note, though, that the UN itself was left behind in this expansion; in the context of the massive humanitarian emergency in East Pakistan/Bangladesh, even Secretary General U Thant of the UN acknowledged that in the early 1970s, the UN was not equipped to deal with humanitarian emergencies (Oliver 1978:20).[1]

Nevertheless, in the late 1970s, a complex of agencies, an "international refugee relief regime," emerged to provide refugee relief under UN coordination. This happened in response first to the Indochinese refugee crises of 1977–83, and later to a seemingly intractable refugee problem in Africa. In the process, refugee protection came to be seen as more than a simple legal problem. Rather it was seen as intertwined with the provision of clean water, shelter, and food, whether in refugee encampments or in refugee settlements. Finally, in the 1990s, focus moved into the issue of "internally displaced persons," or IDPs. These were people legally defined as being in "refugeelike circumstances" despite the fact that they had not crossed a recognized international border. It was noted that their needs were often identical to those of people who had crossed borders.

The story told here is a historical account of how this international refugee relief regime developed. It is very much the story of an international regime, for no one agency dominates refugee relief.[2] At different times and places, different agencies within the international refugee relief regime have dominated relief operations. For example, the Biafra operation (1968–79) was coordinated by the International Committee for the Red Cross, the Indochinese programs in Thailand by UNHCR, and relief programs in Cambodia (1979–83) by UNICEF (United Nations International Children's Emergency Fund—now shortened to United Nations Children's Fund). The Ethiopia crisis (1984–85) was coordinated by USAID, Catholic Relief Services (CRS), and the Lutheran World Federation (LWF). The Rwanda refugee crisis was coordinated by the UNHCR. As of this writing, refugee relief in Albania for Kosovar refugees is being coordinated by a combination of NATO (North Atlantic Treaty Organization, a military treaty) and UNHCR. Of the international agencies, UNHCR is the only agency to specialize solely in refugee work. But this involvement is far from being a monopoly; other agencies have played central roles.

Between the World Wars

Hoover's Famine Relief

Two recurrent issues emerged after World War II, which brought about the development of the refugee relief bureaucracies and which continue to be at the core of refugee relief operations. First is the need to provide food, water, and shelter to civilian victims of conflict—the succor that the Good Samaritan provided; second is the need for internationally guaranteed legal protection for refugees unable to return to their home country. The former is grounded in the commonsense proposition that the right to life is most basic. The latter recognizes that this life everywhere is in a context of a world divided into nation-states that should—and usually do—guarantee such rights to its citizens.

The first modern refugee relief operations were undertaken during and after World War I. The businessman Herbert Hoover made his fortune in mining, but he became the catalyzing force behind deliveries of aid to Belgium during the war and, later, to Russia during the civil war between the White and Red armies (Smith 1984). Both operations involved a combination of material and food supplies, which were to be distributed to millions of noncombatant civilians. Both operations distributed surplus American commodities, but they also relied on advertising and private donations to create distance between themselves and the Allied governments, and thereby maintain the veneer of being apolitical and of being neutral in their provision of humanitarian relief. For the first time, relief programs were measured in millions of tons of commodities distributed, and hundreds of millions of dollars spent.

Neither of Hoover's operations addressed the central cause of the refugee crisis, which was later seen, correctly, to be rooted in the breakdown in the relationship between the state and its citizen. Thus, at the conclusion of the Russian operation in 1920, the new League of Nations concluded that a permanent office to represent stateless persons was needed to resolve the contradiction of lost citizenship. This move was timely because the conclusion of World War I had seen the breakup of three multinational empires: Russia, Ottoman Turkey, and Austria-Hungary. The resulting civil war in Russia and a series of new conflicts among the newly created Balkan states also led to a series of crises in which large populations of civilians suffered. In particular, agreements among the new states provided for the exchange of new populations in accordance with a new policy that each nationality should have its own state. The results were massive population exchanges in the Balkans, the largest between Greece and Turkey, often in the context of war.

High Commissioner for Refugees

The post–World War I order left Europe with many millions of stateless persons: people who could not claim citizenship in any one of the new countries. To accommodate these people the League of Nations in 1921 established an Office of the High Commissioner for Refugees under the leadership of the Norwegian Arctic explorer Fridtjov Nansen. Headquartered in Geneva, the new office was primarily a diplomatic and legal office concerned with making pleas to respect the rights of refugees, many of which came from minority groups in new nation-states. Nansen was assigned special responsibility for Russian, Armenian, Assyrian, Austrian, and German refugees across eastern Europe. His work as High Commissioner was best known for his issuance of travel documents known as Nansen passports to those unable to claim citizenship in any country. At the time, the rationale for the office was seen as a one-time need resulting from the breakup of the empires. After that, the rights of minorities were to be preserved by the nation-states of which they were citizens. In this context, Nansen was able to facilitate the resettlement of millions of refugees from Russia, Greece, Turkey, and other countries. To accomplish this he had to rely on the goodwill of the settlement countries.

But this reliance on the goodwill of the nation-states was a limitation, and the effectiveness for the League of Nations refugee office was reached in the late 1930s when Jews began to be expelled from Nazi Germany. Confronted with a new exodus caused by an explicit state policy, the Office of the High Commissioner pleaded with western European countries and the United States to accept a substantial portion of the Jews forcibly exiled from Germany. Relying only on the power of persuasion, the pleas of the High Commission were largely in vain; in retrospect, the failure to remove Jewish refugees from areas where they would be abused, deported, and eventually executed is recognized as being a major failure in the prewar world order.

The Aftermath of World War II

At the end of World War II in 1945, there were an estimated 12 million to 20 million refugees in Europe. For large numbers of people originally displaced by the defeated Germany, it was a matter of returning home (Stoessinger 1956:52). For a few million, though, this was problematic; large numbers lived in countries occupied during the war by the Soviet Union, and others were survivors of concentration camps with no realistic place to return to. In 1945 and 1946, large numbers of these refugees were repatriated to the Eastern Bloc countries, sometimes forcibly, where some were apparently executed by the new governments, sometimes within earshot of the border (Stoessinger 1956:58, Proudfoot 1956: 214–218).

This experience, combined with the prewar failure to take care of Jewish refugees, led to the enunciation by the United Nations of a *non-refoulement* (literally, "no forcing back") principle, in which it was asserted that no state could forcibly return a refugee who had a well-founded fear of persecution in his or her home country. Likewise, states had the responsibility to provide asylum to refugees who had a "legitimate fear of persecution" on the grounds of race, religion, ethnicity, political views, etc., should they be deported back to their own countries. In 1952, this was enshrined in an international treaty, and the Office of the United Nations High Commissioner for Refugees (UNHCR) was established to protect the legal right of refugees to asylum, and to facilitate voluntary repatriation or integration into new national communities (Pitterman 1984:44). The High Commissioner was provided with $300,000 to establish an office to focus on this legalistic task (Cunliffe 1995).

In 1952, there were still several very specific restrictions on the authority of the UNHCR in its charter. First, it was restricted to resettling refugees within Europe. Second, it was to be "nonoperational," meaning that it would not undertake to directly administer refugee assistance operations, but only facilitate them through the institutions and organizations in host countries. Finally, the charter of the UNHCR was for only five years, and therefore subject to renewal. Ostensibly, this was because it was expected that all refugee operations would be completed, and the need for the UNHCR terminated. In practice, this state of affairs continues today, and the five-year limit also permits the member nations of the UN to keep the UNHCR on a short leash with respect to their own political needs. In more practical terms, it means that planning for periods longer than five years cannot be undertaken. Consistent with this temporary status and with the office's nonoperational role, the UNHCR has never been given a budget to undertake major relief operations on its own initiative.

The Refugee Mandate Expands: The Decolonization of Africa

In the 1960s, the nature of refugee assistance changed. By this time, the post–World War II refugee situations were resolved, and even though there was a brief shift in attention when refugees fled Hungary in 1958, by the early 1960s, it was apparent that there was little refugee work left to do in Europe.

But with decolonization in Africa and Asia, millions of new refugees began to appear. Africa in particular provided a place that the refugee bureaucracies could expand, and in 1963 the UNHCR took its first tentative step outside its home continent by establishing resettlement programs for Rwandans in newly independent Tanganyika (its name was changed to Tanzania in 1964). In this operation, two thousand Rwandan Tutsi refugees were flown from near Goma in the Congo to Tanganyika for resettlement. The new government of Tanganyika was amenable to this program, but only on the condition that the government itself not be directly responsible for the new settlement. The Tanganyikan government also pointed out that it did not have staff or "operational capacity" to implement the new work. The UNHCR, of course, was prohibited by its own charter from being "operational." Consequently, to do the actual work of resettlement, UNHCR approached the Lutheran World Federation (LWF) office in Geneva and asked it to establish an agency to undertake the assistance portion of the resettlement. LWF did this by establishing an office in Tanganyika, and Mwese settlement for Rwandans was built on the shore of Lake Tanganyika (Holborn 1975).

But the biggest relief effort in Africa did not involve UNHCR. The Nigerian Civil War led to the deaths of 1 million to 3 million in Biafra in 1967–70, a conflict which captured the attention of the West. The British and American press reported widely on the starvation occurring, seemingly as the result of a Nigerian government policy that could be characterized as genocide (Jacobs 1987:46–53). Nevertheless, the Nigerian government asked the International Committee for Red Cross (ICRC) to coordinate relief efforts for the survivors. This involved difficult negotiations on both sides of the civil war, and delays in the delivery of relief goods, which probably exacerbated death rates. ICRC was roundly criticized for its slow response, a charge they were ill prepared to refute in the newspapers and magazines where it was made, in part owing to their strong tradition of emphasizing political neutrality and confidentiality (Jacobs 1987; Thompson 1990).

Meanwhile, in the 1960s, UNHCR expanded its work across Africa, particularly in those countries adjacent to the Portuguese colonies of Mozambique, Angola, and Guinea, countries where revolts were being suppressed. In each country, the UNHCR entered into agreements with NGOs (nongovernmental organizations) that were already in place or were specifically formed to deal with refugee issues. Typically, under these agreements, UNHCR negotiated with a Western country to pay for a specific project on behalf of the refugees, which was to be "implemented" by the nongovernmental agency. The nongovernmental agency in turn often had other donors that contributed a portion of the costs in partnership with what the UNHCR was able to raise. UNHCR in turn monitored the implementation of the contract and became "operational" only when issues of individuals' legal rights of refugee status were raised. In response, the UNHCR's bureaucracy expanded, as did the cluster of agencies with which it implemented projects around the world.

The largest of its partners was to be the Lutheran World Federation, which opened offices primarily in Africa during the 1970s. Other large agencies entering into relationships with UNHCR included CARE, International Rescue Committee (IRC), Oxfam, MSF (Médecins sans Frontières), and Catholic Relief Services. Rooted in often asymmetric "partnerships" dominated by UNHCR control of purse strings, the relationships between the UNHCR and its partners were often fractious, despite generally being symbiotic relationships.

Also critical in this emerging mix of the late 1970s and early 1980s were the UN agencies which were independent of the UNHCR. Most prominent was the World Food Programme (WFP), which was "operational" and provided the most important relief item, food, for the UNHCR to distribute via its partner agencies. Other UN agencies involved in relief and refugee work included UNICEF, WHO (World Health Organization), and UNDP (United Nations Development Programme). Out of this alphabet soup of agencies came demands for the greater administrative efficiency implied by centralization. This, however, was resisted by agencies interested in protecting their turf, a primary and consistent criticism of UN agencies in general.

The Indochinese Relief Operation

The constellation of agencies partnered with the UNHCR was given a major boost beginning in 1979 and 1980 when it played a major role in the Cambodia operation in Thailand, and the reception of Vietnamese "boat people" throughout Southeast Asia. In a way not seen since the end of World War II, refugees were considered as being worthy of humanitarian concern. This happened because the needs of refugees, the political interests of the West, the expanding capabilities of the UNHCR, and the attention of the world press coincided.

In 1975, the Communist Khmer Rouge overtook Cambodia and violently emptied the major cities. Having closed down Cambodia's borders, they then tried to establish a utopian agriculturally based state. In humanitarian terms, the consequences were a disaster. Firm numbers are still not available, but by 1978 it was clear that over 1 million Cambodians had died of execution, starvation, and other causes associated with the establishment of the new society.

Refugees bringing rumors about the Khmer Rouge death toll between 1975 and 1978 were frequently heard in Thailand. A few journalists wrote about the rumors, but not in a manner that had caught the attention of the United States, the British, UNHCR, or others interested in refugee relief programs. There were flurries of interest, but overall it was treated less seriously than the Biafran relief program conducted by the ICRC in the late 1960s. It was not until 1979 that the world took notice.

In 1978–79, Indochinese fled both Cambodia and Vietnam. This flight, following closely on the 1975 defeat of the United States' client regimes in those countries, helped justify, particularly for Americans, their long involvement in the Indochinese wars. In effect, it provided an "I told you so" with respect to Communist aggression. The Vietnamese refugees, many of whom had connections in the United States and therefore a constituency, arrived in Malaysia, Thailand, Hong Kong, and other countries on rickety boats telling horrific tales of escape and pirates. This finally attracted the attention of the Western press, a situation Southeast Asian governments exploited by dramatically towing refugees back out to sea, arguing that doing so was necessary in order that their countries not be saddled with an "unfair burden." The cynical strategy, conducted in front of cameras and at the expense of the refugees, actually worked, and Western countries began accepting the boat people for resettlement (see Shawcross 1984; Mason and Brown 1983).

Cambodians arrived in Thailand later and with less dramatic fanfare. Vietnam invaded Cambodia in January 1978, and refugees fleeing both the retreating Khmer Rouge and the Vietnamese invaders began to appear on the Thai-Cambodian border. Thailand responded by quietly forcing the refugees back to Cambodia, often in a fashion calculated to lead to fatalities in minefields, at the hands of Khmer Rouge, or by starvation. The most well-known of these incidents occurred in June 1978, when the Thai military forced between 43,000 and 45,000 refugees back to Cambodia on a path that went alongside a minefield. This raised a furor among the Western embassies in Bangkok, a situation which the Thai prime minister said he was pleased with, as it dramatized the necessity for the West to take responsibility for resettling Cambodians as well as the Vietnamese (Shawcross 1984:88–91).

On behalf of the expelled Cambodians, the small Bangkok offices of the UNHCR and ICRC registered diplomatic protests and made the rounds of both Southeast Asian and Western embassies. ICRC also attempted to establish a humanitarian assistance program via the Vietnamese-sponsored government in Phnom Penh. But, both UNHCR and ICRC were particularly wary of how the Vietnamese would interpret assistance efforts along the Thai border, an area where Khmer Rouge forces were strong. As a result, despite knowledge of desperate suffering on the Thai border, the agencies believed that the most suffering could be averted quickly by means of Phnom Penh–based programs. However, the response to these weak diplomatic efforts was negligible, and the Thai continued with their hard line. Thus, it was not until October 1979, when Cambodian refugees facing famine massed at the Thai border, that a humanitarian response came. In October, a Swedish film crew broadcast pictures of the famine victims to Europe. *Time* magazine also published an eight-page cover story, "Deathwatch in Cambodia." The report, whose coverage came from the border rather than inside Cambodia, began:

> It is a country soaked in blood, devastated by war, and its people are starving to death. . . . Relief agencies believe as many as 2.25 million Cambodians could die of starvation in the next few months unless a vast amount of aid is provided soon. . . . There is nothing ennobling about death by starvation. . . . Soon after food is cut off, the body switches to burning fuel reserves in the liver and fatty tissues. After fat is exhausted, the body accelerates the breakdown of protein in the muscles including the heart, which saps strength. At the same time, the body attempts to husband its resources by cutting energy requirements to the minimum. Pulse rate and blood pressure fall and body temperature drops. Men become impotent; women stop menstruating and nursing mothers fail to produce milk; children stop growing. . . . Death comes in many ways. The intestinal walls become damaged; severe and constant diarrhea may develop." (quoted in Shawcross 1984:171).

The Carter administration, which had a new focus on humanitarianism in foreign policy, responded by generously funding the UNHCR and NGOs to provide relief programs. Thailand accepted this support and requested that the UNHCR coordinate relief efforts.

As a result, the Cambodian operation became the first time when an UNHCR-led international refugee relief regime achieved a significant autonomous role alongside national governments. This position was not rooted in sovereignty, nor in financial resources, but in an ideological commitment to a previously abstract "humanitarianism." This position was established through an appeal to moral authority rooted in the agency's ability to appeal directly the Western public via the press.[3] But the UNHCR still had little practical sovereignty rights outside the diplomatic passports their own officials carry. Financially, the UNHCR continued to be dependent on appeals to donor governments, especially the United States and Japan.

The money collected by the UNHCR in response to this press-driven appeal for Cambodians was far beyond what had been done before. Funds primarily from Western governments were received as fast as they could be spent. Budgets ballooned to a point where the UNHCR was even able to hire a helicopter to ferry staff and reporters to the camps. The initial camp at Sa Kaeo was quickly established, but then abandoned owing to flooding (it had been built in rice fields). A second camp was established at Khao I Dang, and the Japanese agreed to install a state-of-the-art water system. This water system also proved unusable, so more funds were solicited to purchase a water-trucking fleet so that a minimum of water could be trucked in. Between October 1979 and December 1981, the UNHCR and its NGO partners were able to spend $125.7 million in donations, primarily from the United States and Japanese governments. At least $100 million more was collected and spent by ICRC, WFP, and the NGO-partners of the UNHCR (Shawcross 1984:391–393 Waters 1984). Costs included housing and full rations, as the Thai government did not permit refugees to farm outside the crowded camps.

As the Cambodian relief program aged, though, it began to show its rough edges. Within two years programs were cut, camps closed. By 1982, the Thai responded by implementing a "humane deterrence" program in order to encourage Western governments into supporting feeding and third-country settlement programs.[4]

Finally, it was argued more convincingly that the camps had become a "pull" factor, encouraging people to become refugees, rather than simply a response to the "push" of persecution in their home country, a dualism implicit in the internationally recognized definition of a refugee. By recognizing only persecution, the law consigned all other motives to the "pull" factor or economics. Despite the simplicity in the "either-or" dichotomy of the economic migrant/refugee distinction, such decisions were undertaken at the urging of the United States. As a result, it was reasoned, the legal right to asylum remained intact (McNamara 1989). These policies were in place throughout the 1980s. Whether the refugee flow from Cambodia, which eventually stopped, did so as a result of the implementation of these policies or of the gradual pacification of the Khmer Rouge has never been evaluated.

The successes in the Cambodia operation established the pattern of press-driven expansion of the humanitarian bureaucracies, followed by periods of decline in program effectiveness as attention shifted away. I worked at Phanat Nikhom Camp in 1983, and when I arrived, expatriate workers had already made T-shirts advertising the various camp closure dates announced for the Cambodian camps. Each closure had precipitated a "crisis" that was announced to the refugees and refugee workers and in the press. As I recall, there were seven such dates by that point, reflecting "firm deadlines" set by the Thai government and donors in the United States and Europe. But even by this time, it was widely acknowledged that these deadlines were simply Thai efforts at reviving donor interest in funding refugee programs, rather than actual camp closure policies. In fact, the camps were not closed until the 1990s; and then only after a major proportion of Cambodians had been settled in the United States and France, and a lasting peace agreement had been negotiated between the Phnom Penh government and remnants of the Khmer Rouge (Mayotte 1992:93–124; Shawcross 2000:70–82).

African Settlement Programs in the 1970s and 1980s

While the high-profile and high-cost programs emerged in Indochina, other approaches to refugee work were developing, particularly in Africa. By international definitions, which emphasize flight across international borders, Africa had by far the most refugees in the world. African governments did not, however, demonstrate the hostility to newly arriving refugees so common in Southeast Asia, and instead developed reception programs grounded in what they called "traditional African hospitality." Harrell-Bond (1986:16) has noted that such hospitality is extended in spite of the fact that there is a positive incentive to threaten refugees, namely, to attract more support from the international community.[5]

As a result, some of the largest and most extensive refugee assistance programs in the 1980s were in Africa, not Southeast Asia, where the press focused its attention.[6] Relief efforts for refugees from Mozambique, Angola, South Africa, Burundi, Sudan, and Ethiopia served millions—even though Africa represented only about one third of the UNHCR program budget—whereas the programs in Southeast Asia served hundreds of thousands. One consequence of this austerity was that "closed" camps in which refugees were not allowed to farm were impossible in Africa, as rations were inadequate for survival. Thus, in Africa most refugees were not in camps or settlements, and even those in camps were expected to farm and thereby raise a portion of their own subsistence. What rations there were, were considered "supplemental" and included only basic dried goods; certainly they did not include the fresh pork and vegetables I saw distributed in the Thai camps in 1982–83.[7]

Massive resettlement programs in countries like Botswana, Zambia, Malawi, Swaziland, Zimbabwe, Uganda, and Tanzania also reflected the broader willingness of African governments to permit resettlement schemes that had the potential for continuing into an indefinite future. Typically, refugees were allotted lands in remote areas to establish new homesteads.[8] This permitted refugees to work and subsist far away from fighting in ongoing civil wars in countries like Mozambique and Angola. They did this often with only minimal financial and food subsidies from the international refugee relief regime. As a result, there was less pressure for quick repatriation/resettlement schemes as emphasized in Southeast Asia.

Another result in Africa was the concept of "relief through development" and an emphasis on refugee self-sufficiency in food production during the 1980s. Irrespective of criticisms concerning its implementation, this provided a marked contrast to the Southeast Asian programs (see, for example, Rogge 1985; Harrell-Bond 1986; Waters 1999a). Policies for resettlement, which were formalized in the UNHCR's conferences for donors and hosts of the 1980s, assumed food self-sufficiency in new settlements after a period of three to seven years. Other refugees were acknowledged to have settled and achieved self-sufficiency "spontaneously"; in some circumstances, there were more of these latter refugees than of those who were formally resettled (Cuny and Stein 1989). For both groups, programs of naturalization and integration into new countries were sometimes established. Likewise, as wars and political confrontation in southern Africa dissipated in the 1990s, programs for repatriation were initiated; large numbers of refugees made their way back to Mozambique in particular. Others adopted the citizenship of their new country or, as likely, informally blended into local populations (Malkki 1994; Sommers 1994).

Major African Relief Operations:
Ethiopia, Sudan, and Somalia

As the 1980s ended, better-funded efforts emerged in Africa, and the international refugee relief regime began to experiment with new approaches. Among the initiatives was famine relief that was undertaken in Ethiopia, a protracted food airlift to the southern Sudan, relief operations during civil wars in Liberia and Sierra Leone, and military involvement in Somalia in 1992. Each of these experiences shaped the normative relationships existing among the UN agencies, their NGO partners, and

African governments. The larger relief operations were also focused by press attention, which raised expectations for humanitarian action.

Like the Cambodian operation, the Ethiopia relief operation of 1984–85 was galvanized by press attention. Despite explicit famine warnings from agencies in Ethiopia in early 1984, international response was slow. The United States in particular did not want to prop up the Marxist government whose policies had led to the famine in the first place. It was not until a film by a Kenyan, Mohammed Amin, was broadcast on the BBC and in North America that the world's attention shifted to the famine, which was, in effect, lifted out of the broader political context as a consequence. Largely as a result, massive assistance appeared at the beginning of the operation, followed by pleas to sustain life-sustaining operations and a diminution of press attention. USAID, CRS, and LWF were particularly aggressive in mounting relief programs on the back of this publicity.

Operation Lifeline Sudan was different. Beginning in the late 1980s, when it was coordinated by WFP and the LWF's Nairobi office, Operation Lifeline Sudan has in fact been a "lifeline." WFP commodities have been and continue to be provided to refugees and the internally displaced in the southern Sudan. Deliveries typically occur by truck, but expensive airlifts have taken place during periods when towns have been unreachable because of the rains or the siege tactics of the Sudanese military. Much of the support for this "lifeline" has originated in the United States, which in addition to a humanitarian interest has a political interest in destabilizing the Islamic government in Khartoum.

Ironically, the lifeline has kept alive the rebel force and the communities that shelter them, thus prolonging the war. As a result, the context of such operations includes the death of millions from conflict-induced causes, as well as the flight of hundreds of thousands into refugee camps in Uganda and Kenya in what is arguably the most bloody of the world's conflicts. The government forces' brutality in attacking civilian populations, selling of slaves, and the use of starvation as a tool is regarded as even more repugnant than the excesses of the rebellious forces. But a hypothetical question about whether rebellion is sustained by food aid, and as a result causes more human suffering than would occur in its absence is occasionally asked (Shawcross 2000:282). The question is not only unanswerable, but also probably irrelevant. As critics are quick to point out, relief aid responds to publicity and political needs, not to assessments of how to alleviate human suffering.

Somalia is perhaps the most unusual of the African operations in the humanitarian aid context. Following the overthrow of President Siad Barre in 1991, the country slipped into a civil war in which competing warlords fought over control of the southern part of the country. The collapse of the state apparatus and the fighting over political control permitted famine conditions to emerge in 1992. Aid agencies, especially ICRC and CARE, organized the distribution of food, but unprotected convoys were looted by competing warlords, who sold the grains on local markets to finance their armies.

The agencies in Somalia responded by hiring ever larger militias of their own; for example, Natsios (1997:84) recounts that by the end of 1992 ICRC had employed between 15,000 and 20,000 armed guards to protect food shipments. This only seemed to add to the anarchy, as it stimulated blackmail by militia seeking employment as "guards." As a result, a number of American NGOs, CARE the most prominent, advocated for protection from the United States military. They did so by raising the specter of imminent mass starvation in the context of the large in-country thefts. *Newsweek* magazine described the nature of starvation:

> During the famine in Somalia, perhaps the worst ever recorded, average food intake for adults has dwindled from a satisfactory 1,700 calories a day in 1988 to a hopelessly inadequate 200. . . . In essence the starving body consumes itself, devouring its own fat and muscle while shutting off less important systems to keep the brain and the rest of the central nervous system operating. . . . Loss of fat around the eyes gives them a sunken look, and the face starts to wrinkle in what starvation experts call the old-man syndrome (*Newsweek*, December 21, 1992, p. 38).

In response to press reports, President Bush in late 1992 dispatched U.S. Marines to Somalia for the express purpose of protecting food deliveries. This action received the approval of the UN, which took the unusual step of not giving a member state (Somalia) effective veto power over an operation on its own territory. After the Clinton administration took office, the goal shifted to the reestablishment of civil authority, and command of the operation was shifted to the United Nations. It is estimated that as many as 100,000 people were saved from starvation; the goal of "state building," however, was never achieved, and in 1995 the UN withdrew its last contingent of troops (Natsios 1997).

Overview: the International Refugee Relief Regime

This brief overview of the history of refugee assistance is designed to show how and why the international regime has developed as it has. It is of course by no means exhaustive; many more operations have been undertaken than have been described here. However, it does point to how some of the normative standards for giving assistance first emerged and are developing. Among these principles are the following:

- UN agencies have a central role in the coordination of humanitarian assistance. Notably, this is a coordination role, not a hierarchical role. The UN agencies have little direct supervisory authority over the staffs of the specific NGOs typically implementing actual feeding programs.
- UNHCR should be nonoperational while still coordinating. This principle is to a certain extent a contradiction. Coordination implies some ability to coerce cooperation, whether through the power of the purse or other means that influence assistance policies.
- UN agencies are by their very nature sensitive to the interests of governments, which almost by definition have a seat at the United Nations in New York—analogous to a UN agency's board of directors. At times this results in conflict between the human rights that UN agencies seek to protect and the political excesses of those same governments.
- Though UN agencies do have independent humanitarian agendas, they are particularly sensitive to the priorities of the governments of the Western democracies and Japan, which provide the bulk of their funding. This funding, in turn, reflects not only general humanitarian interests but also domestic political interests, including those of ethnic groups, elites, and constituencies of particular nongovernmental actors.
- Filling the void between coordination and operation is a wide array of nongovernmental organizations, or NGOs, that to varying degrees and in different places have a voice independent of both the UN and host governments. To maintain this independence, the agencies must either have financial independence (for example, the ICRC, whose funding comes directly from countries that have signed the Geneva Convention, or cultivate independent relations with the other influential actor, the international media.
- A special relationship between NGOs and the press has developed, with the result that humanitarian activism via press release and insider leaks can be effective ways to influence policy.
- The Western and Japanese democracies are sensitive to the press, which itself often has no more than a passing interest in a particular place or event. Nevertheless, the nature of complex emergencies means that solutions do not neatly fit within

the popular press's attention span or simple "either/or" dichotomies.

Thus, though the tasks of humanitarian succor are similar to those undertaken by the Good Samaritan along the Judean road, the means are different. The context has shifted from an individual act by a passing stranger to an organization to which acts of mercy are delegated. This is a positive development, since it means that the definition of a neighbor has expanded. Today, in a mass catastrophe far more people can be effectively succored than could have been in the Good Samaritan's day.

Thus, in Rwanda in 1994, when something like 3 million people (figuratively) were lying by the side of the road, hurt and homeless like the man robbed and beaten on the Judean road, the bureaucratized Good Samaritan was called to assist. Even if there had been enough Good Samaritans in central Africa at that time, there were not enough bandages, oil, wine, donkeys, or inns in Rwanda to cope with a catastrophe that large. Only with the use of skills developed by the international refugee relief regime in places like Biafra, Cambodia, and Somalia was this operation possible.

In describing the strengths, weaknesses, and development of the international refugee relief regime, it is easy to forget that these normative relationships and principles are not natural, and are of fairly recent origin. The overlapping agencies—the international refugee relief regime—are a combination of modern bureaucracies seeking to expand while protecting their own turf and at the same time doing the anomalous job of assisting strangers on behalf of distant donors who have a mix of humanitarian and political goals. Because of this capability, the social space in which hundreds of thousands of people can die from famine, massacres, and disease has probably shrunk.

The following chapters describe how the systems that have emerged to provide succor work, particularly in the case of the Rwanda refugee crisis. There are, as will be described, massive inefficiencies in how aid is delivered. This, though, is not a new critique. There is also a widespread awareness that more should have been done, but solutions to this relief situation focus primarily on strengthening the existing assistance regime, not on reexamining the assumptions underlying it. Good examples of this approach to reform are provided by the *Joint Evaluation of Emergency Assistance to Rwanda* (1996) and WFP's James Ingram (1993). Both urge better finance, coordination, and centralization but without, however, examining how current methods of coordination and finance led to these weaknesses in the first place.

However, these structures are inefficient when compared to other organizations—that is, other bureaucracies (for context, see Wilson 1989). It is my contention that the strength of the international refugee relief regime is directly related to the extent to which it has been bureaucratized. If you start with this assumption, the question then arises: How can the strengths of such a bureaucracy be strengthened in order to achieve a more effective relief regime? As will be seen, I conclude that the strengths lie more in relief organizations' character as bureaucracies than in their ability to manipulate emotion and pity.

Notes

1. Thomas Oliver's book *The United Nations in Bangladesh* is instructive on the subject of how quickly the international refugee relief regime expanded between the Bangladesh crisis (1971–72) and the Indochinese crisis (1978–83). Oliver describes what are, by later standards, feeble UN bureaucracies. It took months (not days or hours) for the first relief supplies to arrive in Bangladesh. Furthermore, at that time the amounts of cash and supplies were, by today's standards, minuscule. Just 1 million blankets were requisitioned for a population of 10 million returning refugees, not counting internally displaced persons, in a country of 90 million people (1978:114–115).

The UNHCR also did not play a major role in the Bangladesh crisis of 1971–72, even though this crisis involved the flight of over 10 million refugees from East Pakistan (Bangladesh) into India in late 1971. The Indian government was hesitant about admitting too much foreign assistance for reasons of both pride and political expediency. In December 1971, India invaded East Pakistan and installed the new government of Bangladesh. This permitted the return of the refugees. A massive relief program on behalf of Bangladesh—which had been devastated by a typhoon, massacres by the Pakistani military, and the refugee flight and return—was mounted in 1972. The total death toll was estimated as high as 3 million from a combination of drowning, massacres, and famine. This relief operation involved direct aid from the United States via USAID (the United States Agency for International Development) and the establishment of an independent ad hoc UN relief operation, the United Nations Relief Operation in Dacca (UNROD). While extraordinarily "late" by 1990s standards—the relief took months to reach the Bangladeshis—this operation was considered the most successful UN relief program mounted up to that time (see Oliver 1978; Payne 1973).

2. The literature on "international regimes" is voluminous (see Haggard and Simmons 1987). For example, Puchala and Hopkins say of international regimes: "A regime exists in every substantive issue-area in international relations. . . . Wherever there is regularity in behavior, some kinds of principles, norms or rules must exist . . ." There is some debate about the fine points of this definition, but for this book, it highlights the relevant points. The features of an international refugee relief regime are a substantive issue, the international organizations (e.g. UNHCR, WFP, UNICEF, ICRC), and nongovernmental organizations that abide by regularized normative behavior. The very nature of the work means that there

is little coercive authority by which agreements (both treaty and contractual) can be enforced.

3. UNHCR was awarded the 1981 Nobel Peace Prize for its efforts in protecting Vietnamese boat people.

4. Policies of the humane deterrence program emphasized the austerity of camp life and were meant to discourage "economic adventurers," who, it was believed, comprised the majority of the new refugee arrivals, despite continuing evidence of persecution in Vietnam and war in Cambodia. However, such evaluations were also caught in between Cold War power calculation; indeed, as a consequence, the United States continued to back the Khmer Rouge's claim to Cambodia's seat at the United Nations.

5. In a footnote, Harrell-Bond (1986:16 n.6) notes that Sudanese officials were well aware that Thailand attracted more funds by threatening refugees with expulsion, which was contrary to international law.

6. The largest program in the 1980s was in Pakistan, where large numbers of Afghans settled in camps that doubled as guerilla bases. These camps were amply supported by the United States government via the UNHCR. Large numbers of Afghan refugees defined as such by the UNHCR were in Iran, which did not permit the large assistance programs that Pakistan did. Other major relief programs were in Central America.

7. The disparity between what is provided for refugees in Africa and elsewhere is a continuing source of frustration for some. As the Kosovo operation unfolded, there were flurries of e-mails among groups working in Africa who noted that African refugees are unlikely to receive special meals for diabetics, hot showers, or the amount of water being demanded (and financed) for the Kosovars. I think that this analogy could probably be extended to refugees in Asia. The refugees I saw in Thailand received higher levels of assistance than those in Africa. On the other hand, the Thai government was more harsh with the refugees when it came to movement outside camps and forcible repatriation.

8. See Malkki (1994) and Stein (1996) for descriptions of refugee settlements. See Harrell-Bond (1986) for descriptions of refugee camps in southern Sudan and Uganda in the 1980s. See Sommers (1994) for a description of Burundians in Dar es Salaam.

3

The Strength of Bureaucracy

The quality of mercy is not strained,
It droppeth as the gentle rain from heaven
Upon the place beneath; it is twice blessed
It blesseth him that gives, and him that takes.
> —William Shakespeare, *The Merchant of Venice*

Introduction

Refugee relief is a complex task. It involves organizing relief goods and refugees, and then bringing them together in an efficient fashion. It is often made more complex by the fact that refugee flight tends to be to remote areas, and at least initially, is perceived as being sudden. Thus, to accommodate refugees effectively, it is necessary to bring together resources from around the world quickly and efficiently. The only type of organization capable of marshaling the widely dispersed resources needed to do this is the modern specialized bureaucracy.

The strength of a bureaucracy lies in its breaking tasks down into manageable chunks, which can then be undertaken by officials with specific responsibilities. These officials' jobs are separate from their personalities, but their ability to do them is dependent on well-defined skills. Defined rules govern official actions and relationships. The tasks and the holders of the positions are then organized into a hierarchy of authority. This is bureaucratic organization. Finally, the bureaucracy has a well-defined goal or product. In the case of a private capitalist enterprise, this goal is the generation of profits for shareholders, whereas in government it is to undertake a specific measurable task while maintaining the authority of the group in power.[1] In relief work it is to extend mercy on a mass basis or, more generally, to "sustain humanitarian principles."

Bureaucratic organization is found in virtually all modern enterprises, and for most people living in the modern world it is taken for granted (after Weber 1948:196–198). In fact, bureaucracies are so taken for granted that they are frequently blamed for the ills of modern society, despite the fact that hierarchically organized bureaucracy *is* modern society. This is because other forms of organization—such as blind obedience to the whims of a hereditary chief or king or *ad hoc* consensus with neighbors about life's irritations—are unsuitable for the administration of mass society. Building highways, regulating markets, operating mass education systems equitably, collecting and accounting for taxation, or ensuring that the official responses to a theft in one place are similar to those in another, all require a bureaucratic response, not the whim of a chief or king. The same can be said of the large bureaucratically organized corporations which have created the modern world's wealth. They, too, need systematic rules, regulations, and procedures in order to generate the profits their shareholders demand. Organized rational bureaucracies, no matter what large and small frustrations they may cause, are fundamental to the modern world.

Bureaucratic Goals

Elemental to bureaucracies is the concept of formal rationality. Formal rationality means that for a given end, there are rules, regulations, and social structures designed to optimize the achievement of the organization's goal. Four basic elements emerge from this process: efficiency, predictability, calculability, and control by means of nonhuman technology (Ritzer 1996; Weber 1948). Notice that lacking from these four elements are other incentives for social action, such as affection, charisma, personal loyalty, and a number of other emotional qualities that regulated interaction in the premodern world.

The rationalized bureaucracy seeks to maximize all of its four elements in the service of the given end. Here it is perhaps instructive to briefly review them, for as I will show, in the context of refugee relief programs there is a discontinuity between the elements of rationality and refugee work which makes this work more inefficient than other bureaucratized tasks (after Ritzer 1996:18–19).[2]

The Rationalization of Goals

Efficiency

By efficiency, Weber meant that for businesses, as few inputs went into the generation of profits as possible. In other words, in a bureaucracy there is incentive to deliver the most bang for the buck. As a result, throughout the business, there is an emphasis on cutting costs in order to maximize profits—or at least to maximize results in terms of what the bureaucracy "produces." Relief bureaucracies are of course organized similarly; it is just that efficiency is organized to produce a vaguely de- fined "mercy" rather than financial gain.

Calculability

In becoming more efficient, bureaucracies seek to make their inputs and outputs more "calculable." This cuts across productive and administra- tive tasks. In the modern corporation, profits are calculated easily in terms of easily divisible units of money (preferably in a decimal system, as the British only recently discovered when they abolished shillings). Likewise, there is also an emphasis on calculating the inputs. In manufac- turing, such inputs include the raw material, cost of labor, etc. As recent studies have shown, in service industries, companies seek to quantify customer satisfaction through the use of surveys, tracking complaints, and even tracking compliments (see Hochschild 1983:118–119). At uni- versities, evaluation of faculty is periodically done by students, whose ratings of faculty members are turned into numbers, which are entered into a file. All is in the interest of calculability. In relief operations, calcu- lability is measured in terms of lives saved, kilocalories of food distrib- uted per refugee, money spent per refugee, etc. From such calculations, it is inferred how well the more abstract humanitarian task of delivering mercy is done.

Predictability

Predictability is a third quality Weber ascribed to bureaucracies. Bureau- cracies seek to have their subunits behave in a predictable fashion. Pre- dictability is entrenched in both written rules and regulations, and in the unwritten norms of companies and industries. The holder of a particular office or job knows what to expect (and what not to expect) from holders of other positions within the bureaucracy. Consumers also know what to expect when they purchase a product which is packaged inside a box, and citizens know what type of service to expect when they approach the government service desk at the post office, motor vehicle registry, public school, social welfare office, etc.

Bureaucracies seek to produce a predictable product. Thus, a McDon- ald's consumer knows what to expect of a Big Mac in Moscow or San Francisco. National chains take advantage of consumer desires for pre- dictability when they develop brand loyalty. Even jails and prisons within the same system produce a level of incarceration that is the same from place to place, day in and day out (Ritzer 1996). The point of predictability is that things tend to be consistent within a bureaucracy.

Predictability is particularly important in a justice system founded on principles of deterrence. The point behind deterrence is that undesirable social activity is controlled when potential offenders have a plausible belief that there will be a response. The difficulty in establishing predictable precedents in the humanitarian context is discussed in Chapter 11 where violent death in Rwanda is discussed.

Control

A final element of bureaucracies is the emphasis on seeking to control people, be they workers or consumers, through nonhuman technology, especially rules and machines. Most elemental is the tendency to assign certain tasks (and only certain tasks) to an office or agency. Rules that control employee and customer behavior might focus on where to line up in a queue, when to smile, what to wear, and even how to justify arbitrary rules ("blue suits are more businesslike than red business suits"). Human behavior is controlled by machines when the speed of an assembly line is adjusted, when time-clocks are punched, phone calls are monitored, and fuel consumption is checked.

Bureaucratic control is increased on behalf of the hierarchy. Control means that power and authority move upward toward where information is controlled. A by-product of this need to control is that the data—whether about efficiency, calculability, or predictability—are held in confidentiality; indeed, data are often secret. The tendency to maintain secrets, not surprisingly, is yet another characteristic of the need of the bureaucracy to assert control over the humans within it.

Control as an issue is returned to in Chapter 10 where the assumptions behind engineering technology are discussed, specifically in connection with questions of water engineering. Control over the laws of physics is elemental to water engineering. However, the pumps and equipment of the water engineer also control when and how water can be delivered to refugees. The emotional urgency of refugee crises means that administrations must make decisions without the types of control that bureaucracy normally generates.

The Irrationality of Rationality

Visible only from a distance, the dog, nicknamed the King of Ruffle Bar, had sustained itself for an estimated two years, was apparently in good health, and presumably would have survived in this semi-wild state, barring accidents, for the rest of his natural life. However, some well-meaning soul heard about the dog and reported him to the Society for the Prevention of Cruelty to Animals, thereby setting the bureaucratic wheels in motion. Since the King could not be approached by people, a baited trap was set. According to the *Times* report ". . . every day a police launch from Sheepshead Bay takes off for Ruffle Bar, the uninhabited swampy island of the dog. Every day, a police helicopter hovers for a half hour or more over Ruffle Bar." . . . When questioned, representatives of the ASPCA said: "When we catch the dog we will find a *happy* home for it" [emphasis added].

The ASPCA became obsessed with capturing the dog. Once triggered, the ASPCA involved the police with a remorseless, mindless persistence that is too terrifyingly characteristic of bureaucracies once they are activated. . . . Emotionally [the police] sided with the King, even while carrying out their orders. "Why don't they leave the dog alone?" said one policeman. Another observed, "The dog is as happy as a pig in a puddle." . . .

The delusional aspects have to do with the institutionalized necessity to control "everything," and the widely accepted notion that the bureaucrat knows what is best; never for a moment does he doubt the validity of the bureaucratic solution (*New York Times*, February 20, 1970, quoted in Hall, 1976:10–11).

In this description of bureaucratized rationality regarding the "King of Ruffle Bar" there is also irrationality in the bureaucratic rationality. The irrationality is in the fact that bureaucracies, developed to serve humans, ultimately end up themselves being served by humans. By-products of all this efficiency include many of the neuroses of modern society. Max Weber, writing about nineteenth-century industrial capitalism, called these neuroses the "iron cage." He saw a society that, in all its efficiency, had created mechanized petrifaction in which labored "specialists without spirit, sensualists without heart; this nullity imagines that it has attained a level of civilization never before achieved even though it is at the expense of the highest cultural and spiritual ideals" (Weber 1958:182). This is certainly the case—and the frustration—for the police officers flying the helicopter searching for the King of Ruffle Bar.

The sociologist George Ritzer, writing more recently, renamed the late twentieth-century version of this phenomenon "McDonaldization" and called it the "velvet cage." He too, complimented the outstanding efficiency of rationalized business organization, while pointing out that this process also subordinates human spirit to bureaucratic efficiency. Both terms were meant as backhanded compliments to what the authors viewed as the organizational paradigm for modern life.

Both writers make the point that out of this wonderfully productive way for managing complex tasks, many modern neuroses arise. Among them are inhumane working conditions, efficient Nazi death camps, environmental degradation, the cheapening of culture, and that 1990s neurosis named after the government's largest bureaucracy, "going postal": being overcome by a wave of violent rage. The point is that the necessarily abstract (and unpredictable) rationalism of society, carried to its logical extreme, destroys the humanity of the people who serve within the system. This, it seems, is particularly true in the large impersonal manufacturing corporation. But it is also true in other industries, which sell the most unexpected products. For example, airlines flight attendants are taught to smile on command, Disneyland sells "good feelings," and collection agency employees are taught to growl on command (Hochschild 1983; Ritzer 1996). But for the humanitarian agencies it forces a unique quandary: To become part of an efficient bureaucracy, a humanitarian organization must figure out how to take the humanity out of humanitarianism.

Taking the Humanity out of Humanitarianism: Rationalizing Relief Work

The sum of Weber's theory is that the goal of a bureaucracy is to maximize production of its product. To do this, bureaucracies grow, engulfing the less efficient and less predictable, as they seek to control. For a business this makes a great deal of sense; as it seeks to expand profits, it orders it own hierarchy to focus on this one goal. That the humanness is taken out of this process, or at least redefined according to the goal of seeking profits, is of course irrelevant. Instead, the assumption is that this mode of organization is ideal, rather than only the most productive. A consequence has been that bureaucratic modes of organization are a given. Or to borrow a somewhat old-fashioned word, bureaucratic organization becomes hegemonic, meaning that bureaucratic forms of organization are borrowed from the impersonal capitalist corporation and government and applied to tasks of a different nature. One of these tasks is international refugee relief. And while a bureaucratized form of organization is still probably the most efficient method possible for delivering massive relief to large remote populations, the very nature of the task means that the irrationalities that do emerge are different than those that characterize the dehumanizing impersonality of the corporate and government bureaucracy.

The nature of these irrationalities is best explained by evaluating the five elements discussed above—the goal of the bureaucracy, plus efficiency, calculability, predictability, and control—in the context of refugee relief.

The Essential Problem of International Refugee Relief:
A Vague Goal

What is the overarching purpose of the international refugee relief regime? Is it profits? No, though clearly profits are of concern, particularly for the vendors operating on the periphery. Is it maintenance of power, as it is the purpose of a political party? No, though this too can be an element as international refugee relief programs can enter into the calculations of diplomats focused on international politics. Is it the welfare of the refugees? It should be, but then how do you measure this welfare? Likewise, part of the answer to this last question is that an empirical evaluation of refugee suffering does not predict which crises will be responded to and which will not, although again, this does enter into calculations. What about the notorious "CNN effect"? Is the overarching purpose of the international relief regime to gain the attention of the press? This is perhaps a better predictor of how the international refugee relief regime reacts, but it is at best indirect.

Thus, the best answer even to one of the most powerful people in policy-making positions, U.S. National Security Adviser Anthony Lake, could give to Human Rights Watch was to advise them to "make more noise" (Des Forges 1996:229, 1999:625), even though this has nothing to do with rationalized bureaucratic policy analysis. Implicitly Lake was admitting that he could not, without cooperation from the press, generate the political legitimacy to spend relief funds and take principled stands.[3] But what they are really saying is that an international relief effort requires the concern and sympathy of a wealthy donor government's constituency before action will be taken. Mark Walkup (1997) framed this issue in the following fashion:

> For Humanitarian Organizations [HO], resource generation is dependent upon such factors as image enhancement, donor-centric evaluation criteria, distinctive visibility, and competitive independence. . . . Moreover, efficiency, according to donors (the ones who matter), is sometimes only a measure of how fast an HO can spend money and account for it, not whether the funds have any positive, sustainable impact on the affected population (Walkup 1997:13, 189).

Denis Pingaud, development director of one of the most successful refugee relief NGOs, Médecins sans Frontières, was recently quoted as saying, "When the media go all out on one crisis they drain a lot of donor money to the tele-visual events. . . . And that means there is less money for other places (Ford 1999)." Ironically, he goes on to note, "Nowadays TV crews get to the major crisis before we do," which of course they do, since as Pingaud in effect indicates, publicity-savvy agencies follow the TV cameras to the emergencies, rather than the other way around.

So how do refugee assistance agencies calculate their goal—in social science terms, the "dependent variable"—if it is not through profits? It seems that the dependent variable is perhaps again described in the context of the Good Samaritan: it is in terms of "mercy" and not profits. Rather, what is received is a feeling that the right response was taken, a situation justified in the moral terms of a humanitarian ethic.

In the calculation of such a dependent variable, an important element is also missing: what refugees, the actual consumers of the products purchased and delivered, themselves think, want, or need. Instead, what is important is what others think they need or deserve and those others' evaluation as to whether they received these items or not. Thus, missing in the bureaucratized feedback loop is a response from the actual consumers of the food, water, medical services, and relief supplies. As a result, it does not matter whether the consumers are price-sensitive, willing to legitimate power relations, or even legitimate the transaction. A result is that the other elements of bureaucracy, including efficiency, calculability, predictability, and control, all suffer. Walkup (1997:78) describes this situation in the context of refugee workers, whom he calls "field-level bureaucrats:"

> While field-level bureaucrats have great impact on clients' lives, clients do not have reciprocal influence. Clients are not party to Humanitarian Organization mandates, budgets, or operational guidelines. . . . When clients have grievances about the quality of service or their treatment, they cannot appeal to anyone other than these field-level bureaucrats, who themselves are limited in their capacity to make significant changes in policy.

The basic problem, then, is that the "product" of humanitarian organizations' activities is mushy. The product is difficult to describe, and can be measured only imprecisely and indirectly. Certainly it is not measured in terms of cash dividends paid to shareholders. It is not even measured as precisely as it is in democratic governments, where the "consumers" of governments services such as social welfare programs, regulations, education, highways, defense, etc. give feedback to those in power by means of easily calculable election ballots, campaign contributions, or polling research. Rather, the product is measured in terms of what are in effect needs and "good feelings" of a distant constituency, political advantages of distant countries, and so forth. This is why publicity is so important in the manner in which relief programs are administered. The point is not the good feelings of clients, the refugees, but those on the other end of the mercy calculation, the feelings of the donors. To borrow from Shakespeare, has the help given via the organization blessed him that gives? In the process of answering this question, the quality of the blessings of "him that takes" becomes less relevant.

Three More Problems:
Efficiency, Calculability, and Predictability

The imprecision of goals in refugee crises extends to issues of efficiency, calculability, and predictability. Nevertheless, much has been done in the refugee bureaucracies during the last 50 years to improve measures (i.e., to improve the calculability) of refugee health, well-being, and welfare. This is particularly true in the medical fields. Agencies like MSF and WFP have developed measures of refugee population health that take advantage of scientific techniques. This is why they report on common public health measures like height-for-weight calculations and analyses of morbidity statistics (see Essay 1). MSF and UNHCR have even gone so far as to rationalize what diseases they will treat in an emergency (wounds, diarrhea, and malaria), and which they will not (tuberculosis, AIDS, and sexually transmitted diseases). UNHCR has employees who specialize in the often difficult task of counting hundreds of thousands of refugees. Water provision is also considered an important measure of refugee health, and finely calculated statistics are often generated to suit the needs of the refugee camp administration.

Both MSF and Oxfam have developed tools such as refugee health protocols, procedures for recruiting refugee workers, particularly from Europe, and emergency water treatment kits, enabling these agencies to deliver relief items in a predictable fashion wherever in the world they work. As a consequence, the UNHCR, just like the American tourist visiting the Moscow McDonald's, when confronted with an emergency contracts out to these agencies for a fast and predictable setup of programs. Consequently, UNHCR knows what it is getting and the quality of program that will be delivered.

The need for predictability means that agency bureaucracies seek to fit into the market/business environment that donors expect. "[T]hey have learned that this appeals to donors who are rooted in regulatory and accounting modes of operation found in government or business realms. To gain legitimacy, HOs try to 'fit' with the institution environment of the donors," even when requirements for accountability are unsuitable for the relief environment (Walkup 1997:164). This often excludes chapter but less predictable local contractors.

Predictability improves the performance of actual tasks, but this does not necessarily have an impact on the delivery on the amorphous dependent variable "mercy." In fact, what happens is that when and where refugees receive such programs, measures inevitably improve. On the other hand, as described in the introductory chapter, when and for whom this capability is used varies a great deal. Most notably, in the cases of Cambodia and Ethiopia, it was tendered to refugees who were in the public eye. It also tends to be primarily done with a focus on the short run, and as a result, for example, wounds and acute diarrhea are treated in refugee camps, whereas slow diseases like tuberculosis and sexually transmitted diseases are not.

The emphasis on the short term is because of the dependent variable, which is the measure of success. Successes in delivering clean water and lowering short-term death rates can be translated into immediate good feelings for the distant constituencies the international refugee relief regime serves. This is why the more prestigious and high-profile positions in agencies like UNHCR, MSF, and Oxfam are not doctors, nurses, or engineers, but those who handle the press well. How well the medical or engineering staff actually performs does not matter unless it can be presented in a fashion appreciated by donors.

To ensure that the good feelings are controlled and maintained, donor governments in the United States and Europe fund specific projects via pledging conferences in which the UNHCR and other UN agencies present wish lists of projects. On these wish lists are fundamentals for refugee camp administration, including water and food. Governments then promise to fund particular projects on the basis of their own priorities, releasing funds or commodities to the UN agencies as tax receipts in the donor countries become available. UN agencies in turn contract with NGO partners on the basis of the wish list, with the expectation that money will be received as promised. In fact, much of the money is received late or not at all, resulting in budget-cutting sessions as governments fund—or fail to fund—projects on the basis of their own calculations of deservedness and political advantage. The result is that throughout the fiscal year, UNHCR-funded programs are cut as, inevitably, funding for the full wish list fails to materialize. UN and NGO staff members whose salaries are funded through such budgets are of course acutely aware of the tenuous nature of this funding. But again, what is sought is not completion of the project itself, but donor satisfaction.

As a result, efficiency in this context is only peripherally related to the measures developed to monitor the stability of refugee health, as this does not typically make the evening news. Rather, a plausible case needs to be made that a "near disaster" has been averted. This is a tricky task, as it requires enough "bleeding" to make the news, while convincing the viewer that unless more financial resources are forthcoming a humanitarian emergency will be magnified. Notably, the bleeding needs to be blamed on a plausible "other," and not the inefficiencies of the relief agency itself. In effect, efficiency demands continuing drama—but drama is the antithesis of what an efficient and predictable bureaucracy seeks. This is a tenuous position to hold, and explains why the bureaucracies of the Good Samaritan are ever so sensitive about (and subject to) criticism about management practices.

This leads to Weber's final element, which is control. The Good Samaritan bureaucracy seeks to control, just like any other bureaucracy. However, the ability of a bureaucracy to control matters is dependent on the above three conditions. The disjunctures between efficiency, calculability, predictability, and the vague dependent variable all make control more difficult. As a result, there is a proliferation of agencies and no one agency is able to emerge as the overall sovereign, or even coordinator, as happens with other bureaucracies.

Weber's Final Problem: The Persisting Lack of Control

The final element of Weber's typology is control: bureaucracies seek to control workers and other actors with which they interact through rationalized rules, procedures, and technology. In the international refugee relief regime, the individual bureaucracies seek this control, but none actually ever achieve it. As a result, there is little danger of the emergence of a refugee assistance cartel, or of one agency's coming to dominate all others, despite over 50 years of bureaucratization (see Ingram 1993). In fact, the emergence of a new relief opportunity leads not necessarily to the strengthening of the bureaucracies handling the previous emergency, but to a proliferation of new agencies, each seeking to carve out its own turf. This occurs despite the fact that emergencies, by their very nature, demand a coordinated response.

This variation is reflected in a number of ways. Consider a few of the emergencies briefly described in Chapter 2. First, the lead agency varies in major relief operations. Second, the pattern is not predictable. For example, ICRC has coordinated a number of emergency responses: Biafra (1968), Somalia (1991), and portions of the Cambodian response, and the response in Tanzania to the arrival of Rwandans (1994). In the Cambodia crisis, UNICEF coordinated inside Cambodia; a separate United Nations agency, United Nations Border Relief Operation, or UNBRO, in border camps served Khmer Rouge camps; and UNHCR coordinated inside Thailand. WFP coordinated assistance from Kenya into southern Sudan, while UNHCR did it for Somalis in Kenya. There is a plethora of political explanations as to why a particular agency emerges in a particular country; however, the overall phenomenon of dispersal of authority is ultimately a function of the nature of Good Samaritan bureaucracies. Indeed, when not in an emergency environment UN agencies do tend to specialize and dominate. For example, there is little doubt that world health issues like vaccination programs are coordinated by the World Health Organization. Likewise, the World Bank and International Monetary Fund have formed a very tightly coordinated bureaucracy to control international banking and have usurped development aid from the United Nations Development Programme (UNDP). It is primarily in humanitarian relief work that such consolidation of activities is difficult to identify, and it is not clear which of the international agencies is in charge. In the meantime, NGOs attached to UN agencies also proliferate, seek to dominate, and gain independence.

Walkup (1997:191–192) gave an example of how this lack of central control can translate into practical bureaucratic irrationality in the field:

> A notable example of interagency bickering involved a milling machine that was delivered when Ifo camp opened in Dadaab in 1992. A special building was constructed (now used as the logistics office) to house the large machine used to grind grain into flour. However, it was used only briefly until the [humanitarian organizations] determined it was not possible to grind grain for all the refugees. Stumped by this equity problem (which could have been resolved simply) the [humanitarian organizations] closed it down. It remained unused for almost five years until CARE "rediscovered" it and wanted to allocate its use to the community-based Economic Skills Development program. The idea was to put it into use governed by a cooperative that would pay for its fuel with fees charged to refugee users. However, a debate arose over the machine's ownership. UNHCR claimed it was theirs, but WFP claimed that they had paperwork to show that they purchased it. As a result, it still remains unused. . . .

Resistance to central control is structured into the UN and NGO bureaucracies. In the case of UNHCR charter, there are vague requirements that it not be operational, and simply pass along funds to a range of partners and subcontractors. The central activity in many refugee situations, food requisition and distribution, is in fact only a peripheral concern of UNHCR; instead it is in the purview of the WFP, even though the UNHCR-contracted agency will be the final camp manager doing the high-profile work of scooping maize into refugees' bags. ICRC has different restrictions; due to its interest in preserving principles of confidentiality and independence, it typically has only remote relations with other agencies, and does not seek the role of coordinator in emergencies.

This persistent lack of control is not for lack of interest of individual organizations in expanding. UNHCR expanded a great deal in the Rwanda crisis when USAID and ECHO, the European Community Humanitarian

Organization, for a short period refused to contract directly with NGOs and asked that all NGO requests be passed through UNHCR. But this effort to expand in the long run broke down. An important reason why this broke down when NGOs like CARE, the Red Cross, Lutheran World Federation, and others the UNHCR contracted with had their own constituencies in Europe and North America. These, constituencies sought shifts in overall refugee policy in order that direct government to NGO aid would be resumed. Much of this lobbying occurred in the back-channels that independent access to the press permitted. It also meant that the NGOs needed to challenge the competency of the UNHCR, which undercut that bureaucracy's efforts to assert control. Mark Walkup explained the importance of the press in this process:

> [Humanitarian organizations] rely on the media to spread the news of their good works. Media coverage is also seen as an independent validation of the work of HO, despite the reality that the media are somewhat dependent upon the information provided by the HO themselves. The image of a HO is boosted tremendously by interviews with HO–identified field personnel, photographs and video of HO logos on tents or vehicles, and references to a specific HO in news reports (Walkup 1997:139–140).

In a more diplomatic fashion, Ingram (1993:177–178) writes:

> The lobbying power of NGOs is formidable during emergencies that attract media attention. Governments respond by channeling resources through them. While key NGOs may or may not be more efficient than UN agencies, the practical effect is that in almost all disasters a large number of NGOs is involved on the ground. NGOs often have conflicting aims and agendas, and often insist on working in particular regions of affected countries. The task of harmonizing the total effort, which falls to the UN, is far from easy. Very often the representatives of donor embassies insist on being involved. While their efforts can sometimes be helpful, more often than not they add to the coordination burden.

MSF was (and is) perhaps the most skilled agency at coordinating, and at least in Ngara, their staff were well known for maintaining active lobbying efforts on behalf of repatriation and assistance policies that they favored but that the UNHCR opposed.[4] Many of these recommendations focused on security arrangements for expatriates, war crimes trials, and repatriation policies, all well outside the medical sector to which they were assigned by the UNHCR. Donor governments responded to some of MSF's lobbying efforts (though not all) as a result of this pressure. The result was that UNHCR, the nominal coordinator of MSF, adjusted policies and programs accordingly. Such independence would not have been tolerated in a better-rationalized bureaucracy which had a well-defined way of subsuming competing interest groups.

Morals, Emotions, and Irrationalities

The difference between the Good Samaritan bureaucracy and Weber's rationalized bureaucracy is that the former is much more involved in the emotional process of defining its own objectives. Ultimately, this is a question of defining what is good and bad, appropriate and inappropriate. This is unlike a corporation, which has the well-defined and noncontroversial goal of generating profits on behalf of shareholders. The same question can be turned around to analyze the international refugee relief regime. What is the goal of responding to a particular refugee situation outside of a vaguely agreed-on "humanitarian imperative"? Unlike the goal of a publicly held corporation, on which there is consensus, on the goals of humanitarian organizations there is as yet no consensus. Until this happens, the international refugee relief regime will not be able to coordinate its activities in a way to take full advantage of the strength of its bureaucratic organization.

This situation is likely to continue as long as the debate about the nature of mercy, which is a moral issue, continues. As Weber notes (1958:183), debates on moral issues take place in the world of judgments, of values, and of faith. This is not a strength of bureaucracy, but of politics, theology, and other contexts less constrained by the limits of Weber's iron cage, the rationalized bureaucracy. But, necessarily, the nature of mercy is an issue that the Good Samaritan, whether a bureaucracy or an individual, must confront.

Notes

1. Wilson (1989) has written an important book describing how and why government agencies manage tasks and power in the United States.

2. See also Weber 1948:196–248. Ritzer is a more readable popularizer of Weber's ideas, and is highly recommended for the general reader.

3. Ingram (1993:97) notes that the lobbying power of NGOs is "formidable during emergencies which attract media attention." The two best examples of this are probably Oxfam in the United Kingdom, which, besides releasing issue papers, also has its own press, and Médecins sans Frontières in France. In the case of MSF, *The Economist* (July 10, 1999, p. 46) reports that its founder, Bernard Kouchner, formerly a junior minister of health who in 1999 was appointed the first coordinator of UN operations in Kosovo, is "regularly judged France's most popular

politician." He earned his fame by, among other things, helping found MSF, in 1971, on the principle that humanitarian agencies had a responsibility to make noise when witnessing human rights violations.

4. Médecins sans Frontières was also one of the more aggressive agencies when it came to courting the press. The by-and-large French-speaking agency had an American in Ngara to deal with press relations at a point in May 1994 when the press was prominent there. They were also known for having stickers and flags on their vehicles, and their expatriates were all issued white safari vests emblazoned with MSF logos. Some of their expatriate staff made their image more high-profile by standing up in the back of pickup trucks as they drove to the camps, a dramatic pose that went with their rough-and-tumble public image.

Walkup (1997:140) mentions hearing about an ECHO representative's being particularly aggressive about sticking blue ECHO stickers on as many items as possible. The same policy was adopted in Ngara. ECHO was UNHCR's main donor, and asked that all assets purchased with ECHO money be emblazoned with ECHO stickers. I received a complaint from the UNHCR logistics officer in summer 1994 when this was not done quickly enough on LWF vehicles purchased with ECHO money. One of the LWF water engineers mischievously asked whether ECHO stickers should be put on his water pumps before they were placed in his 30-meter-deep wells.

4

Defining Sides: The Social Structure of Right and Wrong in International Refugee Relief

"It was a feeling," said Miss Marple. "It wasn't really, you know, logical de-
duction. It was based on a kind of emotional reaction or susceptibility to—
well, I can only call it atmosphere. . . . Who could be a killer? What kind of a
killer? What kind of a killing? I could feel then rising up rather slowly, like a
miasma does, an atmosphere. I don't think there is another word that ex-
presses it except evil. Not necessarily that any one of these three was evil, but
they were certainly living in an atmosphere where evil had happened, had
left its shadow or was still threatening them."

—Agatha Christie, *Nemesis*

Hidden in the parable of the Good Samaritan is a moral dilemma for humanitarian bureaucracies. How can they translate into regulations the
fact that their field-level bureaucrat should stop and assist, rather than
pass by on the side as did the busy priest and Levite? If the regulation is
written too loosely, their field bureaucrat will need to stop and inquire
about the health and status of all the poor along the road, and never
reach the scene of the major catastrophe. If it is written too tightly, the
field bureaucrat will not be able to legitimately use agency resources and
will not extend mercy, as indeed did neither the Levite or priest in the
Parable of the Good Samaritan.

Refugee relief implies the presence of war, and thus inherently requires
evaluating enemies and making moral judgments. It also implies defining what is acceptable and not acceptable in the conduct of war, who is a
combatant, who is a refugee, what is a "legitimate fear of persecution,"
when is crossing a border significant, and what is a living ration.

The International Committee for the Red Cross (ICRC) with its policy
of nonalignment has perhaps been most successful at dealing with these

questions. It does this by taking a view that it is in the business of providing impartial assistance and makes no judgments about those they assist. This clarity is reflected in very tightly written regulations, which can result in bureaucratic decisions such as the one Mark Walkup (1997:89) heard about:

> A German ICRC officer in Lokichokio [Sudan] lamented about a situation he recently faced when he flew on a reconnaissance mission into a war-ravaged area in southern Sudan. Upon landing on a remote airstrip, he discovered two people requiring medical evacuation. One was, in his words, "a sloppy-drunk, arrogant, wounded SPLA soldier who had probably killed at least five men, and who was smoking cigarettes and bragging to his friends about going on vacation to the hospital." The other was a young girl who would soon die without treatment of a parasitic infection of one side of her face. Although the plane had sufficient space, the ICRC officer was forced to deny evacuation to the girl because her condition was not war-inflicted. With anger in his voice, the officer said, "Surely the little girl deserved and needed the flight more than that bastard, but ICRC policy restricts transport and medical care only to those who are war-wounded." He revealed that he almost broke fundamental ICRC rules and carried her on board. Instead he faced the task of asking forgiveness of the girl's pleading family, knowing that she would surely die because of his decision.

Their reputation for "strict neutrality" permits ICRC to negotiate with distasteful regimes existing in the very real in-between areas created by principles of national sovereignty. ICRC's assumption is that their presence prevents more violence than a lack of presence implied by strong political judgments about warring protagonists. But following this rule meant the German ICRC officer was presented with the necessity to leave a girl deserving of mercy lying by the side of the road. The result was the "irrationality in the rationality" mentioned earlier. But the real irony is not in what the German ICRC officer saw. Instead, in wrestling with the moral dilemma, he sought to structure the question as one of right and wrong; as a result the soldier became evil because he smoked cigarettes, laughed, joked, and could be assumed (without evidence) to have killed "at least five men." The girl and her family, meanwhile (again without evidence), were assumed to be completely dependent on the one flight to save her life. In effect, the German ICRC officer is creating the atmosphere of good and evil that Miss Marple spoke of in the Agatha Christie novel, and the conundrum presented is one of good and evil, right and wrong. Such judgments are perhaps inherent to the nature of bureaucratized relief. But it also introduces a strong element of passion into what the presumably dispassionate bureaucracy does.

The United Nations High Commissioner for Refugees (UNHCR) is explicitly charged with the legal duty of determining who has a legitimate fear of persecution, and who does not. This duty very much involves the type of decisions that the ICRC man made in the southern Sudan. In settled stable circumstances, this implies a hearing process about asylum requests, in which individual cases are examined in the context of international law. Often these hearings hinge on whether an individual has a legitimate fear of prosecution for crimes or persecution for beliefs or membership in an ethnic group. The former would lead to jail time, the latter, to asylum status. Most refugees, however, never receive this dispassionate hearing, for they arrive as part of a mass movement in which a "legitimate fear of persecution" is assumed, irrespective of individual circumstances. Nevertheless, the legal subculture of the UNHCR is fundamentally concerned with legal judgments. As a result, more so than the ICRC, the UNHCR focuses on whether assistance is provided to war criminals or not. In the absence of a legitimate court system (also a characteristic of mass refugee movements), the UNHCR sees itself confronted with a moral dilemma. Some of the UNHCR's NGO partners also view this moral distinction as important. Médecins sans Frontières (MSF) is particularly aggressive in making judgments (see Destexhe 1995 and 1996; MSF 1995).[1]

But the moral issues involved in refugee relief are far more than general judgments about worthiness. Fundamental to current definitions of refugees is the question of what responsibilities and rights individuals have vis-à-vis the state or a broader humanity. These definitions have shifted over time, but decisions about them are inherently embedded in refugee relief operations. Despite the desire to believe that refugees are simply innocents who can return to their homes after the cessation of hostilities, this is rarely the case. Refugees themselves inevitably assign blame and responsibility for their flight. Likewise, war is a polarizing event in a society, and all members of the society are likely to align with one political group or the other, for whatever reasons. Often, refugees are associated with a political cause that is losing ground in their own country; those associated with a winning cause tend to stay. Thus, though refugees may be innocent victims in a legal sense, they are rarely disinterested bystanders.

Defining Victimhood

To illustrate this point, I will briefly recount the moral dimensions of refugeeism by focusing on definitions of victimhood in three different refugee crises: Cambodians in Thailand in 1975–83, Ethiopians during the 1985 famine, and Somalians in 1992–95. These situations provide well-documented examples of how difficult decisions were made about who was a victim and who was not. In the case of the Cambodians, difficult decisions were made about how to deal with a peasantry associated with and sometimes committed to the brutal Khmer Rouge regime. In Ethiopia, the Western donors found the existing government extremely distasteful: the Communist Mengistu government was responsible for resettlement policies and wars that had made a relief program necessary in the first place. The paradigmatic example of callousness cited in this emergency was the decision of the Mengistu government's eastern European allies to pay for a $250 million tenth-anniversary celebration even as massive starvation raged. Somalia is known for being the paradigmatic example of how media involvement drives policy decisions. It was in response to demands by the press, manipulated by American NGOs, that President George Bush ordered the American troops into the country in December 1992. The point is that in each of these circumstances, the need for humanitarian action was invested with moral terms that implied distinguishing victims from victimizers (see Minear, Scott, and Weiss 1996).

Identifying victims involves the promulgation of rules and policies, which become the bureaucracy and thus take on a life of their own. On this basis financial appeals are made, fixing patterns of "victimhood" for the duration of the crisis. This happens in particular as bureaucratic structures become invested in one explanation or the other. The classic case of this phenomenon is the definition of the Rwanda crisis. Initial assessments that emerged in April 1994 indicated that the fighting was due to centuries-old "tribal hostilities." These explanations received wide exposure in the Western press for a short time, but they also were subject to widespread academic criticism. It was pointed out that this was an overly simplistic generalization, and that the roots of the crisis were in a combination of genocide, ongoing war, ethnic mobilization, external political relations, and economic exploitation (see D. Newbury 1998; C. Newbury 1995). According to this view, the victims in the situation were the refugees from the regime in Kigali. The popular press, however, took these explanations and simplified them into the single explanation "genocide," in which some refugees had played a role. This shifted victimhood from the refugees in Rwanda and Tanzania to the new regime in Kigali (see Minear, Scott, and Weiss 1996:62–67).[2] Charles Bierbauer, senior Washington correspondent for CNN (1996:vii–viii), described how this occurs in what is often an arbitrary fashion:

> News organizations are capable of landing small armies of reporters, producers, photographers, and technicians in remote areas. . . . Collectively they are a Cyclops, a giant that cannot be ignored. Television especially, with its single focused eye, commands attention. For brief but intense periods of

time the media send monocular burning images onto the screens we all watch. Scorched villages in Bosnia. Chopped bodies in Rwanda. A soldier dragged through Somali streets. . . . But for all their ability to focus similarly on such stories, the media are not monolithic. And not entirely dependable. Not every tribe's tragedy is recorded. . . . What attracts? Plight and might. No matter how desperate the indigenous situation, the story gets better when the troops arrive.

Quick and simple judgments are not new; in many respects they are even necessary, given the nature of the bureaucracy. Bureaucratic corporations, which advertise and sell goods, are adept at identifying and targeting categories of people who are most likely to buy bananas, Beanie Babies, or hamburgers. Such well-defined categories are necessary in order for the modern bureaucratic system to work well. They are also well within the scope of what bureaucratic organizations do well: create predictable and calculable categories of people.

But the bureaucratic categorizations of corporations are by their very nature defined in an amoral marketplace. They do not involve issues of basic human rights to assistance, of right and wrong, finding fault, or even of life itself, as decisions about refugee assistance explicitly and implicitly do. Despite the different character of humanitarian bureaucracies, however, the same process of categorization occurs. People are classified as refugees or combatants. They are defined as refugees who have crossed an international border and are eligible for international assistance, or "internally displaced people" who are eligible for some other less vaguely defined assistance. They are defined as refugees eligible for assistance and protection, or "economic migrants" subject to deportation. Or, as happened once in the Rwanda refugee crisis, they were defined as refugees from Rwanda and were given asylum in Burundi; but when they were maliciously burned out of their Burundian camps and fled to Tanzania, they were considered ineligible for asylum in Tanzania because they had abandoned a second country of asylum.

In the cases of the Indochinese refugees, Ethiopia, and Somalia, the international community came to terms with deciding who was "legitimately" a refugee and worthy of assistance and who was not. This occurred in the context of a refugee population made up primarily of women, children, and elderly who were clearly not combatants. This need to categorize is within the nature of the bureaucratic mode of action. But moral decisions are also implicitly made as well.

Returning to the parable of the Good Samaritan, the challenge in each situation is to develop moral rules, meaning that field-level bureaucrats can legitimate a decision to help generously, as the Good Samaritan did, rather than to pass by on the side, as did the priest and the Levite. The rules and regulations framing each situation reflect the search of nominally amoral bureaucracies to solve such questions.

Cambodians in Thailand

In 1975–83, following the invasion of Vietnam by Khmer Rouge Cambodia, over 1 million Indochinese—Vietnamese, Laotians, and Cambodians—fled to Thailand. In response to the pictures of the Vietnamese boat people and the flight of Cambodians, major refugee relief efforts were launched. Most of the Indochinese fleeing to Thailand were Cambodians, and this section focuses on them. However, because humanitarian assistance policies were developed not for the Cambodians but for the Vietnamese and Laotians, these groups will also be briefly discussed.

When it came to identifying victimhood and establishing the moral basis for assistance, Cambodians presented the most ambiguous case of the three groups: between 1975 and 1978, Cambodia was controlled by the brutal and isolationist Khmer Rouge government. Behind the sealed borders of Cambodia over 1 million died, the victims of mass executions, starvation, and neglect. The dead included a substantial proportion of urban people, and substantial numbers of Chinese, Vietnamese, and Cham (Muslim) minorities. Rural Khmer also suffered a great deal. The control of the country was developed by a small clique from a secretive Communist party, the "Khmer Rouge," which had existed in the forests since the 1960s. In response to the corruption of the American-supported government and American bombing of eastern Cambodia during the Vietnam War, much of the rural population aligned itself with the Khmer Rouge before their excesses became apparent.

An inkling of the suffering in Cambodia was heard from refugees between 1975 and 1978, but there was little response from the world. Though reports of the mass exodus from Phnom Penh in May 1975 were acknowledged in the Western press, ideological blinders made the refugees' tales difficult to believe. Some from the Western left actually became apologists for the Khmer Rouge, while those on the right focused on Cold War geopolitical considerations in which massacres in Cambodia were of peripheral interest (Shawcross 1984:45–69). Most notably, Vietnam, Cambodia's eastern neighbor, hosted the largest number of refugees bearing tales. However, because of an alliance between the Communist parties of the two countries against the United States and its allies, Vietnam asserted that all was well with Cambodia's Communist revolution.

Cold War calculations shifted in late 1978, when Vietnam, after repeated border skirmishes with the Khmer Rouge, invaded Cambodia, driving the Khmer Rouge government into the forests along the border with Thailand. In Phnom Penh, a new government made up of former Khmer Rouge cadres and protected by the Vietnamese army was installed.

Focused on Cold War rivalries, the Thai and their Western allies responded with alarm to the Vietnamese invasion; the Thai have a traditional fear of Vietnamese expansionism, which the presence of a battle-hardened Vietnamese army on their border exacerbated.[3] Notably, Vietnam was uninterested in humanitarianism; their primary reason for invading was to secure their border. As for the Western countries, their response was confused; the defeat of the Khmer Rouge was welcomed, but the victory of the Soviet-allied Vietnamese was viewed through the prism of its Cold War strategic implications. Left with the paradox of supporting a victorious friend of their worst enemy (Vietnam) or a persistent but emasculated Khmer Rouge, the Thai and Americans chose the latter (Shawcross 1984:70–76).

For the overwhelming majority of the Cambodian people, the Vietnamese invasion meant freedom. From their view, it was irrelevant that the liberator was a traditional enemy of the Cambodians or the Thai; the point was that the despised and brutal Khmer Rouge lost control of their lives. Still, the war continued into 1979, as the Khmer Rouge retreated toward Thailand in the West. Refugees appeared again along the heavily militarized Thai border. Thailand, claiming that the burden of Vietnamese boat people and Laotians living in the camps was already stressing the country, forcibly returned several thousand people in early 1979. UNHCR, which had a presence in the country, made quiet diplomatic protests. After personal pleas from UN Secretary General Kurt Waldheim to the Thai government and the provision of cash contributions to the government for refugee relief, there was a brief respite in the forcible repatriation reports in early 1979. Then in June, after Thai newspapers complained loudly about the "refugee burden," 45,000 were piled into buses and forced back into Cambodia in a well-mined border area. Unknown thousands died from mines, thirst, and neglect, while the UNHCR quietly attempted to negotiate a settlement with either the Thai or nearby Vietnamese army to provide relief and safe passage. ICRC complained more loudly of the repatriation action, a plea that was rejected angrily the Thai; and ICRC's head delegate was removed (Shawcross 1984:91–93).

Despite the drama quietly taking place in Cambodia, humanitarian interest was in fact focused on people fleeing by sea from Vietnam. By this time, in mid-1979, over 350,000 boat people were in camps, mostly in Malaysia, Hong Kong, Singapore, Indonesia, and Thailand. The international press focused Western humanitarian concern on the boat people, and the Malaysian government guaranteed that members of the Western press witnessed rickety boats being forcibly pushed out to sea. As a result, the West adopted a somewhat contradictory policy; at a UN-coordinated conference in Geneva, it was decided that a quarter million new resettlement spots would be provided for fleeing boat people in the United States, France, and other Western countries. Vietnam, the country whose abuses led to flight in the first place, also agreed to seal its borders, thereby preventing the flight of more refugees. This policy implied closing Vietnam's borders to restrict people who had legitimate fears of persecution. This convenient compromising of refugee rights was agreed to by all governments.

In the meantime, in Cambodia's Vietnamese-controlled areas, peasants who had been relocated during the Khmer Rouge years actively sought missing family members and return to their home villages for the first time in three years. Fighting continued in western Cambodia on the Thai border. But most important, the crops planted were abandoned. This raised the specter of mass famine in addition to the fighting. Writing in a regional magazine, the *Far Eastern Economic Review* in late spring, Nayan Chanda claimed:

> Kampuchea today is described by recent visitors and refugees as a country after a holocaust. In this parched land abandoned towns are littered with skeletons and the debris of war, and hundreds of thousands of dazed people crisscross the country seeking missing relatives and trying to reach their native villages (quoted in Shawcross 1984:96).

This presented the international community with a dilemma: whom to deal with, the discredited Khmer Rouge, who controlled the small population along the accessible Thai border, or the politically suspect Vietnamese, who controlled the masses in a dangerous and inaccessible interior? Consistent with their own established policy of neutrality, ICRC insisted on simultaneously contacting both. During the summer, contacts with both the Vietnamese-backed government and the Khmer Rouge capital Phnom Penh were established with respect to the emerging famine; simultaneously the Khmer Rouge government, which was receiving backing from China and Thailand, also contacted ICRC and the UN for assistance. Finally, individuals working at the American embassy in Bangkok formed the Khmer Emergency Group, which began to establish contingency plans and drummed up diplomatic support for a humanitarian relief operation. These actions together initiated the Cambodia relief operation and set the terms for the four categories of refugees that emerged. Embedded in the definitions were also moral judgments about the Cambodians and their suitability for aid. The four categories were: border civilians associated with Khmer Rouge camps; border civilians associated with the camps of the "Free" Khmer; Cambodians living inside Thailand in UNHCR-sponsored camps; and the vast majority of refugees who remained in Cambodia itself.

In October 1979, the predicted refugee exodus emerged from Cambodia's forests. Unexpectedly, the Thai government reversed policy and asked the UNHCR to take charge of 60,000 "illegal immigrants" on two to four days' notice. UNHCR immediately hired bulldozers, back hoes, and water trucks to clear space for a camp, dig latrines, and bring potable water. The Thai government bused in the refugees on schedule, a mixture of Khmer Rouge soldiers, their families, and civilians who had been forced to travel with the Khmer Rouge (Shawcross 1984:176–179).

Interagency fighting emerged almost immediately, particularly in the context of press interest made stronger by an American government gearing up for an election year and willing to fund generously relief programs in such a high-profile crisis. UNHCR and ICRC were in particular criticized by the Americans for failing to bring staff in anticipation of the release of the refugees, or in response to their actual release. This was done in the context of feverish attention from the international press, whose single Cyclopean eye covered the high-profile visit of First Lady Rosalyn Carter at the end of October. The logjams in publicity, funding, and attention for the Khmer were broken. The focus of the Good Samaritan was now on the Thai-Cambodian border. By the end of the year, there were between 600,000 and 750,000 people in encampments along the border. Many were refugees associated with rebel movements, the largest being the Khmer Rouge, which continued to receive arms from the Chinese and logistical support from the Thai. There were also small armies of Free Khmer as well, which the Americans hoped would provide a non-Communist alternative. Finally, there was an assortment of bandits, warlords, and people of uncertain origin, all armed. As for the hungry people pushing out of Cambodia to the border, they probably had a mix of loyalties, some political but many personal. Of course, such loyalties could shift. Nevertheless, for practical and political reasons, food supplies could be routed only through the four relief categories. As a consequence, the food of the international refugee relief regime ended up being used to subsidize various political ambitions of uncertain origin and intent. Khmer Rouge leaders, Free Khmer, and bandits rushed in to establish conditions for how food would be distributed.

Thus, the stage for the moral dilemma of the Cambodia relief operation was set. Who should be assisted? The border-based refugees via the Khmer Rouge? Or the masses remaining in the interior, where they were controlled by distasteful Vietnamese invaders? How to deal with the potential for forced repatriation by the Thai—virtual blackmail?

The solution reached was to demonize further the Khmer Rouge, while feeding the populations living in areas controlled by them. Of the four major players on the border, they had the disadvantage of having by far the worst record, but also controlled of the largest civilian population, an estimated 1 million inside Cambodia itself and border camps by 1979. The Khmer Rouge also continued to have the legitimacy of a seat in the United Nations, a political plum. Since, technically, the 1 million they controlled were internally displaced persons, the United Nations formed the United Nations Border Relief Operation (UNBRO), through which stocks of World Food Programme (WFP) food were handed over to the commanders of Khmer Rouge refugee encampments.

The encampments were located right on the border; their position inside Cambodia was literally measured in meters.[4] Nevertheless, the diplomatic niceties demanded that the people living there were not "refugees" meriting protection from the UNHCR, but internally displaced persons. The distinction became important to the refugees. In the border encampments, they were more likely to be caught in the fighting between the Vietnamese, Thai, and border leaders. But the markets at the border camps were robust as well, providing incentives for the more enterprising and/or ruthless. This black market was perceived by some relief workers as an indication that there was too little control at the border, and as a consequence, refugees there were "overfed."[5] In contrast, movement within the UNHCR camps was restricted. The advantage of the UNHCR camps was that interviews for overseas resettlement were available to refugees within these camps only.

Westerners interested in isolating Khmer Rouge were unsuccessful. Never able to extract the rhetoric about Khmer Rouge brutality from their practical international politics, diplomats instead tried to avoid shaking hands with the Khmer Rouge representatives at the international conferences they attended together.[6] Stymied by the Thai, Khmer Rouge, Vietnamese, and Chinese political demands, Western humanitarians were in effect presented with choices between assisting militarized populations or not assisting at all. Given this choice, symbolic gestures were the only means by which to respond. Somehow, this helped create in the mind of the donors a picture of refugees as they wanted them to be: hungry, helpless, and apolitical.[7]

In the face of aggressive Thai, Cambodian, and Vietnamese assertions of policy, the one way Westerners in Thailand had to assert their moral views of humanitarianism was by accepting Indochinese for overseas resettlement. For the United States a resettlement program was established following the precedent of the Vietnamese boat people program, whereby refugees were admitted who could establish that they had reason to fear persecution because of prior connections with the United States or had relatives in the United States.[8] Large numbers of Vietnamese and Laotians quickly established such connections, which was made possible by the deep involvement of the United States military in Vietnam and Laos and the evacuation of over 100,000 Vietnamese to the United States in 1975. The United States' involvement with Cambodia had been more indirect, and substantial populations of Cambodians did not go to the United States following the collapse of Indochina in 1975. As a result, the Americans were slow to initiate resettlement programs for Cambodians after 1978, despite the fact that they were the largest refugee population in the region. The irony in this was not lost on the Thai government, which adopted a policy of "no second-country resettlement," meaning no settlement in Thailand, leaving the Cambodians no option except repatriation or third-country resettlement in the West or Japan.

A strong moral element was also injected by the Americans when the programs were established. The Joint Voluntary Agency (JVA), an American contractor with the Department of State, was established in Thailand with an explicit goal of excluding Khmer Rouge and other undesirables (bigamists, drug users, prostitutes, uncured tuberculars, etc.) from the resettlement program. The Thai government, meanwhile, continued to play a role in the process by permitting only refugees in the UNHCR camps to be interviewed, irrespective of whether or not they had a well-founded fear of persecution or met the American criteria. Refugees who were not accepted were occasionally forced back to the border encampments by the Thai military, whereas those on the border who might meet resettlement criteria illicitly entered the camps to be interviewed.

There was never any way to verify how successful JVA was in excluding Khmer Rouge from settlement in the United States. They did develop elaborate questioning procedures, rooted in the collection of intelligence from refugee supplicants. The refugees had little to lose by lying and probably did so a great deal, a situation contributing to the rumor and innuendo about Khmer Rouge activity within the camps. It undoubtedly made JVA decision-making much more difficult, if not impossible. When I talked with the JVA interviewers in 1983, I remember being told that ultimately you could tell whether someone was Khmer Rouge or not by looking into their eyes and by the way that they looked at you while being questioned via the interpreter. In a sense, the final arbiter was the same one that Agatha Christie's Miss Marple used in sensing evil . . . the vague, irrational "atmosphere."

The net sum of the Cambodian relief operation was that the moral questions took a backseat to the demands of international politics. The primary distinction made was between Khmer Rouge and Free Khmer refugees in Cambodia, who were fed by UNBRO, which gave food allotments to their "leaders" for distribution, or directly to refugees who were in the UNHCR camps. Despite the differences in deservingness that this implied, this was by and large an administrative distinction reflecting refugees' different arrival times at the border rather than their abstract deservingness.

Thus, two legitimate questions were raised in the context of the Cambodian refugee relief operation: Do international politics always trump humanitarian goals? Or does the presence of humanitarian operations provide succor to armies? In essence, who is deserving and who is not?

Ethiopia, October 1984: We Are the World

Ethiopia has a history of repeated war and famine, the rebellions in Tigray and Eritrea in the northern part of the country being among the most persistent. The chronic war in Eritrea in particular lasted from 1962 until that country became independent in 1991, and has flared since. Famines in the 1970s led to the downfall of Emperor Haile Selassie and the emergence of a new Marxist government in 1976. This also led to a period of turmoil, as the Marxist government, supported by the Soviet Union and its allies, began a process of villagization in which millions of peasants were moved out of traditional areas and into collectivized villages. Such policies, the continuing wars, and a drought in 1982–84 combined to create famine conditions.

The humanitarian community of the West noticed the coincidence of conditions and began issuing pleas for aid in late 1982. Pressure for aid came from Catholic Relief Services (CRS), which focused on the Americans, and the Lutheran World Federation (LWF), focusing on the Europeans. Trickles of aid appeared. For example, 8,000 tons of grain were pledged by Washington. However, donors were reluctant to assist a government viewed as both wasteful and incompetent. It was frequently pointed out that the luxury facilities in the capital of Addis Ababa had received a $250 million makeover to celebrate the tenth anniversary of the revolution, paid for primarily by Ethiopia's allies in the Soviet Union, East Germany, and other Communist countries. It did not take a long leap of Cold War judgment to conclude that the money would have been better spent on famine relief.

In this context, the United States government, which had the largest assistance famine relief capability, was reluctant to assist. In part this was a product of the Reagan administration's anticommunism; but it was also the result of a number of slights to American-Ethiopian relations stretching back to 1974 and frustration with the futile villagization program. Again, as with Cambodia, there was a political question: How to assist a large starving population under the control of a government which was often cruel, incompetent, and ideologically suspect?

The NGOs working in Ethiopia attempted to fill the void. CRS was particularly aggressive with their lobbying effort in the United States, coordinating the production of op-ed pieces and stories in high-profile papers like the *Washington Post* and *New York Times* in 1984. The result was a shift in American policy, announced in September 1984, which resulted in the approval of 32,559 tons of food to be delivered to CRS in Ethiopia in November 1984 (Solberg 1991:29–34). This amount was nominal, given the scope of the problem; however, it did signal a policy shift, and eventually a total of 400,000 tons were shipped to Ethiopia by the United States (Kaplan 1998:21).

The turnaround was accelerated in October 1984, when a film by the Kenyan Filmmaker Mohammed Amin was broadcast on the BBC news. The film had been made in one of the camps for Tigrayans displaced by the war. Ethiopia suddenly gripped the world's attention. The film was the actual reason for the increase in food shipped from the United States, and not the dire (and accurate) bureaucratic analyses of CRS or other agencies. Within a few days, news programs around the world used excerpts from the film, and it galvanized Western pressure. The most notable consequence was the reversal of the American government policies toward Ethiopia, and interest was fanned through 1985 by rock stars who organized rock concerts and recordings (Band Aid, organized by Bob Geldof, and "We Are the World," a song recorded by a bevy of music stars). As a consequence the interest in Ethiopian relief was sustained well into 1985.

The situation was rife with ironies. The famine relief and the various customs fees the government collected from Western donors were used to beef up the Ethiopian military efforts against rebels in Eritrea, Tigray, and Oromo that were at the root of the problem. As with the Cambodian situation, classification of eligible recipients was postponed. Few attempts were made to distinguish between combatants and noncombatants, and large amounts of food aid, mostly distributed in government-controlled areas, undoubtedly contributed to the survival of the Communist-led government. Though the relief effort undoubtedly saved many victims from famine, it also propped up an incompetent regime at a time when it was under attack and did nothing about resolving the underlying causes of the famine. Again, questions of good guys and bad guys were raised in the context of the largest humanitarian relief effort carried out to that time.

Somalia: Operation Restore Hope

Revolt in Somalia led to the downfall of President Siad Barre in 1990. There was no national authority to replace him; instead, what authority was left was seized by competing warlords who each controlled militias. Typically, the militias were responsible to one of the six large clans that are found in Somalia. This resulted in the immediate flight of refugees into Kenya, where they were accommodated in UNHCR-sponsored camps. Of more pressing concern, though, was the condition of the capital in Mogadishu. In 1990, the city was destroyed and 20,000 to 30,000 civilians were killed during fighting between rival clan militias. In the end, a clan leader, General Aideed, ended up controlling the city, but not the countryside, where there was no effective central government.

During the summer of 1992, the situation profile rose in the American press. Focus was on the port of Mogadishu, and reports from American NGOs that famine was imminent were briefly broadcast. Relief of the countryside was made difficult by the presence of well-armed militia, who controlled transportation routes out of the ports and airports. Food was diverted by these militias, a use which the Western aid agencies considered unacceptable. Most agencies responded by hiring armed guards for their convoys of food; ICRC at one point had 15,000 to 18,000 armed guards on payroll. This quickly came to be seen as a form of blackmail to avoid becoming a target rather than genuine "security precautions."

The UN itself was stymied; as an organization composed of governments, it placed central importance on the need to get permission from governments to mount relief operations within their borders. In Somalia, there was no effective government, although there were plenty of claimants. In summer 1992, the UN's interest in distributing food overcame the political interest in preserving principles of sovereignty, and in December, the United States contributed a military contingent with the express goal of ensuring food deliveries. The cover of the December 14, 1992, issue of *Time* magazine bragged: "Somalia: The U.S to the Rescue." Arrival of the troops was greeted with maximum fanfare from the press, which *Newsweek* described:

> The Marines landed in Somalia, and Operation Restore Hope got off to a smooth start, except for a media circus on the landing beaches, which the military encouraged and then complained about. The real battles lay ahead: to feed starving people, impose order and disarm a country that is awash in guns (*Newsweek*, December 21, 1992, p. 3).

The aid community complained vehemently that food was being diverted, and under the protection of the combined military contingents were portions of the famine averted. It is believed that many lives were saved as a consequence of the intervention, and that this part of the intervention was a success (Natsios 1997).

The armed contingents were transferred to UN command, but this proved not to be sustainable. This happened, I think, in part because a political need to maintain feelings of gratitude on the part of the Somali beneficiaries turned out to be too difficult in the emerging circumstances. Their gratitude was called into doubt in June 1993, when 24 Pakistani peacekeepers were killed guarding a soup kitchen, and the West responded by issuing a warrant for the arrest of General Aideed. On October 3–4, relations between donors and beneficiaries again suffered when U.S. Marines attempting to deliver the warrant were attacked, and three helicopters were shot down. Eighteen Marines and 200 Somalis were killed in the unsuccessful arrest attempt. The future of U.S. assistance to Somalia was brought to a particularly high profile when an U.S. Marine helicopter pilot was captured and subjected to a humiliating interview, and the body of a second Marine was dragged through the streets to the jeering of a Somali crowd. This, among other things, made the moral category of the Somalis as victims particularly difficult to sustain in the press, even though, as Drysdale (1997:130) rationally notes: "The evidence that these highly publicized and emotive tragedies bore no relation to humanitarian peacekeeping needs to be emphatically stated." Nevertheless, for humanitarian peacemaking as a whole, the consequences were far-reaching. The Americans, it was said, developed the "Somalia Syndrome," and this was blamed for their reluctance to engage in peacekeeping activities in Rwanda in 1994 and their hesitancy to be more aggressive in Kosovo in 1999.

As for Aideed and the Somalia operation, the UN effectively withdrew the arrest warrant in November 1993, so that there would be someone to negotiate the release of hostages with. In effect, the UN mandate had shifted in March 1993 from the delivery of relief goods to "nation building," which continued until 1995, when the final troops were withdrawn. Somalia itself averted the massive famine that loomed in 1992–93, but also has yet to establish a credible national government in Mogadishu.

The Paradox of Victimhood in International Relief

Common to all three of these cases is a need to maintain a credible sense of victimhood. A moral category created for the Western donors, it gets taken up and used by rationalized bureaucracies. This is despite a fundamental contradiction: rationalized bureaucracies are incapable of having such emotional commitments. It is not a category inherent to the situations themselves, nor does it reflect preexisting social categories. In each case, victimhood was a product of Western needs and interests. Indeed, until the international refugee relief regime focuses on them, the individual Cambodians, Ethiopians, and Somalians who became defined as victims were just as likely to view themselves as enemies, friends, the starving poor, hustlers, homeless, or loyalists. But the old categories are irrelevant to the abstract category victimhood; legitimated by the Western press, it is needed to trigger relief programs. Were that not so, the bureaucratic assessments preceding each relief effort would have been used to commit resources much earlier to Ethiopia, Somalia, and Cambodia, and as a consequence, the dire emergencies portrayed on Western television screens may not have even emerged in the first place. Indeed, to a certain level, this type of prevention already is occurring as a result of the famine early-warning systems established in the 1970s and 1980s.[9]

For civil disorder, however, such early-warning systems do not yet apply. The decision to commit massive resources for refugee relief remains embedded in moral distinctions about who is a victim and who is not, a decision that currently is negotiated in the field of public discourse rather than of bureaucratic legalism. This imbues relief operations with a sense of morality whereby judgment of the actions of others becomes legitimated, often in simplistic categories suiting the needs of the donors rather than fitting the refugees themselves. The results are anomalies such as Cambodians receiving assistance in one kind of camp, but not in another. Other examples are the relationships established by the ICRC's armed guards in Somalia and the need to deal with the various factions in Ethiopia. Notably, when these categories became untenable, the operation redefined the nature of victimhood, a situation particularly evident in Somalia. After peacekeepers were attacked and humiliated, the Somalis they had been "helping" were redefined as victimizers.

This tendency to make moral judgments ranges from assessments of the trivial (whether proper gratitude is expressed) to interpretations of eye contact to whether a particular individual is guilty of war crimes or not. In effect, when there is a lack of bureaucratic specialization, it becomes possible to expect all things of all people,[10] a situation that a British aid worker was surprised to find while working in the refugee camps for Rwandans:

> The problems they [the UNHCR and donors] expected us to solve were overwhelming, bigger than life—problems of justice, national reconciliation, human rights. I'm just a community development worker. We were not trained in those things. We are just new to all this, but we had to make decisions about these issues almost every day. (Walkup 1996:77).

In many ways the sentiment expressed here is strange; indeed it is unlikely that the same aid worker would have the same complaint had she remained in Britain. For example, if she dealt daily with drug-addicted babies on her job, I doubt that she would assert that her job in Britain requires personal judgments about drug control policy—because it wouldn't. The bureaucracies of the National Health Service and the judicial system compartmentalize these tasks, and she would be held personally accountable only for her narrowly defined responsibilities. Her competencies in Britain are well defined, and do not include the duties of a jury and judge. If she lost sleep over her job in Britain, I suspect it would be from compassion for the injustice done the drug-addicted baby, not for international drug trade, inner-city poverty, etc., which unquestionably are also likely part of the problem.

Barbara Harrell-Bond (1986) has written about how this moral need to separate deserving victims from the undeserving local populations who were actually hosting them shaped agency programs in the southern Sudan and northern Uganda. In explaining why refugees needed to be separated from local populations assisting them, she made the following observation about the humanitarian community working there in the early 1980s:

> To attract money, refugees must be visible. It is difficult to count the numbers of self-settled refugees . . . even if they could be identified. . . . Given the nature of international aid, host governments have found it impossible to convince donor governments to spend monies earmarked for refugee assistance expanding the economic and social infrastructure which would cope with such dramatic demographic changes.
>
> Distinguishing between victims of mass distress migrations has always been for the convenience of donors, since the immediate physical needs of those who flee across international boundaries are the same as for the internally displaced. . . . Humanitarian agencies assume that refugees always require relief and that material assistance must come from outside the host country (Harrell-Bond 1986:8–9).

She went on to write about how these requirements led humanitarian agencies to assume that refugees

> . . . constitute "a problem," a burden rather than an economic opportunity. Outsiders view African refugees as helpless; as needing outsiders to plan for them and to take care of them. This assumption is the cornerstone of nearly all appeals for funds. Agencies vary in the degree of dignity with which they transmit images of refugees, but all rely on a public which will respond to media portrayal of extreme human suffering and starvation (1986:12–13).

Note that these categories are created in response to the needs of those assisting, not the refugees themselves. She goes on to state that this compassion is a *moral* virtue, which is difficult to measure. The problem is that there is an unspoken assumption that because refugees are helpless, and therefore worthy of compassion, "any obstacle in the path of carrying out humanitarian objectives must be *immoral*. And since the objective is to do good, it is inconceivable that recipients will fail to be grateful" (Harrell-Bond 1986:26). Essentially, this is the catch that led to the problems with

Operation Restore Hope in Somalia. General Aideed came to be viewed as immoral, and this view came to dominate the rational decision-making of the assistance bureaucracies to a point where the only feasible response was to discontinue the program. Similar issues were raised with respect to the Cambodian and Ethiopian relief programs. There, too, the bureaucratically rational decision (in Weber's sense) to intervene was not taken until the highest level of an abstract "deservingness" (as opposed to a rationalized need for assistance) was established. In effect, the extension of mercy demanded the establishment of a high level of compassion before mercy could be shown. Waiting for this meant that the "most good" would be preferred. But it also meant that, in effect, the most compassionate decision could not be made earlier.

This demand for compassion ultimately distorts the implementation of refugee assistance programs and the picture of refugees throughout an operation, as field-level bureaucrats wrestle with the conflicting demands. This paradox is I think nowhere better illustrated than by the following example recalled by Mark Walkup (1997:83–84) in his dissertation:

> I once observed a UNHCR Field Officer in Dadaab [Kenya] trying to get a large group of Somali refugee women to sit down while they waited in line for distribution of plastic sheeting used for shelter construction. When they did not comply with directives to sit, he seized a small tree branch and began beating the women. His beating continued throughout his time there, which he told me was for "monitoring purposes." Also during this time, he approached a small group of refugees gathered between the refugee women and the distribution center and grabbed a teenage boy by the neck and roughly slung him to the ground with an audible thud. His threats with the stick persuaded them to disperse. When he approached me after with stick in hand, he said matter of factly, "Beating refugees with sticks is not in UNHCR policy, but sometimes we have to do it." On the beating, his colleague attested, "Somali women need this because they don't understand like the men." The Field Officer later commented that he hoped this would not go in my report. . . .

Conclusions

The common thread running through these examples is that victims and victimization are not preexisting discrete categories, but are categories created in the context of the moral demands of the international refugee relief regime. Given the nature of international law and bureaucracy, it is not surprising that the bureaucracies bend situations to meet their definitions of refugees as being victims. This is why a primary job of the UNHCR continues to be hearing and adjudicating individual asylum requests. But this has little to do with broader questions of right and wrong in the context of the mass refugee emergencies which are the primary focus of the international refugee relief regime today.

The cases described above illustrate at least two moral dilemmas that are insoluble in the context of refugee relief. First, the category of victim as currently constructed implies a political vacuum for the refugee. The refugee is assumed to have no politics or feelings vis-à-vis the situation that caused flight in the first place. There is no evidence to support this assumption; in fact, there is a wealth of evidence to the contrary. Cambodian peasants do have attitudes toward the Khmer Rouge and the Vietnamese invaders. Certainly the Somali people had political views. But none of these attitudes necessarily fit inside a bureaucratic box developed in foreign capitals to further the geostrategic interests of players of international politics, who also likely control the purse strings of refugee aid. In effect, because refugee flight is inherently political, to assume politics away from refugees is to assume away the politics in politics. In this process, demands emerge for humanitarian superworkers, people able to deal with issues on a level far outside their specialized expertise. As a result, refugees are forced into the preexisting boxes created in the conversation taking place in the press and bureaucracies. Notably, this is not done by people with training in the use of bureaucratized law, but in the press, by nurses, on TV, in newspapers, and by NGOs and others able to shout loud enough to be heard.

Second, mass refugee movements do not lend themselves to the case-by-case legal determination provided for by current bureaucratic procedures. To do so implies preparing case files for every one of the millions of refugees found in the typical movement. The alternative is that judgments are made in political arenas or in the press.

Thus, the issue of morality, as currently constructed, is a by-product of bureaucratic and political posturing as much as it is a higher-level assessment of what is right and good, or wrong and evil. This is because the moral issues involved do not lend themselves to solutions with the available bureaucratic tools. Bureaucracies by their very nature do not deal well with the feelings and intuition found, most appropriately, in Agatha Christie novels. Imagine the problems a bureaucracy would have in handling a detective like Miss Marple. The problem is that Miss Marples's feelings are not predictable or quantifiable, and Miss Marple while efficient, was notoriously difficult to control! The field-level bureaucrats, with their independence and need for multiple skills, are the same. The consequence is that an emphasis on the maintenance of image takes precedence over a rationalized assessment of whether objectives are met.

In such a bureaucratic context, image becomes a primary goal, and program implementation becomes more haphazard.

Notes

1. Such aggressiveness (and lack of attention to detail) can lead to ironies, as noted by Johan Pottier (1996:426) in the case of Rwandan refugees who were quoted in the same article of the 28 July, 1995, French journal *Le Soir.* "According to Carol Faubert for UNHCR, 'The intimidation of "ordinary" refugees by leaders of the old Rwandan administration "no longer occurs," even though extremists continue to effectively spread their disinformation campaign.' " Pottier adds, "MSF writes: 'The instigators of the genocide are taking control of the camps in an increasingly systematic way, and block the return of the refugees. . . . [The instigators] are free to come and go between camps, and manipulate the refugees through controlling the flow of political information" (Pottier's translation).

2. Pottier (1996:405) commented regarding the frequent recourse to dichotomous reasoning he observed in the Rwanda crisis. He writes that there is "a wider ignorance within the 'international community' about political processes. . . . Aid workers, journalists, observers, consumers of media information, all prefer to reduce social complexity through recourse to simple dichotomies."

3. Before the twentieth century, the petty principalities in what is now Cambodia and Laos were vassals of the larger and more powerful Thai and Vietnamese monarchs. Thus, it was in Laos and Cambodia that the two regional powers rubbed up against each other. The Thai as a result developed portions of Laos and Cambodia as buffer states to protect Thailand proper from their greatly feared rival in Vietnam. After the French left Indochina in 1954, Thailand adopted this policy again, backing the pro-Western factions in both countries against the Vietnamese-allied Communist parties. Communist Vietnam in turn supported the insurgency of the Thai Communist party. Thus, in 1978, for the first time in decades a Vietnamese army was on the Thai border, reigniting longstanding fears. The Thai responded by backing whichever Cambodian faction fought the Vietnamese, including the Khmer Rouge, into the 1990s (Shawcross 2000). This led to the cynical observation that "the Thai were willing to fight the Vietnamese to the last Cambodian."

4. See Mayotte 1992:42–83. Between 1979 and 1992 there was shifting across the line from the Cambodian to the Thai side. For the entire period there existed a no man's land which was occupied by the refugees. Whichever side of the line they were on, the refugees were unable to seek protection from the Thai or Cambodian governments. Also, they continued to have an anomalous relationship with the international refugee relief regime. The various leaders, bandits, and warlords effectively maintained their sovereignty.

5. See description in Mason and Brown 1983:36–47, and Shawcross 1984:225–252. Shawcross, in the conclusion to his book, makes a comparison between the amounts spent on each group of refugees. For the period between October 1979 and December 1981 this figure ranged from a high of $1,124 per head for

refugees in the UNHCR camps to a low of about $48 per head for Cambodians who remained at home. Such figures are rough approximations of the "benefits" each received and are also indicative of the "expressed preferences" that Western agencies had for different types of refugee victim behavior.

6. Shawcross (1984:138), in a chapter titled "Washing of Hands," describes how the American delegate to the United Nations found himself shaking the hand of Ieng Sary, foreign minister of the Khmer Rouge. His comment to Shawcross was "I felt like washing my hand." Senior NGO staff described to me meetings with Sary and others from the Khmer Rouge in Bangkok in 1982–83. They described to me the process they went through to avoid shaking hands with him, which was something of an admission of their powerlessness in challenging humanitarian policy.

7. Mason and Brown (1983:172) wrote: "Relief workers tended to perceive the refugee camps as the donors and they themselves would have wanted them to be: filled with hungry and helpless people in desperate need of aid. Relief workers rewarded helplessness with compassion, self-reliance with suspicion. When a young Khmer worker from the feeding center joined the military, relief workers considered him lost. When a public-health trainee was seen trading sandals in the market, she was reprimanded. Implicitly, relief organization policy sought to keep the Khmer people powerless." From this perspective, the militaries and markets were a threat to the aid agencies' ability to control their image, and thereby their ability to fund-raise by exploiting the prolific press images of hunger and helplessness.

8. The United States' program was by far the largest. However, France, Canada, and Australia and other countries also established programs. The criteria for inclusion in each country's programs were different. The "prior connection" criterion was of most interest to the Americans. Other countries took refugees only with minimum skill levels and, especially, language ability. The result was that poor peasants unskilled in the ways of the West but who had served in American-supported military units had the United States as their primary destination. The outstanding generosity of the American program (any eligible refugee irrespective of language or professional skill was resettled in the States) has cost that country billions in public welfare costs for Hmong refugees and others. This outstanding generosity nevertheless occurred in the context of a petty admissions process.

9. The relief operation for Kurds in Kurdistan was conducted in 1991 beyond the eye of the press. It is generally regarded as successful from a humanitarian viewpoint. The legitimating fact in that case was not the press, but American political interests in maintaining an ally who would oppose Saddam Hussein at that time. Notably, this operation was undertaken with minimal press coverage, few NGOs, and a well-defined objective (see Natsios 1997).

10. Oddly, this view of the humanitarian as a "superhuman" has been receiving more currency in recent years, perhaps a serious reaction to a widely disseminated 1995 article in which Slim suggests that a tongue-in-cheek description of the ideal aid worker is somehow relevant: "First, they must take graduate degrees in social anthropology, geography, economics, a dozen or so difficult and

unrelated languages, medicine, and business administration. Second, at a slightly more practical level, they must demonstrate competence in agronomy, hydrology, practical engineering. In addition they must learn to give a credible imitation of saintliness, and it would be well if they could learn sleight-of-hand as well, since they will often be called upon to perform feats of magic."

5

Making Comparisons Between and Within Emergencies

The fact of being reported multiplies the apparent extent of any deplorable event by five- to tenfold (or any figure the reader would care to supply).

—Barbara Tuchman, *A Distant Mirror: The Calamitous Fourteenth Century*

I want to review briefly what Chapters 2 to 4 have established. Chapter 2 was a history of relief efforts in this century. Like other modern endeavors, relief operations have expanded and grown in the last 70 years. They have grown along bureaucratic lines in a manner similar to those found in most modern institutions. Chapter 3 described the nature of modern bureaucracies. It discussed what factors make refugee relief different from other bureaucratic endeavors and, from a theoretical level, where those weaknesses might be expected to be found. It was pointed out that in normal bureaucracies the primary goals are profits or maintenance of power, and these are easily measured. In humanitarian relief bureaucracies, on the other hand, the primary goal, being rooted in morals rather than a rationalized medium like profits or polls or votes, is vaguely defined. As a result, the criterion for success or failure (also called the dependent variable) is rooted in the mercy of the donors, not the actual needs of beneficiaries of the help, or "victims." In Chapter 4, the need to define good guys, bad guys, and victims was discussed. It was noted that this is a process the Good Samaritan bureaucracy is ill-equipped to deal with, and that there is a proliferation of responsibilities where normally there would be a consolidation.

Chapter 4 also describes three different situations (Thailand, Ethiopia and Somalia) in which attempts were made to sort out victims and victimizers and notes that such definition of good and bad was highly situational, and was often rooted in political wishes as well as more abstract humanitarian goals. In the case of Western democracies, this process of identification of victims and victimizers was highly dependent on the focus of the press rather than on the judicial fact-finding implied by the bureaucracies of the Good Samaritan.

By themselves, these observations are interesting. While I hope that I have framed them in a slightly new fashion, I have doubts that any one of these is particularly original. Certainly, points about the "CNN effect" and the inefficiencies of the international refugee relief regime have been made elsewhere. But I want to go one step further.

My goal in the first part of this book was to lay the theoretical foundation as the central thesis of this book: that if the Good Samaritan bureaucracy is understood as such, the international refugee relief regime can be understood better. This differs from the more traditional reforms typically proposed to achieve greater efficiency in the delivery of humanitarian programs, be they incremental improvements in administrative hierarchy and coordination (see Ingram 1993; Natsios 1996; Walkup 1997; JEEAR 1996) or training and technology (Chalinder 1994; Waters 1984), improvements in relief distribution practices (Waters 1988; Pottier 1996; Jaspars 1994; Shoham 1996), prosecution of war criminals (MSF 1995; Destexhe 1996), accountability (Walkup 1997), or better management of press relations (MSF 1995; Bierbauer 1996; Minear, Scott, and Weiss 1996).

My contention is that the underlying logic of the international refugee relief regime is focused by the bureaucratic need to satisfy the emotions of the donor, rather than the rational needs of the refugees for relief services. Because this happens, it is necessary to maintain refugees as plausible victims vis-à-vis the donor, whether or not this definition is useful in an bureaucratic (administrative or legal) sense.

Next I show how these understandings can be used to inform analysis of specific problems that emerged in the Rwanda refugee emergency in Tanzania. This leads to two kinds of comparisons:

- Between emergencies as diverse as Rwanda, Cambodia, Ethiopia, and Tanzania.
- Within technically diverse fields such as water engineering, contingency planning, food distribution, logistics, and evaluations of violent death.

In effect, donor demands for political legitimation, primarily in the form of positive popular press coverage, drive the bureaucracies of the international refugee relief regime rather than the efficient delivery of services to refugees. As will be shown in the examples from the Rwandan operation, a by-product is that protocols and technologies that rest on rational bureaucratic implementation become less effective. Efficiency suffers at all levels of the operation, which by definition is bureaucratic. The result is a lack of rationalization throughout the system. The level of decision-making concerned ranges from decisions about when, where, and how to respond down to what type of water pumps should be selected to identifying who is and isn't eligible for refugee assistance.

Reliability, Validity, and the Study of Emergencies

Like any social science project, assessing the Rwanda refugee relief operation requires reliable and valid measures. Emergencies by their very nature present unique methodological challenges and, I think, for this reason are best studied in a comparative manner, which includes broad context. A different approach would be a focused ethnographic approach, which emphasizes the brief period when a researcher happens to be present. This approach, though often appropriate to study settled circumstances, leads to biases in emergency situations, which are fluid (Waters 1999a:153–54).

But comparative techniques raise two methodological issues: first, the validity of comparative sociology; and second, the reliability of data collected during emergencies, which are periods of rapid social change.

Valid Methods: The Nature of Comparative Sociology

Although data from different emergencies are not in the strictest sense comparable, as they would perhaps be if they resulted from a double-blind medical experiment, similar operations have been described at different times and locations. The question is how to put together different types of studies conducted at different times and places in order to reach general conclusions? This suggests the use of comparative sociological techniques relying on data that are actually available, rather than what is ideally available as in the double-blind experiment. By using historical comparative techniques, one can eliminate or confirm possible alternative explanations (see Goldstone 1991; McGrath 1984; Waters 1995a and 1999b).[1]

The advantage of a comparative approach is that when we look at data from very different emergencies—for example, Thailand in 1979 and Tanzania in 1994—we can start controlling for a broad range of social, cultural, political, and temporal conditions. In doing this, we can study the effects a common factor has on decision-making. For example, a pattern of behavior on the part of the UNHCR that was described for Tanzania could be written off as being idiosyncratic, resulting from the particularities of that situation. If the same pattern were found in the response of the UNHCR to the Cambodian refugees in Thailand, it would be more difficult to write it off to the idiosyncrasies of the Tanzania situation; it could be better described as being a function of the unique institutional culture of the UNHCR. Now, if the pattern were also found in the way that the U.S. government and Catholic Relief Services responded to the Ethiopian famine, it becomes a characteristic of a broader phenomenon attributable to the broader international refugee relief regime. As the comparisons multiply, and an analytical construct like the bureaucratized Good Samaritan is used to describe ever more situations, validity in effect improves to a point where the construct can be useful for analyzing similar situations.

Jan Vansina (1991), a scholar of African history, describes how the validity of such comparative methods is evaluated to describe otherwise unobservable events, in his case, the spread of migrant groups across central Africa before there were written records. He notes that such an approach achieves a higher order of logical validity because it provides explanations for a large number of interconnected events. The point of such an approach is to find as examples disparate cases, and then identify the underlying process common to all (Vansina 1991:250). The emphasis on explaining unusual situations, known in statistics as "outliers," is important, because if this can be done the chances of the model being applicable to other more normal cases that are not part of the original sample improve. In this way, the tests for validity are different than more familiar methods of survey research, which assume that randomly chosen events reflect events that are not chosen.

Applying these principles to the issues discussed here, I am making the following claims:

- There is an international refugee relief regime which is composed of numerous small bureaucracies which all have an expressed goal (dependent variable) of providing refugee relief services around the world.
- This international refugee relief regime, though clearly established on bureaucratic principles, is not able to reach its stated goal of providing such services with efficiency, calculability, predictability, and control. This inability is due to the fact that the goal itself is vaguely defined and shifts quickly.
- The international refugee relief regime is hypersensitive to the impact of the press on donor politics, otherwise known generally as the "CNN effect," a factor that introduces bureaucratically irrational emotion into calculations of bureaucratic success of failure.
- These effects mean that the emergencies actual responded to are, from the point of objective humanitarian need, fairly arbitrary.

More important are the emotional requirements, which tend to be reflected not just in which emergencies are selected, but also in how actual programs are implemented.[2]

Reliability—The Inherent Difficulties in Evaluating Emergency Operations

Barbara Tuchman (1978) summed up the issue of reliability in developing data for her book about what she called Europe's "calamitous fourteenth century," a period of disease, war, and disorganization that saw the continent's population decline by about one third. I believe that, particularly in the context of modern journalism (if it bleeds, it leads), her assessment also has some relevance to the reliability of data collected for a book about emergency operations:

Tuchman's Law

The fact of being reported multiplies the apparent extent of any deplorable event by five- to tenfold (or any figure the reader would care to supply).

Explaining the origins of her "Law" Tuchman notes:

Disaster is rarely as pervasive as it seems from recorded accounts. The fact of being on the record makes it appear continuous and ubiquitous whereas it is more likely to have been sporadic both in time and place. Besides, persistence of the normal is usually greater than the effect of disturbance, as we know from our own times. After absorbing the news of today, one expects to face a world consisting entirely of strikes, crimes, power failures, broken water mains, stalled trains, school shutdowns, muggers, drug addicts, neo-Nazis, and rapists. The fact is that one can come home in the evening—on a lucky day—without having encountered more than one or two of these phenomena (Tuchman 1978:xviii).

The point that Barbara Tuchman is making is that most things are not written down, and what gets written down is not random. What gets written down is what is most interesting or relevant at the moment, most dramatic, or with the benefit of hindsight most significant.

Modern refugee emergencies, with their overt dependence on press attention (broadening Tuchman's Law to things not only written down but also communicated widely) and suffering, probably exceed the "five- to tenfold" discount ratios she recommends. Like Tuchman's study of fourteenth-century disasters (and keeping in mind that the fourteenth century was far more disastrous in human terms than the twentieth), this study of disaster response by the humanitarian bureaucracies needs to take Tuchman's Law into account. Despite press-related assertions to the contrary, refugee camps are usually the most boring of places, in which waiting and milling about are probably the most common activities.

Reliability: The Inherent Instability of Refugee Crises

Modern refugee crises are inherently unstable, leading to three separate issues that should be considered when evaluating the reliability of data (Waters 1999a:154). First, data sets are often unavailable, and those that are typically are collected under difficult conditions, raising issues of reliability.

Second, the inherently unstable nature of emergencies makes the "cross-sectional data" typically available of less value for making broader inference. Most data, quantitative or qualitative, are collected only at one particular time and as a result are cross-sectional, representing what was happening at the time when the data were collected and not the time before or after. This means that health or demographic surveys, budgeting assumptions, registration statistics, morbidity rates, etc., can be used to draw inferences only for the brief window of time they were collected. An important parameter in the development of a refugee situation is time; camps tend to grow, shrink, and change fairly quickly. Unless such statistics are arranged in a time series, they can be of little use except for the short time around which they were collected. Particularly in a refugee situation, you cannot assume that conditions go backward or forward in time in a predictably consistent fashion.

Qualitative data, impressions written down, do sometimes have more depth, although the usual tradeoff is the precision of calculability. Often, however, these writings are also "cross-sectional"; they are done by aid workers and consultants on short contracts, or journalists on short visits. These reports may be more insightful than quantitative data, and in some ways are more appropriate to emergency conditions. But their weakness is that they must be considered in the context of Tuchman's Law. Their authors, too, write down only that which is unusual and eye-catching, irrespective of the fact that most social interaction even in a refugee camp is mundane. To rephrase Barbara Tuchman's tongue-in-cheek aphorism in terms of what a refugee worker might experience: "One expects to face a world consisting entirely of mass murderers, dying children, thieves, cholera victims. The fact is, even in a refugee camp one can come home in the evening without having encountered more than one or two of these phenomena!" (adapted from Tuchman 1978:xviii).

There are of course people trained and capable of seeing past the drama into the mundane nature of social history, as indeed Tuchman was. These people are typically in academia, though, and not refugee camps. There is a paucity of such broad-based analyses because academics are rarely on the scene quickly enough to develop the broader context in which such stories can be developed well.

Journalists are often capable of writing insightful assessments that take into account a broader perspective. However, the nature of deadlines and assignment editors means that only the most persistent are consistently present in a particular emergency long enough to make broader sense of it.[3] But again, longer assignments to a region or emergency are the exception, not the rule, and the vast bulk of what is written about emergencies reflects fleeting impressions of a reporter sent to a site specifically to report on the dramatic elements, not to provide a deeper analysis.

Methods for this Study

I worked in western Tanzania on a rural refugee resettlement project for Burundians in 1984–87, and then in the Rwanda refugee relief operation from 1994 to 1996. In the latter job, I was extensively involved with setting up the operation, especially issues of food transport, trucking, water development, and the management of Chabalisa 2 refugee camp in Karagwe District.

In these positions I learned the benefits of "arguing by anecdote." In the absence of a steady supply of calculable data, this is a technique well developed in most emergency bureaucracies. This type of argument is different from the measured accumulation and weighing of data typically used in a history like Tuchman's. Such anecdotes may not reach the standard for the measured accumulation of data by standard academic writing, but it is nevertheless the basis for the quick decision-making used in emergencies in particular, and bureaucracies in general. Quick decisions based on seemingly incomplete data were the basis for the policies that unfolded during the two years I was in Ngara, as is generally the case in emergencies. Such a method of course opens one to criticism by academics conditioned to more careful (and slower) methods of argumentation, which ultimately result in fewer mistakes, but are too slow for the dynamics of emergency administration. Nevertheless, such techniques based in anecdote are often "the best we can do," and in the absence of anything better need to be assessed and analyzed. An academic shrugging of shoulders and saying "we can't tell" won't do. After all, relief administrators make important decisions on the basis of such data, and there is no reason that academics can't stick their collective necks out of their shells too.

Because I was involved in day-to-day administration of the relief program, I was not able to collect data (qualitative or quantitative) in a systematic fashion. What I was able to do was occasionally take notes, collect memoranda, and news articles. Part of my job was also to do the reporting about the crisis in general for the Lutheran World Federation. Particularly toward the end of my time in Ngara, I was able to devote a greater amount of time to this more introspective activity, and my choice of subjects presented here reflects this somewhat. To this bias toward the Lutheran World Federation's programs, I can only point to Jan Vansina's central point: in comparative social science, the point is to pick the "outliers," and not just what is typical. I suspect that the medical programs also had a great deal of interesting material; they certainly had the largest number of expatriate relief workers and the largest budgets.

Having noted the caveats, it is now time to get on with the Rwanda situation. The Rwanda situation was both an exhilarating and tragic experience. Countless lives were saved, to a considerable extent because of the UNHCR's skill at organizing a response once they were on site. Much of this skill had to do with focusing international attention and raising money and equipment for the initial response. This was a administrative and logistical achievement.

Thus, there is a major humanitarian success story to be told here. But part of the story is that in the end, a major humanitarian principle, a stand against forcible repatriation, was discarded by the UNHCR, or at best ignored. I trust that reconsidering these successes and failures in the context of the bureaucratized Good Samaritan adds to an understanding of how this happened and why.

Notes

1. This section is adapted from my book *Crime and Immigrant Youth* (1999b) and draws heavily on pp. 54–55.

2. Following similar reasoning, Goldstone (1991:57–58) points out that the point of such an approach is to identify a process that has unfolded in a similar but not necessarily identical fashion in a number of different contexts. Such a process is not necessarily a law, but is a causal statement asserting that a particular sequence will emerge because institutions or individuals—in this case the international refugee relief regime—respond in a similar fashion to similar situations. If the proposed construct is a good one, people will respond similarly, and as a result, likely actions can be predicted and/or explained.

3. Two important examples of this are Shawcross's *The Quality of Mercy*, which is about the Cambodia relief operation, and Robert E. Kaplan's *Surrender or Starve: The Wars Behind the Famine*. Lesley Bilinda, a missionary in Rwanda, also wrote an insightful book, *The Colour of Darkness*, about the genocide in Rwanda. Her book focuses on the work of her mission and that of her husband, who was killed in the genocide. She did write one chapter about Benaco, but this chapter reflected the unusual week in October 1994 when she visited, and not the more mundane weeks that followed and preceded it.

6

Explaining Rwandan Genocide, War, and Relief

Explaining Genocide

The special nature of Rwanda in the modern Western imagination emerges out of one word: "genocide." Virtually all accounts written about Rwanda since 1994 take the genocide as their jumping-off point, whether the subject be economics, agriculture, land reform, religion, food security, ethnography, politics, government, or geography. Even *National Geographic*'s description of Rwanda's famous mountain gorillas is necessarily wrapped in the all-encompassing facts of the 1994 genocide (see Sabpek 1995).

There is widespread agreement that the genocide was a social event of such widespread importance that it merits this central position in descriptions of modern Rwanda. Over 500,000 people died in a country of 6 million to 7 million in two to three months. Among those who died were most of the Tutsi population (Tutsi made up about 14 percent of the Rwanda's total pre-genocide population), and a much smaller proportion of the Hutu (about 85 percent of the total pre-genocide population). In addition, several million of the surviving Rwandans fled their homes, at least temporarily, and several hundred thousand Tutsi returned from Burundi, Zaire, Uganda, Tanzania, and elsewhere, where they had been living as refugees since the 1960s.

In this respect, the Rwandan genocide can perhaps be compared to the role of World War II in French, British, German, Chinese, Russian, and Japanese history, and the Civil War in American. There is little doubt that all these crises occurred; what is debated is the causes leading up to events that, in retrospect, do not look as inevitable as they seemed at the time. As with the crises in Europe, Asia, and the United States, explanations are sought for why Rwanda slipped down the road to genocide when it did. Such explanations are particularly relevant to the subject of

"There are no devils left in Hell," the missionary said. "They are all in Rwanda."

May 15, 1994, cover of *Time* magazine

this book because they framed the policy options available to those who addressed the "underlying causes" of the Tanzania refugee crisis. Though this is not a book about the Rwandan genocide, the understandings of events in Rwanda on the part of actors working in Tanzania is very relevant, for such understandings were the bases on which decisions were made, policies established, and events responded to. But, identifying the underlying causes is not just about seeing "facts." It is also about identifying how observable facts are connected to each other by observers' imputing motives, assessing unobservable "underlying causes," and developing a "theory" about how war, genocide, and relief are connected.

As with all explanations of such events having such broad historical import, what is identified as causal implies practical policies to solve the problems raised by the event itself. In Tanzania, this was an ongoing process as the crisis unfolded. As will become apparent, the explanations and policies observers settled on depended not on the complexity of the "complex" emergency but on ad hoc explanations suiting a combination of "the facts" and the institutional interests of the observers. Initially, these interpretations are necessarily based on information recognized as being incomplete. Despite the tentative origins, however, ideas became a part of a received wisdom in the refugee relief bureaucracies. When this happened, institutional interests in perpetuating programs and policies embedded in the earlier interpretations developed.

Stepping back helps us understand what happened to Rwandan refugees in Tanzania. When we do this, we see what choices, explicit or not, were available to better understand the consequences of these choices. Ultimately, we must go back to how policy-makers understood the genocide. To be meaningful and useful, explanations of the genocide must take into account understandings of ethnic conflict, the nature of justice, Rwandan history, modern economics, demographics, military dynamics, and international politics.

Explaining the Rwandan Genocide

Since 1994, a scholarly consensus over what happened in Rwanda has developed. Genocide by its nature involves attempts to obscure actions and devalue the interpretations of political opponents; thus, reassembling this story has been a laborious process. The historical legwork was done first by Gérard Prunier, who published *The Rwanda Crisis* in 1995; an important afterword appeared in the 1997 paperback edition. More recently, Human Rights Watch researchers coordinated by Alison des Forges (1999) published *Leave None to Tell the Story*, a more encompassing historical description of the modern Rwanda. Des Forges's book describes the actions of individuals during the genocide, and the responses (and lack of response) of the international community as the genocide unfolded. This work was developed with the skills of an investigative reporter and the attention to accuracy of a historian and a lawyer. Primarily a history rather than an interpretation, it is likely to remain an important touchstone for interpretations about the response to the genocide (such as this book), for years to come. Finally, Peter Uvin (1998) published an important account, *Aiding Violence: The Development Enterprise in Rwanda*, about the events and assumptions leading up to the genocide. Uvin's book focuses on how foreign aid programs affected social relations in pre-genocide Rwanda. It also includes a well-developed analytical history of these events.

First, I will present a brief historical overview as presented in these three books. In the next section, I will discuss and assess the explanations that have been used to make sense of the events during the genocide and afterward. Prunier's, des Forges's, and Uvin's account are the most accurate historical record we have. The data they collected are the facts that are known; any explanations that organizes them to describe motivations (or impute them to others) must take account of the story they tell in a plausible fashion.

The Rwanda Genocide: The Scholarly Account

Hutu and Tutsi are old social categories in Rwanda. The terms are used to describe competing groups within Rwandan society. Like all ethnic groups, each has an origin story:[1] The Hutu story is about being people of the soil, descended from the Bantu of central Africa. The Tutsi story is about being cattle herders, leaders, and royalty, descended from Nilotic tribes who arrived from the north some hundreds of years ago. The Hutu are traditionally described as being short and stocky; the Tutsi, tall and willowy.

Such stories are widely believed, although anthropologists point out that the two groups are in fact culturally and genetically very similar. Intermarriage rates have been high in the past, and many—probably most—Rwandans can trace actual descent form both groups. Both groups speak the same language and practice the same religions. There was perhaps some truth to the generalization that Tutsi are tall and Hutu are short, though this probably has as much to do with marriage patterns structured by inter-clan relationships, and norms about inter-marriage as with the genetic purity of an ancient migrant group. Nevertheless, particularly during the period of Belgian colonial power (1916–1961), these terms became important as social categories. It is widely believed that this happened because of the dominant Belgians' need to understand the groups as ethnic in the European sense: namely, as groups which are rooted in kinship and ancestry—perhaps like the Belgians. A rigidification of the two groups' identities began when the Belgian colonial government introduced identity cards in 1931 (Uvin 1998:17), rules about patrimonial inheritance of ethnic category, and generally favored the minority Tutsi over the majority Hutu in the awarding of government jobs, education, and positions within the church. Colonial rule was nominally indirect, and occurred via the Tutsi king, whom the Belgians perceived as being analogous to a European monarch, irrespective of alternative views of kingship and clientship already present in Rwanda.[2]

Sensing the winds of democratic change, in 1958 the Belgians changed tack and took notice of the Hutu nationalist party, Parmehutu (Parti du Mouvement de l'Emancipation des Bahutu),[3] which was particularly strong in the southwest (des Forges 1999:38). In 1962, the Belgians granted Rwanda independence, the Parmehutu party assumed power. Parmehutu's authority rested on a nationalistic appeal to Hutu identity as being more Rwandan than the privileged Tutsi. Following a takeover by Parmehutu, Rwanda became a one-party state which excluded the

Tutsi. This takeover led to the first Tutsi diaspora, with most settling in Uganda, Burundi, Congo/Zaire, and Tanzania. This occurred in the context of sporadic massacres of rural Tutsi by Hutu between 1959 and 1964, during which perhaps 20,000 died and 300,000 fled (des Forges 1999:40). As with the later genocide, these massacres were excused or orchestrated by a Rwandan government intent on consolidating its own power by creating a Hutu ethnic identity in opposition to the Tutsi. The new government preserved a Belgian practice of designating ethnic status on the identity cards. Unlike in the past, when the cards were useful for preserving Tutsi privilege, this time the aim was to exclude those of Tutsi status from access to government power, jobs, and other privileges flowing from the state.[4]

In the late 1960s, massacres of Tutsi decreased, and the country moved on to the business of nation building then overtaking the newly independent countries of Africa. Rwanda even began to look good in terms of ethnic relations, at least to foreign aid donors, after General Habyarimana, apparently more moderate, took over in a coup d'etat in 1973 with a goal of moving beyond older Hutu-Tutsi labels. In doing so, he replaced the older one-party state of the Parmehutu with his own party MRND (Mouvement Révolutionnaire National pour le Développement); his power base was in the Hutu northwest. All Rwandans were made members of this party, and, as in the past, other parties were banned.

During the 1970s, and early 1980s, Rwanda gained a reputation as a darling of Western donors. This was in part due to the relationships Habyarimana and his coterie established with aid agencies, whose representatives saw Rwanda as a good place to invest. Roads they gave money to finance were actually built, environmental programs financed by German money were implemented effectively, and Rwanda even marketed its mountain gorillas as a tourist attraction following the success of the film *Gorillas in the Mist*. But this period of prosperity was, as des Forges (1999:46) says with hindsight, "short-lived and superficial." Left unattended was a festering problem: the rapid population growth of both the Hutu and Tutsi population in Rwanda itself, and the growing Rwandan Tutsi refugee population in the neighboring countries. Within the country, the rapidly expanding population led to ever-smaller plots for those farming on the steep Rwandan hills. As in other African countries, this led to the rapid expansion of the urban capital in Kigali as poorly educated young men left the crowded farms for the bright city lights. Further exacerbating the problem was that similar population pressures in Uganda, Congo/Zaire, and Burundi were marginalizing Rwandan Tutsi youth there. Furthermore, the Ugandan and Burundian governments continued to assert that the Tutsi in those countries could not have citizenship rights, and should return to Rwanda, a position Habyarimana resisted throughout the 1980s.

The demographic pressures presented Habyarimana's government with a crisis. The nature of this crisis was forced on the Rwandan government by economic and military events in the late 1980s and early 1990s. Coffee and other commodity prices fell in Rwanda at the same time the IMF and the World Bank demanded economic reforms and a multiparty democratic political system as conditions for continued financial support. Then, in October 1990, a party of Tutsi Rwandans from the refugee diaspora, the Rwanda Patriotic Front (RPF), attacked from Uganda and briefly threatened the capital, Kigali. The attack was quickly repulsed, but the RPF did manage to hold a small corner of the country along the Ugandan border, and from this territory it expelled the Hutu population.

At this point in 1990, the beleaguered Habyarimana government faced important choices about how to rally the country's support and thereby manage the economic and military crises. Countries in similar circumstances have dealt with similar crises in any number of ways, as the countries of Eastern Europe and South Africa demonstrated during the 1990s. Habyarimana's government decided to demonize the resident Tutsi, even though there was little evidence that they had supported the attack, and there was even much evidence that many wished to repel the RPF. This demonization of the Tutsi led to massacres of Rwandan Tutsi between 1991 and 1993 (des Forges 1999:88–95, Uvin 1998:53–81). As part of the anti-Tutsi strategy, the MRND and a new radical Hutu party, the CDR (Coalition pour la Défense de la République) also encouraged the development of Hutu militias composed of young men weaned on propaganda that blamed the Tutsi for the economic and military problems faced by the country.

October 1990–April 1994:
Seeking an End to War While Preparing for Genocide

At the behest of East African leaders and the international community, in 1993 Habyarimana entered into negotiations with the RPF to address the political crisis. The meetings between the Rwandan government and the RPF were held in Arusha, Tanzania. An agreement, the Arusha Accords, to end one-party rule and declare a multiparty democracy was reached in August 1993. As part of the agreement, the UN agreed to provide peacekeeping troops. In the coming months, there were even some minor moves to implement the agreement, including the stationing of a UN force of peacekeepers (implemented in October 1993), a guarantee of ministerial portfolios for the RPF (not implemented), and the garrisoning of an RPF force in Kigali itself (September 1993).

Simultaneously, a similar though more peaceful process was taking place in neighboring Burundi, where the ruling Tutsi party of Burundi in

July 1993 ceded power peacefully to a Hutu party after losing an open election. But Rwandan Hutu ethnic consciousness received a shock in October 1993 when Burundi's Tutsi-led military mounted an unsuccessful coup against the Hutu government. In response, widespread killing of perhaps 100,000 Hutu and Tutsi occurred throughout Burundi, and several hundred thousand Hutu refugees fled to neighboring countries spreading tales of slaughter at the hands of a Tutsi-led military.[5]

The massacres in neighboring Burundi sent emotional shockwaves into Rwanda, along with several hundred thousand Burundian Hutu refugees. Ethnic polarization was reinforced, despite the Arusha Accords, and radical Hutu, already dissatisfied with the power-sharing aspects of the Arusha Accords, responded by purchasing arms overseas to supply their militia. By January 1994, Hutu leaders were apparently planning a "final solution" by generating lists of their political opponents for assassination.

Some of the UN officials monitoring the Arusha Accords were aware of such preparations, and sent communiqués to New York warning about the preparations for mass murder. A communication from the leader of the UN peacekeeping force, General Romeo Dallaire of Canada, later became notorious. On January 11, 1994, he informed UN headquarters in New York that he would seize weapons imported by militia groups, despite the fact that it was not completely clear that this was allowed by his deployment orders. The office of the then head of UN Peacekeeping Operations, Kofi Annan, blocked this move, and General Dallaire was unable to take the action he thought was necessary.

In early 1994 the situation in both Rwanda and Burundi continued to be watched carefully, particularly by locals, but also by the international community. There were rumors of coups in both countries preceding a summit meeting in Dar Es Salaam, Tanzania, in early April. On April 6, the presidents of the two Hutu-led countries flew back together on President Habyarimana's plane. The plan was for Habyarimana to deplane in Kigali, and then for the plane to go on to Burundi's capital, Bujumbura, a half-hour's flight to the south. But on the approach into Kigali, the plane was shot down, and both presidents were killed. Within the hour, units of President Habyarimana's Presidential Guard had established roadblocks and were seeking out political opponents for assassination. The genocide had started.

Genocide, War, and Flight

During the next six weeks, what was later called the "fastest and quickest killing machine" in modern times operated in Rwanda. The first killings were organized by the militias, but they were subsequently joined by the

regular army. The *Interahamwe* militia, the "youth wing" of the CDR, became most notorious and was deployed via offices of the central Rwandan government itself. Any officials reluctant to participate risked being
killed.

Rwanda's civil war also began anew, as the RPF forces in the north began marching southward soon after the plane crash, leading eventually
to their capture of Kigali in July; by August they had control of the whole
country. This time, the RPF said, the civil war was to "stop the genocide,"
in addition to overthrowing the MRND government. In the process of
overthrowing the government the RPF soon gained a reputation for brutality among the Rwandan Hutu population. At least 10,000 Hutu civilians were killed in eastern Rwanda, as the RPF swept through that area
in April and early May (des Forges 1999:702–722; Prunier 1997a:359–61).
Though technically not a killing of genocidal nature, the often arbitrary
nature of the killing and the fear it generated were more than enough to
stimulate flight. Hundreds of thousands Hutu fled to Tanzania, a move
the retreating MRND government encouraged, because it wanted to
deny the advancing RPF any type of popular legitimacy. In Tanzania, the
Hutu joined the few Tutsi who also had escaped earlier in the month.

The international response to the killing was confused. In the context
of war and massacre, information from Rwanda became difficult to get
and analyze. Nevertheless, it was quickly evident that the killing was of
an unusually brutal nature. By the end of April, the word "genocide" was
being used by some among the human rights activist community. The
ever-diplomatic UN and Western countries, however, feared using the
word "genocide" because international treaty obligations required intervention in that case; they resisted this definition until the end of May. By
mid-June, the French, a traditional ally of the Habyarimana regime, managed to place troops in the southwestern sector of Rwanda, despite the
protestations of the advancing RPF. The French saved several of thousands of potential Tutsi victims, but their presence also permitted the
rump MRND forces to regroup and retreat into Zairean refugee camps.

This is the story that historians have been able to reconstruct after the
fact. But how did the situation look to decision-makers and partisans at
the time? What did they think was happening, and why did they do
what they did? The six explanations below point to various background
factors. Of course, policy-makers did not subscribe to any one of these
explanations to the exclusion of the others, but policies often incorpo-
rated the assumptions behind one or the other. In other words, these explanations became the analytical frames used by policy-makers in dealing with the refugee crisis. Policy-makers who placed emphasis on the
genocide as a cause for refugee flight were particularly important. But
refugees, Tanzanians, and others often proposed other explanations as

shaping events and motivations. These in turn colored their responses to the international relief regime.

History, Justice, and Social Structure: Six Explanations of Genocide

The origin of ethnic conflict and identity is traditionally discussed in terms of history and social structure. "Primordialism" is a common element in the historical approach. Primordialism is the belief that a group has fixed cultural characteristics that are the very essence of the group's culture and that do not change through time. Primordial explanations often focus on the histories that give life to ethnic grievances (Cornell and Hartmann 1998:39–71). In contrast, structuralism (also called instrumentalism) focuses on the immediate social, economic, and political structures as factors giving rise to conflicting group interests. Both types of explanations were common up to the time of the genocide in both Rwandan and international circles.

As the details of how the radical Hutu elite had planned the genocide became known, the plausibility of primordial arguments was challenged. No longer could the genocide be justified as a primordial tribal killing rooted in "ancient hatreds." In response, a new type of historical reasoning emerged, emphasizing the particular importance of mass killing in Rwandan history and asserting that the best way to repair relations was to separate the guilty for punishment, which would permit the innocent to resume pre-genocide relations. The significance of such historical explanations is that justice is asserted as a natural right, without reference to broader issues of political economy, reinforcement of elite power structures, world markets, or other structural considerations.

In contrast to more historical explanations, structural explanations focus on the nature of competing economic and political interests, whether or not the people concerned talk about them or not. On a certain level, primordialism represents what people believe "ought" to be right, moral, and good about themselves and their own and others' actions, whereas structuralism focuses on social inequality and how people actually behave. Each side in any conflict has primordial explanations explaining why they did what they did, even the most extreme evil. No matter how implausible these explanations may appear to outsiders, they are believed within the group itself.

Neither primordialism nor structuralism is the whole story in any particular circumstance; the types of explanations do in fact interact. But typically this interaction is ordered; thus, only *plausible* cultural assumptions about ethnic identity are used by political elites to justify and further their monopoly over power or policy. For example, in Rwanda, the primordial narrative about the two separate "races" was reemphasized by the MRND government when a scapegoat was needed, as prices in coffee declined, IMF austerity measures were adopted, and the ability of the elite to maintain its lifestyle diminished. Thus, a primordial element was overlaid on structural circumstances. The power that elites have, what tools are available, and how relationships are structured by social inequality are the structural constraints. Elites may choose how to manipulate ethnic identity, but they must choose a plausible story that resonates culturally. When they choose skillfully, or fortuitously, the resulting consequences in turn become part of their history. In this way, history proceeds in fits and turns within the ideological limits of the primordial narrative.

From a policy-making perspective, emphases on primordial versus structural conditions present different options to insider and outsider alike. Bureaucracies latch on to an explanation that makes the most sense given the context of the task they must perform, and their own organizational goals; they then develop institutions embedded in the assumptions of those same explanations. Relief agencies searched for a plausible interpretation of what happened in Rwanda in the context of their self-described humanitarianism. Their conclusion was that all refugees were innocent victims. This became a problem in the Rwanda relief operation as it became clear that refugee assistance was probably being extended to people guilty of genocide, as well as the innocent victims assumed by humanitarian bureaucracies.

Explanation 1: Fixed Primordial Ethnic Categorization

The simplest primordial explanations focus on the origin of Hutu and Tutsi as social categories. It is noted that Hutu and Tutsi are old social categories, reflecting occupational specialization in pre-colonial Rwanda. The Hutu were farmers, and the Tutsi were cattle herders and rulers. There was frequent intermarriage between the groups. As there is no direct evidence that massacre or genocide were part of this world, it is assumed that neither occurred. Often, in the primordial view, relationships between Hutu and Tutsi are described as being regulated by norms about obedience to authority which helped the two groups peacefully coexist.

The arrival of colonial rulers (first the Germans in 1892, then the Belgians in 1916) meant that the older categories Hutu and Tutsi were subverted to benefit the newcomers. To fit Belgian preconceptions of race, the country was divided into two groups who were socially segregated. In the Belgian scheme, it was assumed the Tutsi were the "natural" ruling race, and it was through the Tutsi king and his court that the Belgians ruled. To solidify this policy, as well as facilitate control by the Belgians, obligatory identity cards were issued, beginning in 1931, in which ethnic identity was specified. Consistent with Belgian concepts of inheritance, this identity was automatically passed from father to children. In the process, these two identities gained a social significance that they had not had before.

Time magazine on May 18, 1994, presented such a primordial explanation of the fighting that had erupted in Rwanda the month before:

> . . . Historians could point to Rwanda as a case study in what happens to a former colony when suppressed tribal rivalries are released into a power vacuum. It is a familiar lesson: an estimated 1 million Hindus and Muslims died in communal fighting after the British pulled out of India; the departure of the Belgians from the Congo set off savage ethnic-regional warfare; the collapse of the Soviet Union ignited a murderous rivalry between Abkhazians and Georgians for control of Georgia. Rwanda's pre-independence history held special ironies: while colonial rule was far less strict in Rwanda than in South Africa or Rhodesia, the legacy of Belgian rule all but guaranteed the violence that has erupted.
>
> Europeans who stumbled into Rwanda a century ago found a country ruled by tall, willowy Tutsi cattle lords under a magical Tutsi king, while darker-skinned, stockier Hutu farmers tended the land, grew the food, kept the Tutsi clothed and fed. They lived in symbiotic harmony. "They were a reasonably contented rural society," says Basil Davidson, a leading British historian of Africa. "There was no hatred between the two groups. That came only with the colonial system."

In 1958, according to the primordial story, the Hutu elite asserted itself. In the process, the Tutsi king of Rwanda died under suspicious circumstances, and Tutsi were for the first time subject to persecution by Hutu (see Newbury 1988:180–206; Prunier 1995:37–34, 61–67; des Forges 1999:38–40). This policy was developed by Belgians newly sensitive to the democratic winds then sweeping Africa. After all, Hutu made up about 85 percent of Rwanda's population, and continued Tutsi rule was difficult to justify (Prunier 1997:61–64, Uvin 1998:19–21).

Tutsi remaining in Rwanda after independence, in 1961, were pushed out of positions of political authority, and few avenues for political participation were left for them. Hutu elites from the southwest replaced the Tutsi in government, and through the power of their majority they elected a Hutu nationalist party, the Parmahutu, in 1961. Violence against Tutsi continued sporadically, with the result that by 1964, there was a significant Rwandan diaspora living mostly in Burundi and Uganda, but also Tanzania, Zaire, Europe, and North America.[6] Meanwhile, Tutsi remaining in Rwanda herded cattle or moved into the commercial sector, where they formed a merchant minority of sorts. Nevertheless, despite these violent events, Rwanda was considered to be at an advantage compared to its neighbor to the south, Burundi, where a minority Tutsi-dominated government maintained control, and major massacres and refugee flight had been common occurrences between 1961 and 1988 (Lemarchand 1994; Malkki 1995).

Despite peace in Rwanda during the 1970s and 1980s, the Hutu-led government refused to let the Tutsi diaspora return to Rwanda, irrespective of requests from the UNHCR, the refugees, and the Ugandan government. This refusal, along with opportunities for military training in the army of the Uganda's President Museveni in the 1980s, and financial contributions from Tutsi professionals living in Europe and North America, led to the establishment of the Rwanda Patriotic Front (RPF) in the late 1980s. The ideology of this group was grounded in the belief that the Rwandan government was hopelessly corrupt, and for this reason, it was the duty of the diaspora to retake the country (Reed 1995).

In October 1990, the RPF attacked from Uganda. Radical Hutu militias responded by attacking civilian Tutsi populations in Rwanda in the first major massacre of peasants since the 1960s. According to primordial views, this led to the further alienation of the Tutsi population from the Hutu government, with a resulting radicalization of ethnic ideologies on the part of resident Hutu and Tutsi. The radicalization of the Hutu by government elites led to the emergence of radio stations devoted to hate-stimulating broadcasts, the *Interahamwe* militia, and other elements necessary to the genocide. Particularly in the context of Rwandan culture, where obedience to authority had always been highly valued, such primordial attachments made the manipulation of the Hutu for genocidal purposes possible. Radicalization of the Tutsi led to support for the RPF and the invasion from Uganda.

Embedded in such a primordial description are assumptions that also imply solutions to the Rwandan crisis. For example, there is an assumption that confrontation will be a problem as long as the two primordial ethnic categories persist. As a result, policies focus on either segregating the groups, under the assumption that they cannot be reconciled, or eliminating the power one group has over the other. The humanitarian community focused on the latter solution, and on the fact that the war did in fact break the power of the Hutu elite who used the primordial story so destructively. The follow-up conclusion for the humanitarian community was that the refugees, who were primarily apolitical peasant masses, were part of "the problem" only insofar as they were manipulated by elite groups. The elimination of the genocidal Hutu elite from power in Rwanda meant that the innocent peasants could return without fear and begin farming again as they had in the primeval past.

Explanation 2: Cycles of Impunity and Justice

As the scope and nature of the genocide became clear and widely acknowledged, it also became apparent that the killing was not the natural
outbreak of the pure primordialist, but had been implemented as a consequence of a specific policy of extermination, without precedent in ancient
hatreds. As a result, the primordial formulation was no longer adequate to
explain the genocide—or as a basis for other policies. In response to this
insight, the international community came up with a watered-down primordial interpretation; it began to see what happened in Rwanda as being
the result of a "cycle of impunity." The reasoning went that when mass
killing and extermination campaigns began, the lack of legal or political
response meant that perpetrators came to view their activities as legitimate, particularly insofar as they facilitated the achievement of political
goals.

In this interpretation of Rwandan history, there was no effective response by the international community to massacres of Tutsi in Rwanda
in the 1960s or again in the 1990s, after the attack by the RPF. In both
cases, war crimes were committed by the Hutu military on Tutsi civilians
in clear violation of international law. The impunity with which these
massacres were undertaken meant that war crimes escalated until the
genocide of 1994 was a logical and foreseeable consequence.

Given this new assumption, the obvious solutions were first, the threat
of military action when war crimes are committed,[7] and a predictable
process of trial and punishment of those guilty of war crimes and genocide. If it is assumed that genocide is the result of impunity, the forceful
opposition to war crimes is a necessary and reasonable prerequisite for
"breaking the cycle of impunity which gave rise to the genocide in the
first place" (USAID 1998). According to this argument, given the nature
of genocide, ethnic hatred is normal and expected. As with the "purer"
primordial versions, lacking here is an acknowledgement of the structural arguments that economic inequality and desperation on the part of
a political elite seeking to preserve power are also elements.

The cycle-of-impunity argument is currently used to justify the continuing monopolization of political power by the RPF. Acting President
Kagame of Rwanda was implicitly using this type of argument when he
was quoted as saying (IRIN 2000):

It is stupid for some people to say that the genocide was as a result of the
downing of Habyarimana's aircraft. Such people do not know the history of
Rwanda. Genocide started in 1959. It was continued in the following
years—1963, 1967, 1973. Of course we had killings in the 1990s when our
struggle was going on. If you remember, in 1993 we had to halt the negotia-

tion process in Arusha because there were killings in the north and demand that the government should stop them. Towards the conclusion of the Arusha peace process, one colonel close to Habyarimana openly told people that he was going to Rwanda to plan an apocalypse. What is happening today is an attempt by some people to revise history by distorting facts.

The principle that genocide continues as a result of "cycles of impunity," developed in response to the Rwanda crisis, was applied by NATO in Kosovo in 1999. The NATO bombing of Kosovo was in large part justified because it was assumed that if a similar international response had been undertaken in Rwanda, the genocide would have been prevented. In essence the reason that the Rwandan government went ahead with a policy of genocide was that they did not fear retribution from the international community in the form of preventive military action of war crimes prosecutions. As a theory for analyzing how states respond to ethnic conflict, war crimes trials, and international intervention, the jury is still out on whether this explanation actually explains anything. It will be some years before retrospective analyses of the Rwandan and former Yugoslavia crises can help determine whether preventive measures taken in the light of the cycle-of-impunity theory are effective in preventing war crimes. In the case of the Rwanda crisis, there is a consensus emerging that in the few cases where outsiders protested or even intervened in the genocide, at least some lives were saved, and the projection of force was an effective deterrent (des Forges 1999:24–27). Given that the War Crimes Tribunals, as well as the courts in Rwanda have not as of this writing (April 2000) yet convicted large numbers of defendants, no real assessment of the effectiveness of war crimes prosecutions in "breaking the cycle of impunity" can yet be made.

Explanation 3:
Rwanda's Position Within the International Economic Order

Left out of the historical approaches is the role of the international economy in ordering Rwandan society. Many have pointed out that Rwanda seemed by the mid-1980s to have made steps toward ethnic reconciliation.[8] To cite Prunier (1997a:349–350), the consensus about Rwanda in the 1980s was that unlike its neighbors, it was an ideal place for development projects underwritten by virtuous Europeans. "General Habyarimana was neat, he ran a tight ship, he killed very selectively and with almost total discretion, corruption was minimal. . . . Rwanda was the darling of foreigners. . . . Rwanda was still virtuous, Christian, respectable and boring." This was true particularly when Rwanda was compared to neighboring Burundi, where minority Tutsi stayed in power with all the obvious manifestations of an authoritarian military state; to the corruption of Mobutu's Zaire; to the anarchy of Amin's/Obote's Uganda; and to the poverty of socialist Tanzania. Indeed, it was Burundi, not Rwanda, that had had significant massacres between 1972 and 1990, mostly Hutu massacred by the Tutsi military. During that time, Rwanda had a stable government that by the standards of neighboring countries was relatively progressive (Prunier 1995:78–79, des Forges 1999:45). The only political disruption was in 1972, when an internal coup within the military led to the accession of a *less* ideological leader, President Habyarimana, and the elimination of more militant Hutu nationalists from the southwest. In sum, an analyst looking at only the regional history in, say, 1985 would have figured that Rwanda was the *least* likely country in the region to have an ethnically based genocide within ten years. Burundi, Zaire, and Uganda—all had more pronounced ethnic divisions and more deeply embedded "cycles of impunity" than Rwanda in 1985.

In the 1980s, Rwanda managed aid from Germany and China relatively well. The result was that by 1988, a substantial portion of the road system was paved, there were substantial export earnings from tea and coffee plantations, literacy was improving, and health programs were being extended into the countryside. Indeed, Rwanda, of all the countries in the region, by 1986 had the most reason to hope for the quick emergence of the type of capitalist democracy envisioned by Western development aid donors. For this reason, structural analysts point out, the actual descent into genocide is explained by what happened in the late 1980s and early 1990s rather than by tales of historical antagonisms. Or, as Prunier (1997:350) wrote: "The whole system went wrong for reasons which at first were economic and then turned politico-cultural. Rwanda's slide from relative heaven to absolute hell is a perfect textbook illustration of the theory of dependence."

Rwanda's seemingly real economic and social gains began to crumble in the mid-1980s, when a number of factors crippled the country's growth. First, in 1984–86 tin prices dropped, the Rwandan mines were closed, and the export sector became more dependent on coffee. In late 1989 coffee prices in turn dropped 50 percent, and this, along with drought, triggered the first famine in over 40 years, this one among market-dependent farmers. Catherine Newbury (1995) says that these conditions, coupled with declining land-to-farmer ratios caused by a 3.7 percent population growth rate, meant that many young men were unable to achieve the property and family necessary to achieve "social adulthood." The net result was an expansion of the social margins, in both the rural areas and the cities, as the number of young men who had no land, little education, no jobs, and little hope for the future went up (C. Newbury 1995:14–15; D. Newbury 1998; des Forges 1999:45–46). Structural analysts focus on the origin of class relations and economic inequality. They point out that impoverished populations are particularly susceptible to the demagoguery of primordial ethnic chauvinists.

In the late 1980s and early 1990s, the ruling MRND (Hutu) elite agreed to IMF/World Bank structural adjustment programs needed for continued loans to the government to cope with the financial issues raised by the economic crisis. In exchange for loans needed to preserve the privileges of the ruling clique, the government agreed to new economic policies. At the heart of such programs was "cost-sharing" with the population—meaning, in practice, higher taxes, cuts in government employment, and currency devaluation. As in the rest of Africa, this also required cutbacks in government patronage, sell-offs of government assets, and elimination of exchange controls—policies that the already wealthy were in the best position to take advantage of. Again, in the context of the class-based conditions on which structural analysts focus, the net result was that costs were borne by the more marginal social groups (Uvin 1998:40–50), accentuating issues of inequality.

In the face of rising unemployment and the impoverishment of peasant coffee and tea growers, the government sought scapegoats, and the "oppositional role" of the Tutsi was revived. It exploited ethnic chauvinism and the October 1990 invasion of Rwanda from Uganda by the Tutsi-dominated RPF to justify the massacres of civilian Tutsi that occurred in October 1990. Further polarization and fear within the Hutu and Tutsi population were the result. As for the government, it took advantage of the invasion to shift concern away from its own failings as a government and focus on issues of national security.

Those who make structural arguments point out that further radicalization of the Hutu population came in 1993, when the first multiparty elections were held at the insistence of the international community. A Hutu radical party, the CDR, emerged to challenge the more moderate governing MRND party of President Habyarimana. The "Hutu power" ideology of the CDR found new resonance with the dispossessed youth; now the MRND sought to retain these supporters by co-opting and intensifying its own Hutu chauvinism. President Habyarimana himself ended up in a political no-man's-land, and as a result, Hutu radicals attacked his airplane on April 6, 1994, in an attempt to derail the peace agreements that he had reached with the RPF. The attack was a signal for the genocide to begin.[9]

This structural view differs from the more historically focused views because it looks at exogenous (external) political and economic conditions as causes, rather than tribal antagonisms, in-bred hatred, or "cycles of impunity" that emerge naturally out of history. Thus, while analysts focusing on structural conditions may agree that War Crimes Trials are important, they point out that unless underlying conditions are addressed, trials by themselves will not be enough to prevent further violence. Adherents of the structural view do not blame the genocide on the peculiarities of Rwandan culture or trace the conflicts of the 1990s into a vague primordial past, or even back to the 1960s. In the structuralist formulation, the ethnic histories told by the competing parties to outsiders are incidental to the broader economic situation. Thus, the proximate cause for war and genocide is not only primordial ethnicity, but the economic and political conditions leading to the revival of ethnic categories. This view, in effect, says that under certain political and social conditions, ethnic antagonisms anywhere will be revived, with genocide a possible consequence. This is, of course, a scarier view: every ethnic group, by definition, has a primordial story, and so any majority group is at risk to commit genocide given the "right" circumstances.

Like the primordialist view, the structuralist explanations imply policy prescriptions. In particular, the way to avoid future genocide is through economic development benefiting the poor. The point is to avoid a situation where a large pool of poorly educated, dispossessed youth accumulate at the margins of society, be they Hutu, Tutsi, or anything else.

This view has not been dominant in Rwandan policy-making since 1994. However, it is common within NGO and international development bureaucracies and with academic sources.

Explanation 4: Invasion from Uganda

Behind the typical Rwandan version of events is an awareness that fighting in Rwanda started in 1990 when Tutsi exiles invaded from Uganda. Ironically, for different reasons, both the RPF government (currently in power in Rwanda) and Hutu militia make similar arguments, pointing to the invasion from Uganda as significant in explaining the origin (and, by extension, solution) of Rwanda's troubles. RPF representatives claim that the invasion from the north was necessary to stop the genocidal MRND-dominated government. The Hutu claim that the invasion was part of a Tutsi plot to reestablish hegemony in Rwanda.

Consistent with the Tutsi version of this view is the observation that in the 1980s President Habyarimana repeatedly refused repatriation of the Rwandan refugees in Burundi, Uganda, Zaire, and Tanzania. Habyarimana's reluctance even extended to insisting that Rwandans fleeing Obote's Uganda in 1982 were "Ugandan" refugees, and they were to return to Uganda. Indeed, during the 1970s and 1980s, President Habyarimana sought to resettle Rwandan (Tutsi or Hutu) farmers from Rwanda to countries as distant as Gabon (Newbury 1995:14–15). But the Tutsi of the RPF regarded themselves as Rwandans, a self-definition supported by Uganda and the UNHCR. Thus, they regard the culmination of their "invasion" as a homecoming for liberators ready to topple a corrupt and potentially genocidal regime.

The Rwandan Hutu population viewed the RPF invasion from Uganda with terror. The invasion's timing could not have come at a worse time for the already faltering economy. This situation was compounded by the subsequent expulsion of Hutu peasantry from areas captured by the RPF in the northeast in 1990–92. By 1992 some 300,000 Hutu peasants had been displaced by the fighting and were housed in large IDP (internally displaced person) camps immediately outside the RPF zones in Byumba prefecture. This created a large dissatisfied population interested in efforts to reclaim their homes. In response to the Hutu population's fears of the RPF, the government began to train rural peoples in affected areas in militia tactics and massacre, as a matter of "self-defense" (Prunier 1995: 134–138).

Thus, the Hutu take on this invasion explanation is that the genocide was a response to an illegal invasion, and therefore was part of a war. (This position does not acknowledge the qualitative difference between war and genocide.) Meanwhile, the Tutsi/RPF take is that the invasion was necessary to rescue the country from the genocidal intentions of the Hutu leaders, which in their ex post facto analysis were self-evident.[10] Both takes contain persuasive elements that are particularly attractive to aggrieved populations.

One of the policy implications of the invasion explanation is the RPF view that the Tutsi have a "right to return," and therefore the invasion was just. There is a wider Rwandan diaspora, which was unjustly expelled in the 1960s by ethnic extremists and those who were expelled have a natural right to return to their homeland. Such rights of return are common; Israel, Germany, and a number of other countries include in their Constitutions a right for citizens they define as "stranded by history" outside the country to return on the basis of a common ethnic solidarity.

The policy implications of the Hutu take on this invasion explanation is that the Tutsi from Uganda are "foreign invaders" who do not have return rights, and Rwanda is occupied by a foreign army and its government is illegitimate. This is used to justify revolt against the RPF government.

Explanation 5: International Intrigue and Politics

The role of international intrigue in triggering genocide is occasionally mentioned. Pre-genocide Rwanda had close relationships with France, Belgium, and Germany. The RPF had its origins in Uganda, and during its invasion (1990–94) used that country as a safe haven; it is also commonly acknowledged that Uganda was also directly or indirectly a source of supplies for the RPF. The Tutsi-dominated government in Burundi was also apparently sympathetic, and permitted fund-raising for the RPF in the late 1980s.

France had a military relationship with General Habyarimana's Rwanda and supplied his government with arms. There were also close personal relationships between members of the French governing elites and those in Rwanda, including between the families of France's President Mittérrand and President Habyarimana.[11] As a consequence, France came to be considered as an ally of the former government. The establishment of the French military's humanitarian "Zone Turquoise" in southwest Rwanda in June-August 1994 contributed to this belief: The remnants of the old Rwandan government retreated into this zone, and genocidal attacks on Tutsi continued there in places where French soldiers were not present.

There is continued speculation about whether France continued to support the Rwandan exile government after portions of it fled to Zaire. Certainly the Mobutu regime in Zaire provided a route for arms to reach the exiled soldiers. At the time, France's role and actions were unclear, but since then Prunier (1995:285–311) and Alison des Forges (1999:119–21, 184, 668–91) have been able to fill in some of the blanks regarding French involvement.

Belgium is also an important political actor in Rwanda. Belgium is the former colonial power in Burundi, and retains active political and social ties. Belgian troops were central to the UN peacekeeping mission in Rwanda, and it was Belgian members of UNAMIR (the United Nations Assistance Mission to Rwanda, a UN military contingent in Rwanda in 1993–96) who were killed protecting the politically desperate Prime Minister Agathe Uwilingiyimana, a Hutu, at the beginning of the genocide. There have also been persistent rumors that Belgian mercenaries hired by Hutu radicals were involved in the shooting down of President Habyarimana's plane on April 6, 1994. These rumors were widely believed by Rwandan Hutu refugees in 1994, and there is some factual basis to believe that they may be true (Prunier 1995:213–229). Unlike the case of the French, there are no persistent rumors that the Belgian government systematically provided aid to one side or the other in Rwanda's conflicts.

Germany had an unusually close relationship with prewar Rwanda through its overseas development programs. However, this role has not been interpreted as being favorable to one side or the other.

Perhaps the most persistent and plausible claim for international responsibility for Rwanda's genocide is the West's inability to interpret signals that a genocide was going to occur. Warning cables that General Dal-

laire sent in January 1994 were misinterpreted or ignored at UN headquarters in New York and the U.S. State Department in Washington, both
of which wanted to avoid involvement. Had the cables been interpreted
accurately (and courageously), the United States or the UN could have
acted to prevent the genocide (see Gourevitch 1999; des Forges
1999:595–633). President Clinton of the United States and Secretary General Annan of the UN hold this view, and both apologized for this inaction
on their trips to Rwanda in early 1998. Implied in this view is the assumption (or hope) that military action by outsiders at the right moment could
have been an effective deterrent to the actions of the genocidal Rwanda
government, the militias, and the military; the belief that acknowledging a
situation and trying to do something to prevent it from degenerating has
some moral value, even though success is not necessarily guaranteed. Of
course, the idea that *inaction* by the United States and other Western countries, no matter how egregious, is a cause of others' committing genocide
is a logical stretch. Nevertheless, the assumption that the genocide occurred because of inaction by outsiders is explicit Rwandan government
policy today, and is implicit in the apologies of Bill Clinton, Kofi Annan,
and others for failing to act to prevent the genocide.

The Rwandan government continues to have strong suspicions regarding Western aid agencies' contacts with the former Hutu government.
The inability of the West to stop the genocide is typically cited as the basis for this continuing suspicion (Gowing 1998).

Explanation 6: The Demographics of Central Africa

Before 1990, Rwanda and Burundi had the greatest population density in
Africa, and their rate of natural population growth was among the highest. Such a situation in countries highly dependent on agriculture like
Rwanda and Burundi inevitably resulted in population pressure on the
distribution of land. A common occurrence in such situations is that large
numbers of young men leave the farms and emigrate to the cities or
abroad. As a result, the capitals of both Burundi and Rwanda experienced rapid population growth during the 1980s, but without a corre-
sponding increase in urban employment. This created a volatile population of disenfranchised young men susceptible to the appeals of radical
parties peddling ideologies based in race or class.

Demography is not destiny, but it heightens both risk and opportunity
in developing countries like Rwanda and Burundi (Prunier 1997:353; C.
Newbury 1995:14; USCR 1998:41; Waters 1996; D. Newbury 1998; Uvin
1998:180–202).[12] Prunier described this issue in the following manner:

> There is of course one further added cause [of the genocide]: overpopula-
> tion. This [subject] is still a taboo, because human beings are not supposed

to be rats in a laboratory cage, and Christians, Marxists, Islamic fundamentalists, and World Bank experts will all tell you that overpopulation is relative and that God (or modern technology or the *Shari'a*) will provide. But let whoever has not at least once felt murderous in a crowded subway at rush-hour throw the first stone. This author knows of only two cases where over-population has been mentioned in straight unabashed fashion as a direct cause of the Rwandese genocide. One came from a geographer, Jean-Pierre Maison, and the other from Mary Gore, wife of the US Vice-President, who said at the Cairo World Population Conference in September 1994: Rwanda is a tragedy and a warning. "It is a warning about the way in which extremists can manipulate the fears of a population threatened by its own numbers and by its massive poverty."

Whatever else they know, geographers know about land and women know about wombs. Both are to do with nature which they know cannot be pushed beyond a certain point without kicking back."

Peter Uvin (1998:182–83) refines this argument by pointing out that it is not a hard-line Malthusian argument, in which ballooning populations outgrow the food supply. The importance of demographics lies rather in the fact that land scarcity results from decreased agricultural potential, regional economic decline, population movements, disruption of social exchange institutions, and decreased accountability of the state. All such issues contribute to conditions that may lead to genocide. He goes on to point out that "nearly all scholars dealing with Rwanda, including the social scientists who have written the most serious studies of the genocide, align themselves with this position."

Like other structural arguments, demographic arguments imply the need for development aid, if by development aid is understood improving women's education and opportunities, which is closely associated with lowering birth rates. In a context where birth control policies fail, a focus on demographics means that foreign resettlement is occasionally suggested as the only obvious way to lower population densities (see for example discussion in Rutinwa 1996:295–99). It is still too early to know whether attempts to control population growth in Rwanda will fail; it is an important policy area that should be continually assessed.

Conclusion

Each of the six explanations contributes to an understanding of what happened in Rwanda when it did. A number of them are also interrelated. Nevertheless, programs to prescribe solutions have typically emphasized one or the other explanation. Specifically, the international refugee assistance organizations in Tanzania and Zaire assumed that the problem was one of historically grounded dislikes by ethnic elites; their programs were designed to quickly repatriate refugees in the hope that when the elites were forced to share power, the people would learn to get along. This is why programs designed to mitigate problems focus in on measures to encourage Rwandans to reconcile emotionally with each other, be it through the administration of justice, the provision of housing, psycho-social services, or calls for ethnic integration (see, e.g., USCR 1998:42–43).

Left out of such formulations are measures to ensure that class divisions are not reestablished in ways that re-create pre-genocide inequalities. In part, this neglect occurs because it is much more politically difficult and expensive to establish such programs than merely to repatriate refugees. Policies focusing on ensuring that the next generation of Rwandan youth are not marginalized in 15 or 20 years do not have much of a constituency in bureaucracies focused on 1-, 2-, or 5-year budgets.

But the lack of attention to longer-term issues is not due only to difficult financial or political problems. In development circles, it is beginning to be noted that major investment in Rwanda's development was wasted because of such inattention to long-term solutions.[13] Perhaps they have a point. After all, the overall response to the Rwanda situation was not cheap: the estimate for May–December 1994 was that $1.4 billion was spent, more than Rwanda's 1993 total gross domestic product of $1.359 billion (World Bank 1995:166).

Notes

1. This approach is rooted in Max Weber's description of ethnic communities (1948:189), among other traditions.

2. For scholarly accounts of the origins of Rwandan ethnicity, see Newbury 1988; Uvin 1998:13–18; and des Forges 1999:31–37. These accounts all stress the "socially constructed" nature of ethnicity in Rwanda. Uvin's recent account stresses that in Rwanda there are four persistent ethnic groups: majority Hutu, Tutsi, Twa, and Bazungu, or Europeans. The Europeans were individually itinerant but as a group persistent. Initially (1900–62) they were colonialists, missionaries, and businesspeople; after independence (since 1962) they have been aid experts, missionaries, and businesspeople. In both periods, the Bazungu group has had the most economic control, regardless of whether they controlled the power of the state.

3. As the name implies, the party focused on the interests of the Hutus vis-à-vis the Belgians and the Tutsi monarchy. The preponderance of Hutus in the population meant that as long as democratic principles about majority rule were followed, Parmehutu was likely to defeat any royalist party.

4. Burundi, which received independence on the same day in 1962 as Rwanda, continued to be ruled by a Tutsi king until 1966. For most of the period since it has been ruled by the Tutsi-dominated military. In Burundi, despite continuing

ethnic polarization, ethnic designations were removed from identity cards. Certainly ethnic designations on identity cards facilitated genocidal intent in Rwanda, but by itself it is inadequate to explain the persistence (or not) of these particular ethnic categories. Even without the cards, Burundians have no trouble assigning themselves to Hutu and Tutsi categories, sometimes with extremely violent consequences.

5. For an excellent summary time line of the period from 1990 to 1994, see Uvin 1998:70–81.

6. Gourevitch (1995, 1996, 1998), writing in *The New Yorker,* presented the most simplistic accounts of "Hutu Power" ideology, often using sources within the RPF government. As historians, des Forges (1999) and Prunier (1995) present much more scholarly and nuanced accounts, in which they acknowledge other factors besides ideology. Cuenod (1967) wrote an early description of the first Rwandan crisis. Smith (1995) and Reed (1995) wrote a post-invasion account of refugee activity in Uganda.

7. This is the "virtuous power" doctrine adopted by the Clinton administration in Kosovo, described by Layne and Schwartz (2000). According to the virtuous power doctrine, military force shall be used in response to violations of internationally recognized human rights.

8. See also Uvin 1998:40–50.

9. Speculation about who actually attacked the plane continues. Prunier believed in 1995 that the evidence pointed to alienated members of President Habyarimana's own entourage. Des Forges (1999), writing later, professes not to be sure who undertook the attack, and indicates that there is a plausible reason for the RPF or radical members of Habyarimana's own group to have been involved. She speculates also that the French may have had a role, but she is unsure what this might have been (des Forges 1999:181–185).

10. Labeling theorists in criminology call this "retrospective interpretation" and note it is commonly used to explain deviant acts, whether or not there is a causal relationship. Rather it is a trick of memory and interpretation.

11. Prunier (1995 and 1997) devotes major portions of his book to a discussion of the relationship between France and the Habyarimana-MRND regime.

12. Since 1994 there has been a demographic seesaw in Rwanda resulting from genocide, the return of Tutsi refugees from abroad in 1994–95, and the return of Hutu refugees from Tanzania and Zaire in 1996–97. The net result is that despite the substantial mortality in the genocide and war, the population of Rwanda in 1998 was greater than in 1993, the dead having been replaced by refugees from the Tutsi diaspora, Hutu refugees, and babies. Compounding the population problem is the fact that a birth control movement introduced in the 1980s has been replaced since 1974 with pro-natalist views on the part of the peasantry that the dead must be replaced by children, irrespective of government policy. The result is a total fertility rate of an expected 8.3 children during the lifetime of the average Rwandan woman (USCR 1998:41). This is almost the highest national rate in the world today, and approaches the acknowledged absolute limit of human fecundity, 10 children per woman. (The Hutterites of North America, a group that had a strong pro-natalist ideology and good nutrition, had a total fertility rate of

10 children per woman in the early twentieth century; see Nam 1994:179–80). As a consequence, Rwanda's population can be expected to double within 20 to 25 years, as a volatile new group of adolescents come of child-bearing age. Such information obviously relates to the demographic argument that the generation of large numbers of poorly educated, landless youth is a recipe for future sociopolitical volatility.

13. I heard this view expressed by officials from the Department of State at a meeting convened in February 1999 at the Congressional Hunger Center in Washington, D.C.

7

October 1993–October 1994:
The Relief Effort Winds Up

Refugees in Tanzania

There is a tradition of movement—flight and refuge, if you will—in the Great Lakes region of Africa dating back several hundred years. As a result, the populations of the countries bordering on Rwanda and Burundi all speak similar languages, and have similar traditions of cultural contact and movement (see Lemarchand 1970; Waters 1995b). However, international humanitarian efforts to alleviate the suffering caused by such migrations is of more recent vintage. The first international efforts at refugee resettlement began at the time when many African countries obtained their independence in the early 1960s.

Since the 1960s, refugees from the new modern states of Rwanda and Burundi resettled in Uganda, Zaire, Tanzania, and Burundi, with different degrees of involvement by the UNHCR. Settlement schemes, including internationally financed virgin-land settlements in Tanzania and Uganda, were established from the 1960s to the 1980s. Typically, such settlements involved resettling refugees on remote forest areas and then providing partial WFP rations while they established self-sufficiency. Spontaneous urban settlement in Burundi and spontaneous rural settlement in Zaire, Tanzania, and Uganda also took place, all without international support. There were also efforts at naturalizing Rwandans and Burundians in Tanzania and Uganda throughout the 1980s and early 1990s. These efforts had some successes in Tanzania, despite bureaucratic inertia. But the Ugandan government resisted formal naturalization for Rwandans in Uganda, and the several hundred thousand Rwandan refugees in Uganda remained without citizenship rights despite residence there since the early 1960s.[1]

Despite a history of flight and population movement, the capacity of the international community to receive refugees from Rwanda and Bu-

Chabalisa 2 refugee camp for Rwandans was established in October 1994. The layout in a grid pattern made food distribution and camp management particularly easy. (Photo by Michael Hyden.)

rundi was at a low point in 1993. At that time, there had been no major international refugee crisis in the region since August 1988, when small numbers of Burundian Hutu fled to Rwanda. From the perspective of the international community, this crisis "solved itself" when most of the Hutu refugees spontaneously returned to Burundi after the cessation of confrontations (Lemarchand 1994:118–130; MSF 1995:21). Prior to that, the last major flight had been in 1972–74, when several hundred thousand Burundians fled to Tanzania. Indeed, in 1993 there seemed to be an outpouring of peace and goodwill.[2] The first democratic elections in Burundi resulted in a peaceful transition of power from the Tutsi Uprona party (Parti de l'Union et du Progrès National) to the moderate Hutu Frodebu (Front des Démocrates) party, a transition observed by North America's preeminent expert on the region, René Lemarchand. Writing in mid-1993, he concluded with a guarded optimism:

> One aspect of the emerging reality in Burundi is the vision of a multi-party democracy drawing its strength from a civil society free of ethnic conflict; another is that of a singularly fragile polity undermined by the instinctive fears and violent reactions of a Tutsi minority that sees itself at the mercy of a Hutu majority. Exactly what kind of system may ultimately emerge from these contrasting visions is hard to foresee (Lemarchand 1994:187).

As for Rwanda, the war, which had begun in 1990, while unfortunate, seemed to be winding down; an agreement was reached in August 1993 and elections were scheduled. Further afield, Mozambique, which had sent hundreds of thousands of refugees to Tanzania, Malawi, and Zambia over a 25-year period, also was engaged in peace talks. As a result, both the UNHCR and the other refugee assistance agencies in Tanzania were scaling back staff and closing down programs. This meant that vehicles and other assets were being relocated, sold, or handed over to local government authorities. As late as September 1993, no observer expected a new refugee influx into Tanzania in the foreseeable future. Indeed, the opposite was occurring. In September–October 1993, Burundian refugees left Tanzania, many spontaneously and others as part of an official UNHCR-sponsored program, to rejoin the civil society in Burundi Lemarchand (1994) described. Plans were also under way to repatriate Mozambicans.

Thus, when the Tutsi-dominated military in Burundi unsuccessfully attempted to topple the new democratic government on October 23, 1993, there were still hopes that Tanzania would not need to again gear up its refugee reception capacity. This conclusion was easy to reach. After all, the coup plotters *failed*, even though in the process about 100,000 Hutu and Tutsi died. Thus, the international refugee relief regime was caught flatfooted when hundreds of thousands of Hutu peasants fled along old flight paths to Tanzania. The international community was slow to gear up in response, with the result that large numbers of the estimated 245,000 refugees began to sicken and die in the remote forests to which they fled (see *JEEAR* 1996:29; MSF 1995:19–31). Primary responses came from development-focused agencies already in Tanzania, especially the mission hospitals that were in the area. Surveys were also taken by UNHCR and WFP staff, but neither the cash nor food resources these agencies controlled were forthcoming for the Burundians (see Figure 7.1).[3]

Beginning in December 1993, in response to both the high death rates of Burundians in Tanzania and an apparent relaxing of political relations in Burundi, the refugees spontaneously decided to return to Burundi, even as UNHCR and WFP offices were finally opened in western Tanzania. Later evaluations noted, "A refugee population, which had arrived [in Tanzania] in reasonable health, experienced a famine." This occurred in large part because WFP had no contingency stocks and little ready cash with which to make needed local purchases of grain (*JEEAR* 1996:29–30). UNHCR, which did not establish a permanent office until early 1994, also was unable to attract donors to assist isolated refugees in remote forest clearings (see Figure 7.2).

Nevertheless, the first Burundi emergency, despite the mistakes, was a basis for the UNHCR and WFP offices for the Burundians being estab-

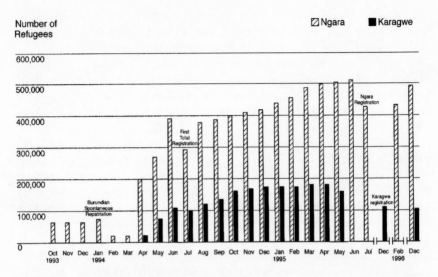

FIGURE 7.1   Graph showing growth and decline in refugee populations in Tanzania's Ngara and Karagwe districts, 1994–96. Note the "declines" in the statistics following registration exercises in July 1994. (*Sources:* Data for October 1993–May 1995 are from UNHCR reports to *JEEAR* 1995; later data are from various UNHCR and WFP sources.)

lished in Kibondo, Kasulu, and Ngara districts in western Tanzania by early 1994. The UNHCR field office in Ngara was to become the center of the Rwanda relief operation and also for the Tanzanian Red Cross, with the assistance of the International Federation of the Red Cross (IFRC). The IFRC also cared for the remaining 8,000 Burundians in a "semipermanent"[4] camp. The assumption was that the refugees would remain until they chose to voluntarily return to Burundi.

With little to do with the few Burundians remaining, the UNHCR staff began drawing up contingency plans to accommodate any potential refugee flight from Burundi. Without a budget, they did what they could: identified a site with water and firewood some distance from the Burundian border, and applied for permission from the Tanzanian and village governments for the use of the site, which was later to be called Benaco. This occupied their time, along with facilitating the passage of relief supplies intended for Burundians in Tanzania to Burundi, where the bulk of the refugees were then located (see Jaspars 1994:6).

Ngara was not to remain a refugee backwater, though. Ngara district borders both Rwanda and Burundi, and the only roads supplying both countries via the port of Dar es Salaam pass through the district. When in early April the world was surprised by the deaths of the presidents of

Dollars (millions)

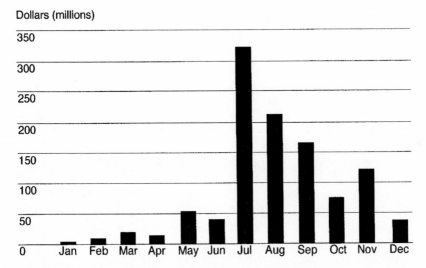

FIGURE 7.2   The United Nations Department of Humanitarian Affairs (DHA) tracked official expenditures by UN agencies (primarily UNHCR and WFP) in 1994. Response to appeals was low until the Ngara influx in May, when there was a stronger appeal. The most expenditures were made in July, which reflects both emergency spending in Zaire and heavy equipment purchases in Tanzania in response to the May–June influx there. (*Source: JEEAR* 1995.)

Rwanda and Burundi in Kigali, Ngara was the logical site for humanitarian contingency preparations for both countries. Africa Watch announced that Burundi was teetering on the edge, and that "it could explode in the coming weeks or months" (Leonard 1994). Fearing a repeat of the Burundian disaster of the previous year, UN staff were put on immediate alert for another Burundian influx. NGO staff (including me) were recruited to expand operations all along the Tanzanian border with Burundi. Most significant, the ICRC positioned food supplies, and the UNHCR assigned two emergency staff, Maureen Connelly and Jacques Franquin, to Ngara in mid-April.[5]

By the end of April it was clear that Rwandans might be involved as well as Burundian refugees. In the first week or two after the April 6 plane attack in Kigali, small numbers of Tutsi refugees (numbering in the tens and hundreds) began to appear in Karagwe and Ngara districts. Hutu also arrived farther to the north, in Karagwe District, escaping from the RPF-controlled areas following the beginning of their April 10 offensive. These groups were given tents at sites slightly removed from the border. Refugee workers were appalled by the machete wounds they saw on the Tutsi refugees and described the refugees' look as dazed, or "shell-shocked." It seemed as if they were incapable of organizing themselves.[6]

A larger crisis loomed, as three things happened in eastern Rwanda during the 20 days following the initial RPF attack. *Interahamwe* militia, apparently commanded from Kigali, attacked out of bases in Kibungo town, near the Tanzanian border. Second, the RPF began its advance on April 10 from its small sector in the north. In their advance they pushed before them hundreds of thousands of the Hutu IDP (internally displaced person) population out of their camps in Byumba prefecture. Byumba town was captured on April 21, and Rusumo in the southeast on April 29–30 (des Forges 1999:295). These Hutu were the displaced who had previously lived in the RPF-controlled areas and had been evacuated in 1991–92. Third, the army of Rwanda, still unsure who was in command and for the first few days not yet taking a major role in the genocide, retreated before the advancing RPF (see Prunier 1995: 213–242).

Among civilian populations, there was confusion from the beginning. One witness from Gahini, in northwestern Rwanda, recounted to me what happened. The Hutu *Interahamwe*, carrying lists of names of people who were to be executed with a machete chop, attacked the hospital. They executed the people on the list and went away. But they returned a short time later to attack all Tutsi, any Hutu who objected to the killing, and any others whom they may have had a personal grudge against. A few days later, a message came from a stranger who claimed to be the vanguard of the advancing RPF. The message was to leave; all who stayed would be killed by the second wave of RPF occupiers, who included execution squads. The surviving populace left, either toward the swamps of Akagera National Park in order to undertake the dangerous crossing to Tanzania on foot through the swamps, or by rushing southward toward the only bridge crossing out of Rwanda, over the Kagera River at the Rasumo bridge, which was controlled by the Rwandan army. As they fled they heard that the RPF execution units did arrive and killed stragglers. For most, though, it was unclear whom they were fleeing from: RPF or *Interahamwe*. What was clear was that many people were dying, and that in late April 1994, Tanzania was a safer place for a Rwandan to be (see des Forges 1999:726–31).

April 25 was still just 19 days after the presidents' plane was shot down, and Rwanda was still newsworthy. There was a dramatic evacuation of foreigners by the United States Marines in Kigali; they brought with them horrific tales of massacres in the city (see, e.g., Gutekunst 1995:22–27). But with the evacuation, live news reports and film from Kigali became less available, and. press attention shifted to the more "visible" story taking place farther south at the Rasumo crossing from Rwanda to Tanzania. The only road crossing along the entire length of the border is a single-lane bridge above the roaring Rasumo Falls, and the Tanzanians granted easy access to the media to film the gathering masses. The shots shifted back and forth from bodies tumbling over the falls to aerial views showing a drama taking place on the Rwanda side of the border at the same time. Tens of thousands, and then hundreds of thousands, pushed up against the Rwandan border post, unable to cross as long as the Rwandan army controlled the bridge. They waited. Pictures broadcast during the last week in April showed a mass of humanity pressing against this single narrow crossing. The MRND-controlled Rwandan government, which still controlled the bridge, refused to let the massing Rwandans pass; the only ones allowed to cross were a small number of expatriates.

On April 28, the block at the bridge broke when Rwandan border guards abandoned the post, leaving the border open. The bridge remained open for some 20 hours on April 28–29. Overwhelmed Tanzanian border guards, having heard of the massacres in Rwanda, required the largely peasant population to leave their machetes, hoes, and other agricultural implements in a large, growing pile. Estimates vary widely, but the *JEEAR* concluded later that 170,000 refugees passed the one-lane Rasumo Bridge on that day.[7] Most traveled on foot, a few on bicycles, and even fewer in automobiles, many of which were the property of the Rwandan government. The three UNHCR officers, who a few days before had been unsure of what emergency they had arrived for, directed the refugees 18 kilometers (11 miles) down the Rasumo Road to the site that had been identified for the Burundians. There the refugees settled down on the mountaintop in Ngara that was to become Benaco Refugee Camp, "the biggest in the world," as UNHCR field officers were soon to brag.

There were two major groups in the arriving population. Half were "experienced" refugees trekking from the IDP camps in Byumba prefecture. The other half included a major portion of the surviving population of Rusumo district, in Kibungo prefecture in southwest Rwanda. Both groups included the MRND leadership who had governed the areas before the plane crash, and some of whom had clearly participated in the genocide. Indeed, at the request of the arriving population, at least one of the organizers of the genocide in Murambi, Byumba, was arrested by the Tanzanians at the request of the fleeing refugees. The bulk of the population, though, were Hutu peasants. At least 75 percent were women and children. Reflecting this relatively normal background, *Time* magazine reported on May 18, 1994:

Yet so far, despair has not triumphed completely. Relief workers are aston-
ished by the cohesion and sense of community they see around them. In
some cases whole villages moved together and reassembled themselves in
the camps; the elders ration food supplies; some priests are presiding over
congregations 1,000 strong. For those who have been witness to mayhem
throughout the past four years of civil war, there were even words of relief.
Compared with the life he had left behind, one refugee told a reporter from
ABC, "here we are tasting the good life." At least here, he explained, no one
was being killed.

The normally staid *Economist* was even more impressed with the lack
of ethnic confrontation in the new camp:

> A few were Tutsi. Fearing trouble, the UN's refugee agency tried to move
> them to a separate camp, but gave up when it became clear that Hutu and
> Tutsi refugees were content to live together. The Red Cross distributed food,
> though most people had enough for a few days. . . . Most of the refugees
> were in reasonable health and only a few had been wounded. . . . But good
> news could swiftly turn to bad. The main camp relies on one small lake, al-
> ready polluted, for water (*The Economist*, May 16, 1994).

The International Refugee Relief Regime Responds

The Burundi refugee crisis had prepared the international refugee relief
regime for this moment well. The elements were in place: representatives
of the two UN agencies charged with refugee relief, UNHCR and WFP,
were present. Ngara was also accessible to the press, and there were opportunities for dramatic film footage both as the refugees crossed the
bridge and as bodies tumbled under it. Indeed, eddies at the foot of the
waterfall did photographers the favor of whirling around 10 or 15 bodies
(depending on the day) in a manner that made the river appear literally
clogged with bodies when viewed through the zoom lens of a *Time*
stringer. In the background, the key financial actors were ready to make
decisions. ECHO and USAID were ready to pay generously for a high-
profile refugee relief operation. Food for the since departed Burundians
was also available for diversion by WFP to the new refugees. Finally, a
number of NGO "implementers"[8] arrived in Ngara looking for ways to
assist, or, more specifically, contract with donors like UNHCR, USAID,
and ECHO to provide services to the refugees (see Borton 1996; von
Bernuth 1996:288).

These were the elements that UNHCR in Geneva had been waiting for
to try out a new plan whereby it would be the primary authority in managing refugee operations: For the first time, the bureaucratic power of

Geneva was among the first on the scene, which gave it an opportunity to test a new emergency response system that had been designed following the conclusion of the Gulf War in 1992. Two elements were key to this. First, early on there was an agreement that funds from ECHO and USAID would be given to UNHCR for distribution to its "implementing partners," i.e. CARE, IRC, LWF, Concern, Red Cross, and the other nongovernmental organizations UNHCR selected. Neither USAID or ECHO would provide donations directly to the NGOs, as they had often done elsewhere in the world; in effect, UNHCR now had power of the purse (Borton 1996:312–313).

Second, it provided a chance to delegate to predetermined European agencies for specific emergency coordination responsibilities. Among these were the Danish Refugee Council, British Overseas Development Agency, United Nations Volunteers, and Emercom/Russia. Each organization was to provide a package of services, including secondment of expatriate technical staff, to be used in the emergency under the coordination of the UNHCR. As a result, over 20 expatriate staff were in Ngara by mid-May, nominally under the UNHCR banner (see Jaspars 1994:15). Finally, at a very early point the Tanzanian government assigned to UNHCR the responsibility for coordinating all expatriate assistance in the refugee camps, effectively offering the UNHCR a sort of sovereignty in dealing with refugee matters.

Now is a good time to review the different groups involved in the Tanzanian operation and their relationship to one another.

The United Nations High Commissioner for Refugees

The United Nations High Commissioner for Refugees (UNHCR) was coordinator of all refugee relief operations. According to its charter, the UNHCR is not an "implementing" agency, except in limited sectors, especially "legal protection issues." This meant in practice that UNHCR awarded contracts to provide services to refugees on behalf of the funding agencies, which were in fact the governments of the United States and nations of the European Community. These contracts were let to nongovernmental organizations such as the Red Cross, CARE, the International Rescue Committee, Concern Worldwide, Christian Outreach, Médecins sans Frontières, and so on. UNHCR's internal divisions, or sectors, reflected the functions that needed to be carried out by the NGOs: Site Preparation and Planning, Logistics, Water and Sanitation, Camp Management/Food Distribution, Social Services, and Medical. UNHCR implemented programs of legal protection and relations with the Tanzanian government itself. These liaison positions were filled temporarily by staff seconded (reassigned) from Europe from May until July 1994. After that, UNHCR hired expatriates on short-term contracts using UNHCR money directly. Behind the scenes, ECHO and USAID maintained UNHCR's authority by refusing to make contributions directly to the nongovernmental organizations, as they had in the past (*JEEAR* 1996:33; von Bernuth 1996). As a result, UNHCR coordinated the distribution of over $200 million dollars in cash and in-kind donations in Tanzania in 1994.

Staff seconded to UNHCR came from the British Overseas Development Agency (ODA) (air and local logistics), the Norwegian Refugee Council (site preparation), Emercom/Russia (trucking), the Swedish Refugee Council (social services and UNHCR office construction), the Danish Refugee Council (site preparation and field officer), Dutch Aid (nutrition), and the UN Volunteers (field and protection officers).

World Food Programme

The World Food Programme (WFP), a UN agency under the coordination of the Food and Agriculture Organization (FAO) in Rome, provided the food for the refugees. As a UN agency, WFP solicited food contributions directly from ECHO (European Community Humanitarian Organization) and USAID (United States Agency for International Development), though it was nominally under the control of the UNHCR in Ngara. WFP's role was so central that it and UNHCR were mutually dependent on each other: the UNHCR counted on the WFP to deliver about 1,500 tons of food to the camps per week.[9] WFP in turn depended on agencies working under UNHCR camp-management contracts to distribute food to the refugees. There was mutual monitoring for quality control, and in addition each agency reported independently to USAID and ECHO. WFP monitored the efficiency of distribution through market and nutritional surveys. UNHCR insisted on the timely delivery of bulk food from WFP donors in Europe and North America (Jaspars 1994; *JEEAR* 1996:87–94; Borton 1996). Both were complex tasks requiring extensive bureaucratic organization to coordinate.

Nongovernmental Organizations

Out of the 20 or 30 nongovernmental organizations (NGOs) that sent representatives to Ngara, UNHCR selected 12 which it would initially fund to work in the camps. The others were sent away, and told that their assistance was not needed; even if they brought donations of cash, staff, or relief items, the assistance was turned down and they were sent away. Among those sent away were large international NGOs like World Vision and Christian Outreach, as well as local NGOs and Tanzanian churches.[10] The 12 selected included those that had worked briefly in the Burundian camps during previous months, plus CARE, which had a large UNHCR-funded program in Kenya, known to Maureen Connelly, the UNHCR officer in charge, from her work there (Borton 1996; Jaspars 1994). This meant that the agencies establishing programs were mostly the large and expensive international emergency agencies, rather than development agencies or agencies with roots in Tanzania. Later in 1994, a number of other agencies began to be admitted by UNHCR as medical agencies like MSF withdrew and services were expanded into school construction, operation of primary schools, and provision for social services.

The cutoff of direct access to USAID and ECHO funds that resulted from UNHCR's new regime created different conditions among the NGOs. Some had a policy of not accepting too much money from the UNHCR, in order that they could maintain their independence of what they believed was an UNHCR insensitivity to refugee needs.[11] Others, like CARE, had a policy of implementing projects only with UNHCR money and were in effect subcontractors to the UNHCR rather than "partners."

USAID and ECHO

The largest share of the spending at Ngara came from monies granted by the governments of European Community nations and the United States to the UNHCR and WFP. The agencies in charge of making these grants were the United States Agency for International Development and the European Community Humanitarian Organization. Their grants had money earmarked for the provision of food commodities, construction of road systems for the camps, water distribution systems, medical services, expatriate salaries and housing, and the salaries of the 20 to 30 UNHCR expatriate staff and 4 to 5 WFP expatriate staff. Although the physical presence of both funding agencies was low-profile, particularly at first, the power of the purse gave them a pervasive influence in broad political decision-making. For example, it was in effect a joint decision by USAID and ECHO that led to the closing down of the camps for Rwandans in 1996 (see Chapter 8). During the summer of 1994, an ECHO monitor had been assigned to the UNHCR as a field officer, but he was not involved in supervising the NGOs and focused on protocol issues. In 1996 the ECHO monitor took more authority over budgetary decisions.

The International Press

Another, less institutionalized, element of the picture was the international press. The influence of the press presence was substantial, and UNHCR went to great lengths to ensure that press access to information and to the camps was controlled. From their perspective, the press was a double-edged sword. To maintain control over press activities at the

Stories Per Week

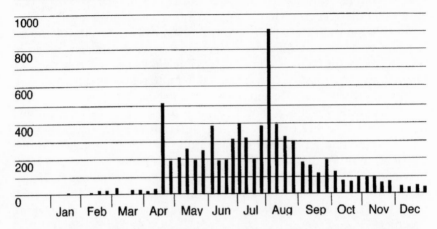

FIGURE 7.3 Press coverage of Rwanda was heaviest in late April, as it became evident that a genocide was taking place; in early June, when the press began to focus on the refugee camps in Tanzania; and especially following the July flight of Rwandans into Zaire. Press coverage lasted for a period of about four months, and then tapered off. Ironically, despite the "CNN effect," no tracking of TV was undertaken that I know of. (*Source: JEEAR.*)

camps, UNHCR brought in media specialists as liaison officers, particularly at the beginning of the operation; one such was Pano Moumtzis, a public relations specialist who has worked in emergency relief around the world. Other agencies, including MSF, CARE, and the Red Cross, also invested in staff to liaise with the international press. What the press wrote about and showed on television generated the political pressure leading to loose purse strings at ECHO and USAID, which is why the press response to the crisis was tracked so closely by all concerned (See Figure 7.3). Broad sympathetic press coverage led to larger refugee bureaucracies who could provide more services. Alternatively, a critical press threatened the standing of any agency, and even the careers of those involved. This love/hate relationship with the press was a central concern as the UNHCR and other agencies sought to both attract and control press coverage (see Gowing 1998).

Setting Up Administrative Systems: Spend Whatever It Takes

In early May 1994, the effects that these relationships would have on the refugee assistance programs were not yet apparent in Ngara. Instead, the focus was on the need to do something—anything—to prevent a recurrence of the Burundi refugee catastrophe of 1993. Unlike the situation with the Burundians, it soon became apparent that this was a disaster made for international intervention. The international press was present to record refugees as they starved, were murdered, or died of disease. This made USAID and ECHO open their checkbooks, and this was like sugar to a bee. The first to take advantage of this situation was the large Italian construction company Cogefar, which had backhoes, graders, and other heavy equipment already on site for a European Union–funded road construction project. These they now offered to rent to UNHCR for camp construction. A private company, Cogefar took advantage of its effective monopoly of this needed equipment and charged multi-million-dollar rents to divert the equipment for UNHCR use during the summer of 1994. Most critical was a four-mile sanitary trench that needed to be dug around the 2km by 2km camp, to provide drainage which would protect the camp's water source from contamination. In the camp there were no toilets, and fecal matter had to be excluded from the water supply at all costs. Other projects included cutting roads for vehicle access and clearing a large site at Benaco for food warehouses.

The NGOs that UNHCR retained set about undertaking tasks on their own initiative, with the advice of the UNHCR. Thus, at Benaco, I was involved with erecting the warehouses; MSF–France installed a pump and water-treatment facilities at a nearby lake which was to become the camp's water source; the Red Cross established outpatient clinics; and so forth. Forty kilometers away, at the UNHCR office in Ngara, daily coordination meetings began. Whoever was present, mostly expatriates, but also some Tanzanians, gathered to exchange notes about what happened, what the press wanted, and what could be expected. By mid-May, UNHCR took control and divided up tasks along sectoral lines, as described above, and made verbal promises (which generally were kept) to reimburse NGOs for their activities. Gradually, as computers and typewriters arrived, written contracts started to become more common, and responsibilities became clearer in the context of what the NGOs brought to the field and UNHCR's preexisting agreements.

Food deliveries began when ICRC lent to the WFP stocks necessary to feed the refugees. The ICRC food stocks were particularly important in Ngara during the first part of the emergency (see Figures 7.4a and 7.4b).[12] This food, mainly dry maize and beans, was distributed by the Tanzanian Red Cross, using lists provided by refugee leaders. There was an awareness that these lists were exaggerated, but for the time being all were relieved that the refugees were being fed and malnutrition was not a problem. The refugees were cooperative; there was no further fighting along ethnic lines, and crime was seemingly nonexistent. At the time, I lived in

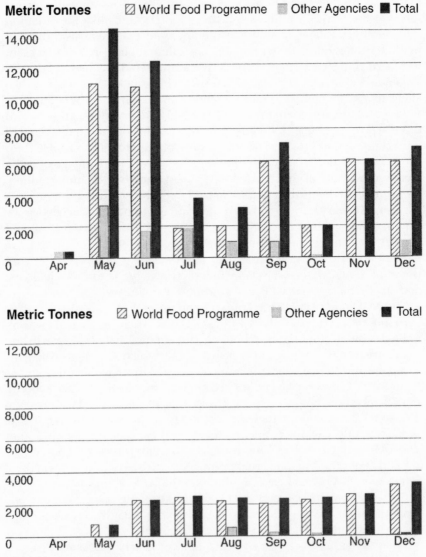

Metric Tonnes ☒ World Food Programme ▦ Other Agencies ■ Total

14,000
12,000
10,000
8,000
6,000
4,000
2,000
0   Apr   May   Jun   Jul   Aug   Sep   Oct   Nov   Dec

Metric Tonnes ☒ World Food Programme ▦ Other Agencies ■ Total

12,000
10,000
8,000
6,000
4,000
2,000
0   Apr   May   Jun   Jul   Aug   Sep   Oct   Nov   Dec

FIGURES 7.4a and 7.4b   The largest source of aid to refugees in Tanzania was in the form of food aid. Early disbursements from the ICRC were important in establishing that population in May 1994. Later in the year there were fluctuations in the food pipeline, such as the one in October, which resulted in declines in rations. Metric tonnage to Karagwe district was less than that to Ngara, particularly in the early months. It is clear that this affected the nutritional status of refugees in Karagwe, but to what extent is not clear. (*Source: JEEAR* 1995.)

Benaco among plastic jerry cans, shovels, plastic sheeting, etc., which remained undisturbed, despite the lack of any security measures. Likewise, a Tutsi nun from Rwanda, who had been living in Tanzania and now lived two or three tents down, wandered unhindered through the camp. Estimates of food distribution indicated a daily distribution between 1,286 and 3,183 kilocalories per day (Jaspars 1994:6–7; Shoham 1996); a survey by MSF–Holland indicated that the average ration was 2,700 kilocalories per refugee per day, but this figure was inflated in part because refugee leaders purposefully inflated population figures in order to get more food, with the result that more food was disbursed than was required to meet planning targets.

MSF–France quickly withdrew from the water sector after installing the pumps it had on hand, deferring to the British NGO, Oxfam, which had water engineers on staff and emergency water-treatment equipment in stock in the UK. Oxfam airlifted complete emergency water systems to the airport in Mwanza, Tanzania, which was trucked to the site. The systems were designed to pump water from Benaco's lake and then sanitize the water and pipe it into the camp. The Oxfam engineers, some of whom had been working in the Burundian camps farther south, installed the systems and they were operational by the end of May. This plant was capable of pumping and cleaning some 1,200 cubic meters of water per day. It was obvious, though, that if the bare minimum of five liters (two gallons) per person per day was to be provided, this yield was inadequate for the refugee population.

Also in May, a well-drilling rig was brought by UNICEF–Uganda to drill 25 boreholes in the region. This was a key addition in the water sector, as it permitted the decongestion of the high population density site at Benaco, where there was water in a lake, to areas that otherwise were without water, and therefore unsuitable for refugees. This activity began by the end of May, and by mid-June, UNICEF and Oxfam had water stations available at a second site 5 kilometers from Benaco, called Lumasi. This camp opened in mid-June, relieving crowding pressures in Benaco and significantly reducing the chance of a cholera epidemic.

The emergency response in the water sector was outstanding in terms of water provision. Within six weeks, the combination of MSF–France, UNHCR, UNICEF, and Oxfam had established two functioning refugee camps with "temporary" water systems to accommodate upwards of 250,000 people. This was done in a remote corner of the world that until then had not had a functioning water system for the small town center of 10,000 to 15,000 people at Ngara. But the operation was very costly. The contracts were negotiated without respect to cost efficiency; materials were flown in from England, as were expatriate Oxfam engineers brought in for two-to-four-week consultancies. The UNHCR approved such expenditures and passed the bills along to ECHO and USAID. MSF–France, UNICEF, and then Oxfam withdrew from the water sector after the high-dollar, high-profile construction contracts were completed.

An even more expensive operation was the transportation program. Truck procurement is notoriously slow in countries like Tanzania; typically it takes six months to order and deliver a standard six-to-ten-ton truck. Since most emergencies require transport of some sort—to haul people, food, equipment, water, and any number of other items to where the refugees are—the UNHCR had made contingency plans. In anticipation of the need, UNHCR in the early 1990s had made a number of standby arrangements, two of which were activated for Ngara. First, ten Nissan flatbed trucks used in the Cambodian relief operation had been put on standby in Dubai. These trucks were airlifted to Mwanza in the second week of May, and arrived in Ngara the next day. The other standby arrangement was an unusual contract with the Russian government's civil defense ministry, Emercom. Emercom had placed 36 small all-terrain Kamaz brand trucks on standby in Bosnia and Russia; they would be operated by a paramilitary unit from the Russian ministry. These trucks began to arrive at the beginning of June. The unit that operated them was self-contained, and at its peak included 56 Russian drivers, mechanics, cooks, administrators, communications experts, and Russian-English translators (see Rehlaender 1994). Many had had experience with trucking and Kamaz during the Russian war in Afghanistan in the 1980s and in the Bosnia relief program; on the basis of this experience they quickly organized themselves as a self-contained "military" field unit. The trucks came with a complete field kit—including food, showers, perimeter fence, tents, vehicle spares, and diesel fuel—which the Russians began setting up at the end of May in Benaco. Quickly the Russians were up and running under the direction of the UNHCR. As with the water system, this was a high-cost operation in which little attention was paid to long-term operating costs. Again, UNHCR passed the bills for air freight and trips back and forth to Russia on to willing paymasters at USAID and ECHO. As with the water system, the trucking operation was considered short-term; the contract with Emercom was for three months, at which point the emergency would be over or the trucks were to be handed over to trained Tanzanian drivers.

Other sectors had similar success in effecting fast but expensive setups. Rented backhoes began digging latrines for refugees, who had few digging tools. Facilities for purchasing services, relief supplies, comforts and conveniences for expatriates, etc. in-country were remote and on the other side of the country, so purchasing was shifted to Nairobi, in neighboring Kenya. Land transport to Nairobi was difficult, so UNHCR rented its own small airplanes to establish an air link with Nairobi (see Jaspars 1994:18–19).

The Ruvubu River separates the main camp at Ngara from the others, but there was no permanent bridge across it, only a hand-cranked ferry. A permanent bridge was planned, but it wouldn't be completed for a year and a half. To facilitate transport between the camps, British ODA air-freighted in a military-style "Mabey" bridge, which was installed under another contract with Cogefar.[13] Aid officials took daily flights to monitor refugee arrivals, and the International Federation of the Red Cross set up a referral hospital in tents, which received more complicated cases from the in-camp outpatient facilities. It was the best in that part of the world. The three MSF agencies (the Netherlands, France, and Spain) had 50 expatriates ready to deliver outpatient medical programs, especially in public health, and by the end of May a measles vaccination program was completed for all under-fives in the camp. New camps were cleared as quickly as possible by Cogefar. One camp, Kayonza, was accidentally located on a mineral concession and had to be unceremoniously abandoned when the mistake was identified.

In May and June 1994, the refugee population in Ngara was the darling of the international media and relief community. The international community responded with an outpouring of generosity and good works. At one point the U.S. Air Force apparently asked to become involved, but the only thing that the UNHCR could think of to ask for was air-drops of firewood. The refugees themselves responded by being well organized, cooperative, articulate (particularly in French), and appropriately grateful.

The First Crack Appears:
Gatete and the Realignment of Refugee Relations

There was a palpable relief among the UNHCR, NGOs, and other agencies working in Ngara in June of 1994. The refugees and agencies worked together well, there was little of the internal squabbling and blaming activity remembered by those who had worked in the Burundian and Somali crises. All worked together well to sustain the refugees. Fears of a cholera epidemic subsided and the camp-management agency of Benaco, the Tanzanian Red Cross, began to organize the refugee house plots into rows. Latrines were dug, and the Oxfam emergency water system was operational. In June, the NGO Concern Worldwide from Ireland began to move substantial portions of the Byumba caseload out of Benaco to the new camp at Lumasi in an orderly fashion (Pottier 1996a:325–27). Relations between the refugees and UNHCR remained good, despite a little bit of under-the-breath grumbling that "they are really all just a bunch of murderers. . . ."

The first potential for a crack in the good feelings started on June 9, when Benaco registered its first murder. Near the Tanzanian marketplace across the street from the camp, a mob surrounded a woman accused of being a witch. She was beaten to death at the edge of the camp, and her body left half covered in the sun. It was explained to a reporter that the woman had been accused of bewitching a person who died (see Rehlaender 1994:42–43, 48). Discussion occurred at the UNHCR meetings, but the participants agreed that while regrettable, such an occurrence was a concern of the Tanzanian government, and noted that some violence was expected in any community of over 300,000 people.

The international community made a different evaluation after a confrontation the following week between a UNHCR official and a refugee leader, known by his last name, Gatete. It became known as the Gatete incident. UNHCR media specialists saw that the incident received wide publicity at the time, and it was the first example of the important role emotionalized incidents would come to play in crisis management. I will describe it in detail here.

When the refugees crossed the Rasumo bridge on April 28–29, a handful were taken into Tanzanian custody and brought to Ngara town. One was Remy Gatete, the government leader of Murambi commune in Byumba district and, of course, a Hutu (Prunier 1995:241). Gatete was arrested on April 28 at the border by the Tanzanian border officials at the request of Rwandans who accused him of being a ringleader in the genocide. He and his family were housed in a tent behind the Ngara town jail. The Tanzanians were presented with a quandary: What to do about such distasteful figures who had not committed crimes on Tanzanian soil?[14] Further, Gatete was identified in the international press as being a leader of the *Interahamwe* and as such, the press believed, would make a good candidate for a war crimes trial. As long as he stayed behind the Ngara jail, the issue somehow remained outside the purview of the international refugee relief regime. However, on about June 14, Tanzanian authorities released Gatete from custody and told him that he could join his people, as long as he did not go to Benaco. Nevertheless, of his own volition he went to Benaco to join his political supporters.

The UNHCR field officer in Benaco, Jacques Franquin, heard about this and called Gatete into his office to inform him that he was ineligible for refugee status under international law because he did not have a well-founded fear of persecution and was therefore ineligible to live in Benaco. Under international law, individuals must demonstrate that they have a fear of persecution because of their political or tribal affiliation— not fear of *prosecution* for crimes they have committed. Anyway, Gatete told Franquin that he would pack his things and return. He did so a few minutes later, followed by about 5,000 of his supporters (3 percent of the total camp population), who carried sticks, stones, and machetes. Gatete told Franquin that he could not leave because "my people will not let me." Tanzanian police who were present defused the situation by giving the megaphone to Gatete so that he could urge his supporters to disperse. Two shots were fired in the air, and at this the Tanzanians ordered UNHCR to release Gatete. Gatete and the crowd left, and the UNHCR officials left for Ngara. The confrontation itself was broadcast live to the NGOs via a VHF radio network established the previous week, which added to the drama. The most dramatic point came when someone from the UNHCR was heard to say: "If there are any deaths here, I am not answerable! Do you hear, Ngara, I am not answerable!"[15]

The next day, an emergency meeting of all NGOs was called by the UNHCR in Ngara. I attended as the representative of LWF. It soon became obvious that the purpose of the meeting was to confirm a policy already established as part of discussions between MSF and UNHCR: that services by all NGOs would cease until Gatete left and refugee leaders expressed remorse for the incident. Franquin and Maureen Connelly, also of UNHCR, described the incident and claimed that 30,000 Hutu refugees were ready to do Gatete's bidding.[16] Staff from the French and Dutch MSF agencies told us what they had heard in the camp.[17] Already, they said, it was becoming apparent that control of the camp was in the hands of criminals like Gatete, who had an absolute control over the Hutu population (MSF 1995:44). Maureen Connelly felt the agencies should reach a consensus as to what they would do and polled the agencies' representatives, starting with the MSFs, for their positions. The representatives indicated that they wanted to discontinue all programs as a protest to the refugees against the involvement of war criminals in the camp.[18] Once this consensus was reached, Connelly indicated that all NGO activity should be suspended pending her meeting with the Hutu refugee leadership the following day. If, after a meeting with the leadership, she was satisfied that the leaders would cooperate with the agencies' delivery services, it was agreed activities could resume. MSF representatives, ever independent, reserved judgment on the situation and left for the Serengeti, where they held a conference to discuss the moral issues involved in working with the Rwandan Hutu population in Benaco. They returned to work about one week later.

At the meeting with the refugee leadership (not including Gatete), Connelly and the leaders inevitably concluded that food and water distribution and medical activities must resume; Connelly said that the leadership was appropriately apologetic, and the agencies (besides MSF) resumed their activities. More important for the overall funding of the program was that more ink was spilled about Benaco in the world press, our work suddenly came to be viewed as dangerous, and funding for security measures became especially easy to get from USAID and ECHO (via UNHCR).

This incident, though not the most significant to the refugee population or Tanzanians,[19] was the basis for redefining relations between the international refugee relief regime coordinated by the UNHCR and the refugees themselves. The headquarters of the NGOs operating in the camps were transferred to a remote hilltop, which was defensible against military action by the refugees. Thus, the Gatete incident set the stage for the adversarial relationship with the refugees that replaced the cooperative one initiated during previous weeks. Given the inherent inequalities in the donor-refugee relationship, such a polarization was probably inevitable. The Gatete incident accentuated further the "at any cost" approach to the establishment of relief operations, but this time the focus was on security for expatriates rather than on feeding the refugees.

Most significant was that immediate decisions were made about resiting food stores out of the camp and to a more secure site on a hill, called K-9, some 15 kilometers from the camp and about midway between the camps and the town of Ngara. This decision was made by the UNHCR, Cogefar, which accepted the earth-moving contract, and CARE, which operated the food warehouses on behalf of UNHCR and WFP.[20] Significantly, it was done without an assessment of needs, or for that matter of the site, which was "surveyed" from the roadside. In addition, UNHCR suggested that all NGO expatriates should establish housing for themselves there. (Several agencies had expatriate staff living among the refugees in the camps, and more were living in Ngara town and on the Anglican mission compound.) On the top of this remote hill there was to be a logistics center, food stores, vehicle storage and repair facilities, and living quarters for several hundred expatriates and Tanzanians. This was done without consideration of the building costs for a small town on a remote hill in the African bush; it was simply announced that funding was no problem as the move was for security reasons. UNHCR explained to us that "the UNHCR would pay for everything involved with the move. Money is not a problem." The UNHCR was apparently able to make such statements because fears in the West of an international incident involving an attack by Rwandans on expatriate refugee workers gave the agency great latitude.

The move had a long-term impact on the refugee operation. In particular it meant that the costs of maintaining a town on a hillside without water, electrical system, market, or sanitation system would be borne independent of the Tanzanian infrastructure in Ngara, and was also emerging around the camp, where a vigorous market quickly came into being. It also meant that there were wrenching shifts in programs. For example, my own agency had to suspend construction of vehicle maintenance facilities, which had already been undertaken near Benaco, because, it was explained that a new facility was to be built. We also had to relocate over 100 Tanzanian employees from the camps to the new town on the hilltop. Momentum was lost as employees actively involved in programs of construction went to wait-and-see mode while another site was first surveyed, and in August, finally leveled.

As for Gatete, he returned to his family in Benaco. He was not to remain long, though. Arrangements were made by the Tanzanian Ministry of Home Affairs, and Gatete was quietly deported by the Tanzanians to Zaire in early July 1994.

The Second Crack Appears: Food Pipeline and Census

The second crack in the picture came from the food pipeline. The program's initial success covered up the logistical issues involved with distributing about 1,500 tons of food per week in the most remote corner of one of the most impoverished countries in the world.[21] Overnight, Ngara went from being a small, remote district with a subsistence economy producing enough food to feed the people there to being the site of a major city that did not produce any food. WFP responded by borrowing 10,000 metric tons of grain from Tanzania's strategic grain reserve—a one-day drive away, in Shinyanga—and purchasing a two-month supply of beans locally. Even these relatively simple local arrangements, though, taxed Tanzania's trucking capacity (Jaspars 1994:5). Nevertheless, adequate food supplies were available through June 1994. But, once nearby sources were exhausted, longer transport lines to the Indian Ocean port of Dar es Salaam, 1,040 kilometers (663 miles) away as the crow flies, were required. There is no paved road across central Tanzania, and the one rail line, built by the German colonialists at the turn of the century, was subject to frequent breakdown. There was also inadequate rolling stock to meet the WFP's need to feed not only Ngara, but also, later, Burundi itself, and still later areas of Rwanda, Burundi, and Zaire.

But in June 1994, the broader issue of coastal transportation routes still lay in the future. The nearby food stocks were exhausted and WFP was still not able to catch up with the rising refugee numbers; what had started as 250,000 refugees had reached 500,000 by the end of June, including 100,000 in Karagwe district (*JEEAR* 1996:33; Jaspars 1994; Borton 1996). Now, finger-pointing at the large UN bureaucracies started. WFP pointed out that a substantial portion of the problem was due to the lack of a census of the refugee population; the refugee leaders provided the numbers of people needing to be fed, and these obviously were higher than the camp population, which inflated tonnage WFP was required to deliver. The WFP, well aware of the problem, blamed UNHCR for delays in taking a census. A census was finally held at the end of June, and the total count of refugees in Tanzania decreased by about 25 percent (see *JEEAR*, 1996:33, Figure 1).[22] There was some short-term relief, but the influx continued, and within a month, another 100,000 refugees had crossed the border into Tanzania. The WFP was right back where it had started. Again it needed to supply 1,500 tons of food per week, as the supplies in-country were again exhausted. Short rations were issued in July, August, and October, a situation Maureen Connelly in June 1995 described as "a continuous emergency, not a sudden influx followed by stability" (*JEEAR* 1996:108 n.3).

July 1994—Still an Emergency?

By July 1994, a number of factors were exacerbating the situation in the refugee camps. First was a staffing shortage. After a vigorous start in May, NGO and UNHCR drastically cut staffing in July 1994. Emergency staff contracts from the UNHCR and other agencies expired, and about 20 people who had established systems on an emergency basis left, including the four top UNHCR staff.[23]

Second, refugees continued to arrive. As RPF units consolidated control along Rwanda's southern border with Tanzania and Burundi, tens of thousands of Hutu refugees began to appear 40 kilometers (25 miles) south of Benaco, having actually crossed a corner of Burundi in order to escape. Unlike the first arrivals, these refugees were likely to be exhausted and suffering from exposure to the elements, having walked a substantial distance and crossed swampy regions. This also occurred at a time before the new agency facilities at K-9 were ready, and remaining staff were left in a state of suspense over when, where, or how they would move.

Third, WFP in August challenged the UNHCR's decision to site the food stores at K-9, which was at the top of a hill where the loaded (and often decrepit) rented Tanzanian trucks were not always capable of climbing without assistance from the Russian Kamaz army trucks. WFP decided to establish food stores east of Lumasi on the main road. The confrontation added to the sour atmosphere persisting between the two UN agencies. This sourness reached a head when UNHCR-Ngara made an end run around WFP, and asked USAID to bypass WFP procurement and distribution networks (*JEEAR* 1995:92; Shoham 1996; Jaspars 1994).

The final insult, as it were, was the loss of Ngara's status as home to the biggest complex of refugee camps in the world. In July and August, 2 million Rwandans fled to Zaire with the defeated Hutu government. Press attention shifted to Zaire, where refugees were dying of cholera and where there was an even larger relief program. A number of agencies even pulled staff out of Ngara and sent them to Zaire, where once again the UNHCR was doling out large contracts for the startup of refugee assistance programs using USAID and ECHO money.

Thus, by July the high-powered relief system in Ngara district had been hit by a number of circumstances that weakened it institutionally. Staff, agencies, and goodwill were sucked out of the operation even as refugee numbers increased, equipment broke down, and food supplies diminished. The one bright spot was that there was still several months' worth of cash reserves in the accounts of agencies unable to spend money fast enough. The period of "spend as fast as you can" had not yet ended, even though it was becoming obvious that it would. According to the *Joint Evaluation of Emergency Assistance to Rwanda (JEEAR)*:

> The extent to which funding was reactive to events was striking. There was a marked contrast in resource availability between the "tap-on" period from mid-July to September, when funding appeared limitless, and other periods when it was less readily available. The factors contributing to this reactive characteristic are many and their relationship complex. Media coverage and the concern of almost all organizations (donor organizations, the military, as well as NGOs and UN agencies) involved in the response for "profile" and "visibility" were clearly significant. What was clear from the study is that the way the system was resourced was sub-optimal, limiting the effectiveness of the response and substantially increasing eventual costs. . . (1996:15)

Out of this environment two questions emerged: how to react in the short run, and what the long-term prospects were. In the short term, the question was "Is this still an emergency?" Clearly the continued arrival of refugees indicated that the situation remained unsettled. The ability of the UNHCR was improved when it moved its offices out of tents and into a complex of prefabricated offices erected by Swedish technicians, contributing to a new atmosphere characterized by hierarchy and attention to procedure. Even the reaction to new refugee emergencies was clearly much more regular and efficient than it had been in May. Certainly, it was a long way beyond the situation a few months earlier when Burundians had starved in the forests due to lack of food and resources.

In July 1994, shortly before finishing her emergency assignment, Maureen Connelly, anticipating a Burundi refugee crisis in the wake of parliamentary elections planned for that month, assembled representatives of the NGOs and asked them whether their organizations were "ready." All agreed that they were ready for an influx of the same size or larger than what had come from Rwanda. The agencies were probably exaggerating their readiness, but the fact that the question could even be posed was an indication of the progress that had been made in refugee reception capacity during the previous two months. Over 200,000 people were being fed and provided with water and medical care. Also, the assemblage was a group of people now experienced in the establishment of large refugee camps, where previously there had been little such expertise. The camp had been successfully set up and run without a major disease epidemic, and assuming the money was available, those assembled were in fact prepared to do it again if called upon.

But the discussion was not limited to the question of readiness. Staff members also acknowledged that when the world's attention had been focused on Ngara, they had enjoyed the press attention in a vicarious way. More important, perhaps, was that as long as press attention continued, political pressure was maintained in Europe and the United States to "do something"—in other words, provide the open checkbook to which the operation had become accustomed. But the staff members also expressed a weariness from the rushing about at the expense of planning or thought. Field workers began to wonder about long-term solutions. What should be the follow-up for a successful emergency relief operation? Field workers recognized that the status quo of a densely packed emergency camp made of grass and plastic could not be maintained. Disease epidemics would always threaten, and political concerns would fester in an idle population so close to the border.

This longer-term thinking was also apparent in discussions emerging about the two possible long-term solutions to the Rwanda refugee problem: permanent resettlement in eastern Africa, and quick repatriation to Rwanda. The only long-term solution the field workers did not consider viable was for the refugees to remain in the camps in Ngara. There, it seemed likely, firewood, water, and security concerns (i.e., proximity to the Rwandan border) would doom Benaco to remain an overcrowded Rwandan "urban" area.

Repatriation and Resettlement

In fact the overall solution to the Rwandan crisis lay far beyond Ngara, or even Tanzania. Decisions were made at UN headquarters in New York and Geneva that the only solution was repatriation to Rwanda, despite the still tenuous control on power enjoyed by the new RPF government in August and September (Reyntjens 1995). In Ngara, this outcome looked extremely unlikely as tens of thousands of Rwandan refugees continued to arrive through November and into early 1995. In addition, corpses, many of whom were apparently execution victims of the new RPF rulers, continued appearing floating in the Kagera River at the Rasumo bridge "body catchment" on an almost daily basis. Policy-makers in camp start-ups in far away cities such as Washington, D.C, and Brussels, where the checks are written, quaked at the potential costs involved.

Into this mix stepped President Ali Hassan Mwinyi of Tanzania in October 1994. At Benaco he announced to the press and the international community that Tanzania was prepared to provide land for the resettlement of all Rwandan refugees along the southern border with Mozambique, on the condition that the international community picked up the resettlement costs. Underlying his offer was the belief, held also by other Tanzanians, that the underlying cause of the Rwandan conflict was demographic pressures and structural inequalities that made any reconciliation between Hutu refugees and the new Tutsi government unlikely.

In Ngara, UNHCR and the NGOs did some informal planning to assess how to move 100,000 to 500,000 refugees across Tanzania's southern hinterland. They worked on the assumption that all transport would be paid for by the international community. Calculations showed that an airlift of unheard-of proportions combined with a one-and-a-half-year rental of Tanzania's railways would be necessary. But irrespective of costs, the international community in the capitals failed to respond to President Mwinyi's offer, and the proposal soon sank, for two reasons. First, the members of Tanzania's parliament that represented the southern region opposed it. Second, there was a sudden shift in Tanzanian public opinion after the murder of a Tanzanian evangelist in the Benaco market.

The Murder of the Evangelist David

The Tanzanian public has traditionally had a welcoming attitude toward refugees; it considers it a duty as a good neighbor to see that they are received humanely (Rutinwa 1996; Gasarasi 1984). The policy of containing the refugee influx in remote corners of Tanzania in 1994 helped Tanzanians to maintain this belief. The Tanzanian public assumes that refugees themselves will behave as good neighbors, as indeed the Rwandans seemed to do. Also beneficial was the fact that a substantial new economy developed around the refugees. The net result was that for most Tanzanians the refugees were out of sight; they knew only what the more entrepreneurial friends told them, or what they read in the newspapers. And up until October, the newspapers were reporting that the refugees were accepting Tanzanian hospitality with gratitude.

In October 1994, there was a sudden shift in this perception as a result of an incident in the Benaco camp. David was a well-known and popular Tanzanian, a 195-centimeter (six-foot-five) evangelist in a Dar es Salaam church who originally came from Arusha. David and a Swiss colleague named Werner arrived in Benaco in October 1994 to deliver Pentacostal Bible tracts to the refugees. They went into the camp after notifying the Tanzanian authorities, but without consulting with the UNHCR. The tracts were in Swahili, not Kinyarwanda, and had on the cover a drawing of serpents around a man. David disappeared while distributing the Bible tracts in the camp; he disappeared in the middle of the crowded marketplace after a mysterious-sounding whistle was blown. Apparently, David's height and the tracts were misinterpreted as being "RPF." It took three days of negotiations by the Tanzanian authorities to recover his body. The day after David had disappeared, refugee leaders produced the body of a murder victim, claiming that it was David. The Swiss missionary who was the only one in the area able to identify David refused to identify the body as David's. On the third day David's body was produced; his head had been crushed, apparently shortly after his disappearance (see Waters 1995b, 1997). Tanzanian authorities provided an escort for the body to the airstrip, where an aircraft chartered by his church took him back to Dar es Salaam. In Dar es Salaam there was a large funeral, which was well-covered in the Tanzanian press.

A second incident in early November led to further Tanzanian reservations about the presence of the Rwandan refugees. As part of the normalization of diplomatic relations with Rwanda, the government of Tanzania agreed to see that refugees returned a number of Rwandan government vehicles that they had brought with them when they came to Benaco. The refugees did this, but in the case of a vehicle brought by the former governor of Kibungo prefecture, they switched license plates and sent back an older car. This deception was quickly discovered, and the governor was called into the police station. In response, a large crowd rushed the police station, and the police fired shots into the air. Refugees in turn blocked access to the camp by pulling culverts across the road, as a demonstration of their power. Two Rwandans were beaten to death in the melee when they jumped out of a car owned by Concern Worldwide and tried to run away from the crowd. The governor was soon released by the Tanzanians, and agency activities resumed normally.

The Tanzanians seized on both issues to drive public opinion in the direction of rejecting permanent resettlement in the southern region. Ironically, international reaction was muted. In part this was because a number of UNHCR officials had been cycled out of the camp, and those remaining were not willing or able to use the potential emotionalism of the confrontations to attract more press attention. This stance probably also reflected the distance the UNHCR took from the Tanzanians, who had effectively delegated all daily management decisions for the Rwandan refugees to the UNHCR. In late 1994, when there were 500,000 refugees in Ngara, only three Tanzanian administrators and a small contingent of police were assigned full time to refugee issues.

Ngara, November 1994

By November 1994, Ngara had settled into the routines, relationships, and procedures that were to dominate the rest of the operation. As Maureen Connelly (who returned in November after a four-month absence) asserted, the crisis continued. But the nature of the crises had changed; they were managed and routinized along the principles established by the staff in the first six weeks, very few of whom remained. The problem was that these routines were dependent on norms established in the setup stage of the operation, when information was scarce, finance was plentiful, CNN's presence was taken for granted, and UNHCR coordination was unquestioned. During the next two years, the newly established bureaucracy's ability to cope with refugee influx improved. The WFP's food pipeline functioned better, and refugee health stabilized, becoming in many respects better than it had been in Rwanda or was in neighboring Tanzanian villages (see Essay 1). As for food distribution, the refugee leaders' control was challenged, and the camp management agencies gradually took responsibilities for food distribution away from the more corrupt refugee leaders.

Despite the fact that the operation was functioning successfully, the camp's days were numbered. Particularly in the UN's New York headquarters, and in Geneva, Washington, and Brussels there was increasing dissatisfaction with the political conditions in the Great Lakes region, and funding by ECHO and USAID soon withered. In the end, 2 million refugees were removed from the UNHCR's rolls in the largest forcible repatriation since World War II.

Notes

1. A number of papers have been written about different aspects of refugee reception in Tanzania. See Malkki 1995; Gorman 1993; Sommers 1993; Daley 1994; Smith 1995; Waters 1995b, 1989, and 1988 for a few of the more recent papers. Khiddu-Makubuya 1994; Whitaker 1999; Prunier 1995; and Smith 1995 discuss the history of Rwandan refugees in Uganda. Stein (1996) and Gasarasi (1984) have written general histories of refugee relief operations in Tanzania. Cuenod (1967) wrote the earliest scholarly account of Rwandan refugee reception in Uganda and Tanzania that I know of.

2. The agency I worked for, Lutheran World Federation, had been involved in resettling these refugees in large settlements between 1972 and 1990. However,

by 1993, headquarters in Geneva had begun to ask whether there was need for a "refugee service" in Tanzania, since at that time there were no new refugees in the region.

3. Several nongovernmental agencies did arrive in time to set up operations (notably LWF in Ngara and Kibondo, Caritas in Ngara, MSF–France in Kasulu, and the Tanzanian Red Cross in Ngara). In addition, the Anglican church's hospitals in the area such as Muragwanza (Ngara prefecture), Kabanga (Kasulu prefecture), and Shunga (Kasulu prefecture) were overwhelmed by the refugee influx. They received little support from the international refugee relief regime during the early days of the influx.

4. Up until 1993, Tanzania had a policy of housing refugees in permanent settlements. Refugees placed in permanent settlements were given access to enough land to support themselves through farming until they were able to return to their home country. In these settlements UNHCR constructed permanent infrastructure, including brick schools and dispensaries, roads, and administrative buildings. Burundians received in the 1970s and Mozambicans in the 1980s and early 1990s were maintained in such settlements.

The category "semipermanent" was introduced in 1993 for refugees fleeing from Burundi. These refugees were provided with house plots and a small area to farm. The area for farming was not enough for subsistence, however, and it was expected that they would receive WFP rations until they were repatriated to Burundi. When the Rwandans arrived in April and May 1994, they were placed in "temporary" camps, because of their large numbers. No permanent buildings were constructed, and refugees received only enough land to build a grass and plastic hut; they were not permitted to farm, and it was assumed that WFP rations would be their primary food source.

5. This brought the total number of UNHCR expatriate staff in Ngara to three at the end of April. Both Maureen Connelly and Jacques Franquin remained involved in the reception of the Rwandan refugee influx. As coordinator, Connelly was to play the key role in establishing how assistance was delivered. The third UNHCR expatriate on site was Andres Jimenez. He finished his assignment in Ngara in late May, and as far as I know, did not become involved in the long-term relief operation.

6. Personal communication from Bernhard Staub and Adamasu Simeso, April 30, 1994. Lisa Henry and Lazarus Mezza also told me about visiting these refugees in April 1994.

7. Published accounts usually refer to a figure of 250,000 refugees. This was a first guess and/or a planning figure. On the basis of census data, the total number who crossed into Tanzania is believed to be about 170,000 (see *JEEAR* 3:2–5 and Jaspars 1994:4–5). This figure may also be high, but is certainly closer to the truth than the more widely cited 250,000 figure.

8. As described in Chapter 2, UNHCR is not allowed to implement refugee relief programs itself. Rather its brief is to use money donated by governments to shape relief programs by contracting with other agencies for specific services to refugees. UNHCR then "monitors" disbursements. In most countries, this means that the UNHCR makes payments to and monitors governmental agencies within the host country who provide services within refugee camps. The exception is

when there is no capacity within the host country government to provide skilled staff to provide such services. This is the case in Tanzania, and other poor countries. In these cases, the UNHCR contracts with international NGOs like the IFRC (International Federation of the Red Cross and Red Crescent Societies), CARE, Médecins sans Frontières, etc., to provide the services. Consequently, these agencies often have an odd relationship with the UNHCR; they are not commercial contractors per se, but partners, or implementers. Independent of this financial tie, UNHCR is also often the designated coordinator for the agencies who rush in to assist in a refugee emergency.

9. Food rations were measured in a variety of ways, depending on which point in the pipeline was analyzed. In 1995, WFP needed to make 1,500 tons available weekly in the Ngara complex of camps, which included the four camps near Benaco and Kitali Hills. This involved trucking the commodities received at the distant port of Dar es Salaam across Tanzania to warehouses, typically on 40-ton trucks. The trucking NGO, Lutheran World Federation, was responsible for taking what was needed from the warehouses and delivering it to the distribution point in each camp, where the camp management NGO scooped it into the refugees' bags. This process involved receiving and dispatching 37.5 40-ton truckloads per week and was coordinated by UNHCR.

Distribution cycles in the camps were either weekly or every other week. At these distributions, the camp management NGOs would scoop into the bag of each family a ration for one or two weeks, for each member of the family. The formula used was based on a daily per capita ration of 420 grams of maize grain or 350 grams of maize meal, 120 grams of pulses, 25 grams of vegetable oil, and 5 grams of salt. Theoretically this provided a per capita ration of 2,045 calories (see Shohan 1996:342). Frequent breaks in the pipeline meant that this ideal was rarely met.

The equity of the food distribution system was checked in at least two ways. First, a third NGO periodically conducted food-bag surveys, randomly checking how much of each type of food was in a refugee's bag as he or she left the distribution center. This is how we knew that the actual amount of food received per refugee was typically between 1,600 and 1,900 kilocalories per day. Malnutrition rates were also regularly calculated using height-to-weight surveys conducted by the NGOs operating outpatient clinics.

10. Churches in western Tanzania are among the strongest elements of civil society. Nevertheless, they were effectively excluded from the setup of the operation by the UNHCR, even though for the first months of the operation, the UNHCR had offices in the Anglican mission compound in Ngara, and continues to have offices in the Anglican compound in Kasulu. One Tanzanian related to me how an Anglican bishop bringing a shipment of used clothing provided by Tanzanians was chased away from Benaco by the UNHCR field officer. The churches of his diocese had already been deeply involved in the response to the Burundian refugees through the provision of medical care, before the UNHCR arrived. "We are professionals," it was explained to the bishop, and do not need minor agencies. Ironically, in 1999 the UNHCR approached this bishop to take over social services for a number of camps for Congolese and Burundians.

UNHCR's aloof relationship with Tanzanian agencies reflects its current "relief only" policy. The Tanzanian agencies often are relatively weak and are therefore in need of "capacity building," but those at UNHCR do not view themselves as responsible for developing local capacity to deal with future refugee influx. This at times leads to acrimonious relations between the UNHCR and what Tanzanian institutions are present.

11. World Vision was the agency that learned most quickly how heavy-handed UNHCR coordination was to be in Ngara. In the first days after the influx, World Vision took blankets to the border to distribute to refugees, despite UNHCR orders not to do so on the grounds that this would provide an incentive to establish settlements on the border, away from Benaco. Despite World Vision's long experience in Tanzania, they were not awarded a sector by UNHCR when the contracts were organized. Consequently, World Vision never did become involved in the Rwanda relief operation in Tanzania.

My own agency, LWF, had a policy going in of a 70/30 split between UNHCR funds and church-generated money. This was relaxed a bit when it became apparent that traditional sources of funds from European Community governments would not be available. MSF had a policy of establishing clinics and systems with their own funds, but very quickly switched over to 100 percent UNHCR funding. The Red Cross societies had independent sources of funds around the world and were never overly dependent on UNHCR. CARE, World Concern, Christian Outreach, and other agencies were virtually 100 percent dependent on UNHCR funding.

12. See Jaspars (1994) for a complete account.

13. The bridge was first installed in July 1994, during the dry season. Highwater marks were miscalculated, and Cogefar received a second contract in 1995 to raise the bridge.

14. Another was a man who was made governor of Kibungo prefecture shortly after the genocide began, apparently assisted in the implementation of the genocide, and then fled to Tanzania.

15. Quote from Rehlaender (1994:5). Translation from German by the author.

16. UNHCR representatives asserted to reporters the same day that it had determined that he had unusual power within the camp, and that "at least thirty thousand refugees dance to his tune" (see Rehlaender 1994). This assertion was made without consultation with the Tanzanians or any broader understanding of the volatile nature of charismatic power (in the sense of Max Weber's descriptions of charisma), such as Gatete did indeed have at that moment. Ironically, the Tanzanian police officer who gave Gatete the megaphone seemed to have a finer sense of this. It also did not reconcile the fact that this same population had turned Gatete in at the border. No indictment for war crimes or genocide had been listed for Gatete on the Web site for the International Criminal Tribunal for Rwanda (ICTR) as of July 1999. As of autumn 2000 the indictments were no longer on the Web site.

17. MSF–Holland had operated clinics inside Rwanda during the early days of the genocide. Many of their local employees were Tutsis, and a large number were killed during the genocide, sometimes in front of their expatriate colleagues. As a result, MSF as an agency closed its clinics in Rwanda and the expa-

triates and the surviving local staff fled to Tanzania. These staff, who by and large were Tutsis, became the source of their information about plots within the Hutu camps. This information, which in July and August 1994 included accusations and rumors of poisonings within MSF facilities, was—to borrow Barbara Tuchman's term—amplified in the meetings coordinated by the UNHCR.

18. As a representative for LWF, I indicated that we saw no reason to discontinue programs, but would defer to the consensus of the group.

19. Interviews with refugees and Tanzanians at the time indicated that there was little understanding of why the international community was peeved with the refugee leadership. This was because discussion among the expatriates took place in English, in Ngara, 40 kilometers away. The Tanzanian government at the time was changing district commissioners, and this meeting was the first for the new head of district government, a military man, Brigadier General Sylvester Hamedi. Refugee leaders, who dealt with the expatriates in French, did not pass the gist of the discussion on to the Kinyarwanda-speaking refugee masses in any organized fashion. Indeed, they had little interest in doing so.

20. Both CARE and UNHCR staff making this decision had had immediate experience with Somali refugee programs, where such compounds were considered standard. In large part, this was due to security concerns, which had been foremost during these crises. As described in previous chapters and in Walkup (1997), there often was an adversarial relationship between relief agencies and the refugees during this emergency. In many respects this mentality surprised me. My own experience with refugee work had been in Thailand and Tanzania, where expatriates lived in towns or camps among the populations they were assisting.

21. The per-refugee, per-day ration for a food supplement in the Great Lakes region was 420 grams of whole cereal, 120 grams of beans, 25 grams of oil, and 5 grams of salt. If the food pipeline worked well, this is what the refugees would receive. Fifty grams of "corn-soya blend" was also included at the time Ngara was established (Jaspars 1994:4–5). Note that these are synthetic figures, and in practice the refugees received a food distribution every one or two weeks. This supplement was a rather bland mix of food, but adequate to sustain life, assuming that it was equitably distributed across the population. Depending on the type of food distributed, this was usually resulted in an average food basket of 1800 calories per person per day. As mentioned in the text, distributions were higher earlier in the crisis. Later in 1995–96, in some camps, figures dropped below 1,800 kilocalories per day in some weeks (see Chapter 8 and Essay 1).

22. As Crisp (1999) recently pointed out, refugee censuses are critical for management and accountability. However, there have been few systematic studies of their accuracy. As he also points out (and as is discussed in Chapters 3 and 4), such censuses are inherently difficult to administer involving as they do definitions of who is a refugee and therefore countable and who is not.

23. Maureen Connelly, Jacques Franquin, Karl Steinacker, and Corrinne Faletto all left in July. Connelly, Franquin, and Steinacker were all assigned permanently to Ngara some months later. In the interim, the senior posts were either vacant or held by temporary appointees. Connelly, Franquin, and Steinacker all returned with permanent assignments to Ngara in October and November.

8

October 1994–December 1996: Normalized Crisis— The Operation Winds Down

By November 1994, a short-term successful but expensive relief program was in place. The policy consensus was already clear, at least at the New York and Geneva levels: there would be a repatriation. The UN secretary-general's special envoy for Rwanda, Ambassador Shahrayar Khan, arrived in Benaco from Kigali in early November to reiterate this point in a meeting for the NGOs. The assumptions behind the repatriation policy were that the presumably apolitical Hutu refugees would welcome the opportunity to return, and they would be welcomed by the new RPF-dominated government.[1] Further relief operations and programs were to be undertaken with these assumptions in mind. Repatriation was a policy that the institutional players—the Tanzanian and Rwandan governments, the United Nations agencies and their NGO partners, and the donor governments—agreed on.

But the view on the ground was different, and questions were raised about whether it was realistic to expect a substantial voluntary repatriation at a time when refugees were still fleeing Rwanda for Tanzania; the number of bodies recovered daily from the Kagera River was actually increasing. Maureen Connelly initiated a planning exercise on November 14 whose purpose was to solicit comments from the staff on repatriation and on resettlement within Tanzania. Repatriation in the November 1994 memo was considered unlikely, primarily for two reasons:

- Spontaneous repatriation cannot be supported immediately both for the internal situation in Rwanda and the political pressure put on people inside the Tanzanian camps.
- [Repatriation] requires close, coordinated planning within Rwanda to ensure that repatriation does not lead to a deteriora-

Keza camp was established in February 1996 for Rwandans and Burundians fleeing Burundi. (Photos by Dagmar Waters.)

tion of the conditions required to sustain repatriation and development within Rwanda, thus leading to further violence and a breakdown of the society.

Local officers of the UNHCR and NGOs were also interested in resettlement in Tanzania and presented a planning document, described as a "nonpaper," that sketched out a scenario where 300,000 refugees would return to Rwanda and 300,000 would be resettled in various regions of Tanzania.

Despite such initiatives, however, in late 1994 assumptions of quick voluntary return and reconciliation within Rwanda dominated higher-level policy development, even though events in Tanzania, Rwanda, and Zaire indicated that such a solution was unlikely. Oddly, the UNHCR in Tanzania was caught in the middle. Its field officers reported the continuing arrival of fleeing Rwandans, massacre reports, and other indicators that voluntary repatriation was not possible in the short term. But UNHCR's donors in Washington, New York, and Europe accused them of discouraging and delaying voluntary refugee repatriation. In part, this reflected the warming of the Western governments to the new government in Kigali, which had been recognized by all and had assumed Rwanda's UN seat.

The donors' leverage came from the power of their purse, and toward the end of 1994, NGO requests for further UNHCR funding became more difficult to fill. The first NGOs to feel the pinch were the specialized medical agencies like MSF, which had used the bulk of its money to develop expatriate-intense outpatient clinics. In particular, UNHCR staff in Ngara criticized the France-based food agency, Agence Internationale Contre la Faim (AICF) (Shoham 1996). AICF's focus was on specialized feeding of malnourished children; this was labor-intensive, and as a result had a high cost-per-beneficiary ratio at a time when overall refugee nutrition was improving. Donations to the World Food Programme also suffered when policy-makers in Europe and North America apparently acted on their hopes for repatriation by resisting requests to expand food deliveries to central Africa, despite the new arrivals and their additional food requirements. The consequence was that breaks began to appear in the food pipeline. This pipeline began in warehouses in the West, where maize and bean surpluses were stored, extended in a slow and ponderous fashion to Western ports, into ship holds, to docks in the ports of Mombassa and Dar es Salaam, by truck and rail transport across Africa, and finally to a growing population of refugees in Tanzania, Burundi, and Zaire in central Africa (see *JEEAR* 1996:87–110). It took several months for the food to travel the pipeline's length, and keeping it filled with the proper amounts of food required anticipating how many refugees would be present in the future, and how much they would eat.

The donors in the West optimistically predicted that many of the refugees would be repatriated and put less food in the pipeline. No one anticipated what actually happened: that refugee populations throughout the Great Lakes region would continue to grow into 1996.

Thus, even as the capability to receive and house refugees actually improved, field workers predicted an ever-increasing disaster, though the type of disaster predicted varied. The MSF agencies focused on the role that murderers played in the camps in Zaire and Tanzania, and used this as a rationale to withdraw from an operation that was also seeing the end of the well-funded emergency contracts.[2] Other agencies were angered by breaks in the food pipeline. The local UNHCR offices in Ngara and Karagwe remained silent while this happened; they had orders from Geneva to avoid confrontation with WFP. UNHCR did, though, encourage NGOs to complain loudly, which they did, in a strongly worded and widely disseminated memo in which they predicted food riots and armed insurrection in Tanzania in the event that WFP did not increase food deliveries.[3] But despite these worries—and several weeks of half rations—no such emergency ever emerged in Ngara, as Shoham (1996:342) has pointed out. The reason was that, independent of the NGOs, refugees had developed sources of food and cash within the local economy to supplement the WFP rations.

The dramatic aspects of the situation again became important in this context. Assumptions about the nature of refugee organization and politics naturally gravitated toward the sensational; and the role of genocide in creating the refugee crisis was central to the Western imagination, even as the event itself became more remote in time. Since the sensational genocide had successfully generated sympathy and financial support in 1994, the UNHCR again emphasized this aspect, along with threats of contagious disease, threats to security of expatriates, and the threats to the operation's integrity posed by a further refugee influx.

The chronic irony of the condition was that the United Nations adopted an aggressive voluntary repatriation policy rooted in the assumption that conditions in Rwanda were appropriate for a return, even as new refugees were arriving in 1995–96. Adding to the irony was the fact that the international refugee relief community in Ngara was becoming more effective at handling the crisis through the quick reception of refugees and the establishment of new refugee camps. At the same time, new predictions of disaster continually emerged—whether the cause was seen to be disease, political instability, insufficient water provision, refugee unrest, *Interahamwe* activity, etc. The *JEEAR* observed: "The situation has never quite stabilized and agencies have been continually needing to increase the scale of their programmes. Another factor contributing to the post-emergency situation in Ngara was that from mid-July [1994] onwards the focus of international attention moved to Goma [the head-quarters of the Zairean operation], resulting in the transfer of resources and personnel away from Tanzania" (12).

November 1994—A Remote Camp, Water Crises, and Emergency Agencies Depart

Hopes had been raised for a quick resolution of the refugee crisis through voluntary repatriation by the visit of Ambassador Khan in early November 1994. Arriving by helicopter in Benaco and accompanied by a very obviously armed bodyguard, he met with NGO representatives in a tent. He emphasized that in his face-to-face meetings with President Bizimungu of Rwanda, the safety of returning refugees had been assured. When I queried Khan about the continuing arrival of bodies in the Kagera River, he expressed surprise, since the president had assured him that the southeast of the country was under control.[4] He also expressed the view that if a repatriation did not occur in the coming weeks, he believed it would not occur at all (see Waters 1999a).

But in the meantime, political and military conditions in Burundi were again deteriorating, and in mid-November 1994, a new influx of refugees appeared to the south of Ngara at the same time that the number of bodies floating down the Kagera River increased. It is not known exactly where the bodies were coming from, but these refugees were Rwandans who had been housed in refugee camps in Burundi in the months since Rwanda's genocide. A few Burundians also arrived. Initially, the new influx was housed in the Benaco complex of camps, creating further demands for food and water and aggravating crowding at a time when sporadic cases of cholera were being treated (see *JEEAR* 1996:69). Even though this epidemic was dealt with capably by the established water, sanitation, and public health agencies, the cholera warning flag, which had already been raised in Goma, was now raised at Benaco.[5]

A positive effect of these circumstances was that a new camp at Kitali Hills, some 50 kilometers (about 30 miles) away, was quickly approved. The site had been surveyed in September 1994 as a possible decongestion site for refugees already in the Benaco complex, which, UNHCR pointed out, would be unsustainable in the long-run because of shortages of firewood and water. The only survey that had been done there, though, was a "wind-screen" survey of water and firewood resources done by UNHCR and NGO consultants from inside vehicles. This survey had indicated that the site was unsuitable for a camp owing to a lack of surface water and a probable lack of groundwater. But despite these shortcomings, the continuing arrival of refugees demanded its use. By March 3, 1995, there were only 23,815 refugees living there. This caseload was managed easily from food warehouses in the Benaco area, and by means of two new water trucks that began transporting water 60 kilometers (37 miles) from Benaco.

Back at the main camp centers, progress was consolidated. In Karagwe, a second decongestion camp was established at the end of 1994 to accommodate 40,000 refugees who had settled in a floodplain during the initial influx. The new camp, Chabalisa 2, was the first to have a semblance of planning, which was possible only because there was no further influx in the north after about August 1994 (see Essays 1–3). As a result, transfers were made to the camp some four kilometers (about three miles) away in a systematic fashion. Carefully surveyed house plots were assigned, and the refugees systematically resettled over a two-month period that ended in December 1994. In the Benaco camp complex, the economy, especially, the markets, blossomed, and Benaco camp became known for its urban amenities, including bars, guest houses, retail outlets, and, as trading in WFP refugee rations took place, its grain market (Waters 1999a).

In the midst of this, the expatriates were focused on two technical issues and two political ones. The two technical issues were a perceived emerging water crisis with a threat of a cholera epidemic, and the establishment of a dependable food pipeline of WFP commodities. The two political issues were, first, the demand of Western donors that voluntary repatriation be encouraged and, second, the need to generate sympathy for the refugees who were still arriving in Tanzania. Thus, the picture presented needed to be one of technical competence at the same time that technical systems were falling apart. On the political level there was a need to explain why refugees should volunteer to return to Rwanda at the same time others were being expelled from their homes there. In the context of these contradictions, the expatriates adopted funding, publicity, and political policies that had inherent inconsistencies. This was especially apparent in the water sector, where the field workers repeatedly stressed the cholera danger in memos and at meetings of the medical, water, and sanitation agencies.

The Cholera Card

Cholera perhaps inspires more terror in Westerners than any other disease (McNeill 1977:230–31). Not without reason: its power had most recently been observed in Zaire, where an estimated 20,000 to 30,000 refugees died of the disease in July 1994 (*JEEAR* 68–75). Death from cholera is quick and horrifying, following an excruciating loss of fluids from violent dysentery. Cholera is caused by a bacterium that is usually water-borne; it breaks out in conditions of crowding and poor sanitation.

In the West, its effects were most devastating in nineteenth-century cities such as London, where it moved around in the piped water supply. In Africa cholera is still seasonal, appearing in many East African towns toward the end of the dry season, when water supplies are not flushed by periodic rains, cleanliness standards decline because of scarce water, and crowded conditions facilitate fecal-oral transmission of disease.

Sanitarians can easily control cholera, like other fecal-borne diarrhea/enteric diseases, by adding chlorine to the water and by providing enough water to promote cleanliness. Thus, provision of money for water supply is central to an operation whose purpose is the basic survival of refugees. In a context where money and financial efficiency were not central to successful engineering, and population concentration was viewed as a political given, medical and engineering solutions guaranteeing refugee protection from cholera and other water-borne diseases were quickly achieved. For the water sector, this meant that millions of dollars were made available for quickly conceived projects. Special isolation units were also established in late 1994, in the event that cholera cases did occur.

Urban Societies? The Refugees' World

While the expatriate Good Samaritans were focused on the logistics in providing adequate supplies of food and water to a group of people they were beginning to view as of politically dubious moral worth, the refugees themselves were establishing a large functioning urban community. Concerns about Rwanda continued to be dominant, and announcements on RPF radio were deconstructed assiduously by refugees. More relevant to daily life were the establishment of the new relationships and routines in their new "homes" in the Tanzanian refugee camps.

By the beginning of 1996 the four camps of the Benaco camp complex had 400,000 to 500,000 refugees and took on the characteristics of an urban conglomeration. There was a specialization of activity there too. For example, the food and water that the expatriates were so concerned about quickly became marketable commodities; the rented trucks delivering the World Food Programme commodities were known to arrive and then return with supplies of grain, oil, and beans purchased by Tanzanian traders. Refugees also dealt with the water shortages from the five liters per day provided by the water system by developing sources of their own. During the rainy season (eight months of the year), this included sources from roofs, and the swampy areas along the lower reaches of the camps. Other urban activities quickly developed too. Churches and mosques were established, bars opened, furniture manufactured, and handicraft industries developed.

HIV infection probably expanded rapidly as new relationships were established, and judging from the number of births in the camp in late 1995, new family relationships established (see Essay 4). The militia training that had been so prominent before the death of David apparently declined to a point where once again they were low profile enough to be at least "secret," meaning it was no longer an issue in UNHCR coordination meetings. Primary schooling was reestablished using a Kinyarwanda curriculum developed by UNESCO in schoolrooms built with UNHCR plastic. Cultural troupes were also reestablished.

Food distribution came under closer control of NGOs, which established a variety of monitoring systems. Unlike in Zaire, there was no evidence that the preexisting leadership from Rwanda controlled substantial food distribution. NGOs like Concern International in Lumasi were in fact justifiably proud of having changed leadership within the camps in late 1994 and 1995 when financial payments to refugee leaders were withdrawn (Pottier 1996a). As Shoham (1996) noted, most distribution in the camps was done by NGOs directly to family groups, and not through the refugee leadership. Finally, by early 1995, systematic "food basket monitoring" programs were implemented to check refugee nutritional status both at the distribution points and via established mother-child health programs which organized home visits (see Essay 1).

In many respects, the camps had the characteristics of an urban society. Time permitted the resiliency of refugee self-initiative and market forces to fill the gaps in what the UN and affiliated agencies were able to provide in terms of material sustenance, and a broad number of services emerged among what had become an urban population. The existence of the camps remained dependent on WFP largesse, which for the Ngara camps in 1996 included approximately 1,500 metric tonnes of maize, beans, and oil per week.

The success from the refugee perspective is perhaps best viewed through the lens of the demographics. After the horror of a flight from Rwanda, genocide, and war the population settled into a very conservative wait-and-see attitude. Somehow satisfied with the otherwise grim circumstances of the boring, uneventful refugee lifestyle found in refugee camps everywhere, refugees developed routines to fill their time. Days revolved around collecting rations, walking to and from small and distant fields, angling for the few jobs available with agencies, church activity, and general hustling in a forceful and sometimes self-protecting manner. Most important, like other Third World refugee populations, the Rwandans began to reestablish families and have children. Mortality rates dropped from the high rates that occurred shortly after arrival, and birth rates began to climb in mid-1995. Statistics available from Chabalisa 2 camp indicate that by the end of 1995 there were approximately 30 births per week, in a population of 37,000, which is a crude birth rate of 4.2 percent (see Essay 1).

April 1995:
Food Crisis, the Border Closes, and Massacres in Rwanda

The expatriates' concerns were different, focused on maintaining a dependent population that was still growing because of continued arrivals from Burundi. The influx from Burundi stretched the capacity of the Ngara-headquartered operation, which was given responsibility for providing water and food. Local sources of water were considered unavailable, so trucking operations were begun from 60 kilometers (37 miles) away. Trucks also were detailed to bring food from the WFP extended delivery point (EDP) in the Benaco complex. Camp management, sanitation, and medical services were delivered by the smaller, more resilient agencies like GOAL (an Irish NGO), Norwegian People's Aid (NPA), and the International Rescue Committee (IRC), which had made good use of Tanzanian and refugee labor but which in the past had been considered too weak to compete with expatriate-dominated agencies like CARE, AICF, and MSF. Adding to the sense of crisis were vague complaints about food delivery and uncertainties in delivery schedules, the passions of which were influenced by continuing verbal attacks in meetings on WFP.

Finally, aerial reports from the border in March 1995 indicated that the influx from Burundi could continue indefinitely. With the UNHCR-coordinated operation near its emotional and financial limits, resignation began to set in. Agencies became aware that they could no longer indefinitely expand programs, and the luster of working in Tanzania wore thinner. The Tanzanian government, which under the direction of Kagera Regional Commissioner Philip Mangula had maintained a policy of open reception, also was being strained, and elements of their military became more concerned about border security. In response, on April 8, 1995, for the first time since the influx began, Tanzania forcefully closed the border to further refugees from Burundi and Rwanda. The Tanzanians emphasized that this policy was consistent with international wishes that all refugees return to Rwanda voluntarily at the earliest possible date, and that there be no resettlement. To a certain degree, the border closing had the desired response, as under pressure from the growing anarchy in Burundi, Rwandans began to return to their own country without seeking asylum in Tanzania. Finally talks concerning the possibility of voluntary return began. UNHCR in Ngara switched sides and joined the repatriation drumbeat most enthusiastically as it became apparent that their own analyses of the situation in Rwanda, based on reports from the continued arrival of refugees, were not being well received in Geneva.

Hopes of this return were derailed, though, by massacres in Rwanda itself. Between April 16 and 20, at least 4,000 refugees in Kibeho Displaced Person Center in western Rwanda died after being fired on by the Rwandan military in a military movement that lasted several days. In the short term the result was that the trickle of voluntary repatriations from Tanzania virtually dried up, which opened the UNHCR to accusations from donors of discouraging repatriation, despite the supposed reemergence of peaceful conditions in Rwanda itself.

Now, though without any particularly clear evidence, UNHCR became more convinced that there was in fact intimidation of potential returnees within the camp complex itself. To counter this, the UNHCR helped fund a refugee camp newspaper and radio station through the Jesuit Refugee Service.[6] The stated purpose of this effort was to provide unbiased information about conditions in Rwanda, in the belief information coming from the UNHCR would be accepted as more legitimate than what the refugees heard from each other or how they interpreted Radio Rwanda's pro-RPF broadcasts.

Summer 1995:
Rationalizing Genocide and Voluntary Repatriation

The Kibeho massacres were the end of the honeymoon period between the government of Rwanda and all but its most enthusiastic supporters.[7] The massacres presented a conundrum for the UNHCR in Tanzania, too. Refugee arguments about the political circumstances in Rwanda made more sense in the context of what had happened in Kibeho, so in spite of the entreaties of young expatriate UNHCR repatriation officers, programs slowed. And in far-away capitals, donors continued to be frustrated and pleas by the UNHCR for money to fund existing programs went unheeded. But a problem emerged. In the heady days of generous financing, Both Ngara and Karagwe had developed budgeting assumptions that savings could be generated only by a decline in refugee caseload generated by repatriation. But the fleet of eight buses brought from Kigali to transport the expected repatriated refugees often roamed the camps with few if any returnees on board.

The UNHCR bureaucracy sought to develop a plausible story as to why the voluntary repatriation policies were effective. As with all such explanations, they sought justification through an arrangement of the most compelling social facts. A description of this view follows.

At the same time, I talked to two African leaders about the situation, and they had made different analyses of the same situation. Their views bear repeating here. Philip Mangula was the regional commissioner of Kagera and had been intimately involved with the development of Tanzania's open-door refugee policy since 1994. The Bishop Mvurubanda was from Gahini, Rwanda, and had been introduced to me through Robert and Patricia Wilson, British missionaries who had worked with him in Rwanda for seventeen years.

UNHCR Repatriation Policies

The UNHCR was founded on the principle that all persons with a legitimate fear of arbitrary political persecution have the right to asylum. This implies a legal proceeding that generally does not have the potential to be implemented, and this was the case for the Rwandans. As a result, assertion of this right is typically made on the basis of a particular situation, the idea being that refugees will voluntarily return home once political changes have occurred. Implied in this are a whole series of evaluations undertaken by refugees, hosts, and the home country. At its root, the assumption is that the refugee is the one best able to evaluate a situation, which is why the UNHCR will for the sake of principle resist the forced repatriation of refugees.

The focus on voluntary repatriation results in the UNHCR's classifying the refugees according to perceived repatriation ability, which is important for their own purposes, rather than in ways that are based on meaningful social distinctions in the Rwandan population itself. In July 1995, Maureen Connelly first related the social divisions to me in a form that became dogma throughout the UNHCR and other agencies. In large part this reflected the classic need of her bureaucracy to define and classify in order to rationalize decisions and policy. She explained that there were three social groups within the camps: (1) the vast mass of peasants, who had nothing to fear from returning, (2) the intellectual elite, who would return to Rwanda but would lose their professional and social status under the new regime, and (3) a small group of leaders who were guilty of genocide, and therefore unable to return at all. The logic followed that the only reason that the first two groups remained in Tanzania was a fear of the latter group, who were the "intimidators," and who were using the others as a human shield.[8]

Evidence from the camps in Zaire indicated that there was probably some merit to this argument, although even when the Hutu militia were at the height of their power in those camps, there was back-and-forth movement to Rwanda. Despite evidence to the contrary, the focus on the power of a mysterious group of intimidators was assumed to be similar in the Tanzanian camps.[9] This happened even though there was much more evidence of back-and-forth movement between Rwanda and the Tanzanian camps (see Essays 5 and 6). More conveniently, it provided a bogeyman to explain the failure of the voluntary repatriation program being encouraged by the UNHCR.

Philip Mangula

In mid-July 1995, I met with Regional Commissioner of Kagera Region Philip Mangula to discuss his concern with the refugees. Mangula had been active in receiving refugees from the first day of the crisis, often traveling to remote sites where refugees crossed into Tanzania. Within the Tanzanian government, where there was a diversity of opinion about how to handle the refugee crisis, his was an influential voice for moderation and refugee reception. In this position he was sometimes at odds with military authorities, who advocated stricter controls at the borders and forcible repatriation. At times, he was also at loggerheads with UNHCR over overall policy, particularly with respect to security, enforcement of Tanzanian labor law, and advocating on behalf of Tanzanians working with the expatriate-dominated organizations. As a consequence, he was in a politically tenuous position both within Tanzania and with respect to the UNHCR. This led to the loss of his seat in Parliament in the October 1995 elections, though he did remain regional commissioner of the Kagera region.

Our talk in July 1995 focused on a trip to Rwanda he had just completed. He had attended a memorial service at a church in Kibungo, where 8,000 corpses had been lying in the church and its yard since April 1994. He was shocked, particularly when told by the Rwandan authorities that two of the refugees he knew (the ex-governor of Kibungo and the administrative head of Rusumo district) were guilty of organizing the massacre. He was shocked at the description and the guilt of the men he knew and talked at length about how the killings had taken place with the use of chloroform and had been organized by the one with "red eyes."

My surprise was at his surprise. In expatriate circles it had been long accepted that these two were war criminals. What struck me as odd was that Mangula's understanding of this circumstance was based on what he heard and saw from the Rwandans, and not what could be read in the *New York Times.*

Mangula also talked about the wider refugee problem. He was concerned about the 400,000 to 600,000 "old case" Tutsi refugees, who had occupied the homes of the refugees in the Tanzanian camps. But he was also concerned about the human rights situation in Rwanda; Rwanda's leader, Paul Kagame, apparently had offered to come and speak to the refugees at Benaco, a move that Mangula thought too risky to attempt.

He joked that the only place the refugees would be moving back to was
Akagera National Park in Rwanda, and acknowledged that not all would
ever be able to return.

Bishop Mvurubande

I also met with the Bishop Augustin Mvurubande of Gahini, Rwanda, in
July 1995 (see Essay 8). Bishop Augustin was living in the Anglican
church compound in Ngara, and was trying to facilitate cross-border
communication to further peace and reconciliation, a position notably
different than that of the Rwandan government, which was calling for
"justice." But Bishop Mvurubande believed very strongly that the church
had a special role to play in reconciliation, and had requested the chance
to return to Gahini to put his conviction into practice. This process was
stymied by his fear that once he reentered Rwanda he would no longer
have refugee status, and would be unable to return to Tanzania. His proposal made a great deal of sense to me. In Tanzania and Rwanda, bishops
and churches are among the strongest elements of the phenomenon political scientists describe as civil society. Unfortunately, the UNHCR, which
is notoriously secular in its outlook, preferred to work through government channels, and avoided church relations as a result.

Gahini, where the bishop's church was, had been subjected to attack by
both Interahamwe and later the RPF (see also Bilinda 1996, and des
Forges 1999:706). As a result, the bishop had a distrust of both elements.
His wife, who is Tutsi, had had a major portion of her family killed by *Interahamwe*. Ten pastors from his church had perished during the conflict,
roughly half at the hands of *Interahamwe* and half at the hands of RPF invading forces. Parts of his own family had been killed by RPF as well.

December 1995: Financial Crisis

During a visit to Ngara in October 1995, USAID Administrator Brian Atwood and EU Commissioner Emma Bonino stressed to the local UNHCR
office and NGOs that they were closing the financial tap in an attempt to
force quick repatriation.[10] Despite the fact that this was contrary to international law and UNHCR mandates, UNHCR-Ngara no longer had the
heart to object. The UNHCR made further attempts to induce repatriation through broadcasts, and they organized a series of "go and see" visits.

The slow-down in the USAID and ECHO cash flow resulted in
UNHCR's not paying its NGO partners' bills. I was acutely aware of this
because in December of 1995, the financial crisis included outstanding
unpaid bills of $4.1 million from the agency I worked for, the Lutheran

World Federation. LWF felt it necessary to threaten suspension of diesel disbursements to UNHCR vehicles to induce payment from UNHCR.

Apparently UNHCR was being forced to juggle payments to creditors, of whom we were one, in an attempt to preserve the program. Field staff from NGOs and UNHCR blamed each other for the financial mess, even though the people in the field were far beyond the problem. Chronically over-committed, the relationship between UNHCR and its partners was further strained at all levels.

"The Day After You Will Be Dogs": Voluntary Repatriation Politics in 1995–96

Repatriation policies were more and more frustrated during the summer of 1995, to the consternation of UNHCR donors. A crisis in the operation occurred in September 1995, when Tanzania expelled three UNHCR ex-patriates, including Jacques Franquin, on 24 hours' notice. The expulsions were in response to UNHCR's provision of food to refugees who had illegally snuck into Kitali Camp after the border had been closed. The expulsions caused a further decline in expatriate-Tanzanian relations, a situation exacerbated when 100 expatriates went to the airstrip to bid the expelled UNHCR expatriates farewell, and Franquin made a dramatic farewell speech.

Despite the continuing influx and escalating confrontations between the cash-strapped operation and its partners, hopes for repatriation continued to increase. Rumors were rife. It was rumored, for example, that entire refugee communes would return. There was even a modest acceleration of repatriation when the RPF-selected prefects of Byumba and Kibungo prefectures in Rwanda visited and made speeches to refugees asking them to return. As usual, the refugees dissected and analyzed events and messages from Rwanda for their real meaning. A quote from the new prefect of Byumba, who visited the Ngara camps in October 1995, was widely cited: "Today you are guests in Tanzania, tomorrow you will be cows, and the next day you will be dogs." This statement was every bit as ambiguous to Rwandan ears as it is to mine. Its possible meanings were widely discussed by refugees. Of particular concern was the comparison to dogs, which is a strong insult in both Tanzania and Rwanda. Did it mean that the Tanzanians would treat them like dogs after the international community stopped looking, or if they did not return? The refugees' analyses of this statement would have done any postmodern semiotician proud. Nevertheless, the visit did in a modest way have the desired result, and there was a brief uptick in voluntary repatriation from Benaco. About 800 refugees per week began to return voluntarily, the majority of whom seemed to be peasant women and children. According the repatriation drivers, none of them could read or write.

Mbuba and Keza:
The Maturation of Refugee Reception Capabilities

In January 1996, the Burundi military moved into Muyinga camp for Rwandans in northwestern Burundi. Refugees were ordered to return to Rwanda, the camped was burned, and over 20,000 refugees fled into Tanzania. The Tanzanian military relaxed military controls, and they were received at the border by Tanzanian villagers. Briefly Tanzania resumed its generous refugee asylum policy.

The response to this influx by the international community in Ngara was quick, reflecting the maturation of the refugee reception capability in Tanzania. The Tanzanian Red Cross and Concern International quickly organized transit camps to distribute high-protein biscuits. Oxfam established a water purification plant, while LWF mobilized UNHCR-owned bulldozers, graders, and other heavy equipment and activated the Russian truck fleet (which had been idled as surplus) to remove the refugees from the border areas. Twelve thousand refugees were removed between January 20 and 25 in this fashion; by February 3, 8,000 more had arrived.

Also contributing to the success of the operation was the experience of the refugees. The majority were Rwandans who had lived as refugees in Burundi for up to one and a half years. In Tanzania, they quickly organized themselves in a manner that could be dealt with easily by the NGOs. This included a general cooperation with the bureaucratic norms of the international refugee relief regime for the distribution of food, provision of medical care, organization into subunits with leaders, registration, water, and sanitary conditions, and other conditions facilitating the distribution of international aid. Also contributing to their resettlement was the fact that they brought with them the blue and white UN-supplied plastic from the Burundian camps, which they used to quickly build rudimentary shelters.

The net result of the effort was a humanitarian and logistical success. The capability of the Ngara operation had expanded greatly since the first influx from Burundi only a year and a half previously. But, as the forcible repatriation was to demonstrate ten months later, this was politically irrelevant. In retrospect, this could have been seen from the responses of the UNHCR and their donors to influx. As described above, UNHCR was already hard-pressed to meet their obligations to the LWF and others. In January 1996, internal squabbling within UNHCR also meant that the most senior positions at the UNHCR Ngara office were again vacant as a result of transfers and extended leaves. Confronted with the refugee influx, on-site UNHCR staff did respond by drawing on as yet unused stocks of food and financial accounts on hand, and permitting the use of UNHCR-owned equipment. However, this was done without promises from their donors at USAID or ECHO for replenishment, reflecting Atwood and Bonino's continuing "quick repatriation only" policy. Ultimately the IFRC stepped into the financial void with emergency funds. The Lutheran World Federation also responded by soliciting church donors in Europe and North America for independent money to operate heavy equipment to set up camps and drill for water.

It was also apparent at this time that divisions were emerging within the Tanzanian government. In response to the breach of the Tanzanian border by the refugees and continued fighting near Tanzania's border with Burundi, artillery began to appear along roads. The military presence of Brigadier General Msuya, a hawk within the Tanzanian government, became more prominent, and it was whispered (not so quietly) among Tanzanians that an invasion of Burundi was imminent during the dry season of 1996.

Oddly enough, this occurred at a time when analyses by George Chaponda, a UNHCR specialist in repatriation programs, were indicating that any voluntary repatriation to Rwanda was unlikely. Chaponda, who ultimately took over coordination of the Ngara office in early 1995, emphasized in his report that the Rwandan refugee situation was among the most complex he had ever seen, and that claims (or rather wishes) to the contrary should be discounted.

Summer 1996: Aging Infrastructure, Perpetual Refugees, and Forcible Repatriation

The refugee operation was mature by the summer of 1996. Over 500,000 refugees were living in Tanzania, and a local consensus was reached that the situation in the existing camps would continue indefinitely. On the broader international front, new information was emerging through which outside observers began to view the operation. *The Joint Evaluation of Emergency Assistance to Rwanda*, published by the Danish International Development Agency Danida, praised the overall effectiveness of the operation in Tanzania. But it also blamed the international refugee relief regime, particularly as it operated in Zaire, for the failed prosecution of the perpetrators of genocide. The international refugee relief regime, oddly enough, tacitly accepted this blame, even though no agency had policing or judicial authority.

More important, the Mobutu regime in Zaire began to fragment, owing in part to the destabilization in the east associated with the Rwandan refugee camps. Rebels from the *Banyamulenge* ethnic group—supported by the RPF government in Rwanda and led eventually by Laurent Kabila—conquered substantial portions of Zaire. Hutu militia gained the upper hand in the Zairean camps and began to assert sovereignty, often violently, over the camps and the corner of Zaire where they were located. The Rwandan government in Kigali responded by supporting the *Banyamulenge* rebels, who were opposing the rump Rwandan government. The response of the international community was to prepare a Canadian-led force that would reestablish security around the camps on behalf of the international humanitarian community. The Canadian troops never arrived, though, because in the meantime, the *Banyamulenge* and their allies directly supported by the Rwandan Patriotic Army occupied the Zairean camps and dispersed the refugees. About 650,000 of the 1 million refugees moved silently and apprehensively back to Rwanda, where they were ordered back to their home districts. The other 350,000 fled into Zaire, where they became the focus for military activity in coming months. Oddly, the United States led a group of governments at the time denying there were refugees left in Zaire. Of these 350,000 many died of violence, hunger, disease, and other causes. A portion were repatriated by air later in 1997 (Human Rights Watch 1997:13, Lemarchand 1999). Eventually some were airlifted by UNHCR back to Rwanda from central Zaire. But hundreds of thousands of Rwandans disappeared into Zaire by fleeing, dying, or simply disappearing into surrounding countries well beyond the lenses of CNN. This human tragedy has been called a "quiet genocide" by observers like René Lemarchand (1999).

The activity in Zaire/Congo did not necessarily have anything directly to do with the refugee situation in Tanzania.[11] Nevertheless, the Tanzanians, with the acquiescence of the UNHCR and its donors, organized a forcible repatriation from Tanzania back to Rwanda. Most refugees resisted by disobeying, marching as a semiorganized column farther into Tanzania either along main roads or into an unpopulated game reserve near the camp. This flight continued for two days until relatively peaceful confrontations with the Tanzanian military occurred. Under orders by the military, the refugees halted, the direction of flight was reversed, and a mass return to Rwanda began. Simultaneously, the Tanzanian military organized a massive refugee column in Karagwe, which walked 130 kilometers (80 miles) over a period of about one week. The UNHCR facilitated this by providing high-protein biscuits and water at specified sites, while complying with Tanzanian orders that all relief operations in the camps were to be discontinued.

During a two-week period in late December 1996, 400,000 to 500,000 refugees crossed back into Rwanda by foot (Lemarchand 1999:196). Objections to the move from the international community were muted, even though there were not the military imperatives found in Zaire. The general assumption was that what occurred was best; that unless the issue were forced, the refugees would not return, and would continue to be a drain on the international community, and a threat to regional political stability.[12] In the interest of expedience, the rhetoric of protecting international humanitarian principles against forced repatriation was dropped.

Only small numbers of refugees, numbering in the hundreds, remained officially in Tanzania. The Karagwe camps were closed and the campsites returned to bush. Benaco and Msuhura camps in Ngara district were also closed. Lumasi has been kept open, and as of mid-2000 continues to be used as a spillover camp for Burundians who have continued to arrive in Tanzania. Other camps, including Kitali Hills and Keza, have been kept open for Burundians.

Operations to expel Rwandans from Tanzania continued in 1997, although Tanzania did reopen the transit camp at Mbuba for Rwandan refugees in 1998. By late 1998, there were some 4,000 Rwandans housed there under the protection of the UNHCR; this was less than 1 percent of the number of Rwandans who had sought asylum in Tanzania since 1994. This number was again increasing in 1999, with reports on the "Relief Web" Web site of the UN Department of Humanitarian Affairs indicating that 20,000 to 40,000 Rwandans were being housed in Tanzania. It is also credibly pointed out that many of the putatively Burundian refugees in Tanzania are in fact from Rwanda. In Tanzania, though, they pass as Burundians in order to receive asylum.

Postmortem: How Sustainable Were the Tanzanian Camps?

The threats to the Tanzanian camps were, during their existence, perceived as being rooted in material needs. Water, firewood, food supplies, security, disease outbreaks, and overcrowding were perceived as potential causes for their downfall. Ultimately, though, none of these conditions were the cause of the breakup of the camps. Rather, the breakup was because the international community underestimated the refugees' resilience, even in conditions of privation. Far from being on the verge of ecological collapse because of water and firewood shortages, as predicted, the camps were at the time of their dispersal in late 1996 differentiating into communities facing more and more toward Tanzania and away from Rwanda. Even the internal camp politics were improving. Distribution of relief items in the Rwandan camps in Tanzania was not tightly controlled by Interahamwe, nor was there evidence that the camps had a military capability for invading Rwanda. Indeed, the camps were not that different from camps in other parts of the world that lasted many more years and continue to exist.

The Rwandan repatriation was settled not on the basis of the technical reasons typically pointed to, but because Western donors were unable to sustain moral imperatives for the assistance program to continue. The situation of the Rwandan refugees in the camps was no longer framed as one whose driving imperative was humanitarian need, but rather as one defined by perceptions of how genocide had occurred. As a result, the largest forcible repatriation since World War II became possible.

Notes

1. There had in fact been flip-flops on the issue in UNHCR. In July 1994, confronted with the mass flight to Zaire, UNHCR quickly negotiated an agreement with the approximately week-old government in Kigali, which was still fighting a war. In September, UNHCR pronounced the situation in Rwanda as being too unsettled for a quick return and reversed themselves again by November (Pottier 1996:424).

2. MSF–France at the same time also withdrew from UNHCR medical contracts in Kibondo for Burundian refugees who had no imaginable association with the genocide. They withdrew from Kibondo on the grounds that they were an emergency organization, and that these camps were in "care-and-maintenance" phase, and no longer required their services. The International Rescue Committee (IRC) took over the contracts for medical services in Kibondo.

3. The memo, which was developed in March 1995, appears below. Notably, this is part of the context in which the Tanzanian border was closed to refugees for the first time in April 1995.

FORUM OF N.G.O's in the Ngara District, Tanzania
[March 1995]

Regarding: the Present Food Crisis in Kagera District (Tanzania) and Surrounding Regions . . .

The situation is such that food rationing at the present level will only last for two weeks. The present ration is 1900 Kcal which is the internationally recognised minimum level. Implications for health and nutrition in decreasing relations below 1900 Kcal is disastrous. . . . If no food is forthcoming immediately within the next two weeks, it is unlikely that N.G.O's in this area will be able to operate either efficiently or safely. The effect of 640,000 starving refugees from the Kagera region is very serious both in terms of security and the local population's environment.

There has been no food donated to the Rwandan-Burundi Refugees since October 1994. . . .

The forced mass return of Rwandan Refugees is completely unacceptable in the present political climate, and so would be the widespread destruction caused by desperate refugees in Kagera region. To avoid a possible outbreak of mass violence and uncontrollable instability urgent food supplies are needed now. . . .

The situation is such that the question of N.G.O. evacuation has now become paramount. The safety of refugees, Tanzanians and aid workers within this region is likely to deteriorate. . . .
[signed]
AEF [Japan], AICF [France], CARE, CONCERN [Ireland], Christian Outreach/Tear Fund Alliance [UK], DRA [Holland], GTZ [Germany], IRC [USA], MSF Holland, MSF Spain, NPA [Norway], Oxfam [UK]

The memo is more interesting for how it frames problems than for its analysis. Rations dropping below 1,900 Kcal does not always cause food riots and result in refugees' marauding neighboring Tanzanian fields, organizing raids on expatriate living compounds, or kidnapping expatriate workers. Yet such occurrences were predicted both in the memo and orally in meetings (see also Shoham 1996). The central point is that this memo represents a return to the management of "crisis" rather than systematic inference and analysis of the existing refugee situation.

Agencies from Ngara that did not sign the memo included LWF, the Tanzanian Red Cross, the International Federation of the Red Cross, the Islamic Relief Organization, ICRC, and Caritas. I do not know whether agencies working in Karagwe, like Memisa or Save the Children, were approached or not. The point is that the major international NGOs in Ngara acquiesced to the UNHCR's verbal encouragement to sign the petition. The two MSF agencies and AICF both left Ngara shortly after the memo was circulated.

4. Des Forges (1999:728–731) describes the context for this assertion. An internal report by Bob Gersony was prepared in September 1994, which detailed RPF executions in eastern Rwanda. One of the pieces of data cited was that during the last week in August and the first week in September, an average of five bodies were pulled from the Akagera River (see Chapter 11).

5. A great deal of resources were successfully put into cholera prevention in Tanzania. Partly as a result, the major sanitation problem throughout the crisis was not cholera, but bloody diarrhea. Indeed, since late 1993, when Burundian refugees first arrived, bloody diarrhea was to be the primary cause of death in the refugee populations. The main outbreak in Benaco was from May to September 1994 (*JEEAR* 1996). This distinction was probably maintained in part because whenever cholera did appear, there was an effective response. Bloody diarrhea, like cholera, is highly correlated with sanitation conditions, water quality, and water provision.

6. Content of this radio station's broadcasts became an issue between UNHCR and JRS. Some at UNHCR considered it to be "repatriation radio." JRS did not consider the promotion of UNHCR repatriation policies to be appropriate, and resisted UNHCR efforts to focus the radio programs on this issue (personal communication, Mark Raper, S.J., July 1999).

7. Philip Gourevitch (1998:198–208) has written an account of the massacres and their aftermath from the perspective inside Rwanda. Whatever the motives were or whoever may be blamed for the massacres, it was clear that they had a chilling effect on repatriation efforts in Tanzania. See also Prunier 1997:362–363.

8. Another typology that gained some popularity was developed by the United States Committee for Refugees (1998) which said that there were five salient social groups in Rwanda: Tutsis who survived the genocide; Hutus remaining inside Rwanda after the genocide; Tutsi refugees who returned in 1994 after having fled to Uganda in 1959–64; Hutu refugees who returned from the Zairean, Tanzanian, and Burundi camps in 1996; Tutsis who returned from Zaire and Burundi. This may well represent a snapshot or reality in 1997 and 1998. However, it also reflects the need of bureaucracies to classify, even in a context where such reality is fast-changing. This becomes a problem when one particular classification scheme becomes rigidified by bureaucratic fiat and has long-lasting consequences for future social action. Johan Pottier has discussed this problem in his article "Relief and Repatriation: Views from Rwandan Refugees; Lessons for Humanitarian Workers."

9. The refugees in Tanzania were by and large Hutu from eastern Rwanda who arrived in May–November 1994. In late 1994 and throughout 1995, 400,000 to 600,000 Tutsi who had lived in Burundi, Zaire, Uganda, and Tanzania resettled in Rwanda. Many occupied the houses abandoned by the Hutu refugees.

10. Observing before this visit, Pottier (1996:423) reports that refugees were predicting that camps would be closed for exactly this reason: the cost of the camps would become primary, and an informed political reading secondary.

11. In 1997 the name of Zaire was changed to the Democratic Republic of the Congo.

12. There are persistent rumors that the United States was involved with the shift in policy. The expulsion, it is speculated, was taken at the behest of the Clinton administration, which has established a close relationships with the new RPF government in Kigali. The Clinton administration also had aggressive policies regarding the development of mechanisms for the prosecution of war criminals, particularly those who differ with official United States policy.

BUREAUCRATIZING
THE GOOD SAMARITAN

In Part 1 the elements of refugee crises were discussed: the political, financial, moral, and technical aspects. This has been developed in a fashion to help understand and explain what happened to the Rwandans in Tanzania. The point of doing this is to illustrate the potential relevance of the concept of the "Bureaucratized Good Samaritan" in understanding the strengths and weaknesses of the international refugee relief regime. It is, I hope, a fairly straightforward story told as narrative about how the international refugee relief regime developed, the moral assumptions underlying it, and finally how it operated in one crisis, Rwanda.

In Part Two, I show how the Bureaucratized Good Samaritan shaped decision-making in three different sectors of the emergency effort in Tanzania: contingency planning, water provision, and responses to violent death and genocide. All three sectors were approached in a bureaucratic fashion using rationally derived organizational principles. Indeed, each sector is approached in this fashion in other situations. Indeed, in the cases of water provision and judgments about violent death, whole schools and colleges of engineering and law exist to train a body of specialists in a predictable fashion. However, in the context of the Bureaucratized Good Samaritan with its emphasis on emotional press-driven decision-making, the principles developed within each field, which are by definition rationalized, are distorted. These chapters point out that they become distorted in a patterned manner, which results in equally patterned mistakes.

The advantage of looking at these sectors at such a "micro" level is that the patterns identified can be used to establish principles for inferring what the broader weaknesses seen in the Rwanda operation were. This permits us to go to the next step, which is to make inferences about why the Rwandan operation ended up having such an unforeseen result: the forcible return of over one million Rwandans, despite the explicit goal of avoiding this result. As in the three technical sectors, the continuing need to generate emotion means that the strengths of bureaucratic organization cannot be fully utilized. In this process of generating emotion, the analysis of the overall complexity inherent to "complex" emergency was simplified. The end result was that the complexity itself was never factored into the way overall policies developed. Instead, in situations with multiple causes, simple solutions were offered, rejected, and then replaced with yet another simple solution or explanation.

The reliance on simple solutions was made necessary by the political need of funding agencies to legitimate decisions to fund refugee relief in chunks digestible in the emotion-driven popular press. As a result, the bureaucratic analysis, which was more finely tuned to the complexity in a complex emergency, was ignored, despite the fact that plenty of analyses of the Rwanda refugee situation that emphasized the complexity of the issue were available. Privileged in broader public discourse, however, were "one answer" justifications for action, including at different times primeval ethnic hatreds, cholera, and genocide. The implications of this simplification for the Rwanda emergency are discussed in Chapter 12.

But what happened in Rwanda is not unique to the managers of that emergency. Rather, it is the consequence of bureaucratic norms and procedures established during the last 50 years by succeeding elements of the international refugee relief regime. Any attempt at reforming it needs to take account of the fact that the "irrationalities" described in the Rwanda case are embedded in the broader bureaucratic structures and relationships. These structures and relationships reflect the history of refugee relief in places as diverse as Biafra, Thailand, Ethiopia, and Rwanda, where they developed. As I write (September 1999), a similar process is playing itself out in Kosovo and beginning in East Timor. At the end of the Allied war in Yugoslavia, a number of countries pledged troops, police, and money with which to police Kosovo. Two months after the pledges were made, only a small proportion of the enthusiastically pledged resources had arrived, reflecting, again, I think press conference–derived wishes for operational capacity. As in Rwanda, when it actually comes time to correlate needs on the ground with the capacity to mobilize, train, and equip actual personnel, the capacity is quite different. The Kosovo situation, like others before it, is establishing expectations for humanitarian capabilities that are too high. The strengths and weaknesses of these relationships are discussed in Chapter 13.

Finally, Chapter 14 asks the broadest question: How can the inherent limitations of the Bureaucratized Good Samaritan be overcome? Bureaucratic decision-making must be separated from the requirements of the popular press for stories, so that the strengths of both can be realized.

The press with its probing eye is important in maintaining the integrity and honesty of bureaucrats in the international refugee relief regime, who, like bureaucrats everywhere, have an unhealthy need to be secretive. But the manipulation of humanitarian policy to cater to perceived press needs is also unhealthy. It distorts the primary strength of the refugee assistance agencies, which is the ability to coordinate the large complicated bureaucratic task of humanitarian relief.

9

The Limitations of
Contingency Planning

Introduction

In retrospect, it is well known that refugees have been fleeing from
Rwanda and Burundi to Tanzania since 1993. It is also easy, in retrospect,
to see specific flights as resulting from precipitating political actions,
such as the assassination of President Melchior Ndadaye (Burundi 1993),
the death of President Habyarimana (Rwanda 1994), genocide (1994), advance by the RPF (1994), fear of accountability for genocide (1994), consolidation of authority by the invading RPF (mid-1994 to early 1995), attacks on refugee camps in northern Burundi (1996), and the capture of
the Goma region of Zaire by *Banyamulenge* militia (1996).

But these are all ex post-facto explanations, made after events have occurred and are then framed in a manner making sense in the context of
the next policy choice. When the events were occurring, they were not
necessarily framed in the same way. Most notorious as incorrect framings
were the descriptions of fighting in Rwanda in April and May 1994 as
"civil war" and not a "genocide." As critics are quick to point out, framing the events as a genocide would have been a legal and moral conclusion with implications for which policy choices were available. In the
same vein, framing the attack on the president of Burundi in October
1993 as a coup meant that the international community did not believe in
the potential for mass refugee flight; in contrast, coup rumors from Burundi in June 1994 and July 1996 led to the expectation of mass refugee
flight. In effect, the emergency itself changed the basis for how conditions were evaluated. As will be seen below, this analytical shift depended in part on which bureaucracies were present and what their internal interests were.

Anticipating future events and policy options requires more than an
after-the-fact assessment of what happened before. Making useful pre-

dictions it requires analysis in order to infer possibilities in the future. This is contingency planning, and it is done all the time in the refugee business, either explicitly in contingency planning sessions, or implicitly in decisions about where to position staff, offices, materials, and equipment. Such predictions are rooted in assumptions about how potential refugees will respond to future events. How effective these predictions are (and by extension the underlying assumptions) can be evaluated logically. There are four logical results:

1. Positive prediction: Analysis and inference accurately predict the nature of a refugee movement.
2. Negative prediction: No action is taken, and there is no a refugee movement. An extreme example is the implicit policy along the border of Canada and the United States: there are no stocks or plans to accommodate refugees on either side of the border.
3. False positive prediction: A refugee movement is predicted, resources are mobilized, and refugees do not appear. The little boy who cried "wolf" had a problem with too many false positive predictions.
4. False negative predictions: No refugee movement is predicted, and refugees do appear. The international community is caught unawares by a refugee movement

It will be demonstrated that when the international refugee regime is in place, there is a tendency to anticipate refugee movements. This results in more false positives, and fewer false negatives, than would occur if the international refugee regime were not in place.

Inaction (i.e., negatives), means that there will be more false negatives. False negatives generally occur when the more conservative diplomatic and development communities are present. Typically, false negatives happen when predictions are made by bystanders (for example, diplomats) rather than specialists from the international refugee relief regime. Such anticipators do not necessarily have a vested bureaucratic interest in action. Both false negatives and false positives are, basically, mistakes, and are viewed as such by after-the-fact evaluators of a refugee relief operation. Mistakes of both types in turn affect how the predictors are evaluated by each other.

False Negatives and False Positives in the Great Lakes, 1994–96

In the context of refugee relief, the false negatives—when a disaster occurred despite predictions it would not—are the biggest problem. The reason that the flight of Burundians into Tanzania was unexpected is that it was a false negative, a situation where there was an implicit assumption that refugee flight would *not* occur following elections and an assassination. Ironically, much of the success of the Ngara operation is attributable to the preparedness induced by the false negative presented by the earlier 1993 Burundi catastrophe.

False positives—cases when a refugee movement is predicted and nothing happens—also do occur. There was a rapid series of these false positives during the Rwanda crisis in Tanzania, leading to the "boy who called wolf" phenomenon: successive warnings that did not result in the predicted crisis were taken less and less seriously. The origins of the false positives is embedded in the need for press coverage to stimulate funding. *Time* magazine shows up for action, not inaction.

This creates a structural conundrum in the business of predicting refugee movements. The international refugee relief regime, with its emphasis on saving lives and humanitarian aid, is acutely aware of the potential embarrassment of being found flat-footed (false negative) when a refugee movement occurs. They point out, rightly, that a vigilant, proactive relief community can save lives. Not coincidentally, this also implies continued funding for contingency programs, standby capability, and commodity stockpiles. All of this feeds the bureaucratic need to expand.

"Anticipation" on the part of NGOs became an important part of the operation in Tanzania between 1994 and 1996. Early in the crisis, anticipation of further disaster loosened the purse strings of Western donors. UNHCR and NGO staff in Ngara were acutely aware of this and anticipated further crises in which more refugees would need to be accommodated, and relief bureaucracies expanded.

How well were refugee movements anticipated in Tanzania between the first influx in late 1993 and the final forcible repatriation in late 1996? How were refugees' views *perceived*, and their motivations for movement—whether in flight to Tanzania or for potential return to Rwanda— assessed? Movements both out of countries of origin, and back to countries of origin can be analyzed in terms of the four success/failure positions described above; both types of movements are examples of how the refugees' decision-making is perceived by the administrators in the UNHCR and related agencies. (See Table 9.1 for a synopsis of this analysis.)

In this analysis of NGOs' contingency planning, the views of the refugees are secondary. What is important is how the refugees are perceived, not what they say or think. On the basis of these perceptions, preliminary conclusions are reached about the nature of what successful positive predictions, successful negative predictions, false positives, and false negatives tell us about the conditions under which refugees move, and the conditions under which they do not. This can be followed on Table 9.1.

TABLE 9.1 Successes and Failures of Contingency Planning in the Rwanda and Burundi Crises in Tanzania, 1993–1996

Time	Policy Assumptions	Actual Result	Interpretation
Summer 1993	Voluntary repatriation of Burundians; peaceful reintegration in Burundi.	War, Oct. 1993, and flight back to Tanzania.	False positive
Oct.–Nov. 1993	No major refugee flight following coup.	Flight to Tanzania.	False negative
Dec. 1993–Feb. 1994	Establishment of Tanzanian camps for Burundians.	Return to Burundi, few stay in Tanzania.	False positive
Mar.–April 1994 (Burundians)	Death of president, elections result in flight to Tanzania.	No flight.	False positive
Mar.–April 1994 (Rwandans)	Death of president results in small number of Rwandans, but big problem Burundians.		Partial positive; size of flight underestimated
April 1994	Arusha Accords call for systematic reintegration of Tutsis.		False positive
July 1994	Parliamentary elections in Burundi lead to flight predictions.	Elections held without major incident.	False positive
Aug.–Nov. 1994	RPF victory and peace. Voluntary repatriation promoted.	More Rwandans flee.	False negative and false positive
Summer 1994–Early 1995	No policy. Old caseload resettled in Tanzania.	20,000 Tutsi repatriate.	False negative
Dec. 1994–April 1995	Renewed violence in Burundi leads to plans for the reception of several hundred thousand Burundians.	About 45,000 Burundians and 25,000 Rwandans from n. Burundi arrive. Border closed.	Partial positive
Early 1995–Early 1996	UNHCR aggressively promotes voluntary repatriation programs.	About 4,000 refugees accept offer, half of whom are Burundians.	False positive
Jan. 1996	Increased fighting in n. Burundi leads to contingency planning for 150,000 Burundians and Rwandans.	About 30,000 arrive.	Partial positive; size of flight overestimated
April 1996	Increased fighting in Burundi.		
July 1996	Coup in Burundi.	Blow-up.	Few refugees to Tanzania
Oct.–Nov. 1996	Intensification of voluntary repatriation programs.	Forcible repatriation.	False positive (?)

Burundi, 1993–94:
Voluntary Repatriation Followed by Violent Expulsion

The international community focused on refugee movements in Tanzania between 1993 and 1996. Ironically, the story starts with a large voluntary repatriation program. The first major population movement involving the Great Lakes region in 1993 was the return of Burundian refugees who had been living in Tanzania since 1972–74. Returns occurred surreptitiously during the early 1990s, reestablishing social ties between Burundians living inside and outside Burundi. Ironically, Burundians most interested in repatriation were found not along the border settlements, where some assimilation had occurred, but in the remote settlements in the interior of Tanzania where ethnic consciousness was most pronounced (see Malkki 1994).[1]

Substantial portions of the Burundian refugees, perhaps as many as 60,000, made their way back to Burundi following the signing of a tripartite agreement between Burundi, Tanzania, and the UNHCR in 1991 (Lemarchand 1994:172–176). A formal program for the expected repatriation of 60,000 more was scheduled for 1993, a process that was apparently speeded up when tens of thousands quietly left for Burundi spontaneously following President Ndadaye's election in July, even before the official repatriation buses made their first trip.

The first UNHCR-sponsored trips were made in early October 1993, and apparently about 4,000 refugees were transferred to a transit camp at that time. Following the assassination of President Ndadaye on October 21, the repatriation center became a target of the rebellious elements in the army and all refugees were apparently killed. Certainly that was the assumption in Katumba refugee settlement in western Tanzania when I asked about their fate in July 1994; none of their relatives had any word during the preceding year that they were alive, although small numbers of survivors from earlier years had managed to sneak back to Katumba.

Following the Burundi repatriation, there were two quick population movements to and from Tanzania. First, about 250,000 refugees left Burundi in late November and December 1993 for Tanzania, and perhaps another 450,000 left for Rwanda and Zaire. This flight (described in Chapter 5) was not anticipated by the international community, which subsequently blamed itself for being unprepared (it acknowledged the false-negative situation). As a result, a population that arrived in Tanzania healthy suffered from high rates of malnutrition and, ultimately, death. On the assumption that this population would remain in Tanzania, substantial resources were committed to the region by the WFP and UNHCR in late 1994. However, by the time these resources arrived, the unanticipated happened again. By early March, 90 percent of these refugees had returned to Burundi, despite the fears of the international community that that country, which was planning elections, was unstable. Indeed, they even returned as new slayings were reported in Bujumbura (*Los Angeles Times* 1994).

The international relief regime's reading of Burundian political and refugee situation in 1993–94 was poor. Policy did not reflect well what was happening in Burundi, and/or the refugee population. Anticipators were "zero for three" with a false negative (refugees could repatriate safely, and no preparation was needed), followed by another false negative (the assassination would not result in refugee flight, and no preparation was needed), and finally a false positive (refugee relief in Tanzania was required—but then the refugees returned to Burundi spontaneously).

Rwanda and Burundi, 1994

On April 6, 1994, the presidents of both Rwanda and Burundi died in a plane crash in Kigali. This followed further negotiations on a peace agreement between the Rwandans of Habyarimana's ruling MRND (Mouvement Révolutionnaire National pour le Développement) and the RPF in which the repatriation of the Tutsi diaspora refugees from 1960s had been agreed to. It also closely followed assassinations in Kigali in late February 1994 (Prunier 1996:206–207) and massacres in Burundi in early March 1994 (*Los Angeles Times* 1994).

During the early days following the crash, anticipators predicted a refugee flight of Hutu from Burundi to Tanzania. The reasoning went that the coup and the death of a president in October 1993 created conditions for flight, as they had the previous year. The international refugee relief regime paid less attention to Rwanda, where events became more horrific, but which had little history of flight to Tanzania. Unlike Burundi, Rwanda did not have a recent tradition of refugee flight across borders. Nevertheless, with the recent events in Burundi in mind, UNHCR staff were assigned to Ngara in mid-April, in part to supervise the few remaining Burundi refugee assistance programs, but also to make surveys in the interest of preparedness.[2] These were the staff who were on hand when the Rwandans crossed the bridge on April 28–29 and were directed to the campsite that was to become Benaco.

Benaco was the first partial success in terms of preparedness. In large part the success was due to what had happened in Burundi; staff and equipment were on the ground when the refugees arrived. In terms of anticipation and preparedness, this situation can be viewed as a partial success. The size of the influx and its origins were different than what was anticipated, but the degree of preparedness that was present contributed to the success in the operation throughout mid-1994.[3]

The success of the Benaco operation put in Tanzania a large number of expatriates embedded in bureaucracies providing the services refugees would require to stay or return. It also highlighted the issue of what would happen next; more specifically, what event would satisfy donors in the West who funded the operation. Very quickly it became apparent that a massive return to Rwanda was what was desired at the higher bureaucratic levels in Geneva, New York, and Dar es Salaam. As a consequence, field staff searched for signs of this during 1994 and 1995, even as new refugees continued to arrive. The combination of the two conflicting pressures, from the field and from distant capitals, meant that field personnel needed to reconcile policy pressures that were not just inconsistent but mutually contradictory. Either refugee were coming from Rwanda and increasing caseloads and demands, or they were going back and thereby decreasing demands. Logically you could not have both; in Ngara, though, they did.

Nothing Is Anticipated: Two False Negatives, and Two False Positives

The net result for these contradictions for planning assumptions was two false negatives and two false positives. How, why, and when did this occur?

Meetings of UN and NGO staff were held in Ngara in May and June to discuss the potential for further arrivals. The parliamentary elections and national day celebrations in Burundi on July 5 were of particular concern. David Lamb[4] of the *Los Angeles Times* reflected these concerns when he wrote on June 4, 1994:

> All but forgotten by the world, this nation [Burundi] hangs in nerve-racking suspension, balanced between forces that dare pray for conciliation and those who would turn this troubled land into another Rwanda.
>
> The slightest misstep could tip the balance. And after a year in which Burundi witnessed its first free elections, the murder of two of its presidents and a massacre that claimed as many as 100,000 lives, the specter of uncontrollable slaughter in a neighboring land is a very real, very chilling.
>
> "Rwanda is terrifying and terrible," said Avenerand Bakevymusaya, Burundi's minister of labor. "One would think it would have taught us to avoid that kind of madness, but there is a very real danger that what happened there could happen here. The calm you see here now is not a reassuring calm. . . ."
>
> The deep mistrust between the Tutsi and Hutu in Burundi, combined with fears that chaos in Rwanda could inflame extremists on both sides

here, has filled this ramshackle capital with anxiety and a well-founded xenophobia.

The countdown is under way, but no one knows if it is toward war or peace. . . .

The neighborhoods where Tutsi and Hutu once lived side by side and often intermarried have become largely segregated—voluntarily—after violent clashes in Bujumbura over the winter and into the spring [of 1994]. Victims hacked to death were almost always Tutsi; those killed by bullets were Hutu. . . .

Refugee workers across the border from Burundi in Tanzania were well aware of what Lamb was writing about. As Lamb did, they framed the potential for violence against what had happened in Rwanda during previous months, and as a result, expected influxes were described in the hundreds of thousands. "What will happen in Burundi will make what happened last month in Rwanda look like a tea party," thundered one agency head at a UNHCR meeting in late June. UNHCR hastened to point out that July 5 was Burundi's national day, and the date for parliamentary elections, and therefore was a particularly propitious date for a coup and the outbreak of violence resulting in refugee flight. Border monitoring was increased, supply requisitions prepared, staff put on standby, leaves canceled, agencies solemnly committed to preparedness.

Despite the dire predictions, few Burundians materialized, and for the first time since May, there was actually a lull in refugee flight into Tanzania in July 1994. In terms of contingency planning, this was a false positive. The refugee influx which did materialize came in August, and were in fact Rwandans fleeing the final RPF push in the southwest, not Burundians. This meant that despite the misread situation, agencies could justify their preparations for the Burundian situation by pointing to the Rwandan influx. In fact, the Rwandans were not anticipated; in fact, they were not noticed until upward of 10,000 had gathered in remote border villages near the point where the borders of Tanzania, Rwanda, and Burundi meet.

The tens of thousands of Rwandans arriving in August 1994 were primarily residents of southwest Rwanda, who crossed over a small corner of Burundi before fleeing to Tanzania. This moment had not been anticipated, although fortunately the infrastructure was established to accommodate them. The influx—occurring at a time when Rwanda itself was turning to peace and the genocidal *Interahamwe* were finally being controlled—was the opposite of what was expected. Indeed, the widespread speculation among the expatriates in Ngara was that with the decline in hostilities in Kibungo prefecture and the arrival of the planting season, the vast proportion of refugees in Benaco would spontaneously return to

Rwanda. In effect, there was a false positive and a false negative. Repatriation, which *was* expected, did not occur, and flight, which *was not* expected, did occur.

The repatriation situation was even more muddled by the end of 1994. What did materialize in terms of repatriation, though, was unexpected. Refugee Tutsi from earlier diasporas began to appear at the border seeking repatriation to Rwanda. These Tutsi were supporters of the RPF who had lived in Tanzania during the previous 20 to 30 years. From Tanzania, probably 10,000 to 20,000 Tutsi returned to Rwanda between summer 1994 and early 1995. An estimated 700,000 more left Burundi, Uganda, and Zaire; many of the Tutsi from Burundi took over the homesteads vacated by the Hutu refugees in Ngara. This return was orchestrated by the new Rwandan government, which at its core was an organization of the "Rwandans abroad." The influx of the several hundred thousand returnees without coordination or assistance from an international community caught the UNHCR off guard; the UN and international community were more interested in restoring the pre-crisis status quo than facilitating the payment of RPF debts to supporters.

More important for the situation in Benaco, though, was the perception by the Hutu that Tutsi from Burundi had occupied their abandoned farms. This unanticipated move clearly complicated planning for refugee return. In terms of contingency planning, it was a false negative.

Rwanda and Voluntary Repatriation 1995–96: A Series of False Positives

The resolution of the Rwanda refugee crisis was the consistent goal of the UNHCR throughout 1995 and 1996. Special officers were hired to encourage voluntary repatriation, buses were brought to Tanzania, and strategizing sessions were established in order to organize a "grand march" back to Rwanda. I was working in Karagwe at the end of 1995, and the field officers there were particularly optimistic about the potential for a grand march. They were particularly encouraged when the leader of one of the camps in the very north offered to go back and, consistent with beliefs that the refugees were peasants unable to make their own decisions about safety, assumed that the entire camp of over 10,000 refugees would return with him. He eventually returned, but with only his own family. In 1995 and 1996, I was part of this hope, and passed on the rumors and hopes in a series of memorandums my head office in Dar es Salaam requested:

UNHCR Ngara continues to believe that refugees do have a legitimate fear of persecution should they return to Rwanda. They also believe that there is intimidation in the camp for those wishing to return. . . . They [also] say that UNHCR Kigali, the Rwandan Government, and others continue to believe that refugees from Tanzania can return to Rwanda at any time safely. . . . UNHCR Ngara is also emphasizing that conditions within Rwanda vary from commune to commune. . . . (July 31, 1995)

UNHCR continues to hold information meetings describing the conditions under which voluntary repatriation can occur through official channels. UNHCR says that mass meetings are going well. According to UNHCR attendance at the mass meetings to explain repatriation is very encouraging and peaceful. . . . There is a standing order for five trucks on Wednesday and Friday mornings. I talked to a few of our drivers today, and they indicate that they gather at the Benaco Police Station each morning. Before the refugees had to arrive at the police station on their own. A new policy is that the trucks are then sent to the houses of the refugees who have agreed to repatriate with a police escort. This is done in order that the profile of the repatriation can be raised among the refugee community. It also means that the volunteers have fewer chances to back out at the last minute. . . . The drivers indicate that most of the repatriates are women and children, and that all are uneducated (according to one driver, there are 6 men for every 40 women [and that] "none of the refugees repatriated are able to read.". . . The drivers indicate that there is a great deal of fear, but [the refugees] are given no chance to change their minds. . . . (August 31, 1995)

The Prefects of Kibungo and Byumba [Rwanda] visited the camps last Saturday in order to encourage the return of refugees. These were the first visits of Rwanda government officials to the camp. There is an indication that their visit is encouraging repatriation requests. Yesterday's repatriation was full for the first time (about 400). . . . One entire commune of 4,000 people has apparently applied to go back (October 12, 1995) [Note: The commune of 4,000 never materialized]. . . .

Repatriation in Ngara is picking up. . . . The repatriation is being encouraged by the UNHCR which has facilitated the flow of information back and forth from Rwanda. They have had two cross-border visits of refugees organized, and are using tapes and radio to send messages back and forth. . . . The general impression is that intimidation is down. People returning to Rwanda seem happier leaving than before, and they are waved off by family and friends. . . . All concerned say that primarily women and children are going. . . . A number of NGOs are critical of the UNHCR for presenting a "donor-driven" too-optimistic picture of political conditions in Rwanda. MSF Holland is most vocal. . . . All mail is read by Rwandan soldiers at the border and the Rwandan Army at the border is not very pleasant. . . . The return of old-caseload Tutsi is continuing (October 31, 1995).

None of the bureaucratized pushing, cajoling, bribing, or coercing by UNHCR worked on a large scale. Information sharing and the "go and see" programs were an especially prominent part of the voluntary repatriation program. This involved taking refugees to Rwanda, who would go and see what conditions were like at their homes, and then would be returned to the Tanzania camp. Each of the refugees was pre-cleared for the visits by the Tanzanian and Rwandan governments and the UNHCR. Despite these precautions, there were confrontations between returnees and people in the home communes. A number of the visitors returned with tales about how they had heard whispers about the wisdom of not returning. UNHCR could respond with nothing more original than assertions that despite the care with which the individuals were selected, those who brought back negative accounts were simply lying (see Essay 8).

In fact, actual repatriation never did keep up with the birthrate, much less the continuing influx from closing camps in Burundi. The repatriation goals were pursued as a result of UNHCR's belief that the RPF would honor agreements to return land and homes. Even reports by UNHCR repatriation specialists that the Rwandans were far from ready to repatriate voluntarily did not cause shifts in policy. The policy throughout 1995 and 1996 continued to be that all refugees could and should return to Rwanda, and resources were invested in making this expectation come true.

The programming decisions for repatriation were in effect a series of false positives. The assessment of the situation by the UNHCR and donors was that the refugees in Tanzania were ready to repatriate voluntarily, if only material incentives were offered to facilitate it. What later evidence indicates is that these assumptions were wrong, and the refugees were not ready to repatriate. The mistake was similar to that made along the Burundi border in 1994, when predictions were made that Burundi was set to "explode" and send refugee movements into Tanzania. This time though, it reflected bureaucratic wishes from central headquarters.

Burundi 1995–96

Burundi continued to be wracked by violence in late 1994 and into early 1995. The potential for flight from Burundi was a chronic issue. On the basis of visits to Burundi in 1995, a special fact-finder ("rapporteur") from the United Nations, Paulo Sergio Pinheiro, wrote:

> The Special Rapporteur cannot but reiterate the thrust of the final observations in his initial report [submitted in 1995]. The dangers facing Burundi remain considerable and the situation in the country may at any time explode, entailing unbearable consequences for Burundi's population, uncontrollable mass movements within the country and at its borders, and finally [leading] to a loss of control or to a destabilization of the Great Lakes Region. . . . To permit such a situation to develop would be to show scant regard for the re-

sponsibility borne by those directly concerned: Burundians, Africans—with
the rulers of Burundi's neighbours in the front line—Europeans, and the
other actors in the international community (Pinheiro 1996:11).

The idea that Burundi would "explode," as Pinheiro put it in his report, or was somehow balanced "on the edge of a knife" (Balzar
1994:A1), was a chronic theme between 1994 and 1996. The implication
was that when Burundi did explode, the result would be more cata-
strophic than what had been seen in the past in terms of either violent
death or refugee exodus.

In Tanzania, this resulted in a gearing up and relaxation of the contingency apparatus on at least four separate occasions. In each, the specter
of the Rwanda crisis with its massive and quick flight of refugees loomed
large. Less prominent in the planning assumptions was the more mundane experience with Burundi since 1993, in which refugees had "border-
straddled," meaning that there was a back-and-forth movement across
the border as local conditions ebbed and flowed.[5]

Many of the refugee movements were concentrated in northern Burundi along the borders with Rwanda and Tanzania. In early 1995, for the
first time since 1993, substantial numbers of Burundians fled into Tanzania, although there was also a goodly proportion of Rwandans in the
refugee flow. Predictions of massive flows of a magnitude of hundreds of
thousands continued to be bandied about until the Tanzanians forcibly
closed the border to the refugee influx for the first time in April 1995. By
the time the border had closed, there were about 45,000 more Burundians
and 25,000 more Rwandans in Tanzania.[6] Thus, this was a partial success
in terms of preparation and prediction; although the size of the influx
had been overestimated, the continued influx was not a great surprise.
As a result, the refugees were accommodated in a relatively efficient fashion. This was a partially positive prediction.

Renewed fighting in Burundi in December 1995 and January 1996 led
to more concerns about a refugee influx, and contingency plans were established for the arrival of 150,000 in the event the Tanzanian government reopened the border. This did happen, and eventually approximately 30,000, most of whom were Rwandans from refugee camps in
Burundi that had been closed, entered Tanzania. This was done relatively
efficiently, in part due to the overpreparation for 150,000. Again, this was
a partial positive prediction.

The Coup in Burundi: 1996

The low-grade fighting in Burundi had left tens of thousands of dead and
was characterized by some as a "slow genocide." Burundi was widely

viewed as a country in chaos. Observers claimed not to be surprised when the former president Pierre Buyoya took the country over forcibly in a coup on July 26, 1996. A Time.com bulletin announced, "Burundi Finally Blows" on July 31. The coup resulted in a strong reaction from neighboring countries, which immediately clamped on a trade embargo. Ironically, given the recent history of the country, the aftermath of the coup was not any more violent than events in recent months when there was no coup.

Flight to Tanzania was not accelerated by the coup, but by events in November 1996 in Zaire. The victory of the Rwandan army and *Banyamulenge* in Zaire resulted in not only the emptying of Rwandan camps and their inhabitants' return to Rwanda, but also the emptying of Burundian refugee camps in Zaire. This resulted in a move of approximately 100,000 across Burundi and into Tanzania; at the same time, to the north, Rwandans were being evicted by the Tanzanian military.

Both movements were the opposite of what was expected: a false positive (expectation of flight following the coup), and a false negative (the reception of refugees following a forced repatriation).

The Forced Repatriation

The final expulsion of Tanzania's Rwandan refugees occurred in December 1996. The bulk had left Tanzania by Christmas, but roundups in Tanzanian villages were to continue until mid-1997. The expulsion was carried out by the Tanzanian military, while the international community, apparently having dropped its previous objections to forcible expulsion, looked the other way and in some indirect ways actually facilitated the movement. Gérard Prunier (1997a) wrote about the expulsion in February 1997:

> Seizing the opportunity where forceful action would go almost unnoticed in the general commotion, Tanzania declared that all Rwandan refugees, about 530,000, on its soil must leave by the end of the year, and the Tanzanian army quickly moved towards the camps. Seized by panic at the idea of return, and probably also coerced in part by their still-active leadership, several thousand refugees fled in various directions in the hope of reaching the borders of either Kenya or Malawi. The Tanzanian army quickly caught up with them, forced them back towards the camps and from there pushed them on across the border into Rwanda. There was no UNHCR protest and the few aid workers operating in the camps who complained were expelled by the Tanzanian authorities. By Christmas, the camps were emptied (Prunier 1997a).

Thus, in one final unanticipated population movement, the official presence of Rwandan refugees in Tanzania came to an end. The Rwanda crisis in Tanzania was over.

The Limitations of Contingency Planning

What factors underlay the failures and successes in contingency planning in Tanzania? Can patterns in the imprecision of refugee movement predictions be found?

One common thread seems to be planners' overreliance on proximate causes that they assume underlie refugee movements. They focus on "triggering events" like assassination or elections, and don't analyze broader factors that influence why refugees move when they do. What they miss is that a "triggering" event is a final, culminating event and, as this analysis shows, only sometimes causes a refugee flight. Such events are only the ultimate proximate causes. Interpreting triggering events as the proximate cause does not furnish enough information for the anticipation of refugee movement.

Not surprisingly, bureaucracies also use predictions to pursue their own self-interest, which they often do via the press, where both successful predictions and bureaucratic competitors' incorrect predictions, or failure to anticipate, are highlighted. Of course a fundamental aspect of prediction is that there will always be some "failures." Having said that, I do believe that this assessment of the Rwanda and Burundi data point to some conclusions as to why refugees move and under what conditions.

Why Refugees Move

There seem to be six primary reasons why refugees move. Each one has policy implications.

1. Rising Political Expectations

Mass refugee flight is most likely to occur during a time of rising political expectations. It is less likely to occur in times of political tension.

Since 1993, there have been two major mass refugee flights: in 1993 from Burundi, and in 1994 from Rwanda. Both of these flights happened at a time of rising political expectations: In the case of Burundi it followed the democratic election of a Hutu president and the repatriation of Hutu refugees after 20 years in Tanzania. In the case of Rwanda, the flight followed a peace agreement and political agreement between warring parties. In both cases, there was a consensus in the national and international communities that the political situation was getting better.

For this reason—the refugees themselves and the international community—were unprepared for the subsequent refugee exodus. For the international community, it meant that relief programs were inadequate to receive both groups. The Rwandans were more fortunate than the Burundians, because the relief programs designed to receive Burundians (though they were too late to help them much) were already in place. The mass exodus of Rwandans was not anticipated.

These examples suggest that mass refugee flows can occur at times of rising expectations, rather than during times of high political or military tension. During times of high tension when political violence is somehow expected, mass flight seems less likely. A possible reason why such times of positive expectations are so volatile is that they involve reorientation in intergroup dynamics: "My enemy is now my neighbor, and all is now forgiven." But such "outbreaks of goodwill" are fragile. When such mass reorientation suddenly fails, as it did in the cases of both Rwanda and Burundi in 1993–94, confusion and fear emerge quickly, and the result is confused flight to a neighboring country.

This circumstance does not necessarily precede every mass refugee flight—the case of Rwandans into Zaire in July 1994 and the Cambodians in Thailand are obvious exceptions. But it does point to a politically liminal area that should be observed by those responsible for assessing the potential of refugee flight.

From this observation follows the next conclusion:

2. Flight Across a Border Area

Mass refugee flight that occurs during a time of rising political expectations is more likely to be across a broad border area. Expected flight during fighting is more likely to be localized and the influxes smaller.

As the conflict in Burundi grew older, locals were probably better able to evaluate the need for flight. As a result, later exoduses tended to be local, rather than general. International agencies, however, fearing a repeat of the massive general exoduses of 1993–94, planned for the latter.

3. Ignoring Refugees' Active Political Role

Governmental actors routinely ignore the de facto political role of the refugees themselves as actors in the international refugee regime.

The result is that governments and the aid bureaucracy assume refugees are responsive only to material factors such as assurances of physical safety, food provision, resettlement assistance, and security of land. This is consistent with the morals of refugee assistance whereby aid workers assume that refugees are innocent bystanders in the conflict, not part of it, and constitute a political *tabula rasa*. The assumption that a refugee population is a political *tabula rasa* is just as unreasonable as it would be for any other population. Ignoring the inherently political origins of flight is probably an important reason that repatriation programs were so unsuccessful.

4. Population Density

The likelihood of refugee flight and repatriation may be influenced by population density. However, this very much depends on how the population is defined; despite their intuitive appeal, population densities probably explain very little.

A characteristic of refugee movement in 1993–96 was the back-and-forth movement across the Tanzanian border. High population densities in Rwanda and Burundi may very well contribute to the conditions leading to strife. However, there is no evidence that the likelihood of movement inevitably increases with population density. There has been too much back-and-forth movement to justify this conclusion.

5. Repatriation and "Border Straddling"

"Border straddling" has been a consistent strategy of Burundians, but not apparently of Rwandans. This practice makes spontaneous repatriation of Burundians more likely.

As a strategy for dealing with localized strife, movement across the border into Tanzania and back to Burundi has been a consistent strategy. An intuitive sense of this is perhaps the reason why refugee influxes of Burundians into Tanzania have been predicted more accurately than those of Rwandans. This could be an artifact of cultural knowledge specific to the Burundian population.

6. Effects of Closing and Opening Borders

The effects of closing and opening borders are not completely clear. However, it is clear that such governmental policies are never as effective as policy-makers may wish.

Immigration policy all over the world is made in the context of both what is possible and what is wished for. Whatever the explicit policy, though, immigrants always sense the permeability of a border, whether it be that between the United States and Mexico, or Tanzania and Rwanda/Burundi. In this respect, refugees are social players who have wishes of their own. Even if their wishes lack legal standing, those expressed by their feet have as much effect on policy development as laws.

Notes

1. In anticipation of this return, French-language classes began in the early 1990s, as dreams of return were rekindled in refugees who had been away from Burundi for 20 years or had been born in Tanzania.

2. The *Joint Evaluation of the Emergency Assistance to Rwanda* (1996, vol. 3, p. 36) briefly discusses this preparedness. According to this report, the emergency response team arrived on April 20 and identified the site for Benaco on the morning of April 29, and the refugees arrived that evening. My recollection is that the identification of the site had been initiated by Andres Jimenez, the UNHCR field officer assigned to Ngara earlier in 1994 to supervise UNHCR's programs for the approximately 10,000 Burundian refugees at Lukole camp. Missionary doctors serving at Murgwanza Hospital in Ngara related to me in summer 1999 that a number of UNHCR staff were present in Ngara in early 1994, some on short-term assignments to simply collect information. See also Jaspars (1994).

3. Also of note was the role of the Western press. *JEEAR* (1996) pointed out that the press, which had been in South Africa in anticipation of widespread violence in connection with the elections in that country, was disappointed when there was a peaceful transition from the Nationalist party government to that of the victorious African National Congress. The antidote to this disappointment, *JEEAR* reasoned, was the opportunity to cover the violence in Rwanda, which was best observed from Tanzania. There may be some truth in this. But it is doubtful that the story would have been any different than the coverage of the Burundi massacres and refugee flight five months earlier had the international community not already been present in Ngara—in the form of the Red Cross's Sheila Wilson and UNHCR's Maureen Connelly—to focus press attention on refugees and bodies in the river.

4. Unlike many of the journalists reporting on Ngara, Lamb had extensive experience in Africa, even having written a book about the continent in the early 1980s. The book reflected his experience as Nairobi bureau chief for the *Los Angeles Times* from 1976 to 1979.

5. This border straddling had been observed on Tanzania's border with Burundi regularly since the first large refugee flight in 1972. This activity is facilitated by the regular passage of information across the Tanzania-Burundi border, which, unlike that between Rwanda and Tanzania, does not have major river or swamp barriers.

6. At the time the Tanzanians closed the border with Burundi, there were about 250,000 Rwandan refugees in Muyinga province of Burundi. The camps for Rwandans were being closed by the Burundian military, and the refugees were being told to return to Rwanda. Instead, virtually all of the refugees headed for Tanzania.

These refugees were by and large apolitical peasants from Rwanda. According to the special fact-finder of the Security Council, Paulo Sergio Pinheiro, "Contrary to the situation in the refugee camps in Zaire, Rwandan refugees in the Burundi camps are not armed, there are no militia leaders, and there seem to be no soldiers of the former armed forces of Rwanda (FAR)."

10

Bureaucratizing the Good Samaritan: Water Crises

Water is a dry subject, so to speak. This is particularly true in the context of the press's interest in refugee relief, where much of the focus is on the dead and dying. *Time* and other popular magazines do, of course, make good attempts at jazzing up the topic of sanitation with dramatic prose like the following:

> Early on there was already a winner in the war, whose triumph will be unaffected by whatever the politicians or soldiers decide. It is the victory of disease. Sanitation is impossible; typhoid, dysentery, cholera are all menacing the refugees, especially the children. Malarial mosquitoes swarm above the swamps. As the rainy season continues in the mountains, the dry cough of pneumonia and tuberculosis echoes through the camps. (Gibbs, 1994)

Unfortunately, the immediate clarity of such emotional appeals rarely lasts as long as sound solutions take to develop. Actual solutions to the problems of drinking water and sanitation to a lay audience are clouded by the technical calculations of engineers. Engineering, with its dependence on nonhuman technology, controls available options, irrespective of human wishes. Unlike unfulfilled contingency plans (Chapter 9), where failures can be explained away in a fog of emotional jargon, unsuccessful water engineering results in stockpiles of unused, abandoned, and broken equipment. For this reason, it is easier to observe the limitations of the Good Samaritan bureaucracy in the water sector than in other sectors.

Water systems are large, complex, and expensive, and by their nature, demand careful engineering if they are to work as planned. As with other large and expensive engineering works, systematic rational planning is necessary to create complex water systems. Underlying systematic planning is the assumption that getting the most water for every dollar spent, pipe laid, pump primed, and concrete slab poured is a desirable outcome. Thus, the engineer's tools reflect characteristics of Weber's concept of rationality, including the elements of efficiency, predictability, calculability, and control. Although Weber's thoughts about rationalization and bureaucratic organization are not taught in engineering schools, the elements he wrote about certainly are. Thus, in well-engineered water systems, pump sizes, pipeline design, population counts, and delivery systems match the amount of water available, be it underground in an unseen aquifer, or aboveground in a lake or river whose water must be purified for human use. Further, the installations are geared to the intended level of use by means of precise calculations that would intimidate a math phobic.

In the case of Ngara, or any emergency for that matter, such a careful methodical approach could not be used owing to the very nature of refugee relief. Population figures were not predetermined, length of stay was uncertain, and projects were funded in response to emotional appeals, especially the fear of cholera, rather than rational cost-benefit calculations. Despite this, the underlying engineering assumptions remain the same. Principles of design, planning, procurement, and installation require a slow, methodical process. But in an emergency where speed is necessary and population counts are imprecise, engineers necessarily relax their assumptions concerning the type of data necessary to provide water quickly, whether they acknowledge it or not. In other words, they must accomplish a certain task without following the procedures that their discipline really requires. The result is a decline in the amount of control (in Weber's sense) that engineers have over the results.

This chapter is about how relaxing rationalized engineering assumptions in the areas of data requirements, procurement, populations, and so forth affected the water sector in Ngara. The consequences can be seen in the abandoned and mothballed water systems that seem to be a feature of not just the camps in Tanzania but of other emergency operations as well. The fault lies not with the engineers, but with an implied acceptance of increased risk of failure as engineering standards are relaxed. This is in large part a result of a dilemma inherent to emergency work: In order to meet the emergency, quality standards must be relaxed. Were textbook standards to be maintained, of course, good water systems would have been built eventually in a place like Ngara, but they probably would have been too late to effectively combat disease.

The dilemma in an emergency is really a question of which engineering assumptions concerning water supply will be relaxed; logically there are only two possibilities. Either, installation of water supplies is delayed until data are collected and design specifications are met, a strategy that entails a short-term risk of epidemics of water-shortage diseases. Or general engineering standards for careful and systematic planning will be relaxed, and cost overruns and failures of inappropriate equipment will be tolerated. The latter is what happens in the context of a modern emergency grounded in the emotional demands of CNN and donors. In effect, the short-term humanitarian disaster is controlled, but there is a concomitant implied assumption that there will be breakdowns in equipment.

Risks are implicitly accepted when the well-publicized pressure to "do something" is high. Emergency administrators grasp the optimistic best guesses of engineers who happen to be on the spot, which in turn becomes an incentive for engineers to generate estimates that solve the administrators' immediate problems with expanding refugee populations. In this environment, assumptions and presumptions are quickly made and become fact. As is described below, in Ngara this happened in the assessments of groundwater, procurement, and water rationing decisions.

Also implicit is that when the consequences of relaxing engineering assumptions develop, and as a consequence an inventory of unused, broken, and mothballed equipment accumulates, the press will be gone, and can be called back to announce another "crisis." The paradox of the bureaucratized Good Samaritan means that even after minimum standards have been reached and "lives saved," and more careful data collection becomes possible, standards for quick decision-making established during the emergency phase become standard, and risks of project failure continue to be taken. In effect, a deal is made with the engineering devils: the danger of water-shortage diseases (cholera, dysentery, etc.) is postponed in the hope that before the system collapses, the refugee situation will have resolved itself politically.[1]

Water Provision in Ngara: 1994

The original site of the Benaco camp was chosen because there was adequate water in a small dammed stream left by the road construction project some 15 years before, adequate quantities of firewood, and easy access to a main highway. For legal reasons, it was also important that the local and national officials in Tanzania approved. The survey of the contingency site was probably no more than a quick walk-around and did not involve assessment of how fast the small lake was replenished by the springs feeding it.[2]

After refugees arrived, filling initial water needs focused on developing the lake. MSF–France installed a pump in early May 1994, so refugees would not climb into the lake with buckets and potentially contaminate it with the bacteria that cause dysentery, cholera, and other diseases.

Within six weeks the Oxfam Emergency Unit also installed a temporary water treatment plant, using a kit airlifted to Tanzania for the purpose. Finally, UNHCR contracted to dig a trench around the hill on which the campsite was situated. The point of this was to channel any runoff carrying human fecal matter away from the lakeside water source.

During the first weeks, all in Ngara held their breath to see whether the dreaded cholera epidemic emerged or not. Death rates due to enteric diseases were high, but were considered to be under control, by international standards. The key point in June 1994 was that the emergency water treatment plant was operational, and adequate supplies of water were available.[3] It was the end of the rainy season, and although this contributed to the discomfort of refugees, it meant that there was a substantial flow replenishing the lake, no matter how much water was pumped by Oxfam.

All were concerned, though, that the lake situation was but a temporary solution. As the situation was described in *JEEAR* (1996:77): "It was recognized from the outset that the capacity of the lake to provide a guaranteed year-round supply was questionable and that it would need to be complemented from other sources." Drilling for groundwater was considered critical because it would provide the needed complement and also permit an expansion of the settlement area. UNICEF–Uganda sent a well-drilling team to the camp with a rig, and they began drilling in late May 1994.[4]

The UNICEF team were master drillers, but were unfamiliar with the geology of the area. Brief consultations with local Tanzanian technicians made it clear that geological advice was unavailable because there were no hydrogeologists in the area, and the Tanzanians had little experience with the drilling capacity of a rig like UNICEF's. The team decided to drill wells at the low points around the campsites, in hopes of hitting quartzite layers through which water flows readily.[5] Instead, they found water in the much less permeable slates, which are the rocky remnants of the clay floors of ancient seas. The slates, which do not crumble as readily as the quartzites, conduct water only very slowly. (The soils around Benaco are composed mainly of soft slates and crumbly quartzites.) Nevertheless, the yields in several of the wells were adequate to establish a new refugee camp at Lumasi. In June 1994, this was critical, because refugees continued to arrive in large numbers, depleting the resources available on the hill at Benaco. As part of their drilling program, UNICEF lined the top 50 meters of each well with plastic casing, even though the wells themselves were all deeper. This is standard practice to guarantee against ground contamination, and is also standard practice in hard-rock drilling. Pumps were placed in the hole (typically 30 centimeters in diameter), and then lowered into the hole below the casing.

In June 1994, agencies were called together to make estimates about the water delivery program for the Benaco camps. Four tentative planning decisions were made at that time. First, a planning figure of 275,000 refugees would be used, and each refugee would be provided with 10 liters (four gallons) per day.[6] This was a high population estimate, well above the numbers that were expected to flee from Rwanda to Ngara.[7]

Second, a decision was made to develop the wells with pumps manufactured by the Monopump company, which at that time were available in the United Kingdom and were widely used in Tanzania. These pumps would replace the submersible pumps from the Oxfam inventory, which were then being installed. Monopump, eager for an order that they did not need to bid for, promised delivery of the pumps in six weeks. UN-HCR, Oxfam, and LWF accepted these promises, despite knowledge that such orders typically took considerably longer. This decision was made because standard procedures recommend one type of pump, meaning smaller spare parts inventories than for multiple pump models, and a single training program for technicians. Then, the Danish submarine pumps would be replaced.

Third, it was noted that the reports of the UNICEF drillers indicated that water supplies in the existing wells would be adequate if all were developed to capacity. Finally, it was decided that LWF would install and operate the pumps while Oxfam continued installing pipelines. Oxfam would quickly withdraw from water-provision activities and would hand over its equipment to LWF. These decisions were made with the limited data available at the time, but the assumptions behind them did not hold. The result, as the *Joint Evaluation* noted, was that by 1995 the situation "deteriorated rather than improved." (1996:77)

The first water crisis began when the new wells began to cave in. As mentioned, the soils around Benaco are composed mainly of soft slates and crumbly quartzites. As water is pumped out of these stones, a cavity forms around the pump, and eventually the well itself caves in on the pump. This what the lining is supposed to protect against. Given the heavy pumping in Benaco, this occurred in some wells in a matter of weeks. When the well caves in, the pump is irreparably damaged.

This problem was first identified in August of 1994 when two Norwegian geologists made a quick visit. Subsequent visits by three British geologists and later an Austrian confirmed this analysis. The lack of lining meant that the wells around Benaco and Lumasi would slowly but surely collapse, and the water supply for a substantial portion of the refugee population with it. The first well collapsed in September 1994, and slowly the other UNICEF-drilled wells began to follow.

But, instead of using the time bought by the UNICEF-drilled wells to redesign the well-drilling program, the next series of quick water-engineering decisions were made, using the same emergency focus in which the first tentative decisions were taken. Three conditions in particular were to result from inadequate analysis and planning:

1. Low spots for drilling were chosen again without any systematic attention to the hydrogeology of the area. This meant that only slates were drilled, even though quartzite ridges were also nearby.
2. A seemingly commonsense assumption was made that the lake would not sustain continued pumping during the dry season. This was made without any survey of where water in the lake was coming from.
3. The ultimate refugee population was again underestimated.

Cholera Is Coming—Let's Spend a Lot of Money

Water provision in refugee camps is measured in liters of clean water produced (and consumed) per person per day. This is simply the total amount of water pumped through gauges, divided by the total number of people. But what is the minimum required for healthful living? For bare subsistence? How are you sure you are counting the right number of people? Right number of liters? What level is a refugee assistance program obligated to provide? Figures having legitimacy in the relief community ranged from the goal of 20 liters daily, which the World Health Organization has determined is the minimum needed for healthful living, to a low of 5 liters per person per day. The 5-liter limit is considered the bare minimum needed to control diseases, particularly cholera (Chalinder 1994).

Water amounts provided in the Ngara camps were closely monitored, whereas those in Karagwe, where the NGO presence was lighter, were less so. Initial estimates based on registration figures supplied by leaders in June 1994 indicated that between the Oxfam plant and the wells, water was being supplied at a rate of about 10 liters per person per day (*JEEAR* 1996:77). This figure dropped as more refugees arrived, but then at the beginning of July, when population figures were adjusted downward following the UNHCR's registration program, it jumped back up to 10 liters per person per day. This administrative adjustment occurred as the Oxfam plant was brought to full capacity and the new boreholes were brought on line in July and August. This proved to be the last time the water situation in Ngara was to be viewed with complacency.

In September 1994, planners were presented with the issue of whether to continue equipping more of the UNICEF boreholes with pumps, knowing that they would perhaps collapse within a few weeks, or abandon them until more boreholes were drilled. Monopumps, which cost about £4,000 each, were in short supply, the original emergency order was late, owing to delays in the UK, and risking them in the collapsing boreholes was potentially embarrassing.[8] Concern also mounted as to whether the lake would last through the dry season, given a pumping rate of 1,200 cubic meters per day through the Oxfam treatment plant. It was obvious to the untrained eye that the level of the lake was dropping. Straight-line calculations based on the assumption that there would be no replenishment of the lake from underground aquifers, and that the lake would supply 40 percent of the water for the new planning figure of 400,000 people, showed that the lake would be exhausted at various times throughout the dry season of 1994. Each of these drops implied that the availability of water provided by the UNHCR would fall below the magic five-liter figure, which was feared by all.

The possibility of reaching this statistical watershed was the cue to raise the cholera flag. The threat of cholera was a potent symbol, particularly following the disaster in Zaire, where a cholera epidemic in July resulted in 20,000 to 30,000 deaths (see Prunier 1995:302–304). The apparent collapse of the boreholes in Ngara and the assumption that water provision under 5 liters per day would cause (as opposed to risk) disease epidemics was widely touted at meetings by the engineers from Oxfam and LWF, as well as the public health agencies, particularly the staff of the MSF agencies. Oxfam advocated aggressive action by bringing in consultants to assess the situation. Three hydrogeologists were brought between September and December to evaluate the situation. UNHCR pressed other engineers to make estimates for what it would cost to pump from the Ruvubu River, 10 kilometers away over the 400-meter-high ridge, and down to the camps. Brought to attention by the cholera scare and dropping production figures from the unlined wells, UNHCR's donors quickly funded each new effort.[9]

Most extravagant was a water-trucking program designed to supplant the entire Benaco water system, which came to be viewed as failing. The Rasumo River Filter Scheme for Camp Water involved installing a water-pumping plant at the intersection of the Ruvubu and Kagera rivers. Within sight of the Rwandan border station on the opposite side of the bridge, a pump station was to be installed that could load water trucks with water on a round-the-clock basis. Notably, no formal survey was done, and permission from local Tanzanian officials was not obtained; these actions were postponed owing to the emergency situation, a detail that UNHCR planned to take care of during a two-week purchasing period. The one-and-a-half-page proposal, including a budget, was typed on November 11, 1994.

This program was funded with $797,300 that an LWF engineer was authorized by the UNHCR to spend on a two-week shopping trip to the

UK and on airfreight to Mwanza. The 40 water trucks, fuel, and the spare parts remained unbudgeted, even though the design implied by the purchases was an expenditure of over $2 million in capital expenses alone. But by the time the engineer reached Dar es Salaam, the Tanzanian government objected to the Rasumo site. Instead of being canceled, the project was rescheduled for a remote lake near the Ruvubu River, some 17 kilometers (about 10 miles) from the camp. When the engineer returned with the chartered airfreight flight after Christmas, the equipment was diverted to this site. A laterite road was built, at a cost of over $100,000, under a quickly negotiated contract with the Cogefar construction company.

Ultimately, the pumping station on the Ruvubu was built with the equipment from the UK, but it still needed to be trucked to the Benaco camps. But by the time the water came on-line in February, only ten UNHCR-purchased trucks were available, and drivers were lacking. One of the new drivers hired to drive a water truck quickly rolled one. Later, it was found that the entire fleet itself was unstable. The trucks did not have baffles in the tanks and the sloshing of the water made them unstable, causing them to tip easily. The new water plant proved more expensive to operate than expected. Meanwhile, however, water supplies through the temporary Oxfam plant and boreholes unexpectedly held up. As a result, the remote water plant and remaining water trucks were mothballed in May 1994, after three months of operation.

Two Tanzanian well-drilling rigs also arrived, but then were dismissed when it was determined that they could not drill to desired specifications. In the rush to do something, no one from Ngara had taken the elementary precaution of determining whether the equipment was adequate for their purposes. A rig donated by the Japanese government arrived, and the operator (not the rig) was deemed inadequate to the task, despite the fact that the UNHCR had presumably preapproved the donation.

Finally, Ngara played a role in a regional planning failure. In July 1994, the United States Army had airlifted to Goma, Zaire, two reverse osmosis water purification units capable of producing 57,600 liters of high-quality water per day. These units produced too little water for the large population in Goma and were mothballed in Kigali after three days of use (*JEEAR* 1996:71). The United States ambassador to Tanzania was approached by UNHCR–Ngara in October–November 1994 to see if the units could be brought to Tanzania. The transfer was approved, and the units were brought to Ngara with some fanfare. Engineering staff in Ngara soon discovered that the units had arrived without directions, and that operation required an expensive consulting contract with a Texas company. Subsequently, the units were mothballed in Ngara, although the units were eventually cannibalized when spare parts for other equipment were needed.[10]

Finally, in January 1995, the Austrian-provided well-drilling rig began drilling the first new boreholes, which was the latest promised solution to the water problem.[11] This well-drilling rig was the first of the measures taken—rigs, trucks, tankering points, pumping stations, and consulting contracts—to actually increase the volume of water pumped into the camps. They did this by redrilling the collapsed UNICEF-drilled wells in the slates, despite claims that the water table around the boreholes was dropping as a result of overpumping, and also without apparently consulting geological maps which showed that water-bearing quartzite ridges were within three kilometers of the camp.[12]

In the context of repeated failures, the apparent dropping of the water table, and the escalation of water-trucking costs, UNHCR solicited an estimate for a massive pumping station on the Ruvubu River. Administrators at UNHCR—frustrated with hydrogeologists who, in a professionally responsible manner, hedged promises until data were available—reasoned that they should pump only surface water they could see, and that the best source they could see was the Ruvubu River. Pumping over the 1,300-foot-high ridge that lay between the river and the camps would require a massive investment. By 1995, UNHCR had received an estimate of $5.1 million and a minimum construction time of nine months from an engineering consulting firm (see *JEEAR* 1996:77). Given the 1,300-foot-high ridge over the mountains, pumping costs were also expected to be high. Nevertheless, this solution became the focus of UNHCR's hopes over the next months.[13]

Finding Water: Slates and Quartzites

Into this situation, in March 1995, a new well-drilling rig from Norway arrived with yet another hydrogeological consultant. The originator of the August 1994 observation that uncased wells would collapse on pumps, Fridtjov Ruden, also had a passion for bootleather-and-hammer-based hydrogeology, meaning he believed that observations from well logs on water yield had to be backed up by field-based observations correlated with geological mapping. His explorations in the areas immediately around the Benaco area indicated that there were tall quartzite ridges surrounding the camps. The quartzite sandstone is hard and brittle (my children called it "sugar-stone" because they could rub it together to generate a pile of sand). It also has large cracks in it, which means that water is easy to pump out. In contrast, the soft slates weather into rounded surfaces, such as the flat-topped hill on which Benaco itself was built. The harder quartzites weather differently, and as a result form the more jagged parapets, including those surrounding the camps. Thus, for practical reasons, the camps were all perched on relatively flat hilltops of slates, rather on the jagged quartzite regions in the area. Ruden's research and the geological maps all indicated that the slates of Benaco were sitting on top of a bowl-shaped quartzite "syncline," meaning that the water-yielding quartzites were typically thousands of meters down in the ground underneath both the camp itself and the river valleys where UNICEF and the Austrians had drilled their wells. The place where the quartzites were most accessible was slightly above the camp on the lower reaches of the sharp jagged hills.

By the time Ruden arrived in February 1995, however, the UNHCR was focusing on the capacity of the Austrian rig and on finding donors to fund the major Ruvubu pipeline project. With a new burst of self-confidence with respect to water issues, generated primarily by their observation that "the only water source you can trust is the one you can see," they sent Ruden off to the Kitali Hills camp, to which water was still being trucked. A variety of personality issues arose during Ruden's brief time in Ngara, and some UNHCR staff hoped he would fail in Kitali Hills, which, as the result of other geologists' quick "window-screen" surveys from vehicles was believed not to have a groundwater supply.

Ruden remained in Kitali Hills for about three months, during which he successfully drilled and equipped enough wells to provide 12 liters per refugee per day, which was the highest in the region. He then wanted to move into the Benaco area to drill on the still unexplored quartzite ridge above the camp, which Ruden showed was the source of the springs feeding what had come to be called the "miracle lake" at the temporary Oxfam water plant. Ruden's surveys demonstrated that the reason the lake had never been pumped dry, in confoundment of everyone's fears, was that there were three springs oozing out of a "spring horizon" at an elevation of 5,250 feet. Benaco itself had a high point of about 5,100 feet, which meant that the horizon could be exploited with minimal pumping at its nearest point, a chain of ridges about four kilometers from Benaco. The replenishment of Benaco's lake had in fact little to do with miracles, and everything to do with the quartzite spring horizon. Ruden drilled these ridges in August 1995, and LWF submitted a proposal to exploit them at a cost of $400,000 for pumping and piping to Benaco to the UNHCR for funding by its donors. UNHCR did not respond, and LWF offered to pay for the pipeline from the ridges with their own money. UNHCR, focused on the Ruvubu pipeline scheme, rejected this offer too.

In the end, neither Ruden's well-field nor the pipeline were built, owing to what came to be perceived a high cost, the fact that Tanzanians felt such a water-supply system implied a permanence to the refugee camp system, and, ultimately, to the forcible repatriation in December 1996.

Ironically, throughout the period the camps were in place, the miracle lake never gave out, the well-field first drilled by the UNICEF crew continued to pump, and a cholera epidemic never materialized.

The water crisis ended, then, not because of the predicted disaster, but only when the refugees were forcibly repatriated to Rwanda. Ironically, among the reasons given for the repatriation was the high cost of maintaining refugees in Tanzania indefinitely, with water provision plans being among the most expensive items.

The Bureaucratized Good Samaritan and Water Engineering

Water engineering is a highly rationalized profession and practice, one whose nonhuman elements control what its practitioners can do. This is the source of both its effectiveness and, in the context of the international refugee relief regime, its weakness. Engineering involves calculations rooted in the physics of how machinery and materials react with the environment. Engineering faculties all over the world demand that students study a great deal of math, because, as engineering scientists are wont to point out, their activities are rooted in data that, when available, can be used to predict what a pump, pipeline, lake, river, or aquifer will produce. Engineers do not have the same leeway to overlook weaknesses and uncomfortable facts that the more human coordinating and funding agencies did. But by generating emotion, UNHCR could stimulate its donors to pay for ever more expensive project proposals. But no matter what emotions were in play, the principles of engineering did not change; drilling risks did not shift, weak planning continued to result in premature obsolescence, and broken and unused facilities accumulated.

But, engineers—unlike engineering—are remarkably human, and are subject to the same emotional demand to respond to an emergency situation as the managers of the international legal system, program administrators, and others. Engineers give in to the temptation to emphasize best- or worst-case scenarios according to or despite the lack of data. Cautiously worded "guesstimates" about yields, costs, and capacities of equipment turned into extreme claims about what could or could not be done given the expenditure of certain amounts of money. Lost were the fundamental data. The engineers accepted the inevitability of worst-case scenarios such as the lake drying up, borehole collapse, dropping water tables, cholera epidemics, etc., without qualifications.

Conclusion: Why the Mistakes

I have noted that a number of mistakes were made because engineering decisions were rushed. Were these mistakes due to incorrect hydrogeology? Or to the way hydrogeological issues were managed and funded by administrators? My contention is that the way hydrogeology and well-drilling was handled in Ngara illustrates fundamental weaknesses in the way emergency administrators seek to control nonhuman technologies and bureaucratized procedures, which they do by managing emotional appeals. First, a quick review of the mistakes:

1. The UNICEF crew chose low spots for drilling without any attention to the hydrogeology of the area. This meant that they drilled only slates in locations remote from the camps, even though quartzite ridges were also nearby.
2. Engineers made a commonsense assumption that the lake would not sustain continued pumping during the dry season, without making any survey of where water in the lake was actually coming from.
3. Consistent with practice elsewhere, UNICEF well-drillers lined only for the first 50 meters of the wells, again, without reference to the nature of local geological conditions, with the result that wells began to collapse.
4. The ultimate refugee population was grossly underestimated.

The assumption that the tedious work of geological survey could be short-circuited and quick surveys substituted led to three of the mistakes. Some shortcuts can be taken, but doing this ultimately implies an acceptance of greater risks of failure. The fourth mistake stemmed from the fact that engineering procedures proceed on the basis of specific population figures, and at Ngara, the population to be served could not be accurately forecast, despite the best efforts of UNHCR.

But the water problems in Ngara were not merely mistakes of hydrogeology. A bigger mistake was a failure to appreciate how much control technology exerts on a situation. Just within the water sector, the amount of equipment that was procured and quickly abandoned was considerable: items such as the mothballed reverse osmosis unit from the U.S. Army, the spare Japanese drilling rigs, and an entire water-trucking unit. When the technology asserted its built-in control over the situation, the technology won, regardless of how enthusiastic the engineers may have been originally. Each potential solution was greeted with enthusiasm, to the extent that demands for sound surveying and technique were suspended. Indeed, precisely the sidestepping of such requirements when the UNICEF rig arrived in May 1994 permitted the establishment of more camps, which greatly facilitated Tanzania's ability to receive refugees. That gamble was, to a certain degree, won, and time was gained. But the time wasn't used. The mistake was that the pattern of decision-making never changed once the UNICEF wells in effect gave technicians a window of opportunity to be more careful and follow standard operating procedures. Rather, technicians continued to suspend engineering assumptions. The result was more and faster purchases of equipment. Donors were also caught up in the crisis atmosphere, and willingly funded each new program without a critical evaluation.

Was the Water Situation in Ngara Unique?

My thoughts with respect to water provision go back to my time in Thai refugee camps in 1982–83. In each of the camps I observed, there were massive water systems that were inappropriate to the situation. The most egregious example was the white elephant the Japanese installed in Khao I Dang camp for Cambodians in 1980: a complete water system was installed before any drilling began. Water was not found in the boreholes, and the result was a multi-million-dollar water system that went unused. Compounding that error was the institution of a costly water-trucking program that in 1983 was still trucking water to a camp located in the middle of soggy rice fields. Other camps throughout Thailand were littered with equipment that had been abandoned or was only partially utilized. And in many Thai camps there was still no operating water system (Waters 1984). The magnitude of the "mistakes" was far beyond what happened in Ngara. At least in Ngara water continually flowed from both Oxfam's temporary water plant and the poorly sited boreholes.

At the time, I noted, with youthful temerity, that none of this made much sense. I ran around the Thai camps asking anyone who knew anything about it why it had happened. Everyone shrugged, and indicated that bad decisions had been made, which probably involved kickbacks and corruption. The engineers assumed that proper engineering would have resulted in better results. As with the situation in Tanzania, none of the people involved with the original "emergency"-phase construction project were still around; less than three years later, no one knew who on the UNHCR or Japanese staff had approved the original construction plan for Khao I Dang and was around to answer these questions. Presumably, as in Tanzania, staff turnover during the emergency had been rapid, short-term consultancies had been numerous, and, as a result, institutional memory was nonexistent. Frustrated, and with a youthful bravado, I even railed about Khao I Dang and the other water systems failures in the journal *Disasters* in 1984 (see Waters 1984). All to no effect, I believe. The article was soundly ignored, and I have yet to hear a comment from someone who actually read it. Nor has it been cited in the few publications written about refugee camp water provision (see Chalinder 1994).

The pattern of unused water systems in Thai camps and the chronic lack of usable equipment for refugee camps in Tanzania indicates to me that the inability to implement complex engineering projects is a general phenomenon throughout the international refugee relief regime. This institutional weakness is part and parcel of the international refugee relief regime, and this is reflected in how the regime uses engineering science. Is this related to the bureaucratization of humanitarian activities? Is the nature of "technological control" useful in understanding the problems that emerged? My answer of course is yes. But understanding this question requires taking a critical look at how engineering science controls a context, and in particular water engineering. Water engineering is about buying and installing equipment that can deliver specific and predictable quantities of water. Built in to the technology are assumptions about what information the engineer will have available. This is the "control" that technology asserts over its human actors, including engineers. This control asserts itself, no matter what. To buy the right pump, the engineer needs to know how much water is available, how long the pipeline will be, how many water taps there will be, and how high the water will be pumped. To find out these numbers, time-consuming planning must be done: wells must be pump-tested, sites for water taps identified, and surveys done.

If the engineer guesses (or doesn't know) any of these numbers, the risk that the pump will not be appropriate increases. Or, as in the case of Ngara, if the planning is done, but then demands for water quickly shift because of increasing numbers of refugees or changing political desires, the data collected become less useful. The equipment that was bought under the previous assumptions joins the heaps of abandoned equipment in warehouses. This exertion of control by the technology is what happened in Tanzania, and probably in Khao I Dang in Thailand.

Does it explain how the international refugee relief regime seeks to relieve suffering elsewhere? In sociological terms, is there a common structural explanation for why refugee systems broke down? This subject will be taken up again in Chapters 12–14.

Notes

1. As engineers are quick to point out, neglecting water supply and sanitation has profound consequences. Lack of attention to the tools of the water engineer is a prerequisite for epidemics of the water-borne disease that holds a special terror: cholera. Cholera has rarely been seen in epidemic form in the West since the nineteenth century, yet control of the massive and devastating cholera epidemics of nineteenth-century Europe continues to have a special place in public health and water engineering textbooks. One of the great triumphs of nineteenth-century en-

gineering was the creation of the clean piped-water systems that made modern urban life healthful and long (see McNeill 1977). The quick and horrible death caused by cholera added to the mystique that the disease held for the sanitarians and water engineers (see press descriptions quoted in Prunier 1995:302–305).

This why in the minds off sanitarians and water engineers, cholera and the control of sanitation disease holds a unique place as a threat to refugee populations. The mix of professional mystification, the emergency context, and the clear importance of providing water permit water engineers to exaggerate the centrality of their trade without challenge. Vacuous superlatives like "Water is the single most important provision for any population; people can survive much longer without food than they can without water" (Chalinder 1984:8) are published and treated as policy touchstones, and cited in meetings to justify the expansion of water equipment purchases. In Tanzania, fears of sanitation disease justified large expenditures for water supply equipment without doing preliminary engineering. Ngara is a good example of this dynamic, though it should be emphasized that the introduction of the emotional need to save lives through water provision is a general phenomenon in emergency operations. Again, the pattern of mistakes emerges systematically out of the poor fit between the need for emotional need to "save lives now" and the methodological requirements of water engineering.

2. In November 1995, the Tanganyika Christian Refugee Service Water Development Unit noted that the "Benaco Dam" was "by far most successful water point" in the area. The lake had in fact been created by a dam that had been built by the Italian Benaco Construction Company when they constructed a highway in the early 1990s (see TCRS Water Development Unit 1995:8). Presumably an engineers' report on the dam-siting process is buried somewhere in the archives of either the Benaco Construction Company or the Tanzanian government. As far as I know, though, no effort was made to locate such a report in 1994–95.

3. According to *JEEAR* (1996:77), "In Ngara, water provision was initially at least a success story. . . that provided satisfactory levels of water in the camp. . . ." The water and sanitation report generated on June 18, 1994, by the UNHCR indicated that 300,000 refugees were being supplied with 5.5 liters per person per day. This was before the first refugee census, though; the actual population was probably about 200,000 at that time, and the water ration on the order of 7.5 to 8.0 liters per refugee. The memo of July 29 indicated that 200,000 refugees were left in Benaco (decreases were due to transfers to Lumasi and downward population estimates following a census). The total supplied on that date was 12.7 liters per refugee in Benaco and 11 liters per refugee in Lumasi. A memorandum I wrote indicates that in September, a total of 2.6 million liters per day were being provided to 300,000 to 350,000 refugees.

4. Despite high rainfall levels in Ngara (the rainy season typically lasts from October to May, and about one meter falls each year), there are few lakes or small streams. Most of the rainfall quickly seeps into underground aquifers, runs off into the Ruvubu River, or seeps into the sandy quartzite formations around the camps. As a result, it was not possible to expand refugee camping areas without searching for groundwater.

5. Quartzite stone start out as pure quartz sand, are then buried, and then are heated over millions of years. During this process, the sand turns into a very hard

but brittle rock called quartzite. When bent by geologic forces, this rock cracks easily, permitting the ready flow of underground water (see TCRS 1995).

6. This comes from an August 1, 1994, memo to UNHCR head of sub-office Rick Garlock from Gerry Garvey, an Oxfam technical team leader. Quoting UNICEF statistics, Garvey noted that the total yield for the well-field was expected to be 119 cubic meters per hour. On August 8, Andy Bastable, Oxfam's acting technical leader, began to express Oxfam's reservations about whether the well-field would be sustainable. Nevertheless, he continued to express hopes that 10 liters per refugee could be supplied.

7. The census figure of 229,000 had recently been released by the UNHCR. It was assumed that the number of refugees would not continue to rise much beyond this figure, as at that time it appeared that the war in Rwanda would end soon. The assumption that more refugees would not arrive turned out to be false (see Chapter 9 for a discussion of the difficulty of predicting refugee movements).

8. In response to a perception of slow delivery times and higher costs, at the request of the UNHCR, and on the recommendation of the engineer on the spot, in early 1995 LWF shifted orders from Monopump UK to Monopump South Africa. The assumption was that spares would be interchangeable between the two pumps. In fact, there was only limited interchangeability, as one pump was "left-hand drive" and the other was "right-hand drive." Thus, a third type of pump and a separate spares inventory were added to the program.

9. A damper was initially put on the cholera scare by Rick Garlock, who was on temporary assignment to Ngara as a UNHCR head of suboffice. He pointed out calmly that cholera was inevitable in the context of a crowded refugee camp situation like Benaco, and the trick was to be prepared to isolate, control, and treat cholera, rather than cast blame about. In this context, UNHCR funded the establishment of cholera isolation units by MSF agencies, a brief study of a large pipeline to the camps, and the hiring of a well-drilling rig from eastern Tanzania.

Garlock left in late September, and the UNHCR was left without a leader until Maureen Connelly returned in early November. Connelly was much more susceptible to the pleas of water engineers to fund expensive solutions to what came to be termed the "water crisis." Her experience in April–July had also given her experience in the uses of crisis to shake loose otherwise tight donor cash. The water-crisis red flag worked: in her first weeks back, donors funded the rental of two well-drilling rigs from Tanzania, water-truck rentals, water-truck purchases, a water-trucking scheme, and an Austrian-funded well-drilling program.

Ultimately, 1 case of cholera was treated by MSF–Spain in the cholera isolation unit before November 7, and between December 12 and December 19, 63 suspected cases treated there. The peak day was December 15, when 10 cases were referred. All cases were the result of close personal contact; none was caused by contamination of the general water supply.

10. Similar units were provided by the United States in the Kosovo emergency in May 1999. See Kosovo Fact Sheet #52, 17 May 1999, USAID.

11. R. W. Treves of Water Surveys Botswana was one of several consultants who assessed the well situation. A subcontractor paid for by UNHCR via Oxfam, he described a chaotic drilling situation in a December 1994 trip report, but

blamed the problem on a lack of technical specifications rather than a more general problem with overall planning, which, admittedly was beyond his purview:

> There are two drilling rigs currently working at Ngara. The Benwell rig [One of two private Tanzanian drilling companies which was hired by TCRS with UNHCR funds] is under-powered for the job and is considered incapable of drilling boreholes to specification. An alternative design has been produced so that they can drill temporary boreholes at Ngara. . . . The operators of the Japanese rig are not considered capable of drilling successfully at Ngara so it is suggested that their rig is assessed to see if it is capable of drilling the required holes. If it is, trained personnel should be found to operate this rig.
>
> Three other drilling rigs have been asked to come to work at Ngara. Two of these are NGO rigs, the first is from Austria and representatives of this rig are believed to be on site at present (13/12/94). . . . The other is a Norwegian rig and is expected to arrive in Ngara in January 1995 . . .
>
> A commercial rig (Afridrill) presently drilling at Ngara for mineral exploration has also been asked to drill water supply holes for the camps. The money for this rig is ready and the owners should be contacted again. . . .
>
> The drilling program at Ngara has suffered because of the failure of agencies to write binding technical specifications. . . . Even though drilling NGO's such as AAR [Austrian NGO] they . . . must also be bound to a technical specification so that their work fits in with the overall site plan. They should not have been invited to drill at Ngara without a specialist confirming that they were capable of completing the work.

In his report, Treves did not assess the recharge of water into the lake at Benaco. This job was at the time considered outside the purview of a hydrogeologist.

12. In my role as an administrator for LWF, I visited the Austrian geologist at his office in Benaco in February 1995 after he had been in Tanzania a few weeks. I had the geological maps of the area, which he had not seen, and specifically asked why he had not considered drilling on the quartzite ridge that was visible from the office door. Even though maps had been available in the area for the previous six months, none had been given to him.

13. In a July 15, 1995, document prepared with Daniel Mora-Castro of UNHCR–Geneva, a comprehensive drilling program was also proposed in addition to the $5.1 million pipeline. The total cost of the program to drill and equip wells was estimated at $5 million. The aim of this program was to provide 20 liters per refugee per day to about 226,000 refugees in nine camps outside the Ngara area. Despite the continuing lack of a formal hydrogeological analysis in Ngara, the memo noted (falsely) that the lake at Benaco dries up in the dry season. Neither of the well-drilling schemes nor the river pumping proposals were ever funded.

11

Bureaucratizing the Good Samaritan: Defining Genocide

Introduction

In December 1997, Secretary of State Madeline Albright said that the West should have defined the events in Rwanda as genocide earlier, for example, in April–May 1994, when it was actually happening. Had this determination been made, legal obligations would have been triggered requiring the United States to react to what was happening in Rwanda, potentially including a politically unpalatable military action. Albright was strongly implying that those who said that the United States was "chicken" in the wake of the Somalia debacle and therefore failed to respond to Rwanda were correct (see Destexhe 1996; MSF 1994; Adelman and Suhrke 1996).

Albright and others may be right in assuming the United States was chicken. But it does not completely explain the failure to do something about the situation in Rwanda. Even in the complete absence of "Somalia Syndrome," bureaucratic, legal, political, and diplomatic institutions must react quickly if they are to stop a fast genocide such as that which occurred in Rwanda in April–May 1994. Acting quickly means that there is little room for gray areas—hat somehow international law, diplomacy, and the bureaucracies supporting them can work together like the parts of a clock. This assumes that all involved entities and their staff are honest, fearless, and act in good faith. Can the bureaucracies concerned do this? More specifically, can they do this in a situation like the Rwanda genocide? Can a specialized legal bureaucracy quickly assert control over the process of differentiating genocide, war crimes, war, exactions, collateral damage, and the other plausible categories of violent events in a context like that in Rwanda?

But there is no such bureaucracy, as war criminals from Cambodia, Ethiopia, Somalia, and a host of other countries are well aware; the

process of systematically categorizing different types of violent death internationally has yet to be bureaucratized. Albright's statement ignores what is known about the slow and often muddled process by which events become rationalized and bureaucratized. Bureaucratized law moves slowly; even a mundane thief cannot be classified as such until after a lengthy and bureaucratic procedure in which a court assigns the label.

Genocide, the greatest of crimes, is even more difficult to define, even when evidence is presented clearly. When confronted with evidence of the Holocaust in 1942, Supreme Court Justice Felix Frankfurter said: "I do not believe you. . . . I do not mean that you are lying, I simply said I cannot believe you" (quoted in Shawcross 1984:47). With the benefit of hindsight, Albright seems to be assuming that somehow both this disbelief in the face of great evil can be suspended and that the bureaucratic mechanisms of law can be brought to bear on a case like Rwanda. The bureaucratized Good Samaritan, though, is probably not efficient in the manner implied by Albright. Examining how the violence and genocide were evaluated in Ngara illustrates why this is so.

Classification of unusual events, criminal or not, inherently occur as a halting process in which events are cognitively framed in various ways:

- What has occurred,
- What is familiar? Are there "frames" that can serve as precedents for thinking about these occurrences?
- What is expected or hoped for?
- What are the legal precedents (in the case of events involving the law)?

Such framing occurs within a legal bureaucracy specialized to accomplish this task: even in the case of an ordinary liquor store robbery this process of definition can be uncertain, imprecise, and halting. In the case of extraordinary events like a genocide, the process is even more halting—mistakes and miscalculations occur in framing—before what actually happened is categorized (Goffman 1974:33).

Opposite: Only one of the over 900 bodies from the Kagera River Body Recovery Project was identified, that of Ngirabatware, son of Rubashurwekere of Cyabingu, Ruhengeri prefecture. This card was found in the pants of a victim in August 1994. The card indicates that he was born in 1957, was a peasant, and a Hutu. He had four daughters, born between 1980 and 1992.

The lower photograph is of a body found floating in the Kagera River in March 1995. (Photo by Tony Waters.)

Recognition, identification, and labeling the Rwanda killings as the legal category "genocide" in fact took about four weeks; six more weeks passed before the first intervention by the international community, that of the French military, which secured the southwest corner of Rwanda. Unlike Albright, I think that the process of identifying what happened in Rwanda as genocide happened fairly quickly. I was sitting on the edge of it, watching body after body come down the river, and to be honest, I did not recognize it as genocide. Possibly I was stupid; more likely, though, the actual process of classification is bureaucratic, and framing disparate incidents accurately is therefore uncertain, imprecise, and halting.

In the case of the Rwanda genocide, I argue in this chapter that the delays in legal diagnosis and response had several causes in addition to the "chicken" issue identified publicly by Albright. Notably, these causes are rooted in the very nature of the bureaucratized Good Samaritan.

The first reason that the West did not respond with a quick recognition and labeling was the pattern of obfuscation inherent in the perpetration of genocide. It has been well documented in Europe and Rwanda that the language of genocide was hidden by means of language developed for the purpose of veiling it (see Prunier 1995:239–252). For example, Prunier (1995:241) writes about the "pattern familiar to those seeking to deny genocide. . . . When talking to your supporters, never claim 'credit' for what you are actually doing but hint at the great benefits derived from the nameless thing which has been done, sharing complicity in the unspoken secret with your audience." An example Prunier (1995:241n) offers is a speech by "Provisional President" Theodore Sindikubwabo of Rwanda in a speech he made in May 1994, congratulating his audience on "the return to a quiet situation . . . now that all the troublemakers have been dealt with."

Second, there is a normal confusion in separating types of mass killing into relevant categories. As Justice Frankfurter implied, this is an unusual cognitive task. It involves differentiating events like genocide, mass murder, civil war, collateral damage, exactions, military conflict, summary execution, retribution killings; all terms that carry potentially either euphemistic or dysphemistic meaning.

Thus, in response to the Secretary of State, I will write about how the Rwanda genocide looked from late April 1994 until October 1995, from two perspectives: first, I will give the standard story that has emerged out of scholarly sources, along with better-known accounts of Prunier, des Forges, and others, who provide syntheses and conclusions about events. These analyses are the result of the after-the-fact compilation of what witnesses observed in their own daily interactions.

Second, I will offer a personal account of what I heard and saw in Tanzania between 1994 and 1996. This personal account will I think illustrate how unusual and horrific events become framed as genocide or something else. I myself did not have the cognitive tools to recognize a genocide even as it was literally floating past me in the Kagera River. Rather than a naïveté in the face of the obvious, though, I think that my reaction reflects the fact that a genocide can be observed only from afar. The problem is that as emotionalized Good Samaritans we were expected to make such judgments (see Chapter 4), even though as individuals we did not have the training or bureaucratic tools to do so. Those of us close to events were focused only on the events occurring in our immediate vicinity. But legal classification occurs at a distance, from which perspective is possible, in a bureaucratized prosecutor's office and courtroom, but also in the press and within the purview of international politics.

Genocide and the Rwanda Crisis Unfold

Through 1993, Rwanda's President Habyarimana attempted to convene a government in accord with the August 1993 Arusha Accords. Political observers disagree as to whether his failure was deliberate or not, but what is known is that by the beginning of 1994, Habyarimana was a fading figure, unable to pull his more radical Hutu followers into compliance with the agreements he had negotiated. Distrust of Habyarimana came from both his military opponents in the RPF and as members of his own party opposed to any power-sharing agreements. In early 1994, Hutu radicals associated with Habyarimana instigated killings that included assassinations of opposition leaders and street riots. Indeed, even as Habyarimana continued his public attempts to implement the Arusha power-sharing agreement, rumors of a "final solution" in the works began to be heard in Kigali. The rumors were loud enough that the UNAMIR commanders like General Romeo Dallaire heard them and transmitted warnings to UN headquarters in New York in March 1994.[1]

However, international attention in the region was not directed at the Rwandan situation, but on South Africa, which had elections scheduled for April 1994. In fact, in its April 9, 1994, issue, *The Economist* in its lead article trumpeted fears of a South African bloodbath, while the death of the Rwandan president and the killings received only brief mention in the back pages. Also, in October 1993, Burundi's first democratically elected government was overthrown by that country's Tutsi-dominated military, working through the Uprona (Parti de l'Union et du Progrès National) party. This crisis led to the death of approximately 50,000 to 100,000 Hutu and Tutsi and the flight of some 750,000 refugees to Rwanda, Zaire, and Tanzania (MSF 1995; Prunier 1995:198–212; Lemarchand 1994:xvi–xix). This quickly mushrooming crisis became the regional focus for peacemaking; the large numbers of deaths and the refugee situation meant that diplomatic circles probably interpreted the Burundian crisis as being the more dangerous of the two ongoing crises in Africa. Rumors of a repeat of the October–November massacres in Burundi were common throughout early 1994, and when President Ali Hassan Mwinyi of Tanzania called the regional leaders to Dar es Salaam, Tanzania, for a meeting on early April 6, 1994, it was for a discussion of Burundian as well as the Rwandan problems.

It is easy to say in hindsight that as of April 6, the genocide was beginning. But consider how things would look to you if, like the journalist Marc-Daniel Gutekunst, you were hiding on the streets of Kigali and were phoning reports outside the country. You might observe what Gutekunst (1995) did in early April:

- The presidents of two countries are dead, killed by a mysterious rocket attack.
- Government sources are claiming that the attack on the presidents is the result of RPF treachery.
- RPF radio speaks of a southward military thrust in order to rescue their beleaguered garrison, threatens to fight any French soldiers brought into the country as peacekeepers, and refuses to participate in any negotiations.
- You wonder about the perilous status of Burundi, which only days before had also been a focus of attention and concern.
- You probably remember that the last death of a Burundian president (six months previously) resulted in major massacres and refugee flight.
- You are probably aware of gangs of Hutu militia with lists of specific individuals' name, seeking these people out to kill them. You might be aware that the people on these lists are members of opposition political parties or are of Tutsi ethnic identity.
- Perhaps you hope for help from the United Nations' UNAMIR military forces. But you also are aware that they do not have a mandate or enough weapons to make a significant stand.
- Most immediately, you are worrying about your own safety, and that of the people in your immediate vicinity.

You do not have the big-picture view that would allow you to identify the legal conditions for defining the events around you as a genocide, mass murder, chaos, or general military action. Certainly you do not have enough evidence to form an opinion of legal intent. Nor do you have detailed information from the countryside where Hutu militia are also being sent as part of the genocide. These uncertainties are probably why *The Economist* avoided using the word "genocide" until its May 21 issue. Nevertheless, as Prunier (1995:265) points out, during the next six weeks (from April 7 to mid-May) 500,000 to 800,000 people were killed, most of them Tutsi who were victims of militia units conducting what is now identified as the genocide. But again this is a retrospective estimate. Even RPF radio claimed that the killings were "political, not ethnic" (*The Economist*, April 16), and even the RPF also underestimated the number of dead as late as May 15 at 300,000 (Prunier 1995:262).[2] Outside estimates were even more scarce. Prunier's "first estimates" were based on observations made by Kigali garbage collectors (60,000 bodies picked up by mid-May), and a vague reference to 40,000 bodies buried at the mouth of the Kagera River in western Uganda.[3] The first credible estimate of 1 million dead came on August 24 (Prunier 1995:262–263).

Meanwhile, the term "genocide" has become so overused that it is difficult to separate its rhetorical from legal usage.[4] As far as I can tell the first time that this term was used was on May 2 in the *International Herald Tribune* by a writer from Human Rights Watch. She made the now-obvious point that the war and the genocide were two separate events, and that calling for a military cease-fire did not necessarily stop the genocide.

But the clear-cut nature of these body-count numbers is only part of the story. Besides a body count, a genocide requires the identification of a perpetrator with the power to have an explicit policy of eliminating an ethnic group. In retrospect, it seems obvious that this condition was met by the circumstances. But at the time, with a paucity of reliable sources, efforts to obfuscate genocidal intention on the part of the perpetrators, a simultaneous civil war, spectacular exodus of Hutu refugees to Tanzania, and a conquering army concerned with issues of control, revenge, and exaction, the picture was not coherent.

Refugee Reports

The first major source of information in April–June 1994 was fleeing refugees. Refugees began to appear in Karagwe district of northwestern Tanzania shortly after April 8. Almost by definition, refugees are of one political/ethnic persuasion or the other.[5] As a result, the veracity of their accounts is inevitably treated with skepticism. Their information also tends to be very localized, which renders it of limited use in making generalizations about widespread genocidal intent.[6] Actually observing a violent death is a traumatic experience, in which the most common response is to hide or leave without observing more. The Tutsi who arrived first in Tanzania, the few survivors of what was later called "the genocide," provided explicit accounts of this nature. Also appearing in Tanzania as refugees, however, were Hutu claiming to fear the advancing RPF, who they said were massacring as they advanced. These claims were filtered through the reporting apparatus of the humanitarian agencies, which also had ideas about how the events in Rwanda should be framed.

As the RPF pushed south during April 1994, this combination of refugees: first small numbers of Tutsi, and then Hutu—continued to appear. Finally, large numbers of refugees began to accumulate behind the one bridge from Rwanda to Tanzania at Rasumo. Aerial photos of the bridge broadcast by CNN showed masses of people poised to leave Rwanda, but prevented by Rwandan government (Hutu) border guards from crossing. On April 28 the border guards abandoned the bridge, and during the next hours masses surged into Tanzania. The vast majority were Hutu, but small numbers were Tutsi.[7]

The inherent confusion is revealed in the reports collected by Prunier (1995:265–267) in late 1994. He did this to illustrate what he then saw as the complicity of the international community with the genocidal Hutu government. He also did it to illustrate the disarray among UNHCR and NGO officials confronted with over 100,000 refugees in Tanzania. But these observations illustrate more clearly the disarray inherent in assessing a confusing situation. Therefore, I use his examples here for a different purpose than the one he intended: to illustrate the framing process inherent to the bureaucratic and legal definition of a series of events as constituting genocide. Note that each of the observers is trying to identify inferences that can be made from the only information that they have: stories and observations of refugees arriving in Tanzania.

- On May 3, the UNHCR official Panos Moumtzis observed that few refugees were wounded, so he inferred that the Hutu refugees had not been attacked as a group (Prunier 1995:265). (Moumtzis had been in Ngara less than four days).
- On May 21, the UNHCR field officer Jasper Jensen inferred from the few wounds on people crossing rivers and swamps that the RPF was doing a "clean job," i.e., their killing did not result in very many wounded, but most people who were attacked died. Jensen apparently believed what he was told by the Hutu refugees he had been trying to assist during the two weeks he was in Ngara (Prunier 1995:265–266).
- Marc Prutsalis of Refugees International on May 20 cautiously took an opposite view based on the same lack of information. His inferences reflected an emerging view that reports of RPF atrocities could be discounted. The reasons he gave were (1) the quality of translators, (2) lack of eyewitness accounts by expatriates to RPF killings, (3) the fear factor of contradicting accounts of refugee leaders, and (4) the possibility that some (though not all) refugees are guilty themselves of committing atrocities

(Prunier 1995:266). (At the time seniority among us expatriates was measured in terms of days. Prutsalis arrived in Ngara on the same plane I did on May 2, but reached the opposite conclusion as Jensen.)[8]

Sociology 101 in Ngara:
The Rise and Fall of Random Sampling

I watched the April 28–29 exodus across the Rasumo bridge on CNN while on an airplane over the Atlantic. I had been hired two weeks earlier by the Lutheran World Federation as a logistics officer, in response to the Burundi refugee crisis, which was still seen as a threat. On May 2 I was dropped into the camps nearest the Rasumo Bridge in Ngara district. Being there was something of a dream come true for me as a sociologist long interested in the social world of refugee assistance programs. It was more confusing for me as a normal human being in the process of observing the process of violent death. All of this social interaction was before me. How to observe and make sense of it? Whom to believe? There were Tanzanian villagers, and the newly arrived UN expatriates. Red Cross expatriates and missionaries were there who had watched events unfold. There were refugees.

I made several observations while coming to grips with the idea of genocide. Not everything seen and heard fits easily into such a category; nevertheless, it is important to use that term: seen from the big-picture perspective, the government of Rwanda did implement a program to kill all Tutsi in that country. However, as I will show, in the field, the concept of genocide is still of little practical use for classifying people or ordering daily activity.

My Life as a Witness to Genocide

In the terms of social science, what lawyers and some diplomats do when framing genocide is collect evidence from various sources. A prosecutor then groups it together in order to present an theoretically grounded inference of guilt or innocence. This theory is then evaluated by a court of some sort. Different courts have different criteria for reaching different conclusions. For example, American courts and those of many other countries assume that *individual* guilt is proved "beyond a reasonable doubt," and that evidence is collected under carefully specified rules of search and seizure. While slow, this court has at least two advantages. First, there is little doubt about the legitimacy of its conclusions. Second, it protects the rights of the innocent. Finally, conclusions about groups are avoided by carefully assigning responsibility to the individual.

At another extreme is the more general "court of public opinion." The requirements of the court of public opinion in which the term "genocide" has been used has vague criteria for decisions, assigns collective and individual guilt, has vague rules of evidence, etc. The ability to punish, though, is limited to public humiliation, and development of prejudice and unflattering stereotypes. Legitimacy may be specific only to a particular community, and for only a short period of time.

Both courts are involved in weighing observations collected from the field before framing an issue. Both necessarily discount data that doesn't fit a theory of guilt or innocence. The following account of what I saw and heard about violent death during my time in Tanzania serves to illustrate the random nature of field-level observations, made before a "theory" has emerged to string observations together; to illustrate the extent to which genocide is a bureaucratized legal conclusion, and not a "social fact" that can be observed in the field.

May 2, 1994: Arrival in Ngara

Flying into the area in a small plane, we circled over a camp of orderly white tents. These were the 10,000 Burundian refugees who had arrived the previous year. I was amazed at the size of the camp! Then we flew over the Rwandan camp. We were told that there were 250,000 people scattered in a field. The camp was disorderly. They had no food. No water. No toilets. From the air the people looked like pieces of tissue paper tossed on the fields.

We then landed at a dirt airstrip. We drove past the Burundian camp and straight to the Rwandan camp. What to do? We were a carload of Tanzanians and three expatriates (me, an Irish manager/engineer, and an Ethiopian policy-maker from LWF Geneva headquarters). What were we looking at? My fellow expatriates wondered out loud how many of the Hutu were guilty of mass murder and speculated about whether you could see it in their eyes. I saw a lot of women and children, and wondered what proportion of the population they were. (Later censuses indicated about 70 percent were women and children under 15). I shouted for someone who could speak Swahili and a middle-aged male refugee in the back came forward to chat. He was from Rwanda and wanted to know if any help would come. He was a Hutu, and this was the third or fourth refugee camp that he had lived in since being displaced from his farm by the RPF in northeastern Rwanda in 1992. His name was Leonidas and he obviously knew more than I did. At his request, I took a picture of him and his family.

Next, we took a trip down to the Kagera River. We stopped first at the Tanzanian border post, where there was a large pile of machetes and hoes seized from the refugees. The RPF had controlled the bridge for three days, stopping the direct exodus, although it was clear that along the road refugees were still sneaking across the river and marshes and making their way to the camp. One of my colleagues, the engineer, made a count. Something like 50 refugees along the road in three minutes while we were traveling 60 kilometers (37 miles) per hour. Twenty minutes later we arrived at the river, and wondered what we could do and see. There was a war going on across the river and we had all heard reports of bodies in the river. The river was at full flood from the rains, and we stood above the falls about 300 meters from the river, wary of approaching the river-border itself. Something brown floated by. My more experienced colleagues insisted that it was a body. We stood watching with a few other observers. I did not know whether I was a witness to history, or just plain silly, and I had sincere doubts about how to present myself. I wondered whether it could be a log floating down the flood-swelled river.

We drove for an hour and discussed what we had seen. My engineer colleague asked how many bodies we saw. I responded, "Something like ten or fifteen." He asked me how long we were there. I had forgotten to check my watch but glibly responded, "Oh, maybe ten or fifteen minutes." He observed that that worked out to 42 per hour which is about 1,000 per day. Two years later, I saw a film in which this number actually appeared. That day, though, I still wondered whether they were logs, even though my Ethiopian colleague insisted they were bodies. He was right, but I did not acknowledge this to myself until later.

After an hour or so, we drove up to a mission compound where a UN flag was flying. Inside was a hub of activity. My more senior colleagues went inside to start negotiating with the UNHCR for a piece of the relief action. I chatted with Marc Prutsalis of Refugees International, who was trying hard to figure out how many refugees had fled, and was looking for a way to get a number back to his headquarters in Washington.

In hopes of helping Marc Prutsalis out, and to practice my Swahili, I wandered off and asked a Tanzanian villager who like most of us was hanging around. He told me that the people hanging around were refugees fleeing from Rwanda. I asked someone from the UNHCR what all of the refugees were doing. The person from the UNHCR told me that they were Tanzanians, that the refugees were not here and were all down by the river. Besides, refugees were not supposed to come to this office, but go straight to the camp 40 kilometers (25 miles) away, as this was the only place the UN would offer assistance.

I chatted with the villager some more. He assured me that they were Rwandan refugees coming up from the valley past the UNHCR office because it is a traditional route for casual trade from Rwanda. But, he said, this is the first afternoon that they crossed this far south in flight from the fighting in Rwanda. I asked him how many refugees there were in the large valley below us. He said with passion, "Lots." In the interest of helping Marc, or perhaps someone else, I pressed him for a number, and he responded, "Lots and lots." I started to laugh out loud when I realized that I had just heard the most statistically accurate report of the day.

It was drizzling. I asked the villager what the refugees should do besides stand around. He indicated that this was somehow my responsibility; so because no one else was doing anything, the two of us went and found the school principal and asked him what he was going to do. He said that they could sleep on the concrete floor of the rundown open-air school building. Later I mentioned to one of the expatriates what the teacher had done. The expatriate recommended strongly against doing this because, in his experience, refugees would use the few pieces of schoolhouse furniture for firewood. (Some days later, I checked to see if this had happened. It hadn't. The refugees stayed in the school for the next week or so and restricted their firewood procurement to groves of eucalyptus in the village.)

Another snippet I remember:

On May 2 there were no markets in camp; the only thing I could find for sale was locally brewed beer and a Spanish peseta coin that a refugee wanted to exchange. When I returned on May 4, though, markets were in full swing despite the fact that food distributions had yet to start. By May 4, there were established exchange rates between the Tanzanian shilling and Rwandan franc and a market full of items carried out of Rwanda. Tanzanians were beginning to arrive in order to buy electronics and other items at bargain rates. The economic historian Eric Jones, with his faith in market economy, would be fascinated by the phenomenon.

May 5: Moving into Benaco

Late one afternoon, I was dumped at the edge of the Benaco camp with tools, tents, a Tanzanian senior staff member, three Catholic nuns, and Tanzanian drivers. We had vague instructions to set up a camp. This was easier said than done. I had diarrhea and lay down in the small shade of a bush in order get out of the hot sun. Refugees quickly rushed over to give me a mat to lie on. Vaguely I was aware that the group was organized by Leonidas, the refugee man whose picture I had taken on my first day. Within an hour I also had the only private toilet in a community of what was said to be 250,000. I was a guest of the refugees, and the norms of hospitality reigned.

Dinnertime in Benaco

Toward dusk, there was a commotion behind our tent as 20 to 30 men aggressively jumped on something. There was nowhere for me to run as tales of these refugees' involvement in the ongoing killing passed through my head. For lack of any reasonable thing to do, I wandered over from my bush, wondering whether I needed to do the humanitarian thing and rescue a Tutsi, but not having a clue as to how to go about doing it. In the center of the men I finally saw it, a bloody carcass in the middle, which they are ripping apart by pulling on the limbs. It was a small antelope—called a *duiker.* It had rushed into the tent of a Rwandan Tutsi nun, Sister Agnes, who was part of our encampment. Confused, it had punched a hole through the back of the tent. This was just enough time for the hungry refugees to corral it, and then tear it apart with their hands—all tools used for butchering had been seized at the border.

Sister Agnes

Sister Agnes had been assigned to a school in central Tanzania and was in Benaco to see whether she could find news of nuns from her order who had lived in Kigali. She had heard rumors that the Catholic church had been targeted by Hutu *Interahamwe*, but news of specific convents had not yet developed. She never did find any survivors in Benaco, so instead, she walked around the predominantly Hutu camp trying to comfort whomever she could. I passed along to her the names of several Rwandan Hutu who were relatives a Ph.D. student in Davis. She was unable to find news of them.

VIPs, the Press, and Me

One morning, on about May 14, the UNHCR coordinator, Maureen Connelly, came around one of the cloth warehouses we were erecting. She was escorting the Irish (or was it Dutch?) minister for development cooperation. I said hi, as I did not know what else to say. He was dazed by the whole experience. So was I. VIP and press were common. *Time* and *New York Times* stringers both asked to file stories on our satellite phone and promised to pay us for the cost (they never did).

All press were looking for the quick, concise story that would fill a news slot, or generate pressure on the public to donate to the cause of Rwandan refugee relief. During the first months, I was the subject of films, a satellite phone interview on VISN and the BBC, and a feature story in the German edition of *Geo* magazine. At one point, a stringer from *Time* magazine intent on having a photo of a white hand distributing pastries to new refugees also took pictures of me. CNN cameras were in our camp at one point, and one Sunday morning, a reporter from the *Christian Science Monitor* chanced by. Some material was eventually used, most was not. In retrospect, I will confess to liking the attention even though their stories did not fit my idea of the sociological "complexity" very well.

Agencies and Expatriates Evaluate

The emergency agencies—UNHCR, CARE, MSF, IFRC—were quick to grab the limelight. They had press agents to draw attention to their activities, and contract managers ready to pounce on donors flush with cash. Their cars had large agency stickers, and crisp white agency flags flew from the antennas of expensive short-wave radios, all of which made for good film for CNN news cameras. They also cycled medical volunteers through on emergency contracts as short as four weeks. MSF in particular was known for its large flags and volunteers who would stand up in the back of moving pickup trucks. This was perhaps an effective way to deliver emergency medical care, but was irrelevant to developing long-term relationships with Hutu refugees.

MSF was in a particularly odd situation that had implications for how the genocide was reported. Their relief operation in Rwanda had employed many Tutsi, and as a consequence, *Interahamwe* had attacked clinics in Rwanda and hacked to death many of their staff. The expatriates had been evacuated from Rwanda with a few Tutsi survivors. Nevertheless they had the courage to establish clinics in Benaco. This made for quick, and in many ways effective, operation as they quickly rose above the linguistic limitations of other agencies. But it also meant that the MSF expatriates' primary source of information about the Hutu refugees was the Tutsi staff whom they brought with them. During the early, confused days, this was good. It meant, for instance, that MSF was able to quickly establish medical and sanitation programs at a time when risks of a cholera epidemic were particularly high.

In May 1994, it was widely believed by refugees and others that the war in Rwanda must "stop at the border," that "all were Rwandans." But as relations between Hutu and Tutsi in the camp polarized between June and October, MSF became the major source of information about poisoning plots, threats against Tutsi, and the persistent power of "the killers." The MSF Tutsi medical aides said that Hutu were killing patients. Hutu in the camp said that the Tutsi were poisoning Hutu. No evidence ever surfaced to confirm either accusation. MSF's formidable public relations arm continued to reflect the concerns of the Tutsi staff by placing demands for arrests and trials of perpetrators of genocide at the center of their assistance programs to Rwandans outside Rwanda.

The Dead Body Business

Again, a scene in the harried UNHCR office. It was early June, and one of my superiors, Phillip Wijmans, decided to ask what was to be done about the bodies in the river. Bodies had been appearing bobbing about in the eddies below the Rasumo Falls and could easily be seen from the bridge while facing the falls. Bodies had been there for about two months by that time, swirling around before being periodically flushed down the Kagera to Lake Victoria, whence the Nile flows. The price of fish was reportedly falling all the way down the Nile to Cairo, as people were reluctant to eat fish that might have eaten human flesh. The UNHCR agreed to call a meeting of NGOs concerned with the issue for the following day, and Wijmans and I went as LWF's representatives. Wijmans and I, Maureen Connelly from the UNHCR, and someone from the Red Cross were the only ones to show up. The representative from the Red Cross asked what the meeting was about. I told him, and he left as fast as politely possible. We talked to Connelly and asked her what should be done. She agreed that something should be done, but noted ruefully that the bodies were outside UNHCR's mandate—refugees are by definition alive, and the bodies had not even clearly passed the Rwanda border. But we had to do something, as we took ourselves quite seriously by now. This had something to do with genocide, which made it particularly attractive because it would raise our agency's profile, which to date had suffered from a lack of flags or stickers and our focus on the low-profile business of diesel procurement and trucking food.

Meantime, in Dar es Salaam, LWF's director approached the Dutch and Danish embassies with a plan for a river "cleanup." They agreed to fund the cleanup to the tune of $40,000. The director told me that this was one of the easiest projects to fund he had ever had. We assumed that it would take about two months to remove all of the bodies from areas on either side of the bridge, and that it was a one-off project. Since the area along the river was under the control of the RPF and not the genocidal former government, there would soon be no more bodies appearing: the project and mass grave would be done by August.

But, Are We Really That Important?

At about this time, Wijmans and I decided to take a morning off. Egil Nilssen, a Norwegian acquaintance working for Norwegian People's Aid, had asked if he could do anything for the Catholic missionary priests in a nearby village. We had been taking ourselves quite seriously and agreed that now was a good time to deliver Nilssen's offer. We drove an hour and a half to the village and asked a girl near the mission compound where we could find the fathers. She and her friend said that they would show us and climbed into our car. They directed us down roads that had not been traveled by a car in some months, all the while waving gaily at their friends.

After about half an hour, we arrived at a very modest building. Inside was a young Italian priest who did not feel comfortable speaking English. Nevertheless, he made us comfortable, and offered to show us his prayer room, which was a small room with an altar. We asked about refugees. He shrugged and said that a few from Burundi had been in the village, but had gone back. We told him that we worked with 250,000 refugees a short distance away, and that Egil Nilssen of Norwegian People's Aid would send him anything he needed. He indicated that he needed nothing and was content with his prayer room. The girls piped up that they knew where some other priests were and offered to show us the way. We ended up 100 yards away from where we had started. These priests were much more appreciative of Nilssen's largesse. We returned to the camp and river taking ourselves less seriously.

The Body Project Begins

Mark Ajobe—the man who in May 1994 had coordinated the removal of 11,000 bodies from the mouth of the Kagera River in southern Uganda, downriver from Rasumo for LWF Uganda—came and set up a "body removal team" based on principles of plenty of liquor, food, and cigarettes for "the boys." He pointed out that the cigarettes are particularly important, as it covers the musty-sweet smell of the water-logged bodies. Ajobe, a former officer in the Ugandan army, tended toward military metaphors, as well as principles of solidarity. He hired local youth at wages three or four times the going daily rate to take over 100 bodies out of the pools at the foot of Rasumo Falls, and then added a bounty of 1,000 shillings (about US $1.80) per body. Most bodies were removed via a boom installed on the Tanzanian side of the river, which was a bit ticklish for the Tanzanian and Rwandan military, whose border after all it is. The Rwandans in particular were concerned and inspected the boom to make sure it was not a howitzer.

Ajobe was at times graphic in his stories of particular bodies, reflecting an attempt to find humor or meaning in the macabre operation. He attached personalities to bodies that were particularly difficult to remove from the river because the eddies they bobbed about in were not readily accessible. There was one that he made up about a disemboweled woman and her fetus, still attached by the umbilicus.

By mid-July, over 200 bodies had been retrieved and buried in the mass grave that had been dug. Now, Ajobe was ready to leave the project, and in a sober and solemn moment he came to me to announce that I was now in charge and pointed out that there was nothing in the project that whiskey and cigarettes wouldn't solve. The day before he left, he walked me down to the bridge to introduce me to the RPF soldiers on duty there.

We explained that we continued to pose no threat, and that we simply wanted to remove the bodies from the river. On the way back he introduced me also to the Tanzanian soldiers, who manned a machine gun nest tucked behind some bushes about 100 feet from the bridge. As the battle for Kigali was going on at that time, we took the briefing seriously.

Between June 28 and July 31, we removed 311 bodies from the area around the bridge. Most of the bodies were not freshly killed; a mix of women, men, and children, the victims had been hacked to death, and we knew that they were probably Tutsi victims of the *Interahamwe*.

Sadly, though, this was more than a cleanup operation. By late July, it was clear that new bodies were arriving daily, and were being swept over the falls where once again they were swirling around in the eddies. With the permission of both governments, we installed a rope net across the river to catch them.

The project went smoothly, but was over budget, a fact my director in Dar es Salaam was quick to note. It was over budget for two reasons: Ajobe's administrative policy of unlimited whiskey, cigarettes, and workers; and the problem that fresh bodies continued to be caught in the nets. Nevertheless, Dar es Salaam gave me as the on-site administrator the unenviable task of wrapping up the body project.[9] I was also presented with the necessity of making an administrative decision concerning how much of a body counted for the 1,000-shilling bonus. Is a leg enough? An arm? What about a fetus ripped out its mother's womb? Was this worth 1,000 or 2,000 shillings?

I passed the body statistics along to the UNHCR, which used them as a monitoring tool to infer that conditions in Rwanda were at best unsettled, despite RPF claims to the contrary. As the year went on, the UNHCR–Ngara office used the statistics we collected to continue making a case that voluntary repatriation was unlikely to be a realistic alternative, despite UNHCR–Geneva's claims to the contrary (see Chapter 7).

In early August 1994 I got a new boss in Ngara, an Australian, Gary Sibson, whom I took down to the river and introduced to the RPF military guarding the border post and the approaches to the bridge. We walked down to the bridge where we spoke English with a soldier whose first name was, of all things, Innocent. I explained to him our continuing project, and Mr. Innocent expressed surprise that we were still getting bodies out of the river, which was substantially under the control of the RPF by now. He speculated that these must be old bodies washed out of the reeds. With a straight face, I agreed that this must be so, even though the day before our people had told me that the bodies were in fact fresh, and were still bleeding from head wounds when they arrived. Later Sibson told me that both he and another soldier who was there laughed at the ridiculousness of our conversation.

Murders and Riots in Benaco

In early June, a team from the German magazine *Geo* came to stay in our camp in Benaco. They had a great story idea: they were planning a story about the refugees, and would follow up with the same refugees in a year's time. They got more than they bargained for. They witnessed the beating of a woman who was accused of sorcery. The sociologist in me assured them that this was the first murder in a community of 300,000 to 400,000 people, and that this was not too bad a record. Then, on June 15, they witnessed the confrontation between the refugee leader Remy Gatete and a Belgian UNHCR field officer, Jacques Franquin (see Chapter 7).

At a meeting the day after the Gatete incident, Maureen Connelly asked that all NGO activities be suspended pending a resolution of the situation to her satisfaction. She framed the issue in terms of Gatete's usurping UNHCR's authority in the camp, which she claimed the confrontation represented. She pointed out to the expatriate audience that Gatete was a major war criminal, a fact that had been published in the *New York Times*.[10] (The *New York Times* as a court of law: my sociological imagination reeled.) Connelly arranged for the MSF agencies to say how they would respond. Representatives of each MSF agency (France, Holland, and Spain) expressed their hard-line views about not working with killers, even if it meant that the withdrawal of their services resulted in the death of innocent people. MSF–France's representative, in particular, had a strong view that the refugees were killers, a view substantiated by the Tutsi staff that worked in Benaco at MSF clinics.

The UNHCR concluded that all agencies should cease camp activities until Maureen Connelly paid a visit to the camp to assess the relationships between the refugees and the NGOs. Claiming with a bit of pseudo-psychology that "forceful action is the only thing such killers understand," MSF responded by suspending its own activities until further notice. I later heard that they drove off to the Serengeti, where, stripped of flags and stickers, they had a retreat to discuss the moral significance of their work in the context of genocide. The next day, after her meeting, Connelly told us that refugee leaders agreed to cooperate with NGOs, and we were again permitted to work in the camp. Gatete himself was quietly spirited out of the camp a week or two later by the Tanzanian police.[11]

I still lived in Benaco at the time, and asked some of our Rwandan refugee workers about the incident. They shrugged and indicated that it was not that important. They expressed no sympathy for Gatete but claimed to be confused about why MSF clinics had been shut for a few days. This did not surprise me, since the facility closure had resulted from a conflict between the French-speaking refugee and expatriate elites. Given the limitations in language and communication, there was no way independent information could be communicated by the expatriates to the refugee masses.

Within a week or two, more murders were reported at meetings, and the total reached five. It was still less than the murder rate in Sacramento on a per capita basis, so I was not worried. But the European expatriates who attributed the murders to *Interahamwe* plots flipped out. Oddly, on June 25, the UNHCR Ngara Security Advisory Committee recommended in a widely distributed memo on UNHCR letterhead that the streets in Benaco be named, and recommended Avenue de Belgique, Tutsi Square, and Avenue du MSF as starters. My boss at the time, Leo Norholt, who had 15 years' experience in Africa, hit the roof in the interagency meeting and pointed out that such a memo on UNHCR letterhead was extremely provocative for the Hutu population, which blamed the Belgians for shooting down General Habyarimana's plane and the Tutsi-dominated RPF for causing them to flee to Tanzania.

In August and September, rumors of nocturnal disappearances and murders began to circulate, and were reported at interagency meetings; the UNHCR protection officer described newly disturbed ground, where she had been told bodies had been buried. I asked whether anybody had actually dug up the ground to see whether bodies were buried there, and if so, how the victims died. No one had. Later I offered some of the workers from our body project to dig up the putative grave sites. The protection officer accepted the offer, but it never happened. One reason was that at that time, refugees were arriving at remote villages in Tanzania at a rate of about 3,000 to 4,000 per day. I was involved with trucking the refugees away from the border, which dominated my time. The protection officer was involved with evaluating their accounts of why they were fleeing and assessing what type of legal refugee protection they were entitled to.

President Mwinyi and the Body Project

The president of Tanzania, Ali Hassan Mwinyi, visited the refugee camps in October 1994. Philip Mangula, the regional commissioner of Kagera, felt strongly that President Mwinyi should see the body project and put it first on his tour of the border region. I had met Mangula a couple of times. As I got to know Mangula over the two years I spent in Tanzania, I became more and more impressed with him. In a quiet fashion, he melded the different worlds of the Tanzanian villagers and the international aid community into a humanitarian force serving the half million refugee "guests" in his region. This he did at political risk to himself. Indeed, he lost his seat in Parliament in the 1995 elections.

Anyway, Mangula wanted to take the president to the river for two reasons. First, he wanted to demonstrate that at least one agency is taking a concern for local Tanzanians, and removing bodies was a service to them (the overall refugee operation had been criticized in the national press for ignoring Tanzanians). Second, Mangula wanted to drive home the point that there was continuing fighting right on Tanzania's border, and that the situation in Rwanda was not settled, claims of RPF diplomats to the contrary.

The previous week, the body count had been down to a point where on some days no bodies appeared; we wondered whether we should save one or two as evidence, just in case. We did the right thing, though, and decided not to do this. Anyway, that day three bodies turned up. I received the president when he alighted from the car. No one else got out of the car, and no one introduced him to me. I said hello, oddly disconcerted to see a man who is about eight inches shorter than I but whose picture is on the money in my pocket.

The presidential aides finally reached us. He shook hands with our body project men, and then his aides escorted him to the river's edge. The men showed him how they did their job, and pulled an execution victim who had his hands tied behind his back out of our net. They plopped the body onto a piece of plastic at President Mwinyi's feet. *Spurrr-lop*, the musty sweet smell of the body greeted our nostrils. An aide called attention, and the President's party headed back to his car quickly. I kept wondering whether President Clinton would go to a river border where a war was going on next door. *Spurrr-lop!*

Later that day, President Mwinyi announced that the Tanzanian government wanted the refugees moved to the southern part of Tanzania, where they would not be a security threat, and could be given land to farm until they returned to Rwanda. Only one week later, the evangelist David was killed in the camp by refugees while distributing Bible tracts. This event (related in Chapter 7) shifted the Tanzanians' sympathy away from the Rwandan refugees and their plight.

Perceptions of Genocide: Kibungo, Rwanda, 1995

In July 1995, I met Philip Mangula in Ngara again. He had just returned from Kibungo, Rwanda, and was again wondering about the status of the body project. We had discontinued it in May 1995 owing to a low body count (down to "just" seven in that month), but he wanted to check. This was his first visit to Kibungo since the genocide, and the killing there was what he really wanted to talk about. He kept talking about the church where the bodies of several thousand Tutsi victims had been lying out in the open since they were killed in April 1994. He also repeated the tales of how victims had been chloroformed in order to keep them for killing overnight. What was more shocking to him is the fact that some of the Rwandan leaders he knew from Benaco were accused of this deed. He kept talking about the "red-eyed one," one of the leaders in the camp whose red eyes, as it was believed in African mythology, betrayed him as being of the devil.

Other expatriates who worked in Kibungo also told me about the same bodies; they described how they would pass each day on their way to work and watch them "move" in the sun as they shriveled and dried. At first I was surprised that Mangula was so unaware of something that all the expatriates had been talking about for the last year. Then my socio-logical imagination took over and I marveled at the different ways experience with genocide were evaluated in different cultures. Mangula talked about the eyes of people, while Maureen legitimated her attitudes by citing *New York Times* stories.

1995: Visiting Benaco with a Tutsi Guest

Also in the summer of 1995, I met the Anglican bishop of Gahini, Rwanda, Augustin Mvurubande. He (Hutu) and his wife Virginia (Tutsi) were old friends of a British physiotherapist at the Anglican hospital in Gahini, Trish Wilson. Indeed, I had interviewed the bishop and his wife for one of the issue papers I wrote as part of my job (see Essay 7). They told me of the massacres their families had suffered during the genocide, and the terror involved in passing through *Interahamwe* and RPF road-blocks on their way from Gahini to Zaire in September 1994.

By this time I was living in Ngara town, where our office had moved in late 1994. I had wanted to go down to the camp in Benaco for some time with Trish to visit some of the refugees living there that she knew from Gahini. For too long I had been trapped in offices and meetings, and such a visit was something I looked forward to. An added bonus was that Trish spoke Kinyarwanda fluently.

When we picked up Trish, she asked whether the bishop could come along; he hoped to spend the night in the camp with some of his parish-ioners, who were refugees in the camp, as he often did. While we were picking him up at his small house, his wife came out and asked if she could join us. Without thinking I, of course, said yes. Five minutes later, while driving toward the camp it dawned on me. She was a Tutsi, going into a camp that the UNHCR had been insisting was under the control of Hutu militants. This was also her first trip to the camp. The case of David, the evangelist who died in the middle of a crowded market at Be-naco, occurred to me. I turned to her and asked her if she knew what she was doing. She told me yes, that God was with her. I had visions of the reaction from UNHCR staff and my career before my eyes. She asked if someone like her did not make the trip, how could they ever live together again? She pointed out that the people we were visiting were her lifelong friends. They had grown up together. The bishop unknowingly appealed to my sociological sensibility by pointing out that quite often ethnic identity is only situationally significant. He pointed out that in fact, even after all that had happened in Benaco, there were still Tutsi living in the camps— "even tall ones."

The bishop's wife turned out to be right, and the trip ended up being a success. On the way back she bubbled on about who had had the courage to greet her, and who had shied away, as well as her hopes for a future of peace and reconciliation. During the coming year, she would frequently return to Benaco and began to spend the night there in early 1996.

Witness to Genocide?

I have, purposely, presented a complex variety of relationships. How to make sense of these experiences? There are people representing courage, fervor, arrogance, humility, naïveté, compassion, civility, confusion, and evil. How is such a range of characters organized into a coherent explanation of what happened? What generalizations can be found by putting the characters you met above into the same pot? All of the adjectives described above, inconsistent though they may be, are reasonable ways to organize such experiences.

For example, there was evil in a number of circumstances: the manner in which David died, the necessity to decide whether my body team should receive one or two bounties for a mother and her fetus, the need for Innocent and me to lie to each other that recovered bodies were not fresh, and the presence of a mass murderer like Gatete in Tanzania. At the same time, though, there was a great deal of courage and compassion. Here, I would first point to the Tutsi wife of the bishop, who visited her Hutu friends in camp; Sister Agnes, who walked quietly from tent to tent to comfort Hutu refugees; and the MSF staff who were able to spirit their Tutsi staff out of Rwanda and begin work again in Benaco.

There was an extreme civility in the willingness of Leonidas and his friends to set up camp and dig me a toilet, when they themselves did not have the tools to do so on behalf of their own children. Sister Agnes showed a great deal of compassion, as did the refugees who dug the pit toilet for me. The expatriates attempting to get "numbers" on the refugee influx were something of a mix between astute bureaucrats and petty publicity seekers. And what of the Italian priest and his prayer room? He lived physically in the eye of the refugee crisis seeking God, but was uninterested in the world outside his small remote corner of the village.

Confusion and naïveté were also present in bountiful supply. Oddly, though, what was confused and naïve overlapped a great deal with what was evil. Much of this confusion and naïveté emerged out of the need for strangers to quickly establish relations in an unusual situation. Where were the confusion and naïveté? The Gatete situation comes most quickly to mind. Certainly Gatete himself misread the situation by going to the camp in the first place. The UNHCR's response to Gatete compounded the situation. MSF's response to the Gatete incident could be seen as naïve. And what about Mangula's lack of interest in framing the situation in Rwanda as evil until he saw the church in Kibungo? This could be framed as his naïveté or as UNHCR's inability to frame the issue in culturally relevant terms.

The murder of David was an accident of interpretation, by both the refugees and David. But David ended up dead, and the Tanzanians despised the refugees as a result. In retrospect, we can conclude that David was naïve to go in the camp, and the refugees, evil and brutal. On the other hand, had the bishop's Tutsi wife been murdered when I took her down to the Hutu camp, I would be calling her brave but naïve today, rather than courageous and insightful.

The problem is that the Good Samaritan, when he or she becomes part of a bureaucracy, becomes incapable of dealing with the subtlety developed in both genocidal and refugee situations. This happens because, in a context focused by the emotionalized nature of modern refugee relief, certainty and moral righteousness are demanded, irrespective of whether the bureaucracy has the technical competency to deal with the situation appropriately. In the vacuum, the need of the relief bureaucracy itself to order facts trumps the technical needs of the legal bureaucracies and their ability to generate effective legal cases suffers.

The Problem:
Framing, Recognizing, and Responding to Genocide

Now, back to the apology of Secretary of State Albright for the United States' not having identified what happened as genocide earlier, and more important, not having taken action to stop it before it started. Had she collected my observations, I do not think that she would have reached the conclusion she did: that earlier international intervention could have prevented the genocide. The reason why, is that there was no neat frame leading to a logical intervention policy that her bureaucracy could have acted on. Neat logical analysis was not what the international refugee relief regime could generate. Rather the American policy was a response to persistent press reports questioning the role of the international community in "permitting" genocide, and not a measured analyti-

cal assessment of whether this was the most appropriate incident on
which to establish a precedent for the prosecution of war crimes. The
willingness of the international refugee regime to focus on the issue of
"assisting murderers" contributed to the State Department's weakness
for developing policy on the op-ed page of the *New York Times*, and not in
independent assessments.

Also, it sidesteps closer examination of the issue of the existing
statute against genocide, which is probably inadequate for what Albright
desired to use it for. This statute was ultimately the "frame" that Albright
and others used. The international legal system, imprecise though it may
be, classifies different types of killing according to intent. Thus, killing
that is organized by a government to exterminate an ethnic group is
genocide; a finding of genocide requires international action to stop it.
This legal frame was established in a retrospective look at the Allied lack
of interest in bombing the railway to Auschwitz. Had the genocide in
Rwanda been similar to that at Auschwitz in its duration and bureaucratized nature, the statute might have worked in the way that Albright
thought it should have.[12]

But the genocide in Rwanda was different from that in Auschwitz. Perhaps events in Rwanda were more analogous to *Kristallnacht*, with its
roving gangs organized by the Nazi party, or maybe to the extermina-
tions by SS-organized "special detachments" in eastern Europe (see
Shawcross 1984:15–17) than to Auschwitz. The Rwandan genocide was
conducted by gangs of machete wielders traveling on foot or vehicle on a
rudimentary road system. Thus, although in a moral and practical sense
the resulting crime of genocide was very similar to that committed in
Auschwitz in the 1940s, I have some doubt as to whether the actual
statute derived from the German situation is applicable. The nub of the
problem is that the logistics of the killing were different. Had international law with respect to genocide been in place after the Armenian
genocide in Turkey in the late nineteenth and early twentieth centuries
rather than not until after the Holocaust, would such a law have obligated the international community to respond to *Kristallnacht*? And
could they have? Could a coherent policy have been formulated using
the bureaucratized military and political tools available?

The Basic Paradox:
Bureaucratic Framing and International Humanitarian Law

The rules of collective memory and cultural restraint have shaped the
post-Holocaust view of genocide (Olick and Levy 1998; Shawcross 1984),
and a wishful "never again" spirit suffuses both the literature and legal
system. That the international legal system did fail to realize its highest

ideal in Rwanda is apparent. What is less apparent is that this fact is not due to the faults of individual actors, but is inherent in the bureaucratic capacity needed to enforce the statute. The standard sociological explanation for this is that situations are "complex," as I have made every effort to show. To some this sounds like amoral relativism. It's not. Rather, it is a recognition that what the international refugee relief organization can do is limited.

This is because there is paradox between the nature of law and policy, and social life. Genocide law, like all criminal law, is embedded in broader social understandings. Policy-makers will inevitably try to simplify, and to do this they will use preexisting categories. Many of these simplifications will be cloaked in the legitimacy and certainty of written law. The problem with this certainty is that the sociologists are in fact right. Social life is complex, and because of the inability of complex bureaucracies grounded in emotion to recognize this, the international system will probably remain caught in its contradictions. Sadly, this means that no matter how much self-criticism Secretary of State Albright may engage in, international law is a weak tool for the prevention of future Rwanda-like genocide.

Notes

1. Prunier (1995:198–212) asks whether this was enough to anticipate the coming "apocalypse." He points out that the allusions and nuances of meaning were deeply embedded in Rwandan culture, which made difficult a "meaningful connection between such obscure cultural allusions and the magnitude of the horror then being planned" (Prunier 1995:209–212). In fairness to the UN's New York bureaucracy, the international context of General Dallaire's warnings also need to be considered. New York was evaluating warnings in a worldwide context, including probably similar warnings from Cambodia, Liberia, Somalia, and Burundi. Bosnia was/is still a hot spot. The site of greatest concern was probably South Africa, where political parties backed by militias were contesting the first multiracial elections in that country amid warnings of potential catastrophe. William Shawcross (2000:84) has recently pointed out that the UN Peacekeeping Office received masses of information in 1994, not all of which proved accurate.

2. The search for precision continues. Alison des Forges in her 1999 book puts the total at 500,000 dead. The total number of dead of course does not matter so much in a prosecution for genocide, which is ultimately about intent and not numbers.

3. Marc Ajobe, the Ugandan coordinator of this body recovery project, told me that the number was 11,000 as of mid-June 1994.

4. William Shawcross's *The Quality of Mercy: Cambodia, Holocaust, and Modern Conscience* includes an extended discussion of this issue with respect to why Khmer Rouge atrocities in Cambodia were defined as genocide so slowly (1984, 45–69).

5. Similar questions about the veracity of refugee reports were raised with respect to Cambodians fleeing the Khmer Rouge before 1978. Their stories were greeted with skepticism, and of course were denied by the Khmer Rouge government itself. But, like Hutu tales of RPF massacres in northeast Rwanda, the accounts proved accurate. As in Rwanda, the group committing the greatest atrocities ultimately lost the war. But just because the refugees' side lost the war doesn't mean that stories they told about massacres are politically motivated lies. Prunier (1997b:360n) indicates that UN officials were aware of at least 30,000 killed by the RPF in northwest Rwanda and Kibungo by November 1994. Several hundred thousand more were to die owing to the policies of the RPF and its allies in 1996–97 when the Zairean camps were emptied (Lemarchand 1999).

6. As part of the body recovery project described below, I was often asked where the 900 bodies pulled out of the Kagera River came from. I never had a straightforward answer, because we never knew enough to evaluate how long the bodies had been in the river. In general, we assumed that the bodies that had been hacked to death and were recovered early in June–August 1994 were *Interahamwe* victims, whereas the execution victims we recovered during the following year were victims of RPF exactions, although we had no way of verifying these assumptions. During a violent spell in northern Burundi in early 1995, the men on the body recovery teams speculated that the victims recovered were from that country. This seemed plausible, and it would not have been the first time bodies from Burundi appeared at the Rasumo bridge. Missionaries from Ngara told me of seeing bodies in the Rasumo bridge pools during violence in Burundi in the late 1980s.

7. *The Economist* in their May 7 issue described the good relations between Hutu and Tutsi refugees. This report, too, was part of the framing process.

8. Time seems to be on the side of Jensen's analysis. Prunier (1995:265–266) thought him prejudiced. But des Forges's (1999) assessment confirms that RPF massacres took place throughout the region in April–July 1994, and with the benefit of more hindsight, Prunier (1997) indicates that the death toll in northwestern and eastern Rwanda from RPF killing was probably at least 30,000 (Prunier 1997:359–60).

But in retrospect I think that both were looking at the wrong thing. They should have looked at the demographics of the refugees. They would have found an extraordinarily small proportion of small children and elderly, which is the real indicator of the hardship that they went through during flight (see Essay 1, and Waters 1996). This would have permitted a statistically sound inference about what was happening.

9. A total of 917 bodies was reported removed between June 28, 1994, and June 1, 1995. Of these 311 were removed in the first month of the project, and were mostly victims of the *Interahamwe*. There was a mixture of children and adult males and females. Eighty-four and 87 bodies were found in the net in November and December, 1994, respectively. These were fresh bodies, and primarily adult males. I assume that the majority were victims of what Destexhe (1996) calls "exactions" by the RPF.

10. I have been unable to locate this story. It may have appeared in another paper.

11. I heard that later in July he was spirited out of the Tanzania by the Ministry of Home Affairs.

12. The July 1999 issue of *American Heritage* (vanden Heuvel 1999) included an article about the nature of the decision-making that went into the decision to bomb or not to bomb the railway to Auschwitz.

12

Why Only the Rwandans?
Relief Operations and Politics

Introduction

In the first chapter I posed the question: Why were the Rwandans forcibly repatriated? Why only the Rwandans? Why were Rwandans forced back to their country, and not the Mozambicans, Afghans, or Khmer Rouge? A facile answer is "politics." But politics is a constant of refugee situations, and not a variable. In fact, nasty politics is a constant. The *Interahamwe* committed war crimes and genocide. But so, probably, did the Khmer Rouge, the Laotian government against the Hmong, Iraq in Kurdistan, factions in the Mozambican wars, Serbs in the former Yugoslavia, Indonesians in East Timor, and the various forces killing Hutu refugees in Zaire/Congo.[1] Currently (September 2000), war crimes and/or genocide are probably being committed in the southern Sudan, Colombia, the Democratic Republic of the Congo (formerly Zaire), Angola, and Burundi. In order to assist refugee masses, the international refugee relief regime has assisted populations under the control of deplorable political movements, including the Khmer Rouge in Cambodia, the Mujahedin in Afghanistan, rebel groups in Liberia, Somali clans, Mengistu's Ethiopia, the Revolutionary United Front in Sierra Leone, etc. Thus, the reason why the Rwanda refugee relief operation collapsed is not to be found in an easy answer like the "politics" of the Rwandans. The *Interahamwe* and Hutu radicals may have well been, for a short period, more brutal than the other bad guys, but this is at best a matter of degree and not a qualitative difference.

Thus, the Rwandans were repatriated not because they or their politics were different, but because the international refugee relief regime was unable to cope with the variations on the problem presented by the Rwandans, and collapsed on its own internal contradictions. This is why the Rwandans were forcibly repatriated. It is my assertion that the answer to the question "Why only the Rwandans?" lies not in the nature of the crimes committed, but in weaknesses inherent in the international refugee relief regime that manifested themselves most forcefully in the case of Rwandan refugees. In effect, the question became: What was it about the Rwanda operation itself that led to the forcible repatriation?

What happened in the case of the Rwandan operation is that there was an emotional buildup generated by what was broadcast about the establishment of Benaco, the genocide and war, and later the cholera epidemic in Goma. This emotional buildup occurred more suddenly than in other emergencies (for example, Cambodia, Ethiopia, and Somalia). The situation in Rwanda was presented as a humanitarian crisis—which indeed it was; but this led to the inference of an abnormally high level of blamelessness on the part of the refugees. In the cases of the Khmer Rouge in Cambodia, General Aideed in Somalia, and the Mengistu government in Ethiopia, an analytical separation of the refugees and their politics from that of the "bad guys" was made before the humanitarian relief operation was initiated. In Rwanda, the speed and volume of refugee flight was unusual. Charity was proffered at a commensurate speed and level, and in this process, underlying assumptions about blamelessness and victimization were pushed to a level too high for any refugee population to achieve. Consequently, "compassion fatigue" set in much more quickly and forcefully than elsewhere.

The early phase of a relief operation is called the "tap-on" phase, and it is the period when procedures are established. As briefly alluded to in Chapter 7, in the Rwanda emergency, "There was a marked contrast in resource availability between the 'tap-on' period from mid-July to September, when funding appeared limitless, and other periods when it was less readily available." (*JEEAR* 1996:14). This tap-on phase, when the UNHCR told its partners "to spend whatever it takes—the money is there," lasted until about September 1994. The funded NGOs responded by developing operating procedures that assumed that money would not be an issue for maintaining relief programs. Although this happened elsewhere as well, for example in the Thai camps for Cambodians, it was in the Rwandan operation that its practical limits were breached.

Just one of the long-term problems created was the opportunity for the Tanzanians to insist on crowded urban-style camps, in which farming was impossible. Had expectations for feeding programs been more modest, probably refugees would have instead been pushed to start farming with the rains in September instead of relying on the generous food distributions. By the time money became an issue, however, the urban camp style was dogma, and transportation for the refugees to another location where they could farm was considered financially prohibitive.

I think that part of the problem was too much food, not because the refugees did not deserve it, but because it meant that the Tanzanian government could restrict refugee movement more severely than they had in the past. This bureaucratic precedent of oversupply had the ultimate effect of curtailing refugee farming activity, meaning that high levels of assistance needed to be maintained, even as the interest of the West in sustaining the camps waned.

The establishment of such high standards affected the refugee assistance bureaucracies themselves. It became bureaucratized dogma that the refugees should be provided with the full measure of food and water provided at the beginning. Then, when the gaps in the food pipelines appeared in early 1995, agencies in Ngara presented a plausible case that food riots and starvation across the region would necessarily ensue if this standard was relaxed. The international refugee relief regime was doing the bureaucratically normal thing—seeking to expand operations from its June 1994 starting point—and they were doing it using the means that had been available in the past, emotional manipulation of the Western public by the media. The point of this continuous emergency state was to repeat the procedures that had worked in the past, rather than to assess and expand refugee reception capacity along the Tanzanian border.

The Strength of Bureaucracy, the Weakness of Emotion

A central lesson is that the strength of the international refugee relief regime comes from its organizational capability—its ability to sustain people in remote areas of the world on short notice. This is the strength of rationalized bureaucracy. The problem is that this strength became dependent on emotion to fund itself. In the process, an illusion was created that the bureaucracy could manage the press to generate funds in the same way that port deliveries and food distribution are bureaucratized and controlled. But the only way to maintain the interest of the press and thereby that of USAID and ECHO was to demonize the refugees themselves by spotlighting the genocide, a status inconsistent with a belief in their status as victims. Thus, despite the fact that the vast majority of refugees could not have had a plausible connection to the genocide, perceptions of apolitical innocence and victim status became more untenable with time. In part, this was because there was no mysterious Pol Pot, General Aideed, or Mengistu on whom the contradictions could be plausibly blamed, so that the refugees could be absolved. In such a context, as critics pointed out, the refugees' staying in Tanzania was incompatible with their presumed apolitical nature, and having political views became equated with having sympathy for the *Interahamwe*. The assumed innocence and deservingness of the refugees could not sustain this repeated assault, and as a result donors became more reluctant to sustain the camps themselves.

Limiting Refugee Contributions

The refugee agencies are not the only factors in the situation. There is an inherent pattern to refugee resettlement and self-sufficiency. Nearest the crisis in time, refugees are at their most vulnerable, and death rates are highest. As time passes, though, refugee life becomes routine and boring, even for a group of people who have suffered through flight and terror. The tasks available tend to fill the day, whether it be in waiting in line for distributions, collecting water, firewood, childcare, education, politics, establishing small gardens, etc. The result is that places like Benaco give off an air of permanence after only a few months, as new relationships are established, birth rates rise, and an urban community, with all its ills, emerges. This air of permanence permitted refugees to improve the situation as they saw it through their own eyes. But the nature of the permanence that develops can be affected by the situation created by the relief program (see, e.g., Malkki 1995).

In any event, refugee resourcefulness and capacity for self-help improve with time. The people who were unable to feed themselves when they arrived in August 1994 were later able to cope with breaks in the "food pipeline" by resorting to social devices unavailable just months earlier. They were stable enough even to begin replacing the infants and toddlers who had died in 1994, which for a substantial portion of the population undoubtedly refocused social energy. More ominously, the urban-style idleness so near the Rwandan border made credible, at least to some refugees, plans to violently retake Rwanda. This was why the militia groups were able to flourish in the camps, at least for a time.

But the experience from Tanzania also shows that when opportunities presented themselves, the refugees channeled effort into resettlement activities and dreams, be they French language classes in Katumba, Swahili language classes in Ngara, clearing farmland, seeking jobs with NGOs, or the formation of political movements. How this resourcefulness develops, though, is highly dependent on the context created. This was a central point of Liisa Malkki's (1994) study of Burundian refugees in Tanzania. Refugees isolated in remote settlements without alternatives developed a radical political movement, with the result that one of the protagonists in Burundi's civil wars of the 1990s had its beginnings in the camps. But refugees living in urban Kigoma invested their efforts and resourcefulness in apolitical pursuits, and in the long run they were more likely to achieve a social status that blended with the urban Tanzanian milieu (see also Sommers 1994).

The relief programs as they developed in Ngara did not recognize this shifting refugee capability for self-sufficiency. The problem with the Rwandans in Tanzania in 1994 was that the relief programs continued to be based on first-arrival conditions and the assumption that total support was necessary. Thus, the short-term practical decision when the operation was first established in May 1994, to house refugees in crowded camp conditions, became bureaucratized dogma. Bureaucratic systems established to maintain this level of dependency developed their own interests, and soon their staffs assumed that there was no other way to deal with the refugees. In the end, policy-makers assumed that there were only two choices for refugees: repatriation or continued existence in crowded Benaco.

Had policy-makers undertaken a more far-reaching analysis, they could perhaps have moved refugees away from the border and given them larger plots, as was done with Burundi refugees farther south in 1993–94. Indeed, President Mwinyi briefly made this offer in October 1994. Instead of accepting it, though, the international refugee relief regime opted for the default condition of continuing with the status quo, irrespective of its unsustainability. This mistake was repeated in 1994 in the Zairean camps, which lay directly on the Rwandan border. In Zaire the consequences were more serious: refugees were left along the border where they first arrived, and no serious efforts were made to move them, or any assistance programs, toward the interior. This decision ultimately played into the hands of radicals organizing cross-border raids.

In each case, the de facto decision to support refugees in crowded camps, once made, created constituencies within the UNHCR, the Tanzanian government, the NGOs, and the other elements of the international refugee relief regime. Refugee world views were interpreted to fit this goal; for example, it was asserted that the vast majority of the refugees were apolitical peasants controlled by the *Interahamwe* and had nothing to fear by returning to Rwanda. People who worked within the relief regime typically asserted this view without any more analysis than that provided by the popular press. They also brushed aside efforts to provide a more complex and nuanced view, such as that of the UNHCR's own George Chaponda. Instead, bureaucracies were conditioned to base decisions on 800-word essays on the *New York Times* op-ed page that focused on "killers in the camps" and "cycles of impunity," rather than on its own analysis and assessments.

The last chance to shift gears from this entrenchment of the emergency relief programs in self-serving bureaucracies was probably in late 1994, when the Tanzanian government and the local UNHCR office briefly proposed resettlement programs. But even this proposal was evaluated only in the context of what was already there—it was conceived as an add-on to existing programs and methods, not as an opportunity to initiate an overall self-help program for refugees. The cost estimates for resettlement were high, including as they did the costs of moving 250,000 people to various remote sites via UNHCR transport, and the program was dismissed out of hand. By default, a policy of perpetuating large crowded refugee camps won. But the camps were not sustainable in the long term.

Notes

1. Destexhe (1996) claims that the only three clear cases of genocide in the twentieth century are the Ottomans against the Armenians, the Germans against the Jews, and the Rwandan Tutsi against the Hutu. This seems overly simplistic to me. It also seems so to René Lemarchand (1999), who counts no less than three genocides in the Great Lakes region of Africa between 1972 and 1997. He classifies the massacres of Burundian Hutu in 1972–74, the *Interahamwe* massacre of Tutsi in 1994, and the apparent elimination of several hundred thousand Hutu in Zaire by RPF and Congo rebels in 1996–97 as genocide.

13

From World War II
to Rwanda and Kosovo

The limitations of the Bureaucratized Good Samaritan were apparent throughout the conduct of the Rwanda refugee relief operation. In a general way they were the following:

1. Lack of a well-defined planning horizon
2. Susceptibility to manipulation by politically interested parties and the press
3. Artificial rigidification of new social boundaries by the assistance bureaucracies

Each of these limitations was inherited from a structure that was brought to Tanzania—from Somalia, Ethiopia, Cambodia, and the other emergencies that the international refugee relief regime responded to. In effect, the response to the Rwanda refugee flight was the sum of the strengths and weaknesses built into the UNHCR and other agencies since the 1950s. There were improvements, particularly in the speed of initial response, in the ability to field staff and coordinate international NGOs effectively, in procurement, and in field-based decision-making. The speed with which the UNHCR was able to furnish Benaco with a potable water supply reflected these improvements. The ability of Oxfam and MSF–France to respond was due to impressive improvements in engineering design and logistics. "Management" of the international press for the UNHCR's purposes was also done well. Coverage was heavy, and was widely credited with stimulating generous short-term responses from Western donors.

But the weaknesses were also inherited from previous emergencies and ultimately led to what from a humanitarian perspective should be viewed as a failure of the international refugee relief regime: the forcible

Refugee girl with cloth doll,
Keza camp, February 1995.
(Photo by Dagmar Waters.)

repatriation of over 1 million Rwandans and the flight of many into the interior of Zaire, where 200,000 to 300,000 disappeared in the forests in 1996–97. As a humanitarian outcome, this was worse than the excesses of the Thai military on the Cambodian border in 1978–79, which did not involve the complicity of the international humanitarian community. The collapse of the Rwandan relief operation also occurred at a time when systems for the provision of food and maintenance of refugees by the international community were breaking down. By their own standards, which required complete support for refugees, the operation was failing.

This breakdown occurred not because of costs, which were not higher than in other emergencies, but because the emphasis on human suffering needed to sustain interest and cash flow changed the morality calculation. Victims worthy of succor became redefined as victimizers needing international tribunals rather than international protection. Meanwhile, political support for the operation in the West was wilting as the portrayal of the crisis shifted from "ancient tribal rivalries" to the evil of genocide. Academics and field bureaucrats objected to both characterizations as simplistic. But, in an operation whose managers self-consciously viewed it as dependent on the press rather than on the rational analysis of their own bureaucracies, only the more simple explanations could be sustained. This shift in the ever-squishy goal of press reception meant that attempts to achieve greater efficiency were stymied as humanitarianism—previously seen as humanitarian relief and protection from forced repatriation—was redefined in the press as justice for genocide survivors and promotion of repatriation. In terms of the biblical parable of the Good Samaritan, no longer was the question framed as one of mercy for an anonymous robbery victim along the side of the road, put there as a result of irrational "ancient tribal rivalries." Now, the victim was still along the side of the road, but he was assumed to be lying there because of his own shame, and therefore not deserving of assistance. Or he was left at the side of the road while the Samaritan—in pursuit of an implicitly higher good for the victim, namely, "justice"—rushed off to apprehend the robbers.

The Emerging Strengths

The international refugee relief regime views itself as being humanitarian, nonaligned, apolitical, and impartial. This goal is enshrined in agencies such as the ICRC and the UN agencies; though it is less explicit in organizations like Médecins Sans Frontières and Oxfam, they all share that goal to some degree. This is reflected in the focus over the last 20 years on improving technical competency in dealing with straight emergency relief programs. Provision of water, establishing medical protocols, UNHCR's stockpiling of trucks in Dubai, UNHCR's contracting with emergency consultants, and the consolidation of financial appeals by USAID and ECHO are all examples of this streamlining of operations. All of these improvements had an impact on the initial response in Ngara, and Benaco was established efficiently and effectively as a consequence. The April–August 1994 phase can be considered an outstanding success. There was no forcible repatriation, the refugees were fed, there were no serious disease outbreaks, and functioning communities were established.

However, when the time frame is extended in either direction, it is doubtful whether the more central humanitarian response has improved significantly since the Cambodian emergency. Before April 1994, the tragedy of the Burundians was neglected by donors uninterested in funding an anonymous emergency. After September 1994, the operation slowly unraveled as high initial expectations of refugee virtue and momentum to develop programs for them could no longer be sustained.

The Role of the Press

The central weakness in the whole scenario is the role the press is permitted to play in policy-making regarding relief. By its nature, the press, as it swings its illuminating light from crisis to crisis and issue to issue, is surprisingly arbitrary and, from the perspective of humanitarian relief organizations, irrational. A camera pointed at a Rwandan, Kosovar, or Timorese refugee is effective in generating attention for those refugees, but not refugees in general. The press's focus is on the particular situation when and where a reporter happens to alight, not on the more general issue of effective refugee relief. Bureaucrats in humanitarian organizations everywhere tremble at the press's potential presence and "impute," or imagine, its presence, even when it is not there. This is of course fine for the press's "watch dog" role regarding bureaucratic arrogance. Massive amounts of bureaucratic excess, inhumanity, laziness, and pulchritude are prevented through the deterrent power of bureaucrats' "imputing" the presence of the press everywhere.

In Max Weber's terms (1948:254–256), the power of the press is charismatic, meaning it depends on unpredictability—for example, a special quality of a clip of film or an article that catches the fancy of the West. The best example of this charisma is Mohammed Amin's film of the Ethiopian famine that was broadcast on BBC news and that practically by itself riveted the attention of the West on famine issues in Ethiopia. Clips of film from the Rwanda crisis, Somalia, Kosovo, and other emergencies were also of this nature. It was arbitrary that there were no such clips that focused on places like Burundi in 1993, Liberia in 1995, East Timor in 1976, Sudan in the 1990s, Colombia in the 1990s, Guatemala in the 1980s, etc. The phenomenon is explained by the "CNN effect," which refers to the importance of film footage in directing the world's attention. I think this explanation is accurate. The problem is that the CNN effect removes the most basic decisions about how and when to mount relief operations from the bureaucracies best prepared effectively to make those decisions.

The press assumes enormous power when it comes to fund-raising. As a mode of fund-raising, depending on the press to publicize humanitarian disasters has become routinized in the bureaucratic structures of the international refugee relief regime. For example, they search for dramatic situations that might be covered, at the expense of the mundane. They hire staff not for their skills in refugee relief, but for their ability to attract the press and thus generate future donations. In this process, the oversimplified answers to oversimplified problems offered up by the popular press become dogma. For example, the cause of the Rwanda refugee crisis is shifted from "primordial hatreds" to simply "genocide"; a more nuanced assessment of both factors was not an option. In the same vein, in 1999 the problem in Kosovo shifted from the KLA, which was described by the U.S. government as being a "terrorist organization" involved in the drug trade, to Slobodan Milosevic within a period of a few months. The problem is that these answers are too simple to provide guidance and goals for the more complex task of institution building, which is needed to improve the world's refugee relief capability.

Organizational Integrity and Press-Driven Funding

It has been shown time after time that press-driven funding, though generous, is not reliable. Reliance on press-driven funding bedevils all of the international refugee relief regime's programs to some extent. Without it, the international refugee relief regime cannot respond effectively, as was the case when Burundi's refugees fled in 1993. Moving back in time, it was seen in the cases of Somalia, Ethiopia, Sudan, and Cambodia as well: in each case, relief programs began long after bureaucratic warnings had been issued. For each crisis relevant bureaucracies issued rational analyses of famine and refugee flight in a timely fashion, but these analyses collected dust on shelves. Only when the press raised the level of attention to an emotional level appropriate for the six o'clock news were programs funded and action taken.[1]

In the case of Ngara there was a second problem with press-driven fund-raising. Here, the blitz of publicity about the Rwanda genocide brought in so much money in a brief period that the UNHCR and NGOs were able to make major decisions without reference to cost efficiency. As a result, it was not necessary to develop bureaucratic procedures reflecting the efficiency that should underlie modern institutions. The influx of money was necessary in the context of an acute emergency, but it should be kept in mind that the level of "acuteness" is primarily a function of the press presence, and not the number of people dying or deserving of mercy, as the case of the Burundians of 1993 demonstrates. Because of the general perception of acuteness, bureaucratic efficiency was pushed aside, and unusual risks were accepted in program development. Rushing from a "do nothing" to a "do everything" phase is not what staid and methodical bureaucracies do best. But in Ngara, as in Cambodia, Somalia, Ethiopia, and other high-profile emergencies, bureaucracies did rush from a "do nothing" to a "do everything" phase.

Consider some of the down-to-earth problems this led to in Ngara:

- Standard hydrogeological standards were relaxed, with the result that boreholes collapsed within six months and the water supply suffered.
- Procurement was done from a broad variety of sources without respect to standardization, with the result that the vehicle fleets and water systems often broke down for lack of spare parts.
- High staff and NGO turnover meant that surveys, social analyses, and consulting information that these staff had generated

was in effect squandered, as the institutional memory was regularly lost.
- Security concerns were overemphasized.
- There was no commitment to train long-term local or refugee staff; the emphasis on emergency personnel meant that as one expensive expatriate left, another was hired.
- Improvements in refugee self-sufficiency capabilities were ignored.

The Fixing of Bureaucratic Assumptions Early in the Process

As I have discussed, in Ngara, bureaucratic systems became entrenched quickly. During the first year of any operation, a wide range of standards are established for how the relief operation will be run, how decisions are taken, what standards are most important, and what is to be done. Many of these standards have little to do with refugees per se, and much to do with the refugee assistance agencies. The standards that are adopted do, however, have longer-term implications for both agencies and refugees. They concern refugee rations, registration procedures, expatriate expectations for security, standards for office space, assumptions of refugee capability, length of contracts, segregation of expatriate and locals, and many other administrative and day-to-day issues. Many of these policies were established to solve an immediate problem. When an agency didn't get its way, both the UN and NGOs engaged in back-alley whispering to the press. The concerns in Ngara about expatriate security generated in June 1994 with respect to the Gatete incident is perhaps the best example of this. Another example of using the press to gain leverage is the March 1995 memo from NGOs complaining about delays in food deliveries. The problem was that when NGOs engaged in such behavior, the critical and predictable standards needed to bureaucratize refugee relief itself were ignored. As a result, less attention was paid to mundane needs for refugee living space, appropriate water provision, effective contingency planning for refugee influx, food rations, and a trucking capabilities.

The water sectors in Ngara and Thailand are also good examples of these problems. Decisions about where to drill, what types of pumps to buy, etc., were made on the basis of short-term availability or the personal preferences of a particular engineer present during the financial "tap-on" phase, and not sustained engineering analysis. Irrespective of the fact that such decisions were assumed to be "temporary," they became permanent as bureaucratic assumptions were fixed. The same can be said of camp design. In both Thailand and Tanzania respectively, Khao I Dang and Benaco were designed as temporary solutions to an immediate crisis. But both violated assumptions about what makes a refugee camp sustainable or not. Khao I Dang persisted despite these assumptions, while Benaco did not. In effect, in lowering standards, accepting higher risks, and throwing the dice, Khao I Dang won, in large part because a resettlement program emerged. Benaco lost.

The Fixing of Moral Assumptions

Also behind the quick decisions are moral assumptions about victimhood that are a more enduring part of refugee relief work. The assumed passivity of refugees was found in many of the operations described here. Indeed, it is what makes the international refugee relief regime *international*, and not a group of agencies focused by various national Red Cross societies, local government agencies, or representatives of, say, the United Nations Development Programme (UNDP). A big part of the reason this occurs (as opposed to development work where the opposite is more typical) is that refugee work is seen as a skill focused on the victims themselves, and not the development of a broader social milieu.

A second moral consideration that emerged sometime between the Cambodian and Rwandan crises is the assumption that mass refugee relief programs are related to the crimes that people in a population have committed. As a result, the assumed guilt of some refugees affected relief policies for all refugees from Rwanda. As a concept, though, this was rarely examined beyond an occasional op-ed piece. Thus, while virtually everyone concerned agreed that war criminals should be prosecuted and fairly tried, it seems odd that bureaucracies whose job is refugee relief and the delivery of food, water, and medical care should do so. In effect, in addition to its core responsibilities, the international refugee relief regime was asked to establish a legal precedent for something as socially complex as an international justice system. This goes against the grain of "bureaucratization," which focuses on specialization of tasks, and not generalization to unrelated fields.

Bureaucracies on Parachutes

In large part, both the weaknesses in program administration and moral underpinnings are limited by the nature of the "parachute bureaucracies" that now make up the international refugee relief regime. The idea behind the "parachute" image is that at any time and any place, the goal is to provide a standard relief package quickly, just as the military parachutes troops into remote battlefields quickly. MSF, IFRC, the Oxfam Emergency Unit, USAID-sponsored disaster and rapid response (DART) teams, and UNHCR have all done this to a greater or lesser extent. Many of the standards they establish make refugee relief more effective, particularly in the short run. But, such "parachute bureaucracies" operating independently from local institutions are expensive, and as a result can be established only during a point when there is a generous press-driven "tap-on" phase of finance. Such agencies are very aware that their constituency is the international press, not the country in which they operate or the refugees themselves. But because they have the highest budgets, press agents, and the most expatriates, they quite often are the most prominent when standards for assistance are established.

In Chapter 3, the strengths and weaknesses of bureaucracies in general were discussed. The strengths were in efficiency in the completion of complex tasks, while their weaknesses were in their rigidification, meaning their inability to respond to change quickly. Here too is a paradox because refugee situations are fluid almost by definition. Nevertheless, the bureaucracies do rigidify as surely as they grow. Turf, responsibilities, and budgets are carved out quickly, irrespective of the type of emergency.

The social analyses that provided the rationale for assistance in the first place become volatile. Given that it is embedded in the needs of the press to sensationalize, it seems relevant to recall Tuchman's Law (Chapter 5), which is really an assault on the manner in which disasters are discussed and evaluated:

> Tuchman's Law: The fact of being reported multiplies the apparent extent of any deplorable event by five- to tenfold (or any figure the reader would care to supply).

Parachute relief bureaucracies, in order to expand, need action to take control of the situation. As a result, Tuchman's multiplier immediately rises. In Ngara, those of us who were interested in development issues called the emergency crowd "adrenaline junkies" because they preferred action to waiting or analyzing. The international relief regime of course sought such people, since action is what is routinized. The point of bringing this up here is to point out that when bureaucrats seeking action arrive, they are likely to find action in one way or the other. But this led to the false positives that compromised the whole effort.

More recently, I watched the effect of action-oriented relief administrators on CNN and read about it in *Time* magazine during the April–July 1999 reports about the ethnic cleansing in Kosovo. Seeking to justify action through bureaucratic norms rooted in calculability, there was again a persistent demand for a body count. The information is not easily calculable; nevertheless, people continue to make estimates and thereby create the impression that the information is calculable.[2] For example, in May 1999, when no one really knew very much, estimates of dead ranged from 4,000, a number based on refugee interviews, to 200,000, which is the number of Kosovar males unaccounted for in the refugee camps. Even when a little bit more was known by mid-June 1999, estimates of Kosovar dead ranged from an assertion of a "possible 10,000 killed, as many as 100 mass grave sites at latest NATO count" in the June 28, 1999, issue of *Time* to President Clinton's assertion in a news conference the same week that tens of thousands had been killed during Serbia's ethnic cleansing. What happened was that different bureaucracies with different interests were generating figures as they pursued their own interests via the press. The process of framing the Kosovo situation as of that week had yet to work itself out. This happened repeatedly as the genocide in Rwanda was framed and continues to be framed. In Kosovo the problem is still working itself out. Predictably, more recent estimates of the dead tend toward the lower end of those made on CNN during the war.

Notes

1. The press and NGOs are oddly aware of the irrationalities of press-driven funding. There is no shortage of articles asking why one emergency is more important than the other. For example, recently an article in the *Christian Science Monitor* by Peter Ford was brought to my attention (1999). In the front-page article, the leader noted: "The Red Cross raised $7 million for Turkey's quake victims. A Congo appeal: $0." In the text of the article, Denis Pingaud, director of development for MSF, is quoted: "When the media go all out on one crisis they drain a lot of donor money to the tele-visual events. . . and that means there is less money for other places." Later in the article, he is again quoted: "Nowadays TV crews get to the major crisis before we do." The explanation for this seeming anomaly is not that TV crews are particularly fast; rather it is that the aid agencies in effect let the TV crews select the crises they respond to. MSF is following the TV crews because that is where their funding base comes from, rather than the other way around. Had MSF selected emergencies on the basis of actual assessments of humanitarian need, they might very well have beat the press to the scene.

2. Gérard Prunier wrote about the difficulties in counting the victims of both the Rwanda genocide and the "exactions" of the RPF government. See Prunier (1995 and 1997b:261–268 and 358–368). Such difficulties are also described in Chapter 10.

14

A Broader Context:
Overcoming the Limitations of the
Bureaucratized Good Samaritan

Millions who would have died are today alive because of the efforts of the international refugee relief regime. In addition, it is clear that the international refugee relief regime has improved its capabilities during the last 20 to 30 years. Equally, though, it is clear that the international refugee relief regime does not realize its full potential for delivering both aid and the protection of humanitarian rights. This book is about why this is so and identifies weaknesses inherent to the bureaucracies delivering aid. Although these weaknesses cannot be eliminated, their effect can perhaps be mitigated. My central point is that to take advantage of bureaucratic strengths, bureaucratic decision-making needs to be further rationalized. This means developing procedures, policies, and technology, which are predictable, efficient, calculable, and give bureaucrats the tools to control the situation. Most important, it means defining precisely what the international refugee relief regime does. In Tanzania, it became involved in a host of complex issues beyond its core responsibilities, which are refugee relief and protection. The peripheral issues like the administration of justice, promotion of reconciliation, and promotion of voluntary repatriation, ultimately compromised the central goals of refugee relief and protection.

Reforming the International Refugee Relief Regime

As a result of this lack of task definition, there continue to be weaknesses in the international refugee relief regime. To review these weaknesses, it is useful to frame them in terms of the five elements of a bureaucracy that were discussed in Chapter 3. These five elements were Weber's four elements—efficiency, calculability, predictability, and control—plus the problem of defining a goal. These can be assessed to identify the reforms these qualities suggest. These were:

- Definition of a goal: careful specification of what the international refugee relief regime is trying to achieve
- The lack of predictability inherent in refugee crises
- The impact that control by bureaucratic procedures and technology has on refugee relief
- The impulse to calculate
- How overall efficiency suffers

Specifying the Goal

A chronic problem is that it is unclear what the goal of the international refugee relief regime is. The international refugee relief regime tried to achieve the following goals in Tanzania:

1. Delivery of a comprehensive relief program (program administration)
   - Doing so in a manner which means that maximum effort is seen and reported on
   - Doing so in a manner that is fiscally responsible and results in comparatively low morbidity and mortality rates
2. Protection of refugee rights (advocacy and enforcement of international refugee law)
   - Protection against forcible repatriation
   - Protection against exploitation by other refugees
3. Promotion of peace, reconciliation, and justice efforts (diplomacy, development, and criminal law)
   - Cross-border visits by selected refugees
   - Identification, exclusion, and prosecution of war criminals and genocide perpetrators
   - Operation of radio stations
4. Humanitarian reporting for the benefit of the press
   - Collecting refugee narratives
   - Evaluating and assessing veracity of refugee reports
   - Reporting and publicizing human rights abuses
5. Generation of reports necessary to sustain political support in donor countries
   - Maintaining support for donations from USAID and ECHO
   - Maintaining support for specific NGO programs
6. Promotion of repatriation and resettlement policies
   - Arranging cross-border visits

- Arrangement of resettlement policies
- Promotion of Tanzanian and Rwandan political policies

The list could be longer. But the point is that one bureaucracy, or even a collection of bureaucracies like the international refugee relief regime, cannot be expected to do every task well. In the case of the international refugee relief regime, what it does best is deliver relief programs and protect refugee rights (items 1 and 2 in the above list). But in Ngara, the UNHCR and its partners went beyond this level, becoming involved in diplomacy, advocacy, administration of justice, and other issues normally undertaken by other bureaucracies. When this occurred, the primary relief and protection functions suffered. For example, the insistence that voluntary repatriation was the only solution for the Rwandan refugees meant that relief programs were compromised. Even water provision policies, which are at the heart of any relief program, were subsumed to the repatriation goal. More central, of course, was the neutralization of the very concept of "voluntary," which inevitably sacrificed the apolitical reputation of the UNHCR and NGOs in the community they sought to assist.

The International Committee for the Red Cross, in contrast to the UNHCR, carefully defines its capabilities and responsibilities as assisting victims of military conflict, and prisoners of war, and limits itself to those activities. It is also consistently the agency most likely to be first in delivering relief to war-affected populations. Finally, it is the least likely to be seen ferrying reporters around refugee camps or, as I recently saw on CNN, dramatically dumping relief goods out of a helicopter emblazoned with WFP stickers in a remote village in Kosovo. The clip made for dramatic footage, but the narrative also indicated that the expensive helicopter was delivering one to two days' rations to a village that was not suffering from a food shortage. I wonder how WFP programs are being bureaucratized in Kosovo as a result of this precedent, and compare this program to the quiet success of ICRC, which was the agency with the in-country stocks of food in Tanzania in May 1994.

James Ingram, the former head of WFP, and Andrew Natsios of World Vision have also noticed that ICRC has had unusual success in developing relief programs. They credit this success to ICRC's long tradition of quietly negotiating with warring parties for humanitarian access. I would credit the success to ICRC's focus on a single complex bureaucratic task, on which all its operational goals have been well focused. Most important is the emphasis on confidentiality, which effectively means that though the press is always free to report on its activities, ICRC does not rely on the press to identify crises or micro-manage its humanitarian work to provide story opportunities. ICRC undoubtedly has numerous "irrationalities in its rationality" (see the example of the German ICRC officer in southern Sudan described on page 50). But inordinate numbers of these examples do not make their way into the press in the manner that the irrationality of "feeding murderers" in Goma and Ngara continued to be hammered on.

There is no reason why the UNHCR, WFP, and the NGOs could not effectively "define out" the peripheral tasks that negatively affect how they respond to refugees. For example, both the promotion of voluntary repatriation programs and the development of an international justice system for prosecution of war crimes are important goals. But they are goals most appropriate for bureaucracies designed for those specific purposes. When policies and procedures of relief agencies are reoriented to take account of such issues, the relief programs themselves inevitably suffer.

Ultimately, defining the goal carefully will require an assertion of will on the part of the funding bureaucracies at ECHO, USAID, and elsewhere. This requires a cultural change, a redirection of attention away from the immediate domestic appetite for news as satisfied by CNN's cameras, to the broader question of how best to develop refugee relief programs. Most important, the location and timing of interventions need to be identified on the basis of systematic assessment of humanitarian risks on the world's borders, not by the press. These assessments are already being quietly generated in foreign ministries, universities, and relief bureaucracies around the world. Nevertheless, leaders cite as the criteria for action not these assessments but photographs and footage shown by the broadcast media, op-ed pages, and advocacy groups (see USAID 1998).

The Problem of Predictability

Bureaucracy abhors a crisis, which by definition is unpredictable. Which is why the international refugee relief regime seeks to routinize planning, be it for standardization of water supply systems, food pipelines, or medical protocols. In effect they seek to routinize crisis management

Planning is done to take the unpredictability out of operations. The irony in emergencies is that planning means making something predictable out of what is unpredicted. But this can be routinized, too, despite the seeming contradiction. For example, fire departments routinize every alarm as being an emergency that is vigorously responded to, even though most are false alarms. In effect, the tolerance for the "boy who called wolf" (the false positives) are routinized and expected because not doing so introduces unacceptable risk. In refugee work, though, the tolerance for false calls has yet to be routinized. Instead, false positives become a criterion for believing that there is a habit of exaggeration. In large part, this is because there are two different sets of bureaucratic actors, the conservative diplomatic reporters and the staff of the more aggressive international refugee relief regime, which have implicitly different criteria for assessment and action.

Predictability was also a bureaucratic strength found in the technology used at the beginning of the crisis in Ngara. In the water sector, the Oxfam emergency water system was used to good effect. The problem was that this initial setup established bureaucratic assumptions that the available procedures could not cope with. This was not the issue of the technology per se, but the assumption that the initial influx would end. This assumption is embedded in water-systems engineering, whose principles are based on fixed populations and are inappropriate for unpredictable refugee populations.

Refugee populations grow, shrink, and change quickly. This is essential if rights to protection and return are to be maintained. Refugees should be dealt with and planned for in terms of years, not months; complex issues cannot be dealt with quickly. Furthermore, dogmatic insistence on voluntary repatriation policies are also unrealistic in the politicized world of the refugee. Repatriation may be appropriate for many refugees, but no refugee crisis is likely to be solved by this "one size fits all" policy. The predictable aspects of refugee movements have not been "engineered" into the technology and procedures developed by emergency agencies like MSF and Oxfam. Indeed, in Tanzania these two agencies in effect engineered their own exits from the systems they established, leaving the UNHCR and other agencies with the more mundane role of operations and maintenance.

This raises an issue about the nature of "parachute bureaucracies," meaning agencies brought from outside with bureaucratic systems rooted elsewhere. In Tanzania, for example, one such agency, Oxfam, literally airlifted in prefab emergency water systems. Such bureaucracies become most necessary when there is little contingency preparation, cost considerations are minimal, and local bureaucratic capacity is weak. Parachute bureaucracies, though, establish unsustainable standards for their successors, who by definition include the agencies best able to develop refugee and local skills. In effect, they were, from the context of local conditions, disconnected and therefore unpredictable. In terms of "predictability," this raises the question of why the international refugee relief regime is not involved in the systematic strengthening of emergency response capability in potential host countries. The agencies that tried to do this in Ngara—LWF, Caritas, and the Tanzanian Red Cross—had difficulties competing with the MSFs and the Oxfam emergency unit during the initial setup period. Equally predictably, they also inherited the setup and the expectations generated by the better financed and "more professional" setup agency.

Why Bureaucratic Control Should Be . . . Controlled

Bureaucratic control is the engine on which operational efficiency is achieved. The strength of control is in large part dependent on the development of procedures and technology guiding decision-making and guaranteeing the quality of service proffered. Innovation can occur before and after a refugee situation, but not during. The bureaucracies in Ngara brought to the situation a strong set of technological and operating procedures. As long as these elements were permitted to control the decision-making, things went as well as could be expected. Refugees were received, fed, and provided with shelter and water, which is what the international refugee regime in its impersonal fashion does best. Procedures were established to maintain control over the relief situation. The problem emerged when UNHCR, following its natural inclination to expand, did so into new fields such as the administration of justice and the advocacy of repatriation programs on behalf of national governments. The UNHCR and its partners were ill suited to perform these complex tasks. The "natural" tendency for the bureaucracies to expand should have been in the direction of refugee reception capacity, which was occurring in January 1996, when refugees from Burundi were received efficiently. But this more appropriate expansion was blocked by the tendency to expand into repatriation politics and the administration of justice, which were inconsistent with the core requirement to provide refugee relief and protection.

Shaping the Impulse to Calculate

The ability to calculate also underlies efficient bureaucracies. Indeed, it is in those fields where calculation reached its highest levels that the international refugee relief regime did its best. Precision was sought, and achieved, in terms of kilocalories per refugee delivered, morbidity and mortality rates, and refugees received and protected. These are of course all indicators of how much succor has been provided along the side of the proverbial road. Had these criteria been the sole bases for assessment, the operation in Ngara would have been viewed as successful. But, these indicators of bureaucratized success were not the basis of assessment; the more emotional issues of genocide, war crimes, and the voluntary repatriation program were. The response of a normal bureaucracy should have been to shout from the highest hilltop that initial relief conditions were outstanding, and that the bureaucracy should be permitted to expand its relief function by establishing more camps, providing more relief, or improving refugee protection capabilities. Instead though, the response was a pandering to the unmeasurable demand for a vague "justice" of the popular press. And when the (calculable) voluntary repatriation program stumbled due to refugee disinterest, the bureaucracies permitted themselves to be labeled as incompetent by their donors for the failure of a program which success was by definition beyond their control.

Seeking Efficiency with Respect to a Well-Defined Goal

Efficiency, measured in the terms of refugees succored per dollar, is an admirable goal. It is also one that can be done more or less effectively. In large part, as I think this analysis shows, this efficiency is ultimately dependent on how well what is being done is defined. Sharpening the goal will have ripple effects on the entirety of an operation.

But refugee relief will never be as bureaucratically efficient as corporate or even social welfare bureaucracies. This is because the feedback mechanism between beneficiaries of the agencies' assistance (refugees), field staff, and donors is inherently weak. There are no profits generated for shareholders or elections held to measure refugee faith in program implementation. The inescapable fact is that evaluation will continue to be donor-centric to some degree. The beneficiaries are still the donors, and must somehow must count the "blessings" of extending mercy. In moral terms, success is mercy, and to extend mercy, as the Good Samaritan did, is simply the right thing to do. But it can be extended more or less efficiently when measured per refugee, per dollar spent, liters of water pumped, and kilocalories distributed.

Relief as a Function of Development

Ultimately, the ability to provide refugee relief is a function of general economic development. It is something the developed countries do automatically as a function. The United States accommodates Cubans, Haitians, Vietnamese, or others with little reference to the international refugee relief regime. In the same manner, Germany accommodates Kurds and Bosnians, and even China in 1978 received Vietnamese. The reason such countries do this is that they have the resources to do so, and it is somehow consistent with political interests.

They do so via domestic institutions, be they governmental, nongovernmental, or part of the Red Cross/Red Crescent movement. Notably, they do it without the prior direction of CNN, although the press may well play a role in spotlighting the more dramatic portions of relief programs. It is in this context that the international refugee relief regime needs to develop refugee reception capability in countries like Tanzania, which are likely to continue receiving refugees. The question of how some of the very poorest countries of the world, some of them producing refugees themselves, will be able to accommodate refugees in the future needs to be answered, and measures to help these countries need to be built into relief policies. Ironically, this was considered elemental to relief programs, particularly in Africa, in the 1980s, a time of skimpier budgets and a different attitude toward refugee relief. Millions of refugees from Mozambique and Angola were removed from the fighting in those countries for years. In the process, the refugee reception capability of countries like Malawi, Zambia, and Tanzania improved. The massive Burundian settlements in Tanzania continue to provide a way for Burundians to shield family and friends from the fighting even today. In this respect, the decisions of the 1970s to accommodate refugees facilitated the capacity of Tanzania's refugee reception capacity in the 1990s.

The Persistence of Refugee Movements

Far from being an anomaly in the postwar world, refugees are a product of the consolidation of the political authority of the modern nation-state and will continue to be so. By definition, they are people socially located in the interstices where a nation-state does not reach. As with the fire department, the question for humanitarians should not be one of "if" or an assertion of "never again." Rather it should be a question of "when" and "how can its effects be mitigated" when it happens?

This means that refugee assistance agencies need to establish mechanisms for the long haul. The relief and protection issues raised when the government in Rwanda changed are rarely solved in the short term. Assuming that there are short-term solutions to problems of refugee movement only means that problems are deferred rather than solved. In the case of Rwanda, long-term development and humanitarian needs would have been better served by diverting the political focus of the camps away from the borders, and toward an organized dispersion of a substantial proportion of the refugee population across Africa. In fact, this happened when the Zairean and Rwandans militaries forcibly dispersed the camps on their border, but at considerable cost of life and suffering. As it is, Rwanda has a substantial Hutu population, which is controlled by the Tutsi-dominated RPF government through the imprisonment of a substantial percentage of the male Hutu population of military age. As René Lemarchand (1999) pointed out recently, such formulas of political exclusion have contributed greatly to the recurrent massacres in the region.

Ironically, the Tanzanians acknowledged the need for dispersion of the Rwandan refugee population in October 1994, when they offered land in the south for rural resettlement. The refugees also asserted it in 1996 when they tried to walk (albeit improbably) en masse to Malawi or some other distant destination. Though the Tanzanian proposal may well have been insufficient to solve the whole problem, it recognized that refugee movements are rarely completely reversible, particularly when there is a sudden and violent shift in political power from one entrenched political party to a completely new one. It also recognized that one of the issues that Rwanda needs to confront in one way or another is the continuing pressure on the land of the substantial rural population. This insight goes well beyond that of the international refugee relief regime's simplistic and implausible assumption that war crimes trials for 5,000, 10,000, or even 130,000 people will "break the cycle of impurity" and solve the broader questions raised by such violent political shifts.

It is also probable that Rwanda will not be the last small authoritarian country to generate refugees along remote borders. Again, this is because often enough, the generation of refugees is a process of political modernization in the context of regional poverty. Asserting "Never again" or assuming that new rules of international behavior will solve this paradox is counterproductive. To continue the fire department analogy, it is well understood that neither fire departments nor fire insurance cause very many fires. Rather, these institutions are acknowledgments that there are imperfections in human societies which have the potential for catastrophe. Planning for such catastrophe does not in and of itself invite it.

The Need to See Evil

The analogy between fire prevention and the international refugee relief regime is not perfect; the human element in a genocide is much greater than in, say, a dangerously wired building. Dealing with the emotions involved in genocide, and the violence typically associated with refugee flight are a necessary part of the resolution of refugee crises. One way to do this is to assign blame. We need to find a bogey-man to blame, to explain away the evil that is before us. In Thailand, Somalia, Ethiopia, etc., the bogey-man was just beyond reach of the courts legitimated the mercy offered to refugees in these crises. The Rwanda situation was different, in part because the international refugee regime had become more efficient than in the past and was able to accommodate everyone outside the country, but also because the really bad guys lost, and as a consequence they too were in the camps being assisted.

So we want and need a bad guy. But a bureaucratic mechanism to provide this bad guy in a legitimate and just fashion is beyond the capability of bureaucratized relief operations; indeed it is a complex legal task unto itself. Criminal law, imperfect as it may be, is the best technical means to legitimately put a face to the evil. But it is a very technical process, and in the context of international laws about genocide and war crimes, still an imperfectly understood tool. The different ways in which people as thoughtful and central to the refugee crisis as Maureen Connelly, Philip Mangula, and Bishop Augustin Mvurubande interpreted reports of killing in Rwanda illustrate how difficult it is to establish a reliable mechanism for meting out justice, even among well-educated people. Providing a sense of justice to the poor and semiliterate, who have little concept of the role of the state in protecting the rights of the innocent, will be more difficult.

Likewise, such a system is more just than having relief workers and reporters gaze into the eyes of refugees in order "sense evil" in order to identify who is deserving of relief and who is not.[1] If for no other reason, the emergence of the war crimes and genocide trials will have the positive effect of legitimizing relief programs for the vast majority of refugees who are as innocent of wrongdoing as the man lying at the side of the ancient Judean road.

Critiquing the International Refugee Relief Regime

I am well aware that my analysis is different than most. Since U Thant first criticized UN agencies for their weak response to the Bangladesh emergency, there have been persistent critiques of the international refugee relief regime. The typical complaint has been that relief has been too chaotic and uncoordinated. The typical prescription has been to designate new "coordinators" for different situations. Sometimes this happens when the UN Secretary General assigns coordinating responsibility to a special representative (Ambassador Shahrayar Khan in Rwanda), a new agency (UNBRO on the Thai-Cambodian border), or an old agency (UNHCR, UNICEF, or UNDP). Other times, ICRC has emerged as a de facto coordinator, even though, so far as I can tell, they have never entered into the close relationships with other field agencies that this implies, as it is against their core operational principles. And thus the "problem of coordination" reemerges.

This occurs, I think because the proverbial cart is put before the horse. Lack of coordination—another name for weak bureaucratic control—occurs because the ultimate goal is too often weakly defined. This opens the "coordinating" bureaucracy to charges of inefficiency as the situation is defined and redefined. In such a context, one bureaucracy fails and another is appointed to take its place.

Were the task more carefully defined, one bureaucracy or the other would probably emerge as the "coordinator" reformers desire. It is very likely that different bureaucracies would emerge in different countries and situations. Which agency, though, is not as important as the goal of creating the powerful bureaucratic mechanisms needed to extend mercy to the hurt and hungry lying along the world's highways.

Notes

1. Agatha Christie in her mystery novel *Nemesis* (pp. 130–131) informs us that Miss Jane Marple had this sense. I have no doubt that Miss Marple did have this sense, as did Hercule Poirot. The ever-rational Sherlock Holmes of course, did not. However, as Miss Marple also points out indirectly, such senses are just that, senses, and difficult to analyze. Meaning you have to take the word of the person having such a skill that it exists; unfortunately the modern rational world would need to license and certify such skills before they could be used to legitimate court decisions.

Oddly, in March 2000, I received an unsolicited mailing from MSF with a headline "I can smell the fear." This is a good example of MSF's focus on generating emotions rather than evaluating critically, as Pottier (1996b) advocates. The problem of course is that MSF's appeal is effective in raising funds in a fashion that the dispassionate (and competent) approach Pottier advocates is not. Ambiguous references to the "smell of fear" are more effective in fundraising appeals than the actuarial tables of risk assessment.

PART THREE

BACKGROUND ESSAYS

Much of my thinking has been done through writing, and much of this writing was done in the context of my bureaucratic duties while working in Tanzania and the United States. This book is a summary of such writing, a process which has been going on since about 1985. Much of my this writing emerged while I was puzzling through what people said at meetings or in refugee camps, and my own efforts at advancing the vision that I and my colleagues at LWF (known in Tanzania as TCRS–Tanganyika Christian Refugee Service) had for how refugee work should be done. The following essays were all in some way part of this thinking process. The essays included here were written between 1989 and 1997, and reflect many of the issues that challenged us in our day-to-day activities. They are included here not as a part of the general argument about the bureaucratized Good Samaritan but as examples of the types of discussions we had in the field. I have tried to choose essays illustrating the parameters in which refugee issues were discussed at the time. Those printed here are the following:

"The Demography of a Camp for Rwandans"
"Chabalisa 2—One Year Later"
"The Chabalisa 2 Market Development Project"
"HIV and AIDS in the Ngara Refugee Camps"
"How Many Refugees Are There in Ngara?"
"Wishing for Repatriation, Late 1995"
"A Bishop in Exile: The Anglican Church in Ngara Camps"
"Some Practical Notes on a Names Taboo in Western Tanzania"

The essays were all written at specific times and places, and for a specific purpose. I would like to both put them into a specific context as well as indicate how they relate to the main theme of this book.

Three of the essays reflect the vision that I shared with my colleagues at LWF for how refugee work should be done (especially Essays 2, 3, and

6). Much more so than other agencies, we believed that Tanzania's refugee relief issues were a long-term concern that Tanzanian institutions should be helped to deal with. In contrast, other agencies believed that their role was to deliver relief, save lives in the short run, and protect refugees from abuse, irrespective of the capabilities or views of local institutions. This is a legitimate difference in vision, and is reflected in many of the different ways that agencies developed policy in Ngara (also see Waters 1999a).

I think that the different views of refugee programs at LWF were in large part the result of the agency's longer history in Tanzania. As described in Chapter 2, LWF began its programs in Tanzania in 1964. The work continued in the 1960s and 1970s in camps for Mozambicans and Burundians. The work with Burundians, most of whom arrived in 1972–74, continued through the 1980s, as large settlements in what had been sparsely populated bush were established for over 100,000 refugees. The development work involved programs building schools in Arusha and general development programs in Singida and Arusha region, and Kibondo district.

These programs were far from the limelight and, as described in Chapter 1, were chaotically funded. One consequence was that there was a heavy emphasis on developing local capacity, which was both cheaper and consistent with the more general development goals. In the process of establishing the refugee settlements, as well as development programs in different parts of Tanzania, LWF necessarily developed programs emphasizing the skills and capabilities of Tanzanian staff. They were so successful at this that in the late 1980s and early 1990s LWF was one of the largest and most influential NGOs in the country. And, consistent with development agencies in many countries, the relatively few expatriates who worked for LWF development and relief programs often spoke the national language, or learned it (in the case of Tanzania this was Swahili). In essence, LWF was a Tanzanian agency with an expatriate presence rather than the other way around.

The relief projects in Ngara and Karagwe in 1994–96, however, were dominated by international agencies run by expatriates who often had some experience with relief projects, but little experience in Tanzania. In the refugee relief operation in Ngara and Karagwe, this meant that LWF's Tanzanian managers sometimes had a tough time presenting themselves as possessing the same level of competence as the expatriate engineers and administrators brought in from Europe. For this reason, the Tanzanians working for LWF and other agencies sometimes became scapegoats for the problems the operation suffered from.

At the time of the refugee emergency in 1994, most agencies, including the UNHCR, responded by hiring more expatriates at ten times what a

Tanzanian professional cost, as described in Chapter 8. This spending did not matter in financially flush times. As USAID and ECHO kept their checkbooks open, expatriates were hired by UNHCR and other NGOs fairly easily. But when the checkbooks closed in late 1994, pressure mounted to lay off expatriates and curtail expatriate-intensive programs. This led to bureaucratic attacks on LWF's programs, some of which were legitimate assaults on our inefficiencies. These assaults (typically verbal, sometimes written) were often expressed as doubts about whether Tanzanian managers were capable of managing complex programs like trucking and water delivery. The bureaucratic assault on LWF's water programs even made its way into the *Joint Evaluation of the Emergency Assistance to Rwanda* (1996:volume 3, Chapter 4).[1]

But at LWF we continued to maintain our identity as an agency able to work well with Tanzanians. The bright spot in our programs was the quality of camp management in Chabalisa 2. This refugee camp had a deserved reputation as being one of the most efficiently and fairly run. The nutritional standards of the refugees were high, and unlike other camps, there were never refugee demonstrations or confrontations ("riots" in the emotion-laden term of the other camp management agencies) about the unfairness of our distribution policies. Nor were there rumors of major food sales to traders as occasionally occurred in some camps.

The expatriate project coordinator, who attended the coordinating meetings at the UNHCR office in Karagwe town, was typically given credit for the good record in Chabalisa 2, even though the actual on-site staff was Tanzanian and Rwandan. This is why a number of the essays (Essays 2, 3, and 6) reflect our need to brag about the capabilities of our Tanzanian staff in this context. In effect, they were preemptive defenses of the capability of our Tanzanian and Rwandan staff. In rereading them, I recognize that the essays were very much written in the context of the moment when bureaucratic maneuverings were taking place. As a result, in retrospect, they appear perhaps too flippant for the serious book I hope this volume will be considered. However, I want to include them because they, like much of the operation, are an emotional response to what was really a bureaucratic problem. It is just that my attempts at eliciting emotion were different than those of the UNHCR and other agencies seeking to perpetuate generous funding policies. Same phenomenon, different goal. A proper bureaucrat would prefer a cost-benefit comparison assessing food distribution in Chabalisa 2, with a comparison to the expatriate-intensive camp management programs run by Concern International or CARE. Such a comparison never happened. In this context, "cute" essays about our camp management programs in Chabalisa 2 were the next best bureaucratic defense we had to offer. They are presented here by and large as they were written during the time I was in Ngara. The date attached to the essay title is the date it was written.

Essay 1 is also about Chabalisa 2. With the assistance of the two LWF project coordinators, Michael Hyden and Denise Barrett, and during my own brief tenure there as acting project coordinator, I was able to collect data about food deliveries, health, and demographics. At the time I thought this data would be useful in managing the camp in the most efficient bureaucratized fashion. In Tanzania, though, I never had a chance to organize the data to my satisfaction. Notably, though the UNHCR was aware that I was collecting data in this fashion, their staff had little interest in using it, and as a result my data analysis was put on hold.

After returning to the United States, I did begin to analyze the data; at one point, I had an interest in publishing the data as an article in an academic journal. While writing this book, though, I became more and more aware that as long as refugee relief programs are dependent on emotion in order to achieve efficiency rather than systematic data collection, the delivery of refugee services remains problematic. Thus the data are included here as an example of what could be, rather than what is. I think it is important to include the data in an abbreviated form in this volume for the benefit of readers who may share my interest and hope that refugee work will become more rationalized.

Essays 4, 5, and 7 were answers to specific questions asked by visitors we had from church agencies in Europe. Since they were intended for a church-based audience, I also responded to requests to personalize the writing in a fashion which appeals to that audience. HIV and AIDS (Essay 4) are important concerns in any Rwandan population. It is also an issue of great interest to the West; indeed, it was one of the best-funded programs in Ngara, being directly funded by USAID via CARE.

Essay 5 is a response to the many normal bureaucratic questions we fielded as to how many refugees there were in Ngara. We never had a good answer. This essay is about the reason why. As described in Chapters 3 and 7, it was one of the first questions asked, because of the obvious need of the bureaucracies for calculability. Refugees have an interest in frustrating this purpose, thereby obtaining more food in order to supplement what is, after all, a fairly meager ration. This is a natural conflict in refugee camp management. As described in Essay 5, though, the numbers published with such certainty are often based on shaky assumptions. This is not due to any ill-will on the part of the international refugee relief regime; rather it is due to the very nature of the process. Despite the certainties of bureaucratic and press accounts, refugee numbers are inherently difficult to determine, and require specialized (bureaucratized) attention.

Just how much specialized attention is required is illustrated by my own efforts at census taking in 1987, which are described in Essay 8. (An earlier version of this essay was published by the journal *Disasters* in 1989.) This is one of my favorite essays, and I am trying to raise its profile a bit by including it here. As a descriptive essay it also fits in well with the bureaucratic pursuit of calculability.

Essay 7 is a short story about how the Anglican church worked in the refugee camps. The international refugee relief regime is of course a firmly secular operation, even though it relies on a number of agencies that have a base in various religious communities. This essay about the Anglican church was written in response to LWF's own church donors, who often had questions about what the church was doing in the refugee camps. I hope it is still of interest to people with those concerns. But I believe that the essay is also of more general interest, as it reflects well the "situational" nature of ethnic identity, especially that of Hutu-Tutsi relations, and is included here primarily for that reason.

Notes

1. The attacks that appeared in the *JEEAR* reflected the problems we had with the management of our water delivery programs in the Benaco camps. In my view, the assertions made about LWF's performance in this sector were erroneous. But this was the program with the most expatriate involvement, and as a result the problems were broadcast most widely, eventually reaching the ears of the *JEEAR* consultants.

Essay 1

The Demography
of a Camp for Rwandans

January 1997

It is well known that the demographic structure of migrant groups is unusual; migration is a process that selects by age, family status, and gender. The most likely age of immigrants is in the economically active years (15 to 30 years) when unmarried people seek work. Immigrant groups may have a disproportionately large number of either males or females, depending on the nature of the work sought (Weeks 1996:218–220).

Refugee groups, though, differ from the typical immigrant group in matters of motivation—refugees, by definition, are not pursuing economic gain but fleeing persecution. The specific demographics of a situation have an effect on the ethnic groups that are subject of the persecution. They also have an effect on age and gender of refugees, for flight itself is demographically selective process (Kunz 1983; Harrell-Bond 1986). The elderly and very young, who are the most vulnerable in any population, are more likely to die during a difficult flight or to be unable to flee in the first place. This in turn can effect the demographic potential within the refugee populations: women in peak fertility years are more likely to be present within the populations, whereas those at ages where mortality is more likely (the very young and the very old) are less likely to be present.

Understanding these issues is important for three reasons.

First, in the short run, understanding refugee demographics is important if relief services are to be delivered effectively. Poor understanding of refugee dynamics has led to policy errors in the provision of relief supplies for targeted portions of the population, as will become apparent below. For example, child mortality is systematically overestimated by formulae which assume that 20 percent of a refugee population is under five (as it is in most rural African areas—see Quist 1995; Médecins sans Frontières 1995); an unusually large number of younger fertile females in the population can mean that fertility patterns will be incorrectly estimated (Waters 1996; Quist 1995; JEEAR 1995); overestimation of the under-five population leads to vaccines and medicines' being over-ordered. The size of the elderly population is also likely to be overestimated.

In a longer term, demographic generalizations are often made having implications for political claims. For example, claims are often made about refugee fertility patterns, death rates, and the relative health of hosts compared to that of the refugee population.[1] The latter claim is often the most politically sensitive owing to the impression held by many that refugees, who are the recipients of international largesse, somehow have an "easier" life than locals if health indicators are better.[2] As is described below, there is some factual basis to such arguments. However, this variation is not due only to international largesse. Low mortality in Chabalisa 2 was also the consequence of the absence of the very young and old who are the ones most likely to die.

Third, a broader theoretical literature dealing with the sociology of refugee populations has emerged, some of it focused on central Africa (Malkki 1995; D. Newbury 1998; Lemarchand 1994; Long 1993; C. Newbury 1995). Implicit to this discussion is how refugee groups grow, contract, and form new social groups (Sommers 1994; Waters 1990; Malkki 1994). The demographic information here describes the basic social material among whom new social accounts, or "ethnohistories," will be generated.

Be that as it may, it is hoped that the following data will form a stronger foundation for discussions in the future. Admittedly, these data are from only one of the 30 or 40 refugee camps in the Great Lakes region and are subject to all the disadvantages of a "sample size of one." However, given their empiricaly grounding, in contrast to the impressionistic demographic conclusions so quickly drawn in policy circles, a number of salient points can be made, including the following (see also Table A1.1):

- Total fertility rates—an estimate of how many children a woman would have—in Chabalisa 2 in 1994–95 may have equaled those in prewar Rwanda by the end of 1995. It took approximately one year for the fertility rates to recover to prewar levels. Crude birth rates—the actual number of children born in a population—on the other hand, were higher owing to the disproportionately large number of fertile females in the refugee population.
- Reported child mortality rates (children under five years old) never equaled those of Tanzania or Rwanda, even during the period shortly after the establishment of the camp, or during the succeeding 15 months (see Table A1.1). Crude mortality levels were also low. This was probably due to a combination of the very small proportion of the population between zero and two years old, and the high level of medical care delivered by the UNHCR and Memisa, a Dutch Catholic agency assigned by UNHCR to provide medical service.
- There was no apparent correlation between delayed food deliveries in April 1994, suboptimal potable water deliveries in late 1995, receipt of a ration rarely exceeding 1,700 kcals per day, and the reported mortality rates. Presumably the low rates of delivered supplies were supplemented by refugee foraging in surrounding areas.
- Neonatal death rates were about 10 percent of all births.

TABLE A1.1   Mortality and Fertility Data for Chabalisa 2 Refugee Camp in 1995

Week	Births	Deaths under 5	Deaths over 59
1	9	4	9
2	2	7	9
3	3	4	8
4	2	2	12
5	–	5	7
6	–	8	1
7	–	3	6
8	4	6	8
9	10	9	10
10	11	3	9
11	–	3	5
12	11	4	2
13	11	3	5
14	5	5	5
15	7	2	6
16	8	2	5
17	–	1	3
18	4	3	2
19	–	1	5
20	9	1	7
21	9	1	4
22	4	4	6
23	11	2	4
24	9	2	6
25	12	5	7
26	28	4	8
27	18	3	7
28	18	2	6
29	15	6	1
30	16	1	5
31	25	0	3
32	20	8	5
33	25	3	6
34	24	4	2
35	25	3	6
36	26	3	5
37	30	3	6
38	38 (to 9/24)	3	8
39	20*	2	2
40	n/a	3	4

October 1995: 156 (35 births per week)
November 1995: 162 (36 births per week)
Total: 927 births for 1995. Crude birth rate of 2.5 percent (24/1,000) on
populations of 37,026. 4.2 percent assuming 30 births per week. CDR 517/37,026,
i.e., 1.4 percent. Natural growth rate would have been 1.1 percent for 1995.
Source: Complimentary records for Chabalisa 2 were photocopied by the author.

- Mortality peaks were reached just after the camp was established in late 1994, and during an epidemic of gastroenteric diseases in February 1995. Otherwise mortality rates were low.
- Approximately one third of all deaths were attributed to malaria. Nevertheless, as with deaths from gastrointestinal disease and malnutrition/starvation, there were notable decreases across time.

The Data: Chabalisa 2 Refugee Camp

A chance to more carefully specify refugee demographics came up in 1994 when Chabalisa 2 camp was established in western Tanzania. Chabalisa 2 was established in September 1994 to accommodate refugees who had arrived in Tanzania between April and August 1994 from two communes in Rwanda. All of the refugees had made a difficult trip by foot across swamplands on the Tanzania-Rwanda border between May and August 1994, and were then received at a campsite named Chabalisa. By the end of August 1994, refugees were occupying swamplands that threatened to be flooded by the rains in September. As a result, a new campsite was established four kilometers away, and approximately 40,000 refugees were moved there. At Chabalisa 2, the refugees were registered and assigned house plots. At the time of registration, each refugee family had to present itself to the nongovernmental agency managing the camp, LWF. The name of the head of household was recorded, as were the age and gender of the household members. This information is reported in Figure A1.1. In December 1992, a sample of 1,404 families (7,480 individuals) was entered into an Excel computer file. From this information, it was possible to calculate age and gender distribution and the family structure of the arrivals.

Data regarding camp fertility was also obtained for the period January 1995–December 1995 from the camp hospital, which was run by Memisa (see Quist 1995). In addition, death registrations for the period October 1994–December 1995 were also obtained for the camp management agency, LWF, which maintained a death register on the basis of information from the hospital. Refugees had incentive to register deaths, in order to be provided with a burial shroud and burial plot.

Information about food distribution was available from April to December 1995. This information was generated by Memisa, which did random surveys at food distribution points every two weeks or so.

Water deliveries ranged from two to five liters per refugee (about one half to one U.S. gallon) per day during the period discussed. Water deliveries were by a combination of piping water from a spring and trucking. Water distribution was coordinated by the agency Oxfam.

The Demographics of Chabalisa 2

Total Population

At the time the camp was founded in September–December 1994, 42,000 refugees were registered. Throughout 1995, a population of 43,000 was assumed for food

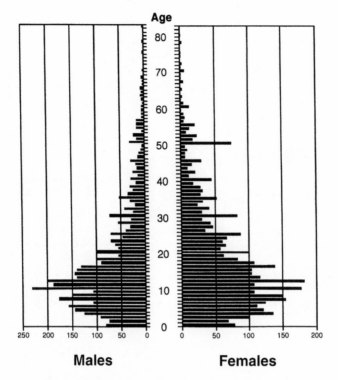

FIGURE A1.1   Age Distribution of Population at Chabalisa 2 Refugee Camp.
Data collected at Chabalisa 2 refugee camp indicated that the refugee population
had an unusual age distribution. Unlike most African populations, the largest
age group is not the very young. Rather, it is the 7-to-15-year-olds of both sexes.
Compared to other African populations, there are also relatively few people over
60. (*Source:* Sample of Chabalisa 2 population done by the author; data collected
under the supervision of Michael Hyden.)

distributions, plot allocations, and other administrative tasks. This figure was adjusted downward to 33,000 in December 1995, after a district-wide UNHCR census of four camps indicated there was a 21 percent overregistration in all
Karagwe camps. It is not clear how much of this overcount had occurred in Chabalisa 2, as camp-by-camp statistics were not released by UNHCR. Because of the
more systematic procedures at the initial registration at Chabalisa (the other
camps relied primarily on refugee generated lists as the refugees arrived directly
from Rwanda), it was assumed that Chabalisa 2 had the most accurate count in
the area. For this reason, this paper assumes a 37,000 refugee camp population in
the calculation of rates.

Age Survey Data

Records of 7,480 refugees from 1,401 families were examined. This is assumed to be 20.2 percent of the total population, and a multiplier of 4.95 was therefore used to generate camp totals for age-specific rates. Half of the records sampled were from each of the two Rwandan communes in Chabalisa 2 present in the camp. Ages for 300 heads of households were randomly assigned due to missing data caused by an omission by one clerk.

Food Distribution and Mortality

As part of the food distribution program, rations were distributed to refugees at a central distribution point every week or two weeks (Table A1.2). During the year,

TABLE A1.2   Food Distribution in 1995

Week	Kcals per person
16	1,647
18	1,600
20	1,692
22	1,710
24	1,468
28	1,770
30	1,409
32	1,614
34	1,641
36	1,655
38	1,677
40	no records
42	3,401 (1700)
44	3,647 (1823)
46	3,748 (1874)
48	3,596 (1798)
50	1,829
51	3,438 (1719)

This table shows statistics from Food Basket Monitoring developed by Memisa on behalf of the World Food Programme. Sampling started at week 16 of 1995, when there were weekly food distributions. After week 42 distributions shifted to a biweekly schedule. Estimates of the weekly rations are therefore given in parentheses. Generation of the data involved random assessment of the rations received by individual refugees as they left the distribution point. Food basket marketing was done by weighing what each family actually received at the food distribution, and then converting the amounts into a figure for kilocalories per day per person.

monitoring data showed that mean rations provided per person ranged between 1,400 and 1,900 kilocalories per person. Low points in distribution did not have an obvious correlation with fluctuations in fertility or mortality. This data do not include what the refugee actually ate. These rations were supplemented by refugees through a range of activities such as foraging, day-labor work, tilling small plots, etc.

Causes of Death

The under-five population had a large proportion of the deaths, as is common in a rural African population (Table A1.3). However, as Table A1.3 shows, the nature of the under-five deaths varied over time. Indeed, in the course of the year there was an overall improvement in the health of children. For example, in October 1994 there were 24 deaths of children between one and five years old, and two neonatal deaths. In contrast, a year later, in October 1995, there were no recorded deaths of one-to-five-year-olds, but there were nine neonatal deaths.

The causes of death were primarily malaria, malnutrition/starvation, and gastrointestinal diseases classified as both diarrhea and dysentery (Table A1.4). The

TABLE A1.3   Monthly Mortality Data

Mortality data	Total	Under 5	Total/day per 10,000	Under 5/day per 10,000	Neonatal under 1 mon.	Infant under 1	CMR modified*
Oct. 94	77	27	0.67	1.74	2	3	1.61
Nov. 94	43	13	0.39	0.87	2	5	0.73
Dec. 94	45	20	0.39	1.29	4	5	1.03
Jan. 95	72	19	0.63	1.26	3	4	1.03
Feb. 95	80	33	0.77	2.36	6	13	1.93
March 95	40	13	0.36	0.84	2	4	0.71
April 95	41	11	0.37	0.73	4	5	0.46
May 95	28	9	0.24	0.58	2	3	0.46
June 95	40	19	0.36	1.27	7	9	0.80
July 95	32	11	0.28	0.71	6	8	0.33
Aug. 95	45	19	0.39	1.27	14	15	0.33
Sept. 95	29	11	0.26	0.71	10	10	0
Oct. 95	14	9	0.12	0.58	9	9	0
Nov. 95	26	14	0.23	0.93	12	13	0.13
Dec. 95	34	20	0.30	1.29	15	17	0.33

*Modified CMR is done with a population of 5,000 under 5. Neonatal deaths are excluded, as these reflect primarily the increase in the birth rate and not overall public health and sanitation standards.

Compiled from the death register maintained by the camp managers. Rates are calculated using an assumed population of 37,000 persons.

TABLE A1.4   Mortality by Disease for Chabalisa 2 Refugee Camp,
October 1994–December 1995

Cause of death	Total	Under 5	Under 1	Under 1 month
Malaria	202	60	31	21
Malnutrition/starvation	103	34	15	8
Gastrointestinal, diarrhea, dysentery	77	30	7	4
Pneumonia	52	23	14	10
Neonatal	22	21	21	21
Childbirth	7	0	0	0
AIDS/HIV	8	1	1	1
Kidney	12	4	1	1
Bacterial	12	4	2	1
Other	149	71	45	31
Totals	644	248	137	98

total number of deaths was highest during the period immediately after the establishment of the camp, but declined toward December 1995 (Table A1.5). This
decline correlates not with fluctuations in food provision, or water provision, but
with time.

Comparative Demographic Data

Standard demographic indicators for Tanzania and Rwanda are found in Table
A1.6. These data indicate that relative to Tanzania and Rwanda, the fertility rates
of the refugee population in Chabalisa 2 were higher and the mortality rates were
lower. In large part this is to be expected from the data in the age pyramid in Figure A1.1. There was a deficit in the age levels vulnerable to mortality, and there
was a large proportion of fertile women without small children.

Discussion: The Demographics of
Chabalisa 2 Refugee Camp

The arriving population had, by African standards, a deficit of children under
five. Typical African populations in rural Tanzania and Rwanda include about 20
percent under-five-year-olds, with the largest number under one year old. The arriving population in Chabalisa 2 had 13 percent under five, with larger numbers
at ages four and five (see Figure A1.1). This probably reflects high death rates of
small children on the trip to Tanzania. Two demographic consequences of this
under-five deficit seem to be decreased overall mortality rates for the camp as a

TABLE A1.5 Mortality by Cause and Month, October 1994–December 1995

Month	Malaria	Malnutrition/Starvation	Gastrointestinal
Oct. 94	20	15	29
Nov. 94	16	12	10
Dec. 94	13	11	0
Jan. 95	21	10	13
Feb. 95	14	17	13
March 95	14	7	6
April 95	15	5	1
May 95	11	3	1
June 95	11	5	2
July 95	20	1	1
Aug. 95	18	0	1
Sept. 95	9	3	0
Oct. 95	3	0	0
Nov. 95	8	3	0
Dec. 95	9	11	0
Totals	202	103	77

TABLE A1.6 Development Indicators in Tanzania and Rwanda, 1989–1994

Indicator	Tanzania	Rwanda
Total fertility rate	5.8	6.8
Maternal mortality/100,000	1,324	748
Dependence ratio	0.94	0.94
Population growth rate	2.6%	2.9%
Life expectancy	51	47
Child malnutrition under 5	28.0%	29.2%
Average household size	n/a	5.0
GNP/capita	$90	$80
IMR	108	84
Under 5 mortality	180	134

Demographic indicators for Tanzania and Rwanda show that the Rwandan refugee population had low mortality rates, and toward the end of their stay, comparatively high fertility rates.

Source: Social Indicators of Development, 1996, Washington: World Bank.

whole, and the rising fertility rates, which were apparent during the latter part of 1995.

Epidemiology

The mortality statistics indicate that the mortality rate of the population of Chabalisa 2 steadily decreased throughout 1995. Infant mortality rates, when corrected for the neonatal death, decreased to an annualized rate of about 12 per 1,000. Nevertheless, about 10 percent of the newborns died owing to a variety of conditions.

There was an epidemic of diarrhea diseases in February, which resulted in a climb in death rates.

In sum, the Chabalisa 2 population was healthy. This is reflected in both declining death rates and increasing fertility rates. This occurred during a time when official food and water distribution fluctuated at levels well below international standards.

The Elder Deficit

Over-65-year-olds were a small proportion of the population in Chabalisa 2. This could mean two things. First, it could mean that fewer over-65-year-olds fled in the first place. This would seem unlikely, as in Rwanda, the elderly population would have had the same reasons to flee as the younger Rwandans. More likely it could be due to the fact that elderly were more vulnerable to death on the road to Tanzania.

The Teenage Surplus

Though there was a deficit of elderly and young in the Chabalisa 2 population, there was an unusually large proportion of youths between the ages of 7 and 21. This will have a long-term fertility implications as the bulge of females enters the reproductive years between 1995 and 2003.

A similar bulge in the male side of the population will mean that there will be a surplus of males entering military age. Given that most Chabalisa 2 refugees have since returned to Rwanda, it is not known what effect this issue will have.

Conclusion

Systematic demographic information about refugee camps is not generally available (for exceptions see Harrell-Bond 1986 and Long 1993). As a result, it is not known whether the data from Chabalisa 2 is typical for refugee populations in general, or even for Rwandan refugees in particular. The data, though, do clarify a number of commonsense assumptions about refugee populations. For example, it is generally assumed that mortality is high during flight, and that as social systems become reestablished (a process that took about one year in Chabalisa 2), fertility rates increase and mortality rates decline. Significantly, a similar pattern seems to have been described in the sketchy demographic data generated by Lynelyn Long for Ban Vinai refugee camp in Thailand. Had refugees remained in Chabalisa 2, the camp would probably have developed in the same way as Ban Vinai.

Notes

1. See Médecins sans Frontières (1995:111) and *MMWR* (1996) for discussions of the upper limits of refugee mortality. They report that death rates of 5 to 10 per 10,000 per day are "frequent." This was not the case in Chabalisa 2; judging from the age survey, this seemed to be due to the demographics of the population which actually arrived. In effect, high mortality either in Rwanda or during the trip to Tanzania meant that few were left in vulnerable age groups in the camp population.

2. Clear-cut evidence of this difference was pointed out by a surgeon who operated on both refugees and Tanzanians and refugees who lived in Karagwe district, Tanzania. He told me that refugees had more subcutaneous fat than locals.

Such dialogue about health status often shapes discussions by nonrefugees about quality of refugee life. Health status, though, should not be confused with overall living conditions. The health status of refugees in the Tanzanian camps was relatively high. However, much more significant for refugee quality of life was the lack of freedom, denial of basic civil rights, and, most important, the lack of a permanent home—the defining feature of refugee status.

Essay 2

Camp Management 1994–95

By Tony Waters and Michael Hyden

October 1995

In August 1994, the UNHCR approached LWF-Ngara about assuming camp management responsibilities for a new camp being opened in Karagwe district in Tanzania. From April to August 1994, the camp at Chabalisa had been receiving wave after wave of refugees from Rwanda. In response, the camp managers, Caritas Tanzania, two other agencies which had withdrawn from camp management, and the UNHCR had been crowding more and more refugees into the camp. Compromises were made, particularly during the dry season, when it was agreed that the only place to house more refugees was in the lowlands. This compromise was made even though all were aware that the land would be uninhabitable once the rains started in October.

LWF-Ngara was ill equipped to cope with this request. It meant establishing an operation over three hours' travel time to the north of our office in Ngara. It also meant pulling staff out of an already stretched operation. In the previous July, we had begun to accept responsibility for the water system. Our trucking operation also continued to be challenged as further waves of refugees arrived, and more water needed to be trucked from the border with Burundi and Rwanda into the Ngara camps. In these respects, however, unfortunately our Ngara operation was no different from other agencies'. Consequently, the urgency of the request from our partners at UNHCR was respected, and LWF agreed to begin operations in Chabalisa immediately.

What Is Camp Management?

The camp managers in each refugee camp are the hands and arms of the UNHCR. In many respects, the camp manager is like the town council. The agency that takes over the camp manager function is the one responsible for assigning plots (120 square meters, or 144 square yards for each family) to refugees, maintaining registration records, and coordinating other agencies such as medical, social services, education, and water in their day-to-day work. Most important, though, the camp management agency organizes the distribution of both food and nonfood items on behalf of the World Food Programme and UNHCR. UNHCR and WFP provide general guidance on such matters in accordance with international standards, but it is the camp management agency that organizes the refugees into lines, and then literally scoops the rations into the refugees' bags. Because of this, the refugees in the camp are very aware of who the camp managers are. More important, the refugees are aware of how fairly and openly their subsistence-level rations are distributed.

Mr. Pantaleon Gambona is LWF's camp manager for Chabalisa 2 refugee camp, and he is justifiably proud of the job that he and his staff have done during the last year. In particular, he points to the fact that there have been no major incidents during distributions during the last year, a claim that none of the other agencies serving Rwandan refugees can make. "We make sure that the refugees understand clearly the limitations under which we operate," he says. "It is important that they understand that when a shortage occurs in WFP's food pipeline, LWF deals as equitably as possible with the situation. This is a sensitive issue to deal with when you might be cutting a weekly maize ration by thirty or fifty percent. After all, this food is what they must live on; by cutting it you are threatening their very existence. In such a circumstance, it becomes very easy for the refugees to blame the distribution agency for the shortage, rather than, say, the shortage of railway wagons, which is the actual cause."

Refugees are by definition vulnerable. What little they do receive they watch carefully and even jealously. For this reason, it is important that they understand the reasons why some people receive more than others, and how target populations are identified to receive food and other items.

Starting in Chabalisa 2

Much of the success in Chabalisa 2 comes from the quick planning that began in September 1994. The camp was laid out in 27 blocks, and each hut received an 8-by-15-meter piece of land. On this land, the refugees were required to build a small hut, typically of grass and sticks that they collect, and covered by one of the most valuable commodities in a refugee's life, a plastic sheet. Shared latrines are dug in the rows in between the huts.

Chabalisa 2 is located around a gentle valley, the camp itself situated on opposite hillsides. Standing on the hilltops, it is possible to see the first work of the plot allocators. The camp itself is in 27 clearly defined blocks of 280 family huts each.

The distribution center is a long building with 14 stalls located near the camp headquarters. Because of the dependent nature of the population, the distribution center is critical to camp management, and was one of the first common buildings to be constructed. The building was designed this way so that the refugees could go to the same stall each week. To avoid confusion, in and out stiles were installed. Because of the urgency of the situation, the camp management infrastructure—the survey, distribution center, latrines, etc.—were installed even as the refugees moved in.

Most important were the toilets, which were being installed by Oxfam. Toilet construction involves the organization of large teams of laborers, and this was the factor that slowed movement into the camp. At times in 1994, it looked as though the state of the new buildings would not keep up with the need to move the refugees out of the old Chabalisa lowlands. Fortunately, though, hard work and good cooperation between the refugees, Oxfam, and UNHCR meant that the refugee population did not expand more rapidly than LWF's ability to receive them.

Effective Camp Management

Refugee Registration

If a plastic sheet is a refugee's most valuable visible possession, the family's ration card is the most valuable document. The ration card is what gives the refugees access to food, a place to build a grass hut, and occasional distributions of jerry cans, soap, plastic sheets, clothing, or other nonfood items.

Accurate registration is a difficult chore for the camp management agency. There is incentive for refugees to exaggerate the number of people in their family or to double-register and receive two ration cards. Registration and issuing the cards is a tricky matter, in which norms of strictness and fairness must be observed. Like income tax fraud, cheating is more likely if it is believed that "everyone else is doing it." From this perspective, it is important for the camp management agency to instill a spirit of "We're all in this together, and we had better make it work."

In the case of Chabalisa 2, this was easier than in other camps; because LWF was able to accept only refugees who had already established themselves at Chabalisa, we did not have to deal with a disorganized arrival from across the border. Refugees were selected at Chabalisa, received a numbered card at that time, and then were transported to Chabalisa 2. At Chabalisa 2, each family presented itself for a ration card which was punched to indicate family size. Aid workers dubbed "shepherds" then took them to the plot that had been saved for them.

Plot Allocation and Dauda Musa

Plot allocation is an ongoing process, and this is where LWF assumes its town council role. Dauda Musa, the head of the plot allocation section, spends much of his time walking around the camp making sure that zoning standards are met, meaning that he looks for abandoned huts, and new huts built outside allocated areas. He also checks to see that all families are maintaining fuel-efficient stoves constructed of mud, dung, and ash, rather than the traditional "three-stone" model.

Musa takes great pride in his work, and likes to take visitors up on the top of the hill so that they can see the straight block pattern. "You should be able to see where everyone is, and easily know how many huts are in each block. This has to tally with the distribution lists which LWF uses for the weekly food distribution," he explains. Among Musa's proudest accomplishments is LWF's plastic roof policy. "Look, every hut has a piece of plastic. And because they are in rows, we know that some are not cheating by building a second hut just to get an extra piece. Finally, all plastic is blue side up! No white tops in Chabalisa 2!" The color is primarily a matter of aesthetics agreed to by Dauda and the camp management, who prefer the blue color. When asked about a single white top in the distance, Dauda sheepishly explained, "We have a few who have sheets of plastic that are white on both sides. That is one of them. But what else can we do?"

Equitable Food Distribution

Food distribution in Chabalisa 2 begins with the storekeeper, who receives bulk food from the central WFP warehouse. Each week, the bulk bags are received for distribution. On each Wednesday, the emptying of the warehouse begins as the food is moved into the distribution center. At the distribution center, refugees queue with their registration cards. After presenting their cards, the week's rations is then scooped into their bags.

There is potential for a perception of unfairness at each stage of the process. At the warehouse, refugees might wonder why bags are left over after the distribution. The same happens at the distribution center. Worse, scoopers may run out of a commodity before finishing with the entire group of refugees.

The key to keeping the distribution fair and accurate is to have the proper scoops. This is not as easy as it sounds, since the bags are measured by weight, while the ration is determined by nutritionists who measure by kilocalories. The scoops themselves are measures of volume. Finally, WFP supplies food that is available for distribution to the refugees, and that depends on what their donors have provided. The staple grain may be sorghum, maize, maize flour, or a high-protein corn-soya blend. If there are chronic shortages of the high-protein blend," the nutritionists may substitute the equivalent kilocalories in maize.

The list of variations goes on, with the result that there may be some confusion and misunderstandings between refugees and the camp managers.

Distribution of Nonfood Items

The UNHCR purchases and collects donations of nonfood items from a variety of sources. Among the basics are plastic sheeting to cover the grass huts, cooking pots, jerry cans, and blankets. These items are typically purchased in bulk, so that every family can receive a basic issue. Other items come in varying quantities. Among the biggest and most generous nonfood item donations that LWF has been involved with was a major clothing donation from the Salvation Army in 1994. Lutheran World Relief (USA) made similar donations through the Christian Council of Tanzania. Soap is also regularly provided. The distribution of both donations was ultimately coordinated by the camp management agencies, which in the case of Chabalisa 2 was LWF. Smaller donations also arrive, and might include extra plastic, hoes, craft kits, maternity kits, etc.

Now that Chabalisa 2 is established, the smaller-quantity items are the focus of distribution. Typically there is not enough to give one to every refugee, so LWF works to target the nonfood item donations for the most appropriate or needy refugees. This requires a lot of footwork on the part of the staff, and good cooperation with the other agencies, like Memisa, which has public health visitors, Save the Children (U.K.), which coordinates social welfare services, or Helpage, which is developing income-generating programs for the elderly and vulnerable. These agencies come in contact with refugees who are particularly vulnerable for one reason or another and make recommendations about how to target donations. As the camp manager, though, LWF has the responsibility for ensuring that the lists accurately reflect needs and verifying that the targeted population actually receives the donation.

The Importance of Effective Local Staff

From the beginning of our work in Chabalisa 2, LWF has been relying on Tanzanian and Rwandan staff to manage the camp. That they have proved effective managers means that systems will be maintained past the point when UNHCR funding for the comparatively expensive expatriates employed by other camp management ends in 1996. The heavy reliance on local staff was in large part made possible by LWF's long experience in Tanzania. Experienced LWF staff from Ngara, Likuyu settlement for Mozambicans, Mishamo, Kigoma, and Ulyankulu project for Burundians, and Handeni settlement for Somalis are all now working in Chabalisa 2 programs. Ironically, although it is often observed by the UNHCR that Chabalisa 2 management is a model for other camps, the fact that heavy responsibilities are assumed by Tanzanian and Rwandan staff is not often connected to this success. One of LWF's recent expatriate volunteers in Chabalisa 2, Ida Grum, from Denmark, complained about this problem. "When visitors come to see the 'model' camp, they look to me for answers. I in turn simply turn to the local staff for the answers. This happens despite the fact that people like the camp manager, Gambona, and Dauda have been here longer and indeed deserve much of the credit for the good work."

What Future for Chabalisa 2?

LWF staff at Chabalisa 2 are justifiably proud of their work. In one short year, they have built on a bare hillside a community of 41,000 people who are able to live together reasonably well. But of necessity, Chabalisa 2 is a temporary settlement; it is still a crowded refugee camp in which people can only wait out a permanent solution to the Rwanda refugee crisis. Certainly the 120-square-meter plots offer little to a population of what were recently self-sufficient farmers. Assuming land is of good quality, a minimum of about two hectares per family is required for self-sufficiency. Clearly Chabalisa 2 does not even offer a fraction of this opportunity.

Currently, the refugees resist suggestions of voluntary repatriation. They continue to hear rumors of killings in Rwanda and point out that the land in the communes from which they come has been occupied by others. As farmers, this is an important question. When can they start farming in order to sustain themselves again? One year of living in the crowded conditions of Chabalisa 2 has yet to offer an obvious answer to the vast majority. As camp managers, it is our hope that we can offer them a safe if austere haven from which the search for more permanent solutions can take place.

Essay 3

The Chabalisa 2
Market Development Project

January 1995

An Introduction to the LWF "Building Code Inspector"

Consolata Mbeikiza's official title is "assistant plot allocator" for LWF's camp management program in Chabalisa 2 camp. Chabalisa 2 is a compact "urban" area of 41,000 people in a remote corner of Tanzania. As with any urban area, the camp requires some discipline and organization if people are to live together in as healthful and safe environment as is possible under the difficult circumstances. Consolata, a Tanzanian in her early twenties, is in effect a building code inspector. It is her job to see that the rules that are adopted for the well-being of the camp are enforced as effectively as possible.

Consolata's rather dry title of "assistant plot allocator" obscures the enthusiasm she has for what is, from her perspective, exciting and challenging. On a recent Saturday afternoon, she explained to me her latest problem: "We had two trucks for hauling garbage from the marketplace yesterday. But it wasn't enough. We need more! When can you send them?"

I had to swallow a couple of times. Frankly, I hadn't heard that the marketplace was in such bad shape; refugee camp marketplaces are usually chaotic places, and to be honest, I had never given the issue a second thought. But Consolata continued anyway, describing what she had been organizing with the camp's "market committee."

"Now we are getting everything in the market organized. The traders have to build proper tables of sticks. And we want the trash out of there. No more heaps of garbage just behind the building. We have to have proper pits, and then get the garbage out of here."

Ever the bureaucrat, I quickly asked who was going to pay for this. This came up because I know that the giant camp at Benaco has a separate line in the budget for marketplace garbage collection. I knew that Chabalisa 2 had no such line. But the question of who would pay had never even occurred to Consolata.

"Pay?" She exclaimed. "Nobody has even brought up the subject. They have to do this themselves. The same goes for building the tables, and they better do it in a straight line, and leave five meters on either side for the road, too."

"Oh?" I asked. "And if they do not, who is going to make them?" I couldn't forget that Consolata was talking about a population that had recently gone through a war. Likewise, I was aware also that at least some of the young men in the camp had been members of the Hutu militias that had committed the geno- cide last year. Who was going to keep them in line?

Consolata was not worried about these questions and had a quick answer: "Me, of course. See that stove over there? That is going to be moved out of the five-meter road easement by Monday." To emphasize the point, she pointed to a nearby hut where a new fuel-efficient design was being finished. "See, she is get- ting ready already." An older man passing by overheard us and started to laugh. I asked him if the stove would be moved by Monday. "Oh yes, of course it will. This is going to be the road."

Consolata's assertions went against every theory of refugee participation that has been preached by the UNHCR and LWF. The theory is that outsiders, be they Tanzanian or Europeans, simply facilitate the "felt needs" of the refugees. Nowhere in the theory is there room for a brash young woman to run around or- dering refugees to pick up trash, make tables, and move stoves. The theory is a product of past practice and is grounded in concrete experience. Such top-down approaches are avoided because they do not work. Refugees, like most people, do not respond well to arbitrary orders from strangers.

Consolata has never read of such theories, but she knows what she wants for "her" market. "Now, we are organizing all the sellers into sections. On those ta- bles over there, tomatoes. Onions are over there. And no more banana beer [*pombe*] drinking or eating is allowed on the road. It just makes a mess. The houses for *pombe* drinking are over there, and the restaurants are over there. Fish is sold way there in the back; you know it stinks. And way over there in the cor- ner is where they slaughter the pigs. Some people don't like that, you know."

Consolata's next goal is to enact building codes for the mud and stick build- ings that make up the marketplace. "Look at that wall," she says pointing at a leaning wall that has started shedding lumps of mud. "Not only is it ugly, but it is also a hazard; the house can crumble at any time on whoever happens to be sit- ting inside." She then shifts my attention to another building. "Now, compare it to that one. They have only used local materials [typically sand, clay, cow dung, and ashes], but there is a thin plaster wall to hold things together. And most im- portant, the walls are straight. That is the way all of the buildings should be done."

The Importance of Language Skills in Chabalisa 2

Later I asked Jean-Claude Bucysenge, one of our senior Rwandan staff members, how Consolata does it. He explained that it was difficult at first. "You know, at first the people in the market did not want to go along with it. But she talked and talked with them, and now they see that it is best for them to organize together in order that the marketplace is better for all concerned. It also helps a lot that she speaks our language, Kinyarwanda well. She can talk to the people easily, and gets along with them well."

Consolata, whose first languages are Kinyambo (the local tribal language) and Kiswahili (Tanzania's national language), explains that she began learning the refugees' language, Kinyarwanda, in April 1994, when Rwandan refugees began to arrive in her home village of Bugene, some 40 kilometers (25 miles) from Chabalisa 2. "I have always known Rwandans, as there were Tutsi refugees from the 1960s living in Bugene. However, they learned our languages, Kiswahili and the local language, Kinyambo, and we did not learn theirs. In April 1994, though, things changed. Thousands of refugees began to arrive in the area, and I began to learn a little. Later, I started working for LWF and living near Chabalisa 2, so then I really had incentive to learn, as did all of the other LWF employees. Now, most of us speak Kinyarwanda, even though it is so different from Kiswahili."

A Meeting with the Market Committee

The Wednesday after Consolata gave me her tour, Dauda Musa, head of the Plot Allocation Unit, took me and Consolata to a meeting of the "market committee," a group of 15 to 20 people who have stalls in the market. Dauda has a philosophical bent, and he explained that for Consolata to make the market project work, it was necessary to "force" the market vendors to cooperate. He elaborated later, though, that this was a "force" that came from verbal persuasion, and not from violence. He says that this is difficult with Rwandan market vendors. Everything for them is business, which is fine, but sometimes they do not see that a day's work together to dig a garbage pit, or make proper tables for their food products, is related to the success of their business." Nevertheless, at the meeting, the committee immediately confronted me with a number of requests.

Could LWF provide tools for the sanitary needs of the market? The answer was yes but only if a plan was presented that would insure that the tools were not stolen.

Could LWF provide pay a salary to the market committee members? UNHCR was paying camp security to provide a similar public service, so why not pay the market committee? The answer was no way. UNHCR and LWF have similar policies about many matters, but not this. After all, the market committee were among the most economically fortunate in the camp, and keeping the market clean and safe was at least as much in their interest as in LWF's. Out of this request though, came an explanation of how market cleanliness policies work.

The market committee wanted LWF to pay for cleaning the market. Currently, the committee members explained, the vendors hire other refugees, typically the handicapped, to clean the market. Each vendor pays the refugee with a bit of produce, so for the day's work, a refugee receives a banana from one person, a bit of clothing from another, some local tobacco from another, etc. These "taxes" are obligatory, and vendors who refuse to pay are sent to the refugee leadership for punishment.

The market committee also wanted additional cleaning in the market. Would LWF provide money to pay them to clean the market another two times per week? This was a trickier question, but still the answer was no. Again it was explained that they were responsible for the market and LWF would only support their own efforts. I even quoted the former president of Tanzania, Julius Nyerere, who had always emphasized the importance of "self-reliance and self-help" in projects such as market improvement.

Working with Rwandans and Tanzanians: Dauda Explains

After experiencing Consolata's enthusiasm, I went away from the meeting a bit concerned. Had my presence as an expatriate raised questions of payment and money that would damage the good work of our plot allocation team? I do not have an answer to this question. Dauda, though, offered an explanation of what he thought had transpired.

"You were offering them the solutions of Tanzania, where we have been brought up believing that individuals must work together for public goods," Dauda explained. "The refugees from Rwanda do not have this background, and are more focused on what is in it for them as an individual. This means that our approach must be adjusted. They are used to the 'force' of physical compulsion or money, and not the 'force' of persuasion, to accomplish group tasks like maintaining the marketplace. I do not believe this is good, but it is a fact that we must work with."

Urban Planning for a Refugee Camp?

Despite the difficulties, Camp Manager Pantaleon Gambona is highly supportive of his plot allocation team's attempts to establish a good standard for what might be called urban planning. "LWF is very proud of the way that Chabalisa 2 looks, whether it is in the neat and pleasing way that the refugee houses are laid out, or the way the market is conducted," he says. "We find that when, in consultation with the refugees, we enforce good planning habits, the results are pleasing for most, and certainly serve the broader benefit of the public. It is bad enough that these people must live as refugees in the first place. There is no reason we cannot work together to make the best of a bad situation, though."

Essay 4

HIV and AIDS in the Ngara Refugee Camps

September 1995

I spent some time in August talking with Judy Benjamin, of CARE's HIV control program in Ngara, and Dr. Rwenkyendele, of the ELCT (Evangelical Lutheran Church in Tanzania, the Northwest Diocese) AIDS prevention program in Bukoba. HIV and AIDS will become a very important issue for the refugee population over the next few years, and I think it is worthwhile briefing LWF's church donors in North America and Europe about how the issue is being handled now.

Before the war Rwanda had a very high HIV infection rate. The best survey indicated that 30 percent of all women seeking prenatal care in urban areas were HIV-positive. The rate in rural areas was considerably lower. These different rates reflected the greater number of sexual contacts by people living in the relatively anonymous world of Rwanda's cities (especially Kigali) than those living in rural areas. Furthermore, social control of sexual behavior remained stronger in the rural areas, where informal social monitoring is easier because everyone knows everybody else.

Benaco camp has a population that was originally half urban and half rural. However, the social habits observed there during the last year indicate that the habits of promiscuity are more like those of urban Rwanda. For this reason, the HIV infection rate is expected to climb toward at least 30 percent of all women seeking prenatal care, as it was in urban Rwanda. Presumably, a similar number of men could also be infected.

There is some feeling among AIDS workers that promiscuity is a bigger problem in the camps than even in urban Kigali, due, they claim, to the lack of activity for the young adult population (no secondary schools, and no jobs), and to difficulty in maintaining normal "social control monitoring" by parents and others—a condition created by the camp environment. There are anecdotal descriptions of despair among young people who have witnessed the death of their peers and family, and have themselves fled to Tanzania. Under such conditions, young people can become very reckless in their sexual habits. The attitude described reminds me of the way social workers in South Los Angeles describe gang members there. The young people say that they have nothing to live for, and will probably die soon anyway. Commercial sex is available in the camps for about 200 Tanzanian shillings (about 33 cents), and many young men and women engage in casual sex. A new fashion for some young men is to boast about their sexual conquests by wearing the rings from condoms as wrist bracelets.

The anonymous nature of a refugee camp adds to this lack of social control. It is easy for young people to avoid monitoring from parents or peers by disappearing into another corner of the camp, where nobody knows them. Because of this anonymity they can behave in ways not possible in a more settled rural or even urban environments. The anonymous nature of this situation will have impacts on the camp population, both immediately and in the long term. Short-term impacts include high rates of crime, higher rates of fertility, and public health problems, in addition to increased promiscuity. In the long-term, AIDS is expected to increase dramatically as a public health concern for the Rwandan refugee population.

So far, AIDS itself is present at relatively low rates in the camps. It is hypothesized that this is because only healthy people were able to flee from Rwanda; individuals with AIDS were too sick to flee. However, the incidence of AIDS is now increasing as those who were HIV-positive when they entered the camp come to the end of the latency period and develop full-blown AIDS.

CARE's HIV-control program focuses on prevention at several levels. Education programs emphasize abstinence by singles, fidelity for those who are married, condom distribution (currently 150,000 per month) to the sexually promiscuous and HIV-positive, and control of sexually transmitted diseases (STDs) such as gonorrhea and syphilis. STD control is perhaps the most effective concrete anti-AIDS measure that can be undertaken, as the ulcers created by gonorrhea and syphilis made the transmission of HIV much more efficient. Convincing the medical NGOs to act aggressively against such otherwise nonlethal diseases, though, has been difficult. Emergency-focused medical agencies will treat acute diseases likely to result in immediate death first. CARE has had some trouble persuading them to take treatment of STDs seriously, as the problem is neither acute nor the consequences of treatment immediate. On the other hand, in the context of a long-term public threat such as AIDS, control of STDs can prevent great loss of life. For example, a 1 percent decrease in the HIV transmission rate in the Ngara camps would be expected to save 4,000 lives in the long run.

Care of the terminally ill AIDS patient is also considered to be part of AIDS-prevention programs. Current protocols at Red Cross Hospital call for the referral of terminally ill patients to the home for care. Rwandans do care well for the terminally ill at home, and CARE has been attempting to reinforce this with the targeted donation of commodities and supplementary food. This has become more difficult since adult supplemental feeding programs were discontinued as part of the recent budget cuts. As a result of the AIDS caseload, the need for adult supplemental feeding programs will probably rise with the AIDS rate. It is unclear how or if this need will be met.

Essay 5

How Many Refugees
Are There in Ngara?

March 1996

Inquiring minds often want to know how many refugees there are in Tanzania? It is a fair question; after all, much of the refugee assistance program is dependent upon refugee counts. Most critically, policies about how much food and water need to be distributed and pumped require a good head count. Medical statistics, mortality rates, and birth rates are based on number of cases per 10,000 people, which implies a good census. Donors are interested, because they want to know how many dollars are being spent per refugee for a particular service. Does it cost $50 per year to maintain a refugee, or $150? Both WFP and UNHCR set budgeting figures when doing their planning.

Officially, there were 472,811 refugees in Ngara as of February 29, 1996. Arriving at such a figure inevitably involves compromises and approximations, a result of practical logistical reasons, bureaucratic inertia, "cheating the system" by refugees, and wishful thinking by agency officials and journalists eager to make the operation seem as big as possible.

But It's Not That Easy

This may be a legitimate question for inquiring minds. But even the total number of refugees is a hard number to get a fix on. People move here and there. Refugees exaggerate numbers to get more rations per person—if you will, rations for "ghosts." During census times, there are inevitably rumors that local Tanzanians are "rented" for the day to make head counts higher and get a higher number punched on the ration card. In addition, most people simply like bigger numbers. As a result the numbers go up and up.

A good example of how difficult it is to keep numbers down was in the first days of the Benaco camp. This was especially apparent at the beginning of the emergency, when everyone wanted to know how many people had crossed the Rasumo River bridge from Rwanda into Tanzania. At that time the UNHCR, claiming that 250,000 had crossed the bridge, called the period April 28–29, 1994, "the largest and fastest exodus" in modern history. Estimates of the total that actually crossed the bridge ran from about 130,000 to a high of 400,000. In a recently published book, whose author should have known better, the number was again reported as 250,000.

What was the actual number? Probably about 70,000—which is a lot, but still is an overestimate of about two times the lowest figure that was bandied about in May 1994. The 70,000 number, though, was arrived at only after the refugees had been in place in refugee camps for seven to eight weeks, and was obtained by means of a large wristbanding exercise in which every single refugee had a non-removable wristband put on in one day. The resulting figure was 229,000, which included not just the 70,000, but also the tens of thousands more who forded the river in May and June.

In contrast, the lists provided by refugee leaders at the time, which constituted the only source UNHCR and WFP had for population, said that there were well over 400,000 in the Ngara camp complex in June 1994. This number was arrived at on the basis of reports of refugee leaders and the distribution of ration cards which had been given to the arriving refugees at the border during the previous weeks. Both ways of counting are easily undermined: refugee leaders had incentives to exaggerate family sizes: it meant more rations for the followers who had elected them. As for the cards, a second card could be obtained by "recycling," i.e., walking back to the border from Benaco and then reappearing in Ngara and getting a second card. Many young men did this.

All involved in the wristbanding initiative knew this, and were aware that the actual numbers were in fact much lower. Indeed, in order to facilitate planning, different programs were using lower figures. As a result in June 1994, food distribution was done on the basis of a count of about 450,000; water systems were being developed for 350,000; and medical statistics were gathered using yet another figure.

No matter how much we all were aware of the potential for fraud, we still like big numbers, and the tendency is to "round up." In a betting pool conducted by the UNHCR staff in late June 1994, before the wristbanding exercise, most estimates were in the 300,000-plus range, which was 33 percent lower than what was actually being used for food distribution. The actual number of people banded was under every single guess, and came to 229,000, a substantial number by most standards, but disappointing for many in the context of the former figure. The 229,000 confirmed in the camps at the end of June, also called into question the count of 250,000 crossing the bridge in the first day.

How Counts Work

A look at three counts that were released by UNHCR for the Ngara area camps in June and July 1995 points at how much numbers can vary (see Table A5.1).

The June lists were estimates developed by the UNHCR in cooperation with refugee leaders. The UNHCR was suspicious though, and let the refugee leaders know it. As a result, they requested the refugees to provide lists of people in their administrative units, which they did, and the number dropped by 45,000 people.

TABLE A5.1   A Comparison of Refugee Counts

Camp	Previous lists (June)	Leaders' lists (June)	Verified (July)
Benaco	190,000	166,886	158,462
Msuhura	100,000	84,246	75,260
Lumasi	126,000	114,616	106,073
Lukole	25,000	21,000	19,050
Kitali	61,000	70,668	62,214
Totals	502,000	457,416	421,059

This is apparently the number that the leaders thought they could get away with without incurring too much wrath from UNHCR and WFP. At a verification exercise conducted in mid-July in which every refugee had to show up and be sprayed behind the ear with florescent dye, the number dropped another 26,000 people, a total decline in population of about 16 percent. Accordingly, the WFP rations provided to all of the camps was cut by 16 percent. The total amount of water provided stayed the same, so actually now the paper figure of water provided to each refugee actually went up 16 percent. When calculated on this lower total population, the birth rate, mortality rate, and other statistics which had been using the 502,000 figure also went up.

How the Population Count Is Done

The best counts in the Tanzanian camps have been done as part of verification exercises. This was last done in July 1995, in Ngara, and December 1995, in Karagwe. All refugees were required to arrive with all family members on one day. All refugees are sprayed with fluorescent dye behind the right ear. At the first booth, each refugee is checked for the fluorescent dye. If they do not have any dye, they are sprayed; the dye is difficult to remove during the first 48 hours after it has been sprayed. The family then reports to the next booth, where the name of the head of family is checked against computerized lists. Finally, they are given a numbered card in which the camp they are assigned to and the number of people in the household is punched. This can be used for collecting rations as well as to verify plot assignments. This is a verification of physical presence, and not individuals. In effect, the exercise is designed to see if an actual body is there.

Attempts are made to keep the day of the verification exercise secret so that refugees cannot hire Tanzanians to be part of their families. This seemed to work in the December 1995 verification exercise in Karagwe District. A small number of families went from previous counts of say, ten persons, down to three who actually showed up. Overall, for the district the count in all five camps was down 22 percent.

How Influxes Are Counted—The Case of Keza

Much of the initial number reports are made when the refugees arrive. Refugees do not arrive through a border control, so the counting is often haphazard. For example, during the January 1996 influx from Burundi, different numbers were provided from least five different sources. A soldier told me how many had passed a particular point that day. A driver then told me how many trips he had made to the transit camp, carrying 60 refugees each time; you could then multiply the number of trips by 60. The manager of the transit camp also had a rough idea of how many he was putting wristbands on and feeding, while the head of the trucking operations had added together the manifests of the number of refugees being sent from the transit camp to Keza. At Keza, the UNHCR took off the wristbands, issued ration cards (as above), and came up with another number.

How Counts Come Undone

Despite the hard work that went into reaching the 421,059 figure above, or the 25,000 figure for Keza, such numbers can become obsolete very quickly, because refugee populations can be very fluid. Refugees repatriate both through official channels and on their own. Lots of babies are born in refugee populations, and a few refugees die. However, the annual natural rate of increase (births minus deaths) is probably about 3 to 4 percent per year.

Other refugees have disappeared into Tanzanian towns and into Kenya and Uganda. Tanzanian police even picked up seven Rwandan refugees on the Mozambican border last month who were on their way to that country! Now that I think of it, even a number of refugees I know have done the disappearing act . . . Ana went to Rwanda to have her baby . . . Mary went to Kenya with her four children . . . Mary's husband went to Poland (!) on a fellowship to get a Ph.D. . . . Petro moved from Chabalisa 2 to Benaco to start a small store. Then there was the Tutsi family I met in Msuhura who picked up and went to Mwanza, in Tanzania, one day. And those are the ones I know; what about the hundreds of thousands I've never met?

But then last October it was pointed out to me that a number of the huts in Lukole camp were new, and had been built by refugees who had recently arrived despite the legal restrictions on entry, and who did not therefore receive food rations. Presumably they will be added during the next verification exercise.

Oh, and then there were the 25,000-plus who slipped across the border legally in January and are now settled in Keza. I talked to a few of them, who were in fact Tanzanians who had been living in Burundi. They had had it with refugee life, and planned to leave for Mwanza as soon as possible. Others were Burundians who had lived in Tanzania some years and had plans already to slip surreptitiously into Tanzania to begin farming in the countryside. And another one I remember was talking about slipping back to Burundi to find his wife and children. I don't know what side of the border they ended up on, even though they were counted as refugees at one or two points.

TABLE A5.2   Fluctuation of Refugee Population in Ngara Camps

Starting figure, July 1995		421,059
5% annual growth rate to March 1996 (9 months)	add	15,000
Official repatriation since July	subtract	6,910
January influx-Keza	add	30,000
Voluntary unofficial repatriation	subtract	10,000?
Leaving for other countries	subtract	10,000?
Unofficially moving into camps	add	10,000?
Recycling and double registration	subtract	5,000
Total		437,969?

Okay, but How Many Refugees Are There in Ngara?

Despite this confusion, we can do some quick adding and subtracting to figure out how the refugee population is probably changing in the Ngara camps (see Table A5.2).

The UNHCR's official count was actually 472,811 on February 29, 1996. You judge now. Which is better? The UNHCR method, or mine? I like big numbers too, so I will acknowledge that we are probably both a bit high. But compromise is always the preference in bureaucracies, so let's split the difference and say the actual number is in the middle. After all, this is how a lot of our figures are arrived at, even if it is not statistically a valid way to go!

The net result is that when all is said and done, a verification exercise done today would probably show that there are slightly more refugees today than in July 1995. The Keza influx, poor response to voluntary repatriation programs, low mortality, and high birth rates all point at such a conclusion. So, how about 450,000 as a figure for the number of refugees in Ngara camps? This can be roughly translated as "half a million" by people trying to impress (say, in press releases and donor appeals), and "up to 500,000" by the more precisely inclined. Both efforts keep with the tradition of rounding all figures upward, which has been going on since the first day.

Essay 6

Wishing for Repatriation, Late 1995

February 1996

I was acting project coordinator at LWF's project in Karagwe during the last two months. The permanent project coordinator, Denise Barrett, arrived in early January, and I have been handing over the operation to her during the last ten days. This involves briefing her on the myriad of daily issues about which a project coordinator must make decisions. Most are mundane issues: leave schedules, night allowance payments, lorry servicing, and so on. Something came up the other day, though, which Denise, at least, thinks is more illustrative of the unique problems that a refugee service agency occasionally faces. At its most simple level, it is a story involving the theft of an employee's belongings. In the background, though, is enough refugee politics, duplicity, and even international intrigue to make the story worth retelling to a broader audience. But to get the whole flavor of the situation, it is necessary to step back to 1994, when the refugee emergency in Tanzania began.

The Story of Pierre and Petro

The story started in September 1994, when LWF–Ngara agreed to take over as the "camp manager" agency for Chabalisa 2 in Karagwe district. One expatriate, Michael Hyden, two refugees, and three Tanzanians were hired to set up the camp and went off in two Russian Kamaz lorries to do so. As an afterthought, Michael hired another Rwandan refugee, Petro, as a cook for the camp he planned to set up. For the refugees to move from the Ngara area camps to the Karagwe camps, it was necessary to get permits from the Tanzanian government. After getting the necessary permits they set off.

A year later Petro was still a cook in the camp. Pierre, one of the two original Rwandan refugees, had become LWF's head of distribution. Neither Petro nor Pierre was satisfied with refugee camp life, and by November 1995, both were dreaming of returning to Rwanda. Both had received messages from friends and family in Rwanda saying that it was safe for them to return. I also knew that both young men, though nominally Hutu, also had Tutsi in their family background. Some months ago, Pierre had told me that his mother is Tutsi. Petro, while working in Michael Hyden's house some months previously, had even sung Rwandan Tutsi songs, which, he told Michael, he could be attacked for in the Hutu refugee camp.

The dream of return was so powerful that Petro volunteered for an UNHCR "go and see" visit, which is a trip back to the home village of the refugee so that they can see the conditions of their home and family. Each volunteer was screened by the UNHCR, Tanzanian government, and Rwandan government, so that they can avoid sending someone who may try to sabotage the program for political purposes. During the visit, the refugees are permitted to visit privately with their families so that there can be a frank discussion of conditions in the refugee camps, as well as in the home village. The refugees are then accompanied back to their home camp in Tanzania by the UNHCR. The purpose of the program is to build confidence in the voluntary repatriation policy that UNHCR is advocating.

I talked to Petro and Pierre just before Petro left. Both were excited, and speculated that they would soon be able leave the refugee camp and return home. Pierre in particular wanted to find an opportunity to study languages at the post-secondary level.

So Petro went to Rwanda in November 1995. I ran into him just after he returned, in early December, and he was breathless to tell his story. He very much wanted to start at the beginning, and narrated how the UNHCR Karagwe office had taken every care to ensure that the refugees on the trip were comfortable. He continued to narrate about how he had been searched at the border by "unfriendly" Rwandan soldiers. Later he was received by the prefect of the province, who was cordial and gave him a letter to facilitate his visit.

Finally, he got to the point of the story, which was his visit with his mother. He was pleased to find her well, and was received cordially. But after that, things went wrong, grievously wrong. He narrated to me that his mother told him privately that he should use his exit permit, and never come back to Rwanda; that he was fortunate to be in Tanzania where he was safe. He went on to relate how he was told that all the young Hutu men were either in jail or dead. That people continue to disappear in the night, and that the government soldiers have sealed the border, stopping all illicit refugee exits. He was told that the head of the district where he lived had spread rumors that Hutu men were not welcome in the area.

I drove away with my head spinning. There had been encouraging signs that the voluntary repatriation program would take off during the previous month. Two to three thousand refugees, most of whom were women and children, had volunteered to be what were presumed to be "scouts" for the men. The UNHCR and the government were issuing press releases about how they expected thousands to be returning to Rwanda daily. The UNHCR even bragged that the Rwandan government had committed itself to accepting 10,000 per day. Buses were purchased and positioned in Ngara for what was expected to be the repatriation of 1996. Who was telling me the truth? Was UNHCR engaging in wishful thinking about the Rwandan government and refugee safety in Rwanda? Were the political leaders of the Hutu refugees manipulating this situation?

Anyway, Petro went on to tell a number of people, including other refugees as well as expatriates, the same story he had told me. I assumed that Pierre of course would no longer have any interest in repatriation as a result of what Petro had told him. I also heard that one of the refugees in Petro's "go and see" group had just about been lynched when he was accused of genocide; only the presence of a UNHCR officer had saved him, so the story went.

The UNHCR Talks About the Visit

Two weeks later, in early January, there was a regular UNHCR coordinating meeting. At the meeting, a UNHCR repatriation officer explained the situation in Rwanda. The driver of Petro's car in Rwanda had heard Petro and another refugee concocting their story to discourage repatriation, he said. This refugee had indeed almost been lynched, but he had encountered an unusual situation, the repatriation officer asserted. The officer pointed out that the matter had been discussed at the national-level tripartite meeting between UNHCR, Rwanda, and Tanzania, where all acknowledged that such things were unavoidable in such a charged situation. The situation is confusing for everyone, after all.

Further complicating matters was the fact that one refugee who had participated in a "go and see" visit in early January had been arrested for genocide, after being duly screened by the UNHCR, Tanzania, and Rwanda. On the visit, he had gone to his home commune in Rwanda and there he was promptly arrested. The subject came up at our meeting, and UNHCR explained to those at the meeting that this refugee had been warned earlier by his friends not to go, as it was well known in the Tanzanian camps that he had participated in the April 1994 massacres. Oddly enough, this came to light only after the fact; it was not apparently well enough known for the UNHCR or Tanzanians who screened him to have caught wind of this explanation before he left in early January.

Finally, at the conclusion of the meeting, we received a stern warning from both the UNHCR and the government that we staff members of NGOs were not to discuss any such issues with the refugees; anything that could be interpreted as discouraging voluntary repatriation would result in our expulsion from Tanzania.

My own view is that there is some truth on all sides. It is apparent that conditions are safe for some in Rwanda, and not for others. Finally, there are at least as many accusations of lying and duplicity as there are actual lies. Most significant, there is a lot of wishful thinking on the part of refugees searching for a future and of the UNHCR searching for a workable policy. Identifying such a policy is extremely difficult, given the emotional, suspicious, and fearful atmosphere in which such decisions are being made.

Anyway, this is all just background to the problem that Denise will confront, which has to do with theft and not refugee repatriation policy. Her problem involves Pierre and, indirectly, Petro. I was briefing Denise on expense vouchers, or one of the other mundane points of Karagwe administration, when Pierre came in with an agitated look on his face. He explained that while he was on a LWF-sponsored trip to see the distribution system in our Kibondo camp, his house had been burglarized, and all of his possessions stolen. It seems that he had left Petro in charge of his house. During the two days when he was on the study trip, the UNHCR had informed Petro that he would lose his refugee status in Chabalisa 2 because he was really from the Ngara camp, whence Michael had taken him the previous year. Shortly thereafter, he went back to Ngara. And Pierre's money was gone. The coincidental departure and disappearance of the money looked suspicious. But was Petro the thief? Or was he the witness?

Pierre, agitated, wanted to follow Petro to Ngara with a policeman so that he could be brought back to Chabalisa 2 as a witness or be placed under arrest, or something. Likewise, it would not do to simply call on the radio for a policeman from Ngara to go find Petro; he was in a camp of 150,000 people, and Pierre was needed there in order to identify him.

So, Denise, what to do? She quickly ticked through the standard administrative decision tree. Sending a car for this purpose, a personal matter, would set a bad precedent. But Pierre is an important employee, so is there another way? What about that Kamaz with the two flat tires? (The Kamaz is a heavy-duty Russian truck maintained in Karagwe as a recovery vehicle). Didn't you tell me that those tires could only be replaced in Ngara, and don't we have to pick up generators for the UNHCR anyway? Okay, I think we have a solution our problems. Generators, tires, and Pierre, I think we have a go. Let us know how things go . . .

Postscript

I went to Chabalisa 2 two days ago, in February 1996, in order to buy some baskets for a neighbor. I saw Pierre, and again he had something urgent to tell me. I wanted to find out what had happened with Petro, the arrest, etc., but instead he wanted to tell me about his own "go and see" visit to Rwanda. He had gone in early January (when the refugee described above had been arrested). He had visited his house, which had been destroyed, and had walked into his neighborhood. He said that many of the refugees' houses were empty, waiting for their owners to return. He said that though "everything has changed," life was returning to normal, and he was thinking of returning in May 1996, when he is due his annual leave from his duties at LWF. He also reported that he visited the LWF office in Kibungo, was well received, and was considering asking for a job there in their repatriation program beginning next May. Certainly, this was very different version of a "go and see" visit than that offered by Petro.

Also encouraging for Pierre was that he had recently received a letter from his uncle who is a Catholic bishop emeritus in Rwanda. Pierre had met a Danish journalist, Ulrik, in December who was to visit Rwanda on behalf of Danchurchaid. Pierre asked Ulrik to visit his uncle to deliver news of him. Ulrik did this, and the bishop, delighted to receive news of his nephew, immediately wrote him a letter. He then did the commonsense thing, and posted it to Pierre in a letter clearly addressed to him at Chabalisa 2 refugee camp. He then gave it to the Rwandan post office, which had it delivered to Tanzania promptly.

What about his trip to Ngara, about Petro? Pierre told me that he had found Petro and had had him arrested. After the police threatened to beat Petro, he admitted to stealing the 200,000 shillings Pierre had saved from his work with LWF. Fifty thousand shillings were returned to Pierre there, but the other 150,000 shillings had already been sent to Mwanza to purchase the stock necessary to open a small retail shop in the Benaco camp. I was told that the police have agreed to seize the stock when it arrives, presumably so that it can be turned over to Pierre.

What About Voluntary Repatriation?

The question donors and visitors always ask about the Rwandan refugees is, when will they go back to Rwanda? Is it safe or is it not? Some people working here have quick answers to these questions. They say that if the Hutu intimidators guilty of genocide were arrested, the rest would go back. They think that the only reason the largely peasant refugee population stays in Tanzania is that they are manipulated by clever leaders who, guilty of genocide, need their "protection" to avoid Rwandan and international courts.

Others say that the government in Rwanda is so hostile to repatriates that few refugees will go back. Those who say this can point to the influx of 20,000 to 25,000 Rwandans into Tanzania from refugee camps that had been closed in Burundi in late January 1996. Given the option of a lorry ride back to Rwanda or a risky flight to Tanzania, this many chose the latter. Now, the rumor is out that the Rwandan government has requested that the Burundian military government forcibly return all Rwandan adult males. My own inclination is to usually side with those staying. If I were asked to make such a choice, I would be hesitant to return under such uncertain circumstances. I do not believe that large numbers of Rwandan refugees will go back voluntarily in the immediate future and agree that the recent influx of Rwandans into Tanzania is a bad sign.

However, this an outsider's way of reasoning and is not how refugees like Petro or Pierre think about their future. Individual refugees focus on what they hear from people they trust on both sides of the border, rather than on the larger global political issues that outsiders focus on. The people refugees listen to might include LWF or UNHCR staff but are more likely to be their friends, enemies, and families. They look at their own individual situation and future and assess their chances. What do they hear in letters sent from Rwanda? Is news permitted to go back and forth? What do those who go back and forth say, and what personal motives shape their views? The messages they receive, though, continue to be and will continue to be confused.

Leaving one's home was an emotional decision that many made quickly in a dangerous situation. Likewise, any decision to return will be an emotional one that is based in the individual relationships refugees have on both sides of the border.

Essay 7

A Bishop in Exile—The Anglican Church in the Ngara Camps

July 1995

I first heard about Bishop Augustin Mvurubande from Trish and Rob Wilson. British medical missionaries who had lived in Rwanda for 15 years. The Wilsons had fled to Tanzania in late April 1994 after the hospital in Gahini, where they worked, had been attacked by the Hutu *Interahamwe*. During the attack, many of their staff and colleagues were killed. Later, advancing Rwanda Patriotic Front (Tutsi) forces entered the town of Gahini and ordered many of the remaining Hutu to leave. The ones who left became the refugees we now serve in Tanzania; many who remained behind were killed.

The Wilsons had met Bishop Augustin in Gahini, where he had been an Anglican pastor and later bishop. He himself was Hutu, whereas his wife was Tutsi. The couple fled Rwanda for Zaire in mid-1994. From there he moved to Ngara in Tanzania because that was where many of his church members and other pastors had gone. The Wilsons had also stayed in Ngara, where they helped provide medical services in the camps.

Rob and Trish mentioned Bishop Augustin to me last January because he had a special desire to return to Gahini in order to promote peace and reconciliation. He proposed to do this by taking personal messages back and forth between refugees in Benaco and those who had remained behind in Gahini. First, though, Bishop Augustin needed transport to Rwanda, and then he needed travel papers in order to be able to return to Tanzania. As a refugee, he would lose rights to international protection at the time he stepped back into his home country, Rwanda.

LWF was unable to assist with the bishop's request. Despite claims to the contrary by all sides, visits to promote peace and reconciliation never actually seem to work out, for a variety of legitimate reasons. For example, the Rwandan (RPF) government wants to examine every returnee to see whether he has committed war crimes, the UNHCR wants only elected "official" leaders involved, and the Tanzanians worry about cross-border security. Finally, many of the leaders in the Tanzanian camps have ambitions of one day seizing power in Rwanda and view the camp population as "theirs"—their future political supporters. They, too, have an interest in frustrating cross-border contacts and keeping the camp population in their sphere.

Despite the fact that this request was denied, we have been able to continue in our relationships with the Bishop Augustin and begin better to understand the difficulties of the route toward peace and reconciliation that he is trying to develop, which he calls a "middle road." By that he means participation by Hutu and Tutsi in all spheres of society. Fundamental to this is building relations between individuals, without recourse to revenge. Today, he lives in a modest house in the Anglican compound in Ngara, where he is the guest of the Tanzanian Anglican bishop of Ngara, Edwin Nyamubi. He is the only Rwandan bishop in the area; others who fled have gone to Nairobi, Zaire, or other places. In cooperation with Bishop Nyamubi, he is helping to rebuild the Christian community among the 600,000 Rwandan refugees in Tanzania.

A Visit to Gahini Commune/Msuhura Camp: The Pressures of a Mixed Marriage

Last January I spent my first day with the bishop. I had asked Trish for a chance to visit with the ordinary refugees she knew from her days in Gahini. I had been spending much of my time in offices doing such things as writing reports, meeting with other expatriates and Tanzanians, escorting donors to project sites, etc. In other words, despite my claim to be a refugee worker I am usually doing things that administrators anywhere in the world would do, without reference to the fact that the purpose of LWF's work is service to the refugees.

Trish offered me a break from these necessary routines. She speaks Kinyarwanda fluently, and as the high-status wife of the former director of Gahini Hospital, she felt a responsibility to visit the people she knows who fled: her gardener, the woman who had done the cooking in her house, the neighbors she had known for so many years. As we were leaving for the drive to the camp on a Saturday afternoon, she was asked whether the bishop, who stays in a nearby house on the Anglican compound, could get a ride to the camp. This is a common request in transportation-poor Tanzania, so we went to his house to pick him up. There I met his wife and children.

As we were getting ready to leave, Trish relayed the request of the bishop's wife to come along. Without thinking, I said yes, not at first realizing the unusual nature of the request. Virginia is a Tutsi, and we were going to go into the heart of a Hutu camp where in previous months anyone resembling a Tutsi was murdered. Since we were going to a place where many people knew Virginia and her ethnic background, she was obviously at great risk for her life. I asked her why she would take such a risk. At the time, she replied that God would protect her, and left it at that. Later she explained that there are many Tutsi living quietly in the camp. Many of them are Tutsi women married to Hutu men, although the bishop claims that there are also a few men as well, "even tall ones," referring to the physical height that is considered basic to Tutsi identity. Nevertheless, tension between Hutu and Tutsi is high at times, and so the bishop's wife usually does not spend the night in the camp, whereas he does. Virginia claims that relations with her Hutu friends in Benaco are better than they have been in the five years since the Tutsi-dominated Rwanda Patriotic Front invaded Rwanda from Uganda in 1990, and especially since the massacre of the Tutsi by Hutu *Interahamwe* last year.

This is the backdrop against which Bishop Augustin and his wife are attempting to develop a "moderate" road. Their work is through the church, which is for many the focus for social activities within the camp. The central point, the bishop explains, is to welcome, not alienate. This is difficult because of what many refugees have seen in the past; many hold only a very distant hope for life beyond refugee camps in the future. For this reason, Bishop Augustin points out that reconciliation with God must come first. Only when a reconciliation has been made with God for the crimes committed, wrongs suffered, and hate felt will it be possible to make a reconciliation with other Rwandans.

Currently, much effort is being put into what is hoped will be a choir competition four times a year for the church youth groups. Choir competitions are almost like a sport in Rwanda, and the refugee youth of Ngara are enthusiastic. The Anglican church is currently sponsoring about 140 choirs, each with 20 to 30 youth members. Each choir writes its own songs for the competition around a particular biblical theme. The theme of the current competition was deliverance, not a particularly surprising theme for a population that has so recently fled its own country. Next quarter's theme will be peace, justice, and reconciliation. Ephesians 2:13–16 is the passage from the Bible that the bishop uses in talking about these issues. These verses reflect well his goal of peace and reconciliation through the church: "But now in Christ Jesus you who once far away have been brought near by the blood of Christ. For he himself is our peace who has made the two one and has destroyed the barrier, the dividing wall of hostility, by abolishing in his flesh the law with its commandments and regulations."

The Choir Competition

The choir competition itself took place under the Lumasi Camp "circus tent," a tent donated by a missionary society from Canada. Trish, Rob, and I were introduced to the audience and then ushered into a nearby mud hut, where we were fed a lunch of rice and peanut sauce and given a soda. There was also a calabash of traditional Rwandan brew, not yet fermented in deference to the Protestant pastors in attendance. In the hut, we prepared the prize envelopes for the winners, while the competition continued in the background. There were 30 prizes in all. The 15 semifinalists received 2,000 shillings ($3.30) each, and the grand prize was 30,000 shillings ($49.50).

Later, Trish brought out a letter from a British missionary who had worked in Gahini in the 1970s. The missionary wanted to know what had happened to the pastors he had worked with so he could include them in his prayers. The answers that Trish received illustrated well the difficulties involved in focusing their choir program, or any other subject dealing with Rwanda today, on subjects like peace and reconciliation.

They went through a list of about 30 pastors. Perhaps 15 to 20 were in the Tanzanian refugee camps. One or two were still in Rwanda, and one was in a Burundian camp. One or two more had disappeared. The rest, 5 or 6, they reported had been killed. By their reckoning, about half of these had been killed by the Hutu *Interahamwe* during their attacks in Gahini in mid-April 1994. The other half they claimed had been killed by the RPF after they took over Gahini in late April. Trish was surprised somewhat that they were willing to discuss such a subject after lunch and viewed it as a positive sign that the recent terrible past was moving further away.

The bishop later explained to me why the choir program was important for the process of peace and reconciliation. He said that the choir competitions expose the people to the gospel in an enjoyable way. This exposure is important, he explains, because people must become united with God, because it is God who protects, not the politicians and big government who promised protection in the past. "Forgiveness comes from God and passes to those around us," he explains. In effect, he argues that the vertical comes before the horizontal, meaning that without God's forgiveness for our own sins, we cannot forgive those around us. And until Hutu and Tutsi forgive those around them, reconciliation cannot begin.

The bishop views the discipleship training required to produce good choral singing as a way to preach the principles of Christian forgiveness. He is well aware that this is by itself not enough, but views it as a start. Particularly important is the fact that the competitions are particularly interesting for the young people, a few of whom were active in the horrors of the past but in whom the future of the refugee communities in Tanzania nevertheless lies. Because of this paradox, he emphasizes that all must be welcome; the point of choirs is not to directly confront, but to present all with the need to seek and offer forgiveness.

Reconciling People Who Don't Talk to Each Other

When I first met the bishop earlier this year, he had hopes of returning to Rwanda himself to personally facilitate the reconciliation process. Sadly, he no longer believes this is possible. Since I met him in January, positions on both sides of the border have hardened, and cross-border communication has decreased as a consequence. There are also further restrictions to travel across the border. In the case of the Rwandans, no one can legally leave the country to visit Benaco, although the UNHCR is trying to initiate a "go and see" program (see Essay 6). Tanzania has also sealed the border as best it can in order to prevent further refugee influxes. Thus, even though relations between Tutsi and Hutu within the Ngara camps may be improving, the refugees are more separated than ever from their families back home.

As a result, communication has been reduced to radio broadcasts from Rwanda which refugees claim include veiled threats; contacts are occasionally made at public conferences in other cities. The bishop recalls attending a conference in Nairobi in December 1994 at which many public claims about peaceful coexistence were made. In private, though, his colleagues from Rwanda warned him not to return.

What is the next step? No one has a good answer. Everyone is aware that something must happen to alleviate the crowded, unstable conditions in Ngara's camps. The groundwater supply is being depleted, firewood supplies are diminishing, and the crowded conditions constantly present the possibility of epidemic disease. These conditions can only be alleviated by spreading out the population, whether in Rwanda, Tanzania, or elsewhere. Everyone involved, including the bishop, believes that voluntary repatriation must play a role, but no one knows what is next. One thing is clear, though: as long as there is no cross-border dialogue, nothing—no matter how necessary—will happen.

The bishop and his wife have a few suggestions about how this process may begin, but little means with which to implement them. They suggest mediated meetings in neutral cities such as Dodoma in central Tanzania, where refugee leaders could meet with representatives of the Rwandan government. They are also critical of current efforts being made by the UNHCR and the governments of Rwanda and Tanzania to design mechanisms for voluntary repatriation because no representatives of the refugees are involved. They point out that without such involvement, the mechanisms designed could very well prove meaningless. Nevertheless, they claim that Tanzania, with its history of mediating the 1993 Arusha Accords, between the RPF and the former Rwandan government, has the best reputation for neutrality and is the best site.

Can the church play a role? Bishop Augustin and his wife believe it must. However, they also note that divisions are deepening between the church in Rwanda and that in the camps of Tanzania. In this respect the church is like other institutions. They point out that the positions within the church that were "vacated" when they fled have been taken over by Tutsi returnees from Uganda, Tanzania, and Burundi. Indeed, there is now a new bishop in Gahini who is a returnee from Uganda. In this respect, the church is not unlike many other institutions being rebuilt in Rwanda after the terrible genocide and war: life in Rwanda will move on, whether the refugees return or not. Perhaps the church in Rwanda has good reasons for doing this; after all, they need to get the work of reconstruction under way for the Rwandans still left in Gahini. Unfortunately, the reasonable dialogue needed to include the 25 to 30 percent of Rwandans living in Tanzania and Zairean refugee camps is not occurring. At the root of any solution is such a dialogue. However, even with good and well-meaning Rwandans on both sides of the border the pain is still recent, and suspicions high. Overcoming this will be a slow, difficult, and necessary process.

Essay 8

Some Practical Notes on a Names Taboo in Western Tanzania

1989

In July 1987, I had occasion to distribute rice and household goods to a small village of Burundian refugees in the Kigoma region of western Tanzania. The refugees had been in the area for about 15 years, and had established themselves in association with a village of the Waha, the most numerous ethnic group in Kigoma region. All were agricultural people who considered themselves to be Hutu or Ha rather than Tutsi. Notably, the groups spoke mutually intelligible languages, and also had very similar cultural practices and beliefs. Nevertheless, as a result of an expulsion order issued by the Tanzanian government, the Burundian households had had their houses burned, and a small relief program was mounted (see Waters 1988).

- The relief goods were distributed by household, with special allowance made for unusual circumstances, especially large family size. The final count was that there were 796 persons living in the village, of whom a slight majority were adults. Most families had 0, 1, or 2 children, though there was one family with 8, and another with 12.

The low birth rate indicated by the count surprised me somewhat; this area of Tanzania was known for a high population growth rate, and in addition, local people had indicated to me during the previous three years I had lived in the area that the refugees from Burundi who were living in the village were even more prolific than the Waha. So why would they say they have only one or two children or none at all? Particularly in these circumstances, for the refugees there was a potential material incentive to have more children, for they could then claim a larger share of the relief goods. Yet they did not have even the four, five, or six children I expected. To rationalize the survey results with these other reports, I simply assumed that there must have been an unusually high infant mortality rate. Thus satisfied, I sent my report to Dar es Salaam.

Adapted from *Disasters* 13, 2 (1989):185–186.

But the problem still bothered me. Two weeks later, I visited a Catholic sister who had been working as a nurse in the area for over 30 years. Somewhat smugly I told her about my little survey, and indicated to her that there must be an un-usually high infant mortality rate among these people because the family sizes were so small. She laughed, and told me no, that it was impossible to take a cen-sus among the Waha or Burundian people in the area. Mentioning a child by name, or even counting a child, it is believed, makes that child potentially visible to malevolent spirits. Thus, any acknowledgment of a child, particularly to strangers, is taboo. The same restrictions apply to cattle or goats, which are an important form of wealth in the area. In effect, asking how many children, cattle, or goats a person has is the same as asking a Westerner about his or her salary or bank account.

A light went on after her explanation, for it shed light not only on the problems with my census but on a number of other observations I had made during the previous three years. It also explained a number of anomalous circumstances I had observed during my time in this part of Tanzania. Several are of interest.

- A Dutch doctor once told me that the Waha women did not know how many children they had; even when three children were standing around a mother, obviously hers, the mother would sometimes ac-knowledge only one pregnancy in response to a direct question by the doctor.

- A contractor I worked with, a mason, was known for being a man rich in cattle and goats. Indeed, he would periodically suspend his work for me because it was his turn to herd the flock. When I casually asked him how many animals he had (I was trying to be polite in a Western sense by showing an interest in his affairs), he said that he had one goat and one cow. Later, when I was married, he gave me a goat as a wedding present. Presuming this was his entire flock, I was taken aback by his generosity. Rethinking the matter in the context of the taboo mentioned above, though I was still impressed with his generosity, I was relieved that he had not been completely impoverished by his gift for our wed-ding.

- The sister who described the taboo to me in the first place explained some of the anomalous situations that developed for her clinic as a con-sequence. Children's names would inexplicably be changed, presum-ably because the child had attracted the attention of malevolent spirits. The names were changed so that the spirits would be fooled as to who the child was. This made maintenance of health records, a major tool for such health clinics, a chancy affair at best.

- I needed a guard at the compound where I worked, and I hired a man who remembered when the Germans had occupied Tanzania, and therefore must have been about 85 years old in 1987. One day he proudly announced to me the birth of a son. I asked him how many children he now had, and he indicated that this was his first. Pressing my question further, I expressed incredulity that a man of his age and experience would be having his first child at age 85. He insisted it was true, so I dropped the subject, once again puzzled by the nature of communication.

Having by now established for the reader that I spent my years in Tanzania as a cultural maladroit, I hasten to add a codicil: I am an American, for whom Tanzanians graciously make exceptions when dealing with spiritual matters. As I was told by the Tanzanians on occasion: it is not possible for me, as an expatriate, to comprehend such spiritual matters, no matter how much my Western-derived rationality asks me to do so. Nor is it considered desirable or purposeful by the Tanzanians for us to focus on the local spirits, for they are not believed to bother outsiders. From the Tanzanian perspective this is a blessing, as who really needs the malevolence this implies?

Although I may not comprehend Tanzanian spiritual matters, I think it is important for expatriates at least to acknowledge the significance such beliefs can have for their work. Aside from the benefits that good manners and cross-cultural understanding always bring, there are material benefits as well. Most expatriates working in Third World countries are there to assist with the material development of physical and human resources. Effective adaptation of these improvements depends on how well such development is adapted to local perceptions and beliefs.

Certainly, the taboo described here did not destroy the effectiveness of my small relief program. Nor did it cause the sister's clinic to collapse, nor did it mean that the Dutch doctor was not able to treat the patient who refused to acknowledge more than one pregnancy. However, questions of program quality are also involved. Accurate record-keeping is likely to improve the quality of many of the types of programs that are components of development, a view shared by Westerners, Tanzanian government officials, and, in a somewhat different way, even Tanzanian villagers. Record-keeping is inherent to the operation of both schools and clinics, institutions badly needed and wanted in even the most remote villages, and by the most isolated villagers. Other activities of modern life are also involved in such record-keeping, from the maintenance of payroll forms to the provision of relief supplies.

Ultimately, local cultural institutions such as this naming taboo are incompatible with development objectives. I suspect that as the schools and clinics that are being developed by the Tanzanian government (sometimes with the assistance of foreigners, often without) take root, this particular taboo, along with other social activities, may well wither. Until it does, though, it should be treated with a sensitivity that will serve both the more traditional Waha and the new institutions emerging in the area.

Bibliography

Adelman, Howard, and Astri Suhrke. 1996. "Early Warning and Response: Why the International Community Failed to Prevent the Genocide." *Disasters* 29(4):295–304.

Balzar, John. 1994. "Burundi Battles Its Demons in Fight to Survive," *Los Angeles Times*, August 15, 1994, p. A1

Bierbauer, Charles. 1996. "Foreword" to Larry Minear, Colin Scott, and Thomas G. Weiss, *The News Media, Civil War, and Humanitarian Action*, pp. vii–viii. Boulder: Lynne Rienner.

Bilinda, Lesley. 1996. *The Colour of Darkness*. London: Hodder and Stoughton.

Borton, John. 1996. An Account of Coordination Mechanisms for Humanitarian Assistance During the International Response to the 1994 Crisis in Rwanda. *Disasters* 20:305–323.

Chalinder, Andrew. 1994. *Water and Sanitation in Emergencies*. London: Relief and Rehabilitation Network.

Cornell, Stephen, and Douglas Hartmann. 1998. *Ethnicity and Race: Making Identities in a Changing World*. Thousand Oaks: Pine Forge Press.

Crisp, Jeff. 1999. "Who Has Counted the Refugees? UNHCR and the Politics of Numbers." *New Issues in Refugee Research*, Working Paper No. 12, in *Journal of Humanitarian Assistance*, posted on August 1, 1999, at the Web site <http://www-jha.sps.cam.ac.uk/c/c012.pdf>.

Cuenod, Jacques. 1967. The Problem of Rwandese and Sudanese Refugees. In *Refugee Problems in Africa*, ed. Sven Hamrell. Uppsala: Scandinavian Institute of African Studies.

Cunliffe, Alex. 1995. "The Refugee Crises: A Study of the United Nations High Commission for Refugees." *Political Studies*. 43:278–290.

Cuny, Frederick C. 1983. *Disasters and Development*. Oxford: Oxford University Press.

Cuny, Frederick C., and Barry Stein. 1989. "Prospects for and Promotion of Spontaneous Repatriation." In *Refugees and International Relations*, ed. Gil Loescher and Laila Monahan, pp. 283–312. Oxford: Oxford University Press.

Dabelstein, Niels. 1996. "Evaluating the International Humanitarian System: Rationale, Process and Management of the Joint Evaluation of the International Response to the Rwanda Genocide." *Disasters* 20(4):287–294.

Daley, Patricia O. 1991. "Gender, Displacement, and Social Reproduction: Settling Burundian Refugees in Tanzania." *Journal of Refugee Studies* 4(3):248–266.

Des Forges, Alison. 1999. *Leave None to Tell the Story: Genocide in Rwanda*. New York: Human Rights Watch.

———. 1996. "Making Noise Effectively: Lessons from the Rwandan Catastrophe." In *Vigilance and Vengeance: NGOs Preventing Ethnic Conflict in Divided Societies*, ed. Robert Rotberg. Washington, D.C.: Brookings Institution Press.

Destexhe, Alain. 1996. *Rwanda and Genocide in the Twentieth Century*. New York: New York University Press.

———. 1995. "The Third Genocide." *Foreign Policy*, pp. 3–17.

Drysdale, John. 1997. "Foreign Military Intervention in Somalia: The Root Cause of the Shift from UN Peacekeeping to Peacemaking and Its Consequences." In *Learning from Somalia*, ed. Walter Clarke, pp. 118–134. Boulder: Westview Press.

Economist. 1994. "Rwanda: In flight." *The Economist*, May 7, 1994, p. 44.

Ford, Peter. 1999. "What About Disasters TV Crews Miss?" *Christian Science Monitor*, August 26, 1999.

Gasarasi, Charles P. 1984. *The Tripartite Approach to the Resettlement and Integration of Rural Refugees in Tanzania*. Uppsala: Scandinavian Institute of African Studies.

Gibbs, Nancy. 1994. "Rwanda's Killing Fields." *Time*, May 16, 1994, pp. 56–58.

Goffman, Erving. 1974. *Frame Analysis: An Essay on the Organization of Experience*. Cambridge: Harvard University Press.

Goldstone, Jack. 1991. *Revolution and Rebellion in the Early Modern World*. Berkeley: University of California Press.

Gordon, Linda. 1990. "The Missing Children: Mortality and Fertility in a Southeast Asian Refugee Population." *International Migration Review* 23(2):219–237.

Gorman, Robert F., ed. 1993. *Refugee Aid and Development: Theory and Practice*. New York: Greenwood.

Gourevitch, Philip. 1998a. *We Wish to Inform You That Tomorrow We Will Be Killed with All Our Families*. New York: Farrar, Straus, and Giroux.

———. 1998b. "The Genocide Fax: The United Nations was Warned About Rwanda. Did Anyone Care? *The New Yorker*, May 11, pp. 42–45

———. 1996. "Is Burundi Next?" *The New Yorker*, February 19, p. 7.

———. 1995. "After the Genocide." *The New Yorker*, December 18, 1995, pp. 78–96.

Gowing, Nick. 1998. "New Challenges and Problems for Information Management in Complex Emergencies: Ominous Lessons from the Great Lakes and Eastern Zaire in late 1996 and Early 1997." Background paper to *Dispatches from Disaster Zones: The Reporting of Humanitarian Emergencies*. London: Reuters Foundation, 1998. Posted on Reuters Foundation Web site, May 28, 1998: <www.foundation.reuters.com/>.

Gutekunst, Marc-Daniel. 1995. "The Mille Collines and Kigali at War." *Issue: A Journal of Opinion* 23(2):22–27.

Haggard, Stephan, and Beth A. Simmons. 1987. "Theories of International Regimes." *International Organization* 41(3):491–517.

Hall, Edward T. 1976. *Beyond Culture*. New York: Anchor Books.

Harrell-Bond, Barbara. 1986. *Imposing Aid: Emergency Assistance to Refugees*. Oxford: Oxford University Press.

Hochschild, Arlie Russell. 1983. *The Managed Heart: Commercialization of Human Feeling*. Berkeley: University of California Press.

Holborn, Louise. 1975. *Refugees: A Problem of Our Time. The Work of the United Nations High Commissioner for Refugees*. Metuchen, N.J.: Scarecrow Press.

Human Rights Watch. 1997. "Zaire Attacked by All Sides." In *Civilians and the War in Eastern Zaire*. Short report no. A901. March.

Ingram, James. 1993. "The Future Architecture of International Refugee Assistance." In *Humanitarianism Across Borders: Sustaining Civilians in Times of War*, ed. Thomas G. Weiss and Larry Minear, pp. 171–194. Boulder: Lynne Rienner.

Integrated Regional Information Networks [IRIN]. 2000. IRIN interview with Acting President Paul Kagame [of Rwanda]. Posted April 7, 2000, on IRIN Web site, <www.reliefweb.int/>.

Jacobs, Dan. 1987. *The Brutality of Nations*. New York: Alfred A. Knopf.

Jaspars, Susanne. 1994. *The Rwandan Refugee Crisis in Tanzania: Initial Successes and Failures in Food Assistance*. Relief and Rehabilitation Network. Network Paper #6. London: ODI.

JEEAR [Joint Evaluation of Emergency Assistance to Rwanda]. 1996. *Study 3: Humanitarian Aid and Effects*. Copenhagen, Denmark: Danida, March.

Kaplan, Robert E. 1998. *Surrender or Starve: The Wars Behind the Famine*. Boulder: Westview Press.

Kenny, George. 1999. "Kosovo: On Ends and Means." *The Nation*, December 27, pp. 25–30.

Khiddu-Makubuya, Edward. 1994. "Voluntary Repatriation by Force: The Case of Rwandan Refugees in Uganda." In *African Refugees: Development Aid and Repatriation*, ed. Howard Adelman and John Sorenson, pp. 143–158. Boulder: Westview Press.

Kunz, Egon. 1983. "Exile and Resettlement: Refugee Theory." *International Migration Review* 1591–92:42–51.

Layne, Christopher, and Benjamin Schwartz. 2000. "Was It a Mistake?" *New York Times*, March 25, 2000.

Lemarchand, René. 1999. "Fire in the Great Lakes." *Current History*, May 1999, pp. 195–201.

———. 1995. Rwanda: the Rationality of Genocide. *Issue: A Journal of Opinion* 23(2):8–11.

———. 1994. *Burundi: Ethnocide as Discourse and Practice*. New York: Cambridge University Press.

———. 1970. *Rwanda and Burundi*. London: Pall Mall.

Leonard, Terry. 1994. *AP Worldstream*, May 20, 1994. "Army Holds Position, Trades Artillery Fire with Rebels." Available on Lexis Nexis. (Associated Press). *Sacramento Bee*, May 21, pp. A1, A20.

Long, Lynelyn. 1993. *Ban Vinai: The Refugee Camp*. New York: Columbia University Press.

Los Angeles Times. 1994. "World News" department. March 10, Section A.

MacDonald, Flora. 1998. "Refugee Crisis in the Great Lakes: Have Any Lessons Been Learned?" *Forced Migration* 1:30–31.

MacKinnon, Neil. 1986. *The Unfriendly Soil: The Loyalist Experience in Nova Scotia*. Kingston: McGill-Kingston University Press.

Malkki, Liisa. 1995. "Refugees and Exile: From Refugee Studies to the National Order of Things." *Annual Review of Anthropology* 24:495–523.

———. 1994. *Purity and Exile: Violence, Memory and National Cosmology Among Hutu Refugees in Tanzania*. Chicago: University of Chicago Press.

Mason, Linda, and Roger Brown. 1983. *Rice, Rivalry and Politics: Managing Cambodian Relief.* Notre Dame: Notre Dame University Press.

Mayotte, Judy. 1992. *Disposable People.* Maryknoll: Orvis Books.

McGrath, Roger. 1984. *Gunfighters, Highwaymen, and Vigilantes: Violence in the Frontier.* Berkeley: University of California Press.

McNamara, Dennis. 1989. "The Origins and Effects of 'Humane Deterrence' Policies in South-east Asia." In *Refugees and International Politics,* ed. Gil Loescher and Laila Monahan. Oxford: Oxford University Press.

McNeill, William. 1977. *Plagues and Peoples.* New York: Anchor Books.

Médecins sans Frontières (MSF). 1995. *Populations in Danger: A Médecins sans Frontières Report.* London: Médecins sans Frontières.

Minear, Larry, Colin Scott, and Thomas G. Weiss. 1996. *The News Media, Civil War, and Humanitarian Action.* Boulder: Lynne Rienner.

MMWR: Morbidity and Mortality Weekly Reports. 1996. "Morbidity and Mortality Surveillance in Rwandan Refugees—Burundi and Zaire, 1994." Atlanta: Centers for Disease Control, February 9.

Nam, Charles. 1994. *Understanding Population Change.* Itasca, Ill.: F. E. Peacock.

Natsios, Andrew W. 1997. "Humanitarian Relief Intervention in Somalia: The Economics of Chaos." In *Learning from Somalia: The Lessons of Armed Humanitarian Intervention,* ed. Walter Clarke and Jeffrey Herbst. Boulder: Westview Press.

———. 1996. "NGOs and the UN System in Complex Humanitarian Emergencies: Conflict or Cooperation." In *NGOs, the UN and Global Government,* ed. Thomas G. Weiss and Leon Gordenker. Boulder: Lynne Rienner.

Newbury, Catherine. 1995. "Background to Genocide in Rwanda." *Issue* (Africa Studies Association) 23(2):12–17.

———. 1988. *The Cohesion of Oppression: Clientship and Ethnicity in Rwanda, 1860–1960.* New York: Columbia University Press.

Newbury, David. 1998. "Understanding Genocide." *African Studies Review* 41(1):73–95.

Olick, Jeffrey K., and Daniel Levy. 1998. "The Holocaust: Collective Memory and Cultural Constraint." *American Sociological Review* 62(6):921–936.

Oliver, Thomas W. 1978. *The United Nations in Bangladesh.* Princeton: Princeton University Press.

Payne, Robert. 1973. *Massacre: The Tragedy at Bangla Desh and the Phenomenon of Mass Slaughter Throughout History.* New York: Macmillan.

Pinheiro, Paulo Sergio. 1996. Initial Report on the Human Rights Situation in Burundi Submitted by the Special Rapporteur, Mr. Paulo Sergio Pinheiro, in Accordance with Commission Resolution 1995/90. At UNHCR's Web site: <www.unhcr.ch/refworld/un/chr/chr96/country/16ad-bdi.htm>.

Pitterman, Shelly. 1984. "International Responses to Refugee Situations: The United Nations High Commissioner for Refugees." In *Refugees and World Politics,* ed. Elizabeth G. Ferris, pp. 42–81. New York: Praeger.

Pottier, Johan. 1996a. "Why Aid Agencies Need Better Understanding of the Communities They Assist: The Experience of Food Aid in Rwandan Refugee Camps." *Disasters* 20(4):324–337.

———. 1996b. "Relief and Repatriation: Views from Refugees, Lessons for Humanitarian Workers." *African Affairs* 95:403–429.

Prunier, Gérard. 1997a. *The Rwanda Crisis, History of a Genocide.* Paperback edition. New York: Columbia University Press.

———. 1997b. "The Geopolitical Situation in the Great Lakes Area in Light of the Kivu Crisis." February 1997. <www.unher.ch/networld/country/writenet/wrilakes.htm/>, U.K.: Write Net.

Quist, Ronald. 1995. End of Mission Report to Memisa, Holland. Unpublished report. October.

Reed, Wm. Cyrus. 1995. "The Rwandan Patriotic Front: Politics and Development in Rwanda." *Issue: A Journal of Opinion* 23(2):48–53.

Rehlaender, Jens. 1994. "Fluchtpunkt Benako." *Geo*, August.

Reyntjens, Filip. 1995. "Subjects of Concern: October 1994." *Issue* (Africa Studies Association) 23(2):39–43.

Ritzer, George. 1996. *The McDonaldization of Society.* Rev. ed. Thousand Oaks, Calif.: Pine Forge Press.

Rosenblatt, Roger. 1994. A Killer in the Eye. *New York Times Magazine*, June 5, 1994, pp. 39–47.

Rutinwa, Bonaventure. 1996. "The Tanzanian Government's Response to the Rwandan Emergency." *Journal of Refugee Studies* 9(3):291–302.

Sabpek, Paul. 1995. "Mountain Gorillas of Africa: Threatened by War." *National Geographic*, October 1995, pp. 58–83.

Schechtman, Joseph B. 1963. *The Refugee in the World: Displacement and Integration.* New York: A. S. Barnes.

Shawcross, William. 2000. *Deliver Us from Evil: Peacekeepers, Warlords, and a World of Endless Conflict.* New York: Simon and Schuster.

———.1984. *The Quality of Mercy: Cambodia, Holocaust, and Modern Conscience.* New York: Simon and Schuster.

Shoham, Jeremy. 1996. "Food and Nutritional Programs During the Rwandan Emergency." *Disasters* 20(4):338–352.

Slim, Hugo. 1995. The Continuing Metamorphosis of the Humanitarian Professional: Some New Colours for a New Chameleon. *Disasters* 19(2):110–126.

Smith, Charles David. 1995. "The Geopolitics of Rwandan Settlement: Uganda and Tanzania." *Issue* (Africa Studies Association) 23(2):48–53.

Smith, Richard Norton. 1984. *An Uncommon Man: The Triumph of Herbert Hoover.* New York: Simon and Schuster.

Solberg, Richard W. 1991. *Miracle in Ethiopia.* New York: Friendship Press.

Sommers, Marc. 1994. "Hiding in Bongoland: Identity Formation and the Clandestine Life for Burundi Refugees in Urban Tanzania." Ph.D. dissertation, Department of Anthropology, Boston University.

Stein, Barry. 1996. "Older Refugee Settlements in Africa." On H-Net. Humanities and Social Sciences on-line: <http://h-net2.msu.edu/~africa/sources/refugee.html>.

Stoessinger, John G. 1956. *The Refugee and the World Community.* Minneapolis: University of Minnesota Press.

TCRS (Tanganyika Christian Refugee Service). 1995. "The Kamantendele Aquifer System." Draft report, November 1996.

Thompson, Joseph E. 1990. *American Policy and African Famine: The Nigeria-Biafra War, 1966–70.* New York: Greenwood.

Tuchman, Barbara W. 1978. *A Distant Mirror: The Calamitous Fourteenth Century*. New York: Alfred A. Knopf.

United States Committee for Refugees. 1998. *Life After Death: Suspicion and Reintegration in Post-Genocide Rwanda*. Written by Jeff Drumtra. Washington, D.C.: U.S. Committee for Refugees.

USAID (U.S. Agency for International Development). 1999. Kosovo Fact Sheet #52, May 17.

————. 1998. Statement to House Committee on International Relations, Subcommittee on International Operations and Human Rights, May 5, by Richard L. McCall, chief of staff to the USAID administrator. Unpublished report.

Uvin, Peter. 1998. *Aiding Violence: The Development Enterprise in Rwanda*. West Hartford: Kumarian Press.

vanden Heuvel, William J. "America and the Holocaust." *American Heritage*, July / August 1999.

Vansina, Jan. 1991. *Paths in the Rainforest*. Madison: University of Wisconsin Press.

Von Bernuth, Rudolph. 1996. "The Voluntary Agency Response and the Challenge of Coordination." *Journal of Refugee Studies* 9(3):281–290.

Walkup, Mark. 1997. "Policy and Behavior in Humanitarian Organizations: The Institutional Origins of Operational Dysfunction." Ph.D. dissertation, University of Florida, Department of Political Science. Ann Arbor: University Microfilms.

Waters, Tony. 1999a. "Assessing the Impact of the Rwandan Refugee Crisis on Development Planning in Rural Tanzania, 1994–1996." *Human Organization* 58(2):152–162.

————. 1999b. *Crime and Immigrant Youth*. Thousand Oaks, Calif.: Sage Publications.

————. 1997. "Conventional Wisdom and Rwanda's Genocide—an Opinion." *Africa Studies Quarterly* 1(3). On-line refereed journal. Posted to Relief Web, UN Department of Humanitarian Affairs, Geneva, December 9, 1997.

————. 1996. "The Demographics of the Rwanda Crisis, or Why Current Voluntary Repatriation Policies Will Not Solve Tanzania's or Zaire's Refugee Crisis." *Journal of Humanitarian Affairs*. On-line refereed journal at www.jha.ac.

————. 1995a. "Towards a Theory of Ethnic Enclave Formation: The Case of Ethnic Germans in Russia and North America." *International Migration Review* 29(2):515–544.

————. 1995b. "The Social Construction of Tutsi in Modern East Africa." *Journal of Modern African Studies* 33(2):243–248.

————. 1990. "The Parameters of Refugeeism and Flight: The Case of Laos." *Disasters*. 14(3):250–258.

————. 1989. "Some Practical Notes on a Names Taboo in Western Tanzania." *Disasters* 13(2):185–86.

————. 1988. "Practical Problems Associated with Refugee Protection in Western Tanzania." *Disasters* 12(3): 189–195.

————. 1984. "A Comparative Analysis of Water Provision in Four Thai Refugee Camps." *Disasters* 8(3):169–173.

Weber, Max. 1958. *The Protestant Ethic and the Spirit of Capitalism*. New York: Macmillan.

————. 1948. *From Max Weber*. New York: Oxford University Press.

Weeks, John. 1996. *Population*. 6th edition. New York: Wadsworth.

Weiss, Thomas G., and Leon Gordenker, eds. 1996. *NGOs, the UN and Global Governance*. Boulder: Lynne Rienner.

Whitaker, Beth Elise. 1999. "Changing Opportunities: Refugees and Host Communities in Western Tanzania." Working Paper 11, New Issues in Refugee Research. *Journal of Humanitarian Assistance*, on-line edition, posted on August 1, 1999: <http://www-jha.sps.cam.ac.uk/c/c011.pdf>.

Wilson, James Q. 1989. Bureaucracy: What Government Agencies Do and Why They Do It. New York: Basic Books.

World Bank. 1995. *World Development Report*. Washington, D.C.: World Bank.

————.1988. *World Development Report*. Washington, D.C.: World Bank.

Index